# Radical Futures? Youth, Politics and Activism in Contemporary Europe

## *The Sociological Review* Monographs

Since 1958, *The Sociological Review* has established a tradition of publishing one or two Monographs a year on issues of general sociological interest. The Monograph is an edited book length collection of refereed research papers which is published and distributed in association with Wiley Blackwell. We are keen to receive innovative collections of work in sociology and related disciplines with a particular emphasis on exploring empirical materials and theoretical frameworks which are currently under-developed.

If you wish to discuss ideas for a Monograph then please contact the Monographs Editor, Steve Brown, Professor of Social and Organisational Psychology, School of Management, University of Leicester, Leicester, LE1 7RH, UK. e-mail: s.d.brown@le.ac.uk

Our latest Monographs include:

Gender and Creative Labour (edited by Bridget Conor, Rosalind Gill & Stephanie Taylor)
Violence and Society: Toward a New Sociology (edited by Jane Kilby and Larry Ray)
Disasters and Politics: Materials, Experiments, Preparedness (edited by Manuel Tironi, Israel Rodriguez-Giralt and Michael Guggenheim)
Urban Rhythms: Mobilities, Space and Interation in the Contemporary City (edited by Robin James Smith and Kevin Hetherington)
Waste Matters (edited by David Evans, Hugh Campbell and Anne Murcott)
Live Methods (edited by Les Back and Nirmal Puwar)
Measure and Value (edited by Lisa Adkins and Celia Lury)
Norbert Elias and Figurational Research: Processual Thinking in Sociology (edited by Norman Gabriel and Stephen Mennell)
Sociological Routes and Political Roots (edited by Michaela Benson and Rolland Munro)
Nature, Society and Environmental Crisis (edited by Bob Carter and Nickie Charles)
Space Travel & Culture: From Apollo to Space Tourism (edited by David Bell and Martin Parker)
Un/Knowing Bodies (edited by Joanna Latimer and Michael Schillmeier)
Remembering Elites (edited by Mike Savage and Karel Williams)
Market Devices (edited by Michel Callon, Yuval Millo and Fabian Muniesa)
Embodying Sociology: Retrospect, Progress and Prospects (edited by Chris Shilling)
Sports Mega-Events: Social Scientific Analyses of a Global Phenomenon (edited by John Horne and Wolfram Manzenreiter)

Other Monographs have been published on consumption; museums; culture and computing; death; gender and bureaucracy; sport plus many other areas. For further information about the Monograph Series, please visit: www.sociologicalreviewmonographs.com

# Radical Futures? Youth, Politics and Activism in Contemporary Europe

Edited by Hilary Pilkington and Gary Pollock

Wiley Blackwell/The Sociological Review

ISBN 9781119062363 and The Sociological Review, 63:S2.

All articles published within this monograph are included within
the ISI Journal Citation Reports® Social Science Citation Index.
Please quote the article DOI when citing monograph content.

*Registered Office*
John Wiley & Sons Ltd, The Atrium, Southern Gate, Chichester, West Sussex, PO19 8SQ, UK

*Editorial Offices*
350 Main Street, Malden, MA 02148-5020, USA
9600 Garsington Road, Oxford, OX4 2DQ, UK
The Atrium, Southern Gate, Chichester, West Sussex, PO19 8SQ, UK

For details of our global editorial offices, for customer services, and for information about how
to apply for permission to reuse the copyright material in this book please see our website at
www.wiley.com/wiley-blackwell.

The right of Hilary Pilkington and Gary Pollock to be identified as the editors of this work has
been asserted in accordance with the UK Copyright, Designs and Patents Act 1988.

Wiley also publishes its books in a variety of electronic formats. Some content that appears in print
may not be available in electronic books. Designations used by companies to distinguish their
products are often claimed as trademarks. All brand names and product names used in this book
are trade names, service marks, trademarks, or registered trademarks of their respective owners. The
publisher is not associated with any product or vendor mentioned in this book.

Limit of Liability/Disclaimer of Warranty: While the publisher and authors have used their best
efforts in preparing this book, they make no representations or warranties with respect to the
accuracy or completeness of the contents of this book and specifically disclaim any implied
warranties of merchantability or fitness for a particular purpose. It is sold on the understanding
that the publisher is not engaged in rendering professional services and neither the publisher nor the
authors shall be liable for damages arising herefrom. If professional advice or other expert
assistance is required, the services of a competent professional should be sought.

First published in 2015 by John Wiley & Sons

*Library of Congress Cataloging-in-Publication Data*

Library of Congress Cataloging-in-Publication data is available for this book

A catalogue record for this title is available from the British Library

Set in TimesNRMT 10/12pt by Aptara Inc.

Printed and bound in the United Kingdom

1   2015

# Contents

# Acknowledgements

Financial support for the research underpinning this volume was provided by the European Union Seventh Framework Programme (MYPLACE project, Grant Agreement number FP7-266831). The editors would like to acknowledge the role of the Commission and thank the Research Programme officers for MYPLACE, Simona Ardovino and Sylvie Rohanova, for their support over four years of implementing an ambitious project in challenging times for the whole of Europe. The research findings, and their interpretation, included in this volume remain the responsibility of individual authors and the MYPLACE consortium.

The editors would like to express their thanks not only to authors contributing to this volume but to the whole MYPLACE team. The collection and analysis of the extensive data underpinning the articles would not have been possible without the dedicated contribution of many researchers, and non-academic partners, not represented among the list of authors in this first collaborative publication from the project. The professionalism and enthusiasm of the whole MYPLACE research team, as well as the patience and good humour of the Project Manager, Martin Price, has sustained the collective work of the project through some periods of intense collaboration and made the project not only productive but genuinely enjoyable.

We extend our thanks also to the *Sociological Review* Monograph Series editor, Chris Shilling, and the *Sociological Review* Editorial Manager, Caroline Baggaley for their critical and encouraging comments and technical support. We would also like to thank those who anonymously reviewed the articles for their constructive and helpful criticism.

Finally, we would like to thank every young person who took the time and effort to contribute to the MYPLACE research, whether in the form of answering a questionnaire survey after school or work or tolerating the interference of an ethnographer in their lives for months, if not years. The project asked some difficult questions. We hope the answers we have started to formulate in this volume do some justice to the young people who were 'bothered' enough to help us find them.

# Series editor's acknowledgements

*The Sociological Review* Monograph series publishes special supplements of the journal in collections of original refereed papers that are included within the ISI Journal Citation Reports and the Social Science Citation Index.

In existence for over fifty years, the series has developed a reputation for publishing innovative projects that reflect the work of senior but also emerging academic figures from around the globe.

These collections could not continue without the considerable goodwill, advice and guidance of members of the Board of *The Sociological Review*, and of those anonymous referees who assess and report on the papers submitted for consideration for these collections. I would like to thank all of those involved in this process, especially Dr Paul Hodkinson for his very considerable input into the collection as a whole, all of the referees, and also the editors of *Radical Futures? Youth, Politics and Activism in Contemporary Europe* for having produced such a stimulating volume.

*The Sociological Review* welcomes ideas for future Monographs and anyone who may be thinking of preparing a proposal should contact Professor Steve Brown, e-mail sb343@leicester.ac.uk, who has now assumed the role of series editor.

Chris Shilling, SSPSSR, University of Kent, UK

# 'Politics are bollocks': youth, politics and activism in contemporary Europe

## Hilary Pilkington and Gary Pollock

**Abstract:** This introductory article introduces the MYPLACE (Memory, Youth, Political Legacy and Civic Engagement) project, the findings of which are the basis of the articles in this volume. MYPLACE maps the relationship between political heritage, current levels and forms of civic and political engagement of young people in Europe, and their potential receptivity to radical and populist political agendas. In this introductory article, the implications of the project's three-way gaze – to the past, present and future – are explored by addressing three questions that run through contributions to this volume: What is politics, and why do many young people say they hate it? How does the past shape the present and the future? Are young people receptive to populist and radical right political agendas? The article outlines the distinctive case study approach to the project and its integrated mixed method design, detailing the common survey, interview, focus group and ethnographic research instruments employed in the project and the principles followed for the analysis of survey and qualitative research data.

**Keywords:** youth, politics, activism, Europe, democratic theory, memory

This collection of articles emanates from a major cross-European research project on the civic and political engagement of young Europeans. The MYPLACE (Memory, Youth, Political Legacy and Civic Engagement) project[1] uses a mixed method (survey, interviews, ethnographies) and case study approach[2] to map the relationship between political heritage, current levels and forms of civic and political engagement of young people in Europe, and their potential receptivity to radical and populist[3] political agendas. Facing three ways – to the past, the present and the future – does not sit easily with the first rule of research design, which is to determine a single research question. It does, however, lend the project a distinctive dynamic traction; it understands youth civic and political engagement as firmly rooted in its structural (including historical and cultural) context whilst recognizing that this changes across time and space and that young people themselves are active agents of that change. Freed from the straitjacket of a single hypothesis drawn from a discrete field of literature, moreover, the project works across and between normally unconnected fields

*The Sociological Review*, 63:S2, pp. 1–35 (2015), DOI: 10.1111/1467-954X.12260

including those of youth studies, democratic theory and participation, memory studies and far right studies. In this introductory article,[4] we situate the project at the intersections of these existing literatures and seek to make critical interventions to them. We do this by addressing three questions that emerged as common threads across contributions to this volume and shape the structure of the volume outlined below: What is politics, and why do many young people say they hate it? How does the past shape the present and the future? Are young people receptive to populist and radical right political agendas?

## What is politics, and why do many young people say they hate it?

The answer to this question is, on the surface, simple. Asked what she visualizes when she calls politics 'boring', a MYPLACE interview respondent explains, 'I'm thinking like all the old people in the House of Parliament, or Commons [...] or whatever it's called, just doing nothing, just sitting there talking really' (Fiona, Nuneaton, UK[5]).

There is little dispute within academic circles that, like Fiona, young people across Europe have disassociated themselves from the formal politics of 'old people'. This disassociation is reflected in a clear decline in electoral participation and other forms of traditional institutional political participation (Klingemann and Fuchs, 1995; Dalton and Wattenberg, 2000; Mair and van Biezen, 2001; Norris, 2003). While this reflects a general population trend, the withdrawal from formal politics has been especially intense among young people. A number of studies have shown that the youngest generations tend to vote less (Kimberlee, 2002; Wattenberg, 2006) and to participate less in formal political organizations such as parties and trades unions (Dalton and Wattenberg, 2000).

More disputed is the question of how we should interpret these 'facts' (Kimberlee, 2002; Brooks and Hodkinson, 2008). For some, the decline in young people's engagement in institutional activities is evidence that the political system is unreceptive to young people's demands or is perceived as such by them (Marsh *et al.*, 2007; Henn *et al.*, 2005). Young people may be failing to vote, for example, not because they are apathetic but because politics appear 'remote and irrelevant' (Kimberlee, 2002: 90) or overly complex and populated by a professional political elite concerned with pursuing a narrow self-serving agenda (Henn and Foard, 2014: 367). This may manifest itself also in a lack of interest in public affairs and/or a sense of absence of personal efficacy concerning the political process (Wattenberg, 2006; Blais *et al.*, 2004). Underpinning this, it is suggested, may be a deeper lack of fit between political institutional models and the kinds of concerns expressed by young people, who have grown up in a socio-economic context of precarity and instability (Kimberlee, 2002). The contribution to this volume by Pollock *et al.* provides further evidence that young people feel remote from a perceived political elite and demonstrate high aggregate levels of populist beliefs that will make mainstream parties uncomfortable.

A second interpretation is that participation by young people has not declined per se but switched focus as new possibilities for political expression have emerged. Young people, it is argued, are not apathetic (Nestlé Family Monitor, 2003) but choose to participate in less professionalized and controlled political activities such as in online forms of participation (Norris, 2001), political consumerism (Stolle *et al.*, 2005) or non-institutionalized activities in general (Norris, 2003). This has led to calls for the broader conceptualization of the political sphere to recognize the engagement of young people in non-formal politics (Marsh *et al.*, 2007; Brooks and Hodkinson, 2008) and claims that young people are not so much apathetic or disengaged as 'engaged sceptics' (Henn and Foard, 2014: 362).

The claim that youth apathy is a 'myth' (Brooks and Hodkinson, 2008: 474), however, has been strongly disputed also. The academic community, claims Furedi (2005: 40), avoids confronting the very real and 'troublesome phenomenon of youth apathy' by 'attempting to define it out of existence', deluding itself that young people are 'engaging in alternative ways'.

## Youth apathy: myth or inconvenient fact?

Such different interpretations of current trends in youth engagement with politics suggest a need to re-examine 'the facts' themselves. The decline of traditional forms of participation, as well as a lack of interest in public affairs and the absence of personal efficacy in the political process, among young people identified in the published academic literature (Kimberlee, 2002; Wattenberg, 2006; Dalton and Wattenberg, 2000; Blais *et al.*, 2004) is not fully borne out by our data. The MYPLACE survey shows significant conventional political engagement alongside high variability; across all locations 71 per cent of respondents who were eligible reported that they had voted in the last national election, ranging from 39 per cent in Nuneaton (UK) to over 80 per cent in the two locations in Denmark and eastern Germany as well as in Podsljeme (Croatia), Agenskalns (Latvia), Vic (Spain) and Kuopio (Finland). Moreover, the 'myth of youth apathy' argument is contingent upon evidence of a parallel increase in non-institutionalized forms of participation among young people (Norris, 2002; Marien *et al.*, 2010), which is a thesis less readily confirmed. Data from the last six ESS rounds (2002–12) suggest that although young people *are* more likely to engage in non-institutional than institutional forms of political activity, trends in levels of non-conventional political participation remain either stable or show a decline (see Appendix, Table A1).[6]

Although the MYPLACE survey captures only a single point in time, it included an unusually detailed question on political activity in which respondents were asked if they had participated in the last 12 months in a total of 23 different activities, thus allowing a nuanced analysis of the levels of young people's engagement in both 'institutional' and 'non-institutional' forms of politics.[7] The frequency of youth participation was grouped in relation to three distinct types of political activity which were constructed on the basis of a factor analysis of 20 different activities: 'public traditional participation',[8] 'private individual participation'[9] and 'protest action'[10] (Soler-i-Martí *et al.*, 2014). The vast majority of young people in all 30 locations in Europe included in the survey had not participated in any 'public traditional' activities in the last year. Non-conventional political activities – protest actions as well as private, individual forms of engagement – are more common; they account for more than half of the total participation in political actions. The findings thus confirm the weak propensity of young people to participate through traditional institutional forms and their greater participation in non-conventional activities.

Furedi's critique of the suggestion that youth political apathy is a 'myth' rests not only on measures of the quantity but also the quality of activity. To put it crudely, 'non-conventional' forms of politics must be equally as 'political' as conventional ones to warrant the conclusion that political participation by young people is not decreasing, just changing. The bigger question of what constitutes 'the political' is returned to below; here it is worth noting that 'private individual participation' requires a lower level of involvement in terms of costs and public visibility. Young people's greater engagement in non-conventional participation, which is 'easier', may be interpreted, therefore, as constituting a downgrading of the significance of the political among young people. The higher 'value' of traditional forms of participation, moreover, appears to be confirmed by young people themselves. When MYPLACE survey respondents were asked what constitutes effective political participation, they evaluated traditional forms most highly; 'voting in elections' received the highest mean response for effectiveness (Mean = 6.85 on a scale of 0–10) and 'being active in a political party' was considered the third most effective form of participation (Mean = 5.41),[11] notwithstanding the almost exclusively negative associations with political parties expressed by young people participating in follow-up semi-structured interviews. This raises questions about the equivalence of different forms of participation and the effectiveness of utilizing the apparent preference of young people for online and virtual forms of participation to stimulate their participation in more traditional forms of participation (such as voting).

## E-democracy: a false dawn?

There has been significant public discussion of, and investment in, E-democracy solutions to the problem of young people's reluctance to engage in traditional political participation, in particular, voting. The potential of social networks, and the new media and communications technologies that facilitate them, for the emergence and maintenance of social and political activism has been confirmed by studies in both the United States (Cohen and Kahne, 2012) and Europe (LSE, 2013). Internet tools and social media can enhance the participation of young people in democratic life not least because the technologies themselves are inherently interactive and encourage young people to enter into multiple dialogues with other individuals or groups. Thus, the Internet and its associated technologies create the opportunities to participate in political discourse by allowing young people to communicate information in a dialogical manner, using sources that they find credible (often received from people within their existing networks) and allowing, via virtual platforms such as Facebook and Twitter, almost instantaneous sharing of images, sound and text. The Internet allows young people to seek information, cross-check news articles, communicate with organizations and their members, get messages across to political teams and send petitions or contact politicians and municipal officials.

However, there is also increasing evidence that online forms of participation are no 'quick fix' for the inclusive and democratically oriented engagement of young people in the political sphere. CivicWeb (a major EU project on virtual activism by young people) concluded that computer-mediated communication technologies (CMCs) supplement established forms of political activity offline rather than providing participatory spaces online for those who are disengaged from politics (CivicWeb, 2009). Since the publication of the CivicWeb report, the virtual terrain has shifted away from the kind of 'top-down' websites, news media or tightly censored blogs delivering information, that were the focus of the CivicWeb study, towards more 'interactive' or 'participatory' modes of communications (online forums, social networking sites or blogs with loosely moderated comment sections). However, the latest studies continue to suggest that the interactive nature of these online platforms extends pre-existing political participation rather than encourages young people who are disinterested or distrustful of politics to engage and does not substitute for the positive relationships that emerge from face-to-face contact (LSE, 2013).

The limitations of online platforms relate also to the kinds of subjectivities and publics that digital technologies facilitate. The Internet increases accessibility and ease of publication, allowing people to consume but also produce political discussion. However, it remains an open question as to how much young people exploit this opportunity and whether it facilitates their connection with mainstream politics. Certainly, the Internet allows young people to interact, maintain their anonymity and compare information sources in a way that makes them feel empowered (Hulme, 2009). However, CMCs inherit social inequalities and power asymmetries, and do not guarantee democratic, equal-opportunity interactions (Herring, 2001). Thus, while Internet technology can fulfil many of the conditions of a successful political public sphere (Habermas, 1991), providing young people with the freedom of speech, expression and assembly needed for a healthy public discourse, the very multiplicity of the Internet may create as many barriers to political engagement as it circumvents. For example, the practice of 'selective exposure', whereby people choose to consume only the information that reinforces their prejudices, has the effect of closing down political debate. Thus 'engagement' in and of itself does not necessarily expand or diversify young people's political horizons. Among and between (oppositional) groups, moreover, a distinctive 'call and response' mode of discursive engagement is often endemic in social media communication and exacerbates positions and ratchets up tension (Pilkington, 2014: 51). Abusive, sexist, racist and homophobic language, as well as gossip, misinformation and 'trolling' are also everyday features of digital culture. The implication of this is that the Internet can create publics that are isolationist and exclusionary in nature, having little or no engagement with those whose interests are opposed to their own.

Ethnographic studies conducted as part of the MYPLACE project suggest that, in fact, there is greater tension and ambivalence among young activists about the uses and abuses of 'new social media' than existing literature might lead us to expect. This is expressed in criticisms of the careless use of social media by others (posting inappropriate messages or giving away information to oppositional groups) as well as a dismissive attitude to the 'keyboard warriors' it shelters: '[...] it's like oh great you click the word "like" and well you're really doing your bit in't ya?' (Tim, English Defence League (EDL), UK). MYPLACE interview respondents also expressed concerns that the Internet was an environment that was easily manipulated by the state for the purposes of surveillance and control. Thus, in evaluating the potential of the development of apparently youth-friendly forms of participation, we have to consider not only *if* digital technologies facilitate youth engagement in politics, but *what* kind of politics that is.

## 'Politics are bollocks': the constitution of the political

> Politics are bollocks. I don't know nothing about politics. I don't follow politics. (Chris, EDL, UK)

Arguments and counter-arguments about the apathy towards, or disconnect from, politics among young people are underpinned by an assumption of the normative 'good' of political engagement. It is this premise, it would appear, that is not shared by those young people who distance themselves from 'the political' by choosing to define their engagement as 'not politics' even when, as in the case of the respondent cited above, they are highly politically active.

This disavowal of politics is found not only among activists. Recent research in the UK found that, when asked, 'If I say politics, what do you say?' in online focus groups with 18 year olds who had been eligible to, but opted not to, vote in the 2010 General Election in the UK, young people's immediate reactions were that politics was 'boring', 'confusing', 'intellegant men talking S**t', 'control', 'influence', 'power', 'money', 'corrupt', 'lies', 'miniplulation'[12] (Henn and Foard, 2014: 367). The MYPLACE research found a similar encoding of the process of politics and the sphere of 'the political' as 'dirty', 'corrupt' and 'deceitful'. Semi-structured interviews with a sub-sample of survey respondents in each research location showed that although meanings attached to 'politics' and 'democracy' vary greatly across Europe, there is a general disappointment with, and rejection of, the institutionalized political sphere and formal political activities. Young people frequently rejected mainstream parties for their lack of clarity, and for not dealing with issues directly: 'It's like talking and not getting anywhere. You have to get out there and say what you mean.' (Johnny, Denmark). Politicians are distrusted because they 'always hide something from people' (Denis, Latvia) or because they distribute resources unjustly or dishonestly. Indeed, in some regions (especially Hungary, Slovakia, Croatia, Estonia, Latvia and Portugal) politicians are openly, and frequently, identified with corruption: 'What came to my mind immediately was corruption.' (Tiago, Portugal). Respondents also generally view the political elite as inhabiting an alien, distant world, having totally different horizons and experiences from (young) people.

This is confirmed by MYPLACE survey data. Even in those countries where young respondents described their society in positive terms or expressed pride in their democracy (Finland, Denmark or Germany for instance), they were highly disappointed in politicians, political parties and the political elite in general. Trust in national parliaments, measured on a 0–10 scale, showed a mean of only 4.50, with just 10 of the 30 research locations (each of two locations in Denmark, Finland, Georgia, plus all four German locations) scoring above 5.0. Trust in parties was even lower with an overall mean of 3.75 on the same scale. Based on responses in agreement or disagreement with two statements – 'Politicians are corrupt' and 'The rich have too much influence over politics' – a scale to measure attitudes to politicians and politics was constructed. On this scale of 0–8 (where 0 = negative views and 8 = positive views), the mean score for respondents across all 30 locations in Europe was 2.46, falling as low as 1.14 (in Greece) and rising only as high as 4.55 (in Denmark).[13]

One way of understanding this contradictory picture in which young people express strong, sometimes passionate, views about something they claim to have no interest in is through the notion of 'anti-politics'. Beck and Beck-Gernsheim (2002: 158) envisage youth (dis)engagement as the practice of a 'politics of youthful anti-politics', consisting in a refusal to care about institutionalized politics while 'unintentionally acting very politically by depriving politics of attention, labour, consent and power'. This is reworked by Farthing (2010) to suggest young people are 'radically unpolitical' while engaged in a new 'politics of fun' based on a transformative agenda, a radically revised 'target', and new forms of participation including active rejection. A more detailed empirical exploration of how new forms of political action may be located in youth cultural leisure practices is provided by Riley *et al.* (2010) who employ Maffesoli's theory of 'neo tribes' to suggest that an 'everyday politics' (a politics of 'pleasure and survival') is practised by young people participating in the electronic dance music scene.

The half-hearted 'consent' invested by young people in the democratic system as they encounter it today is evident from the MYPLACE survey which showed that overall mean satisfaction 'with the way democracy works' across the full survey sample was, on a scale of 0–10, just 5.01.[14] However, the notion of 'anti-politics' tends towards a simplification of a more complex picture. Young people do more than 'simply stay at home' (Beck and Beck-Gernsheim, 2002: 159) and, when they do engage, they are more inclined to do so in unconventional politics – street politics, life-style politics and symbolic action. Moreover, beneath the tangibly tepid support for contemporary democracy, lies some evidence from the MYPLACE survey that young people would be willing to contemplate non-democratic forms of rule as a way to escape the contemporary political malaise. Using a scale for attitudes to the democratic system (based on positive and negative evaluations towards 'Having a democratic, multi-party system' and 'Having an opposition that can freely express its views') indicated that negative attitudes towards the democratic system were clustered, as anticipated, in locations in post-socialist European societies. This pattern is repeated in support for 'autocratic principles' of government (a scale constructed on the basis of attitudes towards 'Having a strong leader who is not constrained by parliament' and 'Having the army rule'). However, this analysis revealed also pockets of dissent from democracy across the European space. In the UK locations, for example, 'Having a democratic, multi-party system' was positively evaluated by less than two-thirds (62.7 per cent) of respondents while more than half (56.1 per cent) saw a strong leader, unconstrained by parliament, as either a 'very good' or 'fairly good' form of government. The paradox to be understood, it would appear, therefore, is that these young people are not so much 'anti' politics but profoundly disillusioned with the current democratic system while continuing to be, in principle, supportive of democratic forms of government and seeking to 'be heard' through it.

### Communication: consensus or conflict?

One of the concerns that runs through contributions to this volume is the need to understand the nature and extent of the critique of liberal democracy being expressed by young people and the potential for reclaiming 'the political' and its investment with new meaning. On this question, contributions by Sik and by Busse *et al.* adopt a broadly Habermasian vision of the public sphere. Busse *et al.* suggest that communication (Habermas, 1984) might act as the mechanism for making representative democratic institutions more permeable and bridging the gap that has opened up between the 'parallel worlds' of formal politics and the informal modes of engagement favoured by young people. Sik, drawing on Habermas's (1984, 1996) theory of communicative rationalization, explores the processes of memory transmission and political socialization as an aspect of the communicative reproduction of lifeworld. In conditions of open debate, he suggests, this results in a democratic political culture while, in the context of ideologically restricted or distorted communication, it leads to the formation of an antidemocratic political culture.

The practice of non-conventional forms of political participation within, for example, new social movements, can be an act of reclaiming and revitalizing the political through the creation of spaces of 'autonomous communication' in which more horizontal, inclusive and substantive debate takes place (Castells, 2012: 11). Participation in such direct forms of democratic process, moreover, is meaningful in itself. In the practice of forms of 'deliberative democracy', preferences are not aggregated and represented through democratic institutions but formed or transformed through the democratic process (Della Porta, 2013: 61). That young people feel more comfortable talking about politics to those with similar views, and with whom they largely agree, is suggested also in the contribution to this volume by Levinsen and Yndigegn. Based on the findings of survey and interview research for MYPLACE in two locations in Odense (Denmark), they find that, contrary to the expectation that dissimilar views would increase discussion, in fact young people tend to avoid discussion with those with whom they disagree.

*The Sociological Review*, 63:S2, pp. 1–35 (2015), DOI: 10.1111/1467-954X.12260

In contrast, contributions to the volume by Grimm and Pilkington and by Pollock *et al.* are shaped by critical interventions in democratic theory that envisage the Habermasian public sphere as potentially exclusionary (Mouffe, 2005; Della Porta, 2013) and question claims that 'consensus', as the outcome of deliberation, is the best way to ensure democratic inclusion. Grimm and Pilkington draw on survey, interview and ethnographic data from the UK, eastern Germany and Russia to argue that frustration with a political process rooted in debate, deliberation and consensus – expressed through the association of politics with 'chatter about nothing, which has no meaning' (Marina, Russia) – is present across countries with very different political heritages and contemporary constitutions of democracy as well as amongst both 'mainstream' youth and political activists. Indeed, even in those cases where country-specific data suggest young people are mostly satisfied with their democratic system and that their criticisms of it are likely to be worked through via liberal reformism (see Busse *et al.,* in this volume, on youth in western Germany), disillusionment with formal politics is expressed by respondents in terms of its constitution in 'endless discussion'. For those for whom formal politics is associated with meaningless debate, the centrality of 'talk' to alternatives based on forms of deliberative democracy may have little appeal also. In imagining what a political sphere that young people would reinvest in might look like, therefore, we might consider radical democratic critiques, which argue that understanding politics as the search for a universal rational consensus reduces it to the design of institutions capable of reconciling all conflicting interests and values, when the essence of democratic politics is, in fact, the legitimate expression of such conflict (Mouffe, 2005: 3).

That a politics young people find meaningful and attractive should be one that engages the emotions as well as the intellect is no surprise. 'Social movements are emotional movements', Castells (2012: 13) reminds us, in as much as protest starts not with a programme or political strategy but with 'the transformation of emotion into action'. Indeed, social movement theory has a long history of understanding collective behaviour as emotionally driven rather than deliberative and interpretative and thus as different from normal, 'rational' behaviour (Edwards, 2014: 37). The centrality of emotions, grievances and beliefs to the collective action engaged in by young people is confirmed by ethnographic studies of more than 40 different groups and movements as part of the MYPLACE project. However, as Crossley (2002: 50) argues, emotions are not necessarily opposed to rationality and it is precisely what he terms 'the reasonable qualities of emotions' that Mizen discusses in his contribution to this volume. Based on a study of activists' reflection on their reasons for joining a local Occupy movement in the UK, he argues that protest and movement activism necessarily involve an emotional dimension, because feelings have to be sufficiently strong for young people to become active and the arousal and organization of feelings are a necessary activity if social movements are to form and develop. However, if emotions are regarded as solely the instinctive preserve of individuals, then they remain susceptible to equations with irrational and unreasonable behaviour (something that social movement theory has been concerned to move away from). Thus, he

argues, although emotions play a clear and decisive role in motivating and sustaining young activists' participation in the local Occupy movement, they are
engaged in a process of 'emotional reasoning' which can take complex and nuanced forms including constant deliberation with the concerns that they come to
hold.

## How does the past shape the present and the future?

The role of political heritage in shaping contemporary civic and political engagement as well as the democratic contours of Europe in the future was foreseen in
the FP7 call – 'Democracy and the shadows of totalitarianism and populism:
the European experience' – under which MYPLACE was funded. Central to the
research design, therefore, was that research should be conducted in countries
representing: post-communist legacies, within which are included the 'authentic'
Bolshevik heritage (Russian Federation), the (more or less) nationalist resistance
to Soviet rule (Georgia, Estonia, Latvia), Central and East European variants
of communism and the experience of both fascist/authoritarian and communist
political heritage (Croatia, eastern Germany, Hungary, Slovakia); and western
European political histories that include periods of fascist (Spain, Portugal,
Greece) or national socialist (Germany) rule and those in which, in contrast,
radical or extreme politics have remained on the fringe or semi-incorporated into
mainstream political agendas (UK, Finland, Denmark). However, in its conceptualization, the project envisaged no 'good' and 'bad' histories or any straight
lines from 'authoritarian' pasts to precarious democratic presents or futures. Its
premise was rather that radical and populist political and philosophical traditions are pan-European and cyclical rather than embedded in discrete national
political cultures or based on rigid classifications of political heritage (totalitarian, communist, fascist) and open to 'healing' through democratization.

As outlined in the contribution to this volume by Popov and Deák, two concerns – not to contribute to the recycling of stigmatized understandings of particular national or regional histories and to ensure the inclusion of the experience
of those countries with no authoritarian political heritage – led to the decision to
understand the 'shadows' under study as not those associated with a particular
ideology or regime type but through the looser notion of 'difficult pasts'. This notion has the advantage also of shifting the ontological focus of the research from
the consideration of competing interpretations of the past itself, to the evaluation of the immanence of the past (Birth, 2006) in the present, and, potentially the
future. Of interest is not how much, or what, young people know about difficult
periods in the past but how particular articulations of the past shape their current
political, civic and social attitudes and behaviour. The immanence of the past is
captured in MYPLACE survey data on how respondents evaluate the impact of
historical events. In composite terms, respondents in Germany and Russia were
on average the most likely to say that historical events were of importance to
their country. When considering particular events, the Second World War com-
manded the consistently highest score, demonstrating its perceived continuing

*The Sociological Review*, 63:S2, pp. 1–35 (2015), DOI: 10.1111/1467-954X.12260

importance for all countries; 85 per cent of young people across all locations regard the Second World War as being important in the history of their country, with the lowest level recorded at 66 per cent in Barreiro (Portugal). Other historical events that continue to have impact reflect locally significant experiences, for example the experience of communism, fascism and the Cold War.

It is important here to clarify the relationship between memory and more institutionalized forms of historical knowledge. Although memory is often seen as an alternative to the official historical narrative (Pine *et al.*, 2004) – indeed as some observers maintain, memory is sometimes employed to challenge the established historiography in societies that undergo political transformations when meanings of national identity and political heritage are re-evaluated (Assmann and Shortt, 2012) – in this volume, Popov and Deák argue that memory and history should not be seen in as opposition to one another. On the contrary, the two are interconnected and shaped by each other. This is evident from the fact that the perspective of the subaltern, marginalized, or simply 'ordinary' is now more often than before included in the writings of professional historians. At the same time, interpretations of events and historical figures central to institutionalized historical narratives are reproduced in popular discourse in the process of national identity construction and negotiation of its meanings.

At the individual level, MYPLACE survey data indicate which variables predict respondents' relation to the historical past. Among socio-demographic variables, parental social class and belonging to the majority (ethnic) group in society are associated with a propensity to believe that historical events and commemorating the past are important among young people. Regression analysis shows that the perception of the importance of history, the past and historical memory/commemoration is influenced by young people's level of political knowledge and interest in politics (Muranyi and Berenyi, 2014). Young people who are most dissatisfied with democracy and consider themselves 'right-wing' are most likely to have been engaged in past-related activities over the last 12 months (this is based on a list of 12 activities such as having watched a film or documentary that was set in recent historical circumstances, having talked with parents or grandparents about the past, having attended a veterans' parade or shown support during a remembrance day etc.).

### Difficult pasts, depressing presents, radical futures?

The current generation of young people is united by the experience of growing up in a Europe that, for the first time, is largely free of both right- and left-wing authoritarian regimes. They share the lack of any first-hand memory of the Cold War and the associated fears and prejudices that divided Europe or, with a few notable exceptions, any direct experience of living under a communist, authoritarian or fascist political regime. They have experienced also the widening of the European Union[15] and increasing channels for physical mobility across Europe as well as a permanent revolution in communications technologies. At the same time, this generation shares also the experience of growing up in the first global crisis of capitalism in the post-World War II period. Moreover, the pressures of conformity and subordination under authoritarian regimes have been replaced with those of the individualization of risk (Beck, 1986) and the compulsion for young people to construct and manage successful personal 'biographies' (Furlong and Cartmel, 1997). As Europe negotiates the current economic recession, the structural conditions in which those challenges are faced become more difficult and the weak social position of young people (especially in employment terms) renders them particularly vulnerable.

These shared generational experiences have implications for young people's political engagement and participation. The financial crisis across Europe from 2008 disrupted the trend towards withdrawal into 'civil privatism' (Habermas, 1976) that had accompanied a period in which modernization and prosperity were assumed. The sudden collapse of the expectation of prosperity meant that the search for new forms of activism – hitherto undertaken by a minority of young people – was extended to those previously depoliticized. How this affects young people's participation strategies specifically is considered by Soler-i-Martí and Ferrer-Fons in their contribution to the volume. Drawing on Bourdieu's (1979, 1985, 1989) concept of 'social space', they suggest these strategies are determined by the position youth occupies in the social space and explore how variations in 'youth transition regimes' (measured in terms of the degree of exposure to risk, the length of young people's pathways to adulthood and welfare state generosity and age-orientation) in different countries position young people more centrally or more marginally in the system of social relations. Drawing on MYPLACE survey data for 12 participating countries, they conclude that in societies where youth transition regimes accord young people positions of greater centrality (Finland, Denmark and Germany followed by the UK, Estonia and Latvia), there is a tendency towards participation (especially institutional participation) as well as protest action. In contrast, in contexts where youth transition regimes place young people in more peripheral positions (Hungary, Slovakia and Croatia as well as Greece, Spain and Portugal), passivity is usually the dominant strategy (alongside less organized and more confrontational forms of protest).

The most intensive period of empirical data collection for the MYPLACE project (2011–12) coincided with the peak of economic crisis in many participating countries. The 'depressing present' thus emerges as an important prism through which young people both interpret the past and engage with the future. However, the interaction between difficult past and depressing present is contextually diverse. For young people in post-socialist contexts, for example, the depressing and frustrating present is perceived not as a radical break from assumed prosperity but as a continuation of the difficult past, where the latter is associated with the whole post-socialist transition period. As Popov and Deák note in their contribution to the volume, when the difficult past is located in the 'living memory' of respondents, closure between past and present is lost (Mah, 2010: 402). The relationship between difficult past and depressing present is also socially structured. The example of the UK, discussed by Popov and Deák, illustrates how respondents from different socio-economic backgrounds bring

*The Sociological Review*, 63:S2, pp. 1–35 (2015), DOI: 10.1111/1467-954X.12260

the past into their evaluations of the present differently: young people from more affluent families contrast the 'depressing present' to a nostalgic image of a 'better past' characterized by less marginality and greater sense of community in working-class milieux; those having grown up themselves on the council housing estates associated with these environments, in contrast, show little nostalgia for them. Finally, as indicated in Grimm and Pilkington's contribution, which considers the role of the perception of the 'silencing' of certain subjects as legitimate topics for political debate, social amnesia may be applied to the present as well as the past. This point is also made in the contribution by Pollock *et al.* which argues that populism may be a misnomer in that certain sets of beliefs are described as 'populist' in order to deny the legitimacy of the complex and often inconsistent beliefs that many young people hold.

Looking to the future, and the potential for receptivity to the populist radical right among young people, however, contributions to this volume by both Sik (on the shift towards anti-democratic political orientations in Hungary) and by Koronaiou *et al.* (on the rise in support for Golden Dawn in Greece) suggest that radicalization cannot be explained solely by economic crisis. Sik argues that structural transformations, such as the financial crisis, do not create a radical political culture but rather act to strengthen processes of political socialization and memory transmission that shape antidemocratic attitudes while weakening processes that form democratic ones. In this sense crisis is a structural catalyst, which triggers already existing but latent cultural potential for radicalization. This renders the various media of transmission of political heritage (museums, archives, family memory practices, school curricula etc.) central to our understanding of how this iterative process occurs and, for this reason, particular 'sites of memory' (*lieux de mémoire*) were the focus of study in every country participating in the MYPLACE project. In this volume, the contribution by Sik is an example of how two *lieux de mémoire* in Budapest, the House of Terror and the Holocaust Memorial Center museums, shape the transmission of memory.

*Intergenerational transmission of political attitudes*

> I can't answer no questions about politics. [ ... ] Ask me a question about politics, and I'll phone me granddad. (Ray, EDL, UK)

The role of the family is indispensable in mnemonic socialization and politicization of the younger generation (Pine *et al.*, 2004; Hirsch, 1999; Jennings *et al.*, 2009; Keightley and Pickering, 2012); it is a particularly important channel for transmission of memories that are opposed to more institutionalized and politically dominant historical discourses. MYPLACE research focusing on the intergenerational transmission of memories and political values showed that the family is particularly important in the politics of history; here, young people perceive memories passed from the older generations of family members to be a more trustworthy source of information than any other institutionalized historical discourse (school curriculum, museums, media, etc.). At the same time, not only memories are passed intergenerationally but also silencing and contradictory interpretations of the 'difficult past' that might lead young people to be confused in their own interpretations of those periods of national history. Since these histories are elements of current political debates, this may have the effect of encouraging 'historical nihilism' and, as a consequence receptivity to more radical political ideas. Intergenerational interviews (with two or three generations of the same family) also demonstrated that 'cognitive mobilization' – discussion of political subjects at home – has a significant impact on young people's perceptions of politics. Although young people do not necessarily share the political views of their parents and/or grandparents, the research showed that they were likely to have more articulated political views if they were exposed to such discussions in the family. However, although the older generation of respondents often initiates the process of memory transmission by telling stories from the family's past, young people are far from passive listeners to these memories. The MYPLACE research revealed how these memories are engaged with by young people critically and in a way that makes them relevant to their present situation. A common example of how young people internalize family memory only if it has direct relevance to their own experience, whilst dismissing it if it is considered inappropriate to contemporary life, is the dismissal of older generations' 'racist' remarks:

> Oh, my granddad was [...] one of the nicest blokes you'd ever see, you'd ever meet but he was a bit of a, tiny bit of a racist. [...] I mean he'd go up to a certain street in this town and it's literally full of Indians and that like, and he'd go, if he's pissed off, he'll open the windows, wide down, 'get out the street, you fucking Pakis'. Like, 'Oh, granddad' [...] (Darrell, Nuneaton, UK)

Moreover, MYPLACE survey data suggest that young people identify more with the political views and values of their peers than their family. In 28 of 30 locations, peers (partner or boyfriend/girlfriend and best friend) are seen as having closer political views to respondents than family (father, mother and grandparents). Indeed, this is one of the cases in which MYPLACE data reveal relatively little significance of context; there is not a great variation across locations on the degree of closeness or distance of family and peers on respondents' political ideas and values. However, multilevel analysis suggests that political activism (participation other than voting) is associated with the closeness of political ideas with family and peers. Young people who are more politically active tend to feel more distant from their family's political ideas compared to more passive young people. In contrast, the level of political activism is positively associated with the closeness of political views with peers. As young people participate more frequently in political actions, so their political views tend to align with those of their peers rather than their families. Thus political engagement may facilitate the establishment of new political preferences, which are independent of family origin.

At the individual level, multilevel modelling also shows that political interest of both father and mother is associated with higher political interest in the

*The Sociological Review*, 63:S2, pp. 1–35 (2015), DOI: 10.1111/1467-954X.12260

respondent (other factors that are important include level of education, age and political knowledge). This tends to confirm existing research that suggests that family has an important influence on political engagement, although it should be borne in mind that the level of parents' political interest is respondent-assessed.

Another measure of influence on young people's political views was frequency of discussion of politics with a range of family members and peers. This measure suggests that politics is discussed most frequently with fathers and peers (girl-friend/boyfriend and best friend) compared with either mothers or grandparents. The contribution to this volume by Levinsen and Yndigegn considers this gender difference in detail on the basis of the findings from both quantitative and qualitative data in Denmark (Odense). They conclude that fathers remain the most frequent discussion partners. Friends and partners (girlfriends/boyfriends) are also frequent discussion partners, and young men discuss politics more frequently with their friends than do young women. Based on the qualitative data, it seems that parental political socialization, to some extent, is rooted in traditional gender roles, where fathers are more likely to be a source of information about societal issues while mothers tend towards giving advice on personal matters. The analysis of the Danish data also suggests that young people with low (perceived) political distance to their father, mother and/or friend discuss politics more frequently. However, the impact of political distance is strongest in discussions with fathers and this seems to be a consequence of negative experiences from prior discussions; when political discussions with parents turn into a fixed pattern of disagreement, there is a tendency to withdraw from the discussion.

## Are young people receptive to populist and radical right political agendas?

In its original conception the MYPLACE project highlighted the potential for the growth in support for radical ideologies of the 'far right' among young people based on evidence that the European political space, especially the European Parliament, was being colonized increasingly by populist and, somewhat paradoxically, Eurosceptic political parties and blocs. Since then (2009), there has been a steady stream of successes of such parties in national parliaments: Golden Dawn took 7 per cent of the vote in Greece in June 2012; the Finns took 19 per cent in Finland, 2011; and Jobbik polled 20 per cent of the vote in Hungary, 2014. These parties also won seats in the 2014 European parliamentary elections where Jobbik polled 15 per cent of the national vote, Golden Dawn 10 per cent and the Finns 13 per cent. More dramatically, Eurosceptic/nationalist parties won the elections for the first time in France (with 25 per cent of the vote) and the UK (27 per cent). Even Germany, whose political and economic investment in the European project has been seemingly unswerving, saw the anti-Euro currency party Alternative für Deutschland poll 7 per cent of the vote and the far right National Democratic Party (1 per cent) also take a seat.[16]

The significance of these trends for the MYPLACE project is heightened by the conventional perception that young people are the most likely to support extreme politics (Fielding, 1981: 56; Mudde, 2014: 1). The 'typical extreme-right voter' in Europe is characterized by Bakić (2009: 201) as 'a twenty five-year-old unemployed man, with below-average education'. Goodwin (2011b: 6) states that those who turn out for 'populist extremist parties'[17] are, in terms of age 'either very young or very old'. In fact, however, the data on whether young people have a particular propensity to support the 'extreme-right' is sparse (Mudde, 2014: 1) and inconclusive. As Kitschelt (2007: 1199) states, with regard to individual socio-demographic criteria and support for the 'radical right', only two facts are incontrovertible: support is weakest among highly educated professionals and greatest among manual workers, those in small business, the unemployed, 'housewives' and pensioners; and such parties attract more men than women. The strongest case for heightened receptivity among young people is made by Arzheimer (2009) who proposes that the young will have a greater propensity to vote for the 'extreme right' because 'they compete with immigrants for scarce resources' (Arzheimer, 2009: 263). Arzheimer's confirmation of this hypothesis, however, is based on data from Eurobarometer surveys in EU member countries (plus Norway) prior to the accession of former socialist countries and over the period 1980–2002. The findings do not reflect, therefore, differences in profiles of supporters in western Europe and former socialist eastern Europe or capture potential changes in socio-demographics of voters as a result of the recent growth of 'new far right' or 'populist radical right' parties and movements.

From the range of different terms employed by those studying the far end of the right-wing political spectrum cited above, it is clear that part of the problem in determining a clear answer to the question of whether young people are particularly receptive to such parties, is the lack of conceptual clarity. Kitschelt (2007: 1178) takes a pragmatic stance on the internal debate concluding that regardless of the conceptual disagreements underpinning the range of concepts used – 'radical populist right' (Mudde, 2007), 'radical right' (Norris, 2005), 'extreme right' (Ignazi, 2003) – all roads lead to general agreement on which electorally successful parties should be included under the various definitions for study. For the purposes of MYPLACE such pragmatism does not suffice, not least because the object of study is individual attitudes and behaviours rather than parties and electoral support for them (as discussed in more detail below). It should be noted here, therefore, that, while the terminology used by cited authors is retained in order to avoid misrepresenting their findings, the position underpinning this volume follows Mudde (2007) in recognizing an important distinction between classic 'extreme' or 'far right' political parties, which are in essence antidemocratic, and a new populist form of the radical right which remains broadly democratic despite opposing some fundamental values of liberal democracy and promoting an ideology that combines nativism, authoritarianism, and populism. This distinction is particularly important to bear in mind when considering examples of ethnographic studies of movements and parties included in contributions to this volume by Koronaiou *et al.* and Grimm and Pilkington. In the case of the former, the object of study is the classic far right Golden Dawn party which, despite its own rejection of its identification as fascist or neo-Nazi, is characterized by a classic fascist ideology based on a mythologized conception of the Greek nation as an organic (biologically unmixed and culturally homogenous) community that exists in a state of degeneration and decline, is confronted by (internal and external) enemies that threaten its unity and survival and is in need of revolutionary national rebirth (palingenesis). In contrast, the two groups considered in the contribution by Grimm and Pilkington – the English Defence League (EDL) and the Russian Run movement – may attract a classic (and undesired) fascist or national socialist fringe but are much closer to single issue social movements with an ultra-patriotic and Islamophobic (in the case of the EDL) or nationalist (in the case of Russian Run) hue. For example, although the EDL is referred to routinely as 'extreme' or 'far right' in the media, from an academic perspective it shows distinct differences from groups traditionally associated with the far right of the political spectrum in that it 'is not driven by a fascist or neo-fascist ideological end goal' (Copsey, 2010: 5), does not reject the principles of a democratic constitutional state or fundamental human equality, does not uphold an ideology of racial supremacy and promotes gender and LGBT rights.

It would appear that the impact of age on support for the far right among young people varies also across different national and regional contexts. In countries like Austria and France, Arzheimer (cited in Mudde, 2014: 4) suggests, young people vote disproportionately for extreme right parties. However, the case of the UK appears to provide counter-evidence of a significant shift in the demographic of support for the far right in recent decades. While support for the National Front[18] (NF) in the 1970s came disproportionately from the young, this relationship is reversed in figures on support for the British National Party[19] (BNP). Thus while 37 per cent of NF supporters studied by Harrop *et al.*[20] in 1977–8 (cited in Goodwin *et al.*, 2010: 199) were under the age of 25, only 11 per cent of supporters in Goodwin's BNP supporter sample[21] (2002–2006) were this young. Moreover, compared to the data from the 1970s, the proportion of supporters aged 35–54 years old increases by 10 percentage points (from 29 per cent to 39 per cent), while the proportion aged 55 or over doubles (from 18 per cent to 36 per cent). Goodwin (2011a: 137) concludes, on the basis of both quantitative and qualitative (interview) data, that, 'Despite its attempts to mobilize new groups of supporters, there is little evidence that the party is successfully recruiting large numbers of young people and women.'

The explanations put forward for the reversal in age profile between the NF movement of the 1970s and early 1980s and the contemporary BNP are rooted in generational discontinuities in political socialization and civic values. In particular, young people are found to be less likely to express racial prejudice and xenophobia and are more open than older generations to living in an ethnically diverse society (Sky News, 2011). It follows that those socialized during the 1970s – a period characterized by intense political conflict over race and immigration – may have retained a greater level of concern with these issues. This age cohort would now be middle-aged or older, which is where the strongest support for the extreme right is found (Goodwin *et al.*, 2010: 199). These findings are confirmed by the intergenerational research conducted as part of the MYPLACE project; young people were found to associate xenophobic and racist views and parties/movements that promote them with the older generation whilst they themselves talk positively about contemporary multicultural Britain. A similar connection is made in interpreting levels of support for right-wing extremism in Germany. Attitude surveys show that the oldest generation tends towards right-wing extremism most strongly and that younger generations tend to be more liberal and cosmopolitan (Schellenberg, 2013: 154). This finding is, again, confirmed by qualitative research on intergenerational transmission of attitudes conducted for MYPLACE in both western and eastern Germany.

The younger generation in East European countries does not follow the West European pattern in being more tolerant than older generations (Levinsen, 2012). Regular surveys on ethnic relations in Russia (conducted by VTsIOM, 1988–2003 and the Levada Centre 2003–2006) over the period 1994–2006 suggest that young people (16–25 years of age) display heightened levels of ethnic intolerance and that young people's xenophobia is of the more radical variant (Gudkov, 2004; Leonova, 2009); in 2006 the proportion of 'open xenophobes' among 16–25 year olds was 14 per cent higher than the sample average (Leonova, 2009: 151). In the Hungarian case, this translates into a quite different profile of support for the populist radical right than in the case of the UK. Analysing a large sample of Jobbik voters, Kovacs (2013: 229) finds that people aged 18–29 represented the largest age group (29 per cent) and were not exclusively from among the 'losers' of transition; rather a 'young and mainly student-dominated group is over-represented among Jobbik voters in almost every region of the country' (2013: 230). A similar stronger expression of xenophobic or nationalist views among younger than older generations was identified in the MYPLACE research in Slovakia.

It is also possible that the connection between youth and the far right is stronger in western European countries when it comes to more direct forms of activism. As Mudde (2014: 4), for example, notes, one problem with relying on voting data for understanding support for the extreme right is that relatively few young people vote for such parties, either because they are too young to vote or because young people in general are less likely to vote. Fielding's classic study of the National Front, for example, found young people to dominate amongst 'activists' within the movement (Fielding, 1981: 56). In sharp contrast to the low recruitment of young people to the BNP, moreover, the English Defence League (EDL) – a consciously 'feet on the street' movement – has been portrayed as youthful. Copsey (2010: 5), for example, describes the EDL as 'a loose coalition of hardcore football hooligans, far-right extremists and politically unsophisticated white working-class youth' while a Facebook hosted survey conducted by DEMOS found 72 per cent of supporters of the EDL to be under the age of 30 (Bartlett and Littler, 2011: 5). In Scandinavia, those joining 'neo-Nazi movements' are characterized as being mostly 16–20 years old (Kimmel, 2007: 205) while in Germany, the Autonome Nationalisten (Autonomous Nationalists), who have been a central feature of the far right scene since 2002, are characterized by their youth and distinctive adoption of stylistic and behavioural patterns of left-wing groups (Schellenberg, 2013: 152).

*The Sociological Review*, 63:S2, pp. 1–35 (2015), DOI: 10.1111/1467-954X.12260

Care should be taken not to overemphasize the representation of young people even in these smaller, more subcultural movements. The overestimation of the proportion of youth active in movements like the EDL is possible as a result of young people being active in the most visible (street) element of the movement; those who demonstrate tend to be younger men whereas older members are more likely to be involved in other activities, including leafleting, flash-demos and legal challenges (Bartlett and Littler, 2010: 5). The fact that the DEMOS survey was conducted via social media is also likely to produce an overestimation of the proportion of young people. The ethnographic study on the EDL undertaken for MYPLACE, indeed, charted a decline rather than increase in interest in the movement among young people over 30 months of fieldwork. Respondents suggested that the shift of the EDL away from its roots in the Casuals (football subculture) and the attempt to rid the movement of those looking for violence is the reason for this. However, the research also identified some tension between older and younger members of the movement; younger members are perceived as unruly, prone to 'kick off' at demonstrations or to use inappropriate language or make inappropriate posts to social media sites. As such they become the object of disciplining or exclusion as the EDL seeks to establish itself as a public awareness raising movement with legitimate concerns rather than an extremist organization of the far right (Pilkington, 2014: 121). A recent Extremis/YouGov survey of the general population confirmed that those aged 40 years and above would be more likely to consider joining the EDL; of those who had heard of the movement, only 5 per cent of 18–24 year olds said they would consider joining, while 13 per cent of 40–59 year olds said they would consider it (Extremis Project, 2012).

## Politics (not parties)

Perhaps the most limiting dimension of the existing literature is that it is confined largely to formally registered (and electorally successful) political parties and voting intentions. As Mieriņa and Koroļeva point out in their contribution to this volume, the groups supporting right-wing extremism and far right parties are small. This makes them difficult to analyse on the basis of general population surveys; a problem compounded by the fact that the group of young people in general surveys is typically small. Reliable data on the strength of support for different populist or extreme ideas among youth in Europe, especially its Eastern part, and what motives drive it, are thus lacking.

While the MYPLACE survey does not suffer from a small sample size for young people, the target age range (16–25 years) means that a significant proportion of respondents were too young to have had the opportunity to vote. While the survey asked respondents both how they had voted and which, if any, political parties they felt close to, these questions produced such a small number of cases of those voting for, or feeling close to, a far right or populist radical right party that the analysis of findings would have no statistical validity. Thus, in their contribution to this volume, Mieriņa and Koroļeva focus on support among youth for 'far right ideology' rather than particular parties or movements, employing measures for xenophobia, welfare exclusionism and negative attitudes towards minorities included in the survey instrument. Their analysis suggests that despite comparatively low immigration rates, young people in post-socialist locations, along with Greek locations, tend to have more negative predispositions and to be more xenophobic and exclusionist towards immigrants than young people in West European locations, especially Germany. However, their analysis of contextual factors suggests that the high prevalence of far right sentiments in East Central Europe is explained not by the post-socialist status as such but rather factors such as little general trust and confidence in politicians, low interest in politics, ethnic nationalism and little contact with other ethnic groups.

This returns us to the question of the significance of the disavowal of politics among young people. A key conclusion from the analysis of MYPLACE survey data by Mieriņa and Koroļeva is that political distrust is one of the strongest predictors of support for far right ideology, whether or not this is ultimately translated into votes. Follow-up interviews from the MYPLACE research, moreover, show that, notwithstanding high variance in the level of tolerance towards radical or extremist movements amongst respondents, the clarity of their messages and their direct and straightforward engagement with current social issues rendered them distinct from the mainstream parties that were heavily criticized. Xenophobia, welfare chauvinism, exclusionism, and anti-minority attitudes are more widespread among young people who have little interest in, or understanding of, politics. This is a finding supported by single country studies. Schellenberg (2013) suggests that National Socialist groups in Germany adopt a populist discourse attacking mainstream political parties and their politicians as elitist, corrupt and profoundly antisocial while Kovacs's (2013) study of the support for the Hungarian Jobbik movement concludes that the binding element between different subgroups of the Jobbik constituency is a strong anti-establishment attitude. This, moreover, appears to be confirmed by qualitative research among university students supporting Jobbik, which suggests that the main motivation for their support was neither extreme nationalism nor xenophobia but 'a profound dislike of the whole political elite of the transition' (Iterson cited in Kovacs, 2013: 229). The article by Pollock *et al.* in this volume shows that anti-establishment sentiment is as much a feature of left-wing as right-wing disillusionment.

This evokes Mouffe's (2005) argument that the incapacity of established democratic parties to put forward significant alternatives fuels the current rise in appeal of 'anti-establishment' parties, which provide people with some form of hope that things could be different. Although, she argues, this is an essentially 'illusory hope', founded on unacceptable mechanisms of xenophobic exclusion, when it is the only channel for the expression of political passions, it is seductive (2005: 71–72). The evidence suggests that support for populist radical right attitudes extends well beyond the levels of a small pathological marginalized minority and constitutes a 'radicalized version of mainstream ideas' (Mudde, 2007: 25–30, 297). This raises the uncomfortable possibility that populist radical right movements may themselves 'articulate albeit in a very problematic way, real democratic demands which are not taken into account by traditional parties' (Mouffe, 2005: 71).

*The Sociological Review*, 63:S2, pp. 1–35 (2015), DOI: 10.1111/1467-954X.12260

## MYPLACE project: approach and methods

Central to the MYPLACE project is its use of multiple research methodologies in 30 case study locations across Europe. Data collection was undertaken using a questionnaire survey, semi-structured interviews, focus groups and participant observation and the results of all these data sources are drawn on in articles included in this volume. Most of these data were collected in parallel in order to provide a holistic understanding of young people's political and civic engagement in the countries studied. The project was sensitive from its inception to the importance of the triangulation of data, building this objective into the design and development of the research instruments. Uniquely, the project has included substantial collaboration with museums (and other public institutions engaged with memory work) in each partner country. Through observation of their work (exhibitions, events and outreach work with youth) as well as focus groups and interviews conducted with young people visiting the institutions, the role of memory in the transmission of political views and readiness for activism is captured in the project. Ethnographic methods were employed to explore the meanings of activism among young people engaged in a range of organizations and movements ranging from student self-organization and youth sections of political parties through anarchist and Occupy groups to ultra-patriotic and radical right-wing movements.

### Case study locations

The countries included in MYPLACE were selected to research contrasting social and political heritages from communist to fascist as well as countries with no such experience. Flyvbjerg (2006) contrasts 'random selection' with 'information oriented selection' where the former delivers representativeness and generalizability and the latter allows small samples to be theoretically productive through the careful selection of contrasting cases or 'critical cases'. MYPLACE uses both strategies. First, the purposive selection of two contrasting locations in each country (four in Germany) was undertaken on the basis of a prior analysis of literature and socio-demographic indicators. This strategy allowed each team to focus on an area where there was evidence to suggest that young people will have a greater propensity to be receptive to radical political agendas than elsewhere. The selection of the contrasting location was not to have a 'control' group in the formal, statistical, sense but enabled a comparative contextual analysis where there were fewer reasons to anticipate a high propensity for receptivity to radical views. The single most significant gain in case study sampling is delivered by having two cases rather than one (Sudman, 1976). This dual location 'theoretical sampling' approach avoids the national partiality of single case studies and represents significant added value in allowing contrasts both within and between countries. MYPLACE articulates 'case' at various levels: country; research locations; activist groupings; and individuals within locations. These 'empirical units' are the inputs from which further 'cases' of findings are generated through conceptual development (Ragin, 1992).

The factors contributing to the propensity for young people to be receptive to radical agendas are likely to be nationally and locally sensitive as well as contingent upon different forms of radicalization. The primary consideration when selecting locations was the importance of local factors and evidence that particular factors may be associated with young people's receptivity to radical political agendas. The following criteria were all considered as *potentially* important in the selection of each location by each team: community segregation and perception of minority groups; underlying socio-economic inequalities; civic engagement; continuity and discontinuity in political heritage; the activity of 'supply' side movements and the integration of populist/radical groups with other youth 'subcultures'; ideological resonance and local democracy; and the extent of political engagement/alienation.

Location specific case studies were used for the questionnaire survey and the follow-up semi-structured interviews. In Germany the four locations were selected in order to capture the importance of the different political heritages of eastern and western parts of the country. The 30 research locations (see Table 1 and Figure 1) represent a rich, diverse and unique source of data on the political attitudes and behaviour of young people across Europe.

*Questionnaire survey*

The questionnaire survey was undertaken in each of the 30 locations using a common questionnaire[22] and a representative sampling strategy of young people aged 16 to 25[23] which aimed to secure 600 interviews per location.[24] The questionnaire includes 82 questions which translate into 385 separate items which measure the attitudes, values and behaviour of these young people on a wide range of political and participatory issues. The survey data was initially analysed by each team using a report template which guided the substantive content of the analysis as well as appropriate statistical techniques to build and test scales. The data were then pooled,[25] resulting in a database of 16,935 respondents and subject to a comparative analysis by location with each team taking responsibility for a specific theme from the questionnaire.[26] Finally, multilevel regression modelling (Hox, 2010) was undertaken, where appropriate, to exploit the research design which nests the data within a hierarchical structure of 30 locations within 14 countries. Cross country analyses of the extreme right (Mieriņa and Koroļeva) of populism (Pollock *et al.*) and of the context of political participation across Europe (Soler-i-Martí and Ferrer-Fons) exploit the comparability of the survey data and show that while there are important location specific experiences and findings, there are nonetheless broader regional patterns which often map on to different welfare state types (Kääriäinen and Lehtonen, 2006).

*Semi-structured interviews*

Follow-up semi-structured interviews were conducted with a sub-sample of 30 of the survey participants in each of the research locations, using theoretical sampling informed by respondents' answers to two key questions in the

**Table 1:** *MYPLACE research locations*

| Country | Location | Hypothesized receptivity to radicalization | Geographic notes |
|---|---|---|---|
| Croatia | Podsljeme | Low | District of Zagreb |
|  | Pescenica Zitnjak | High | District of Zagreb |
| Denmark | Odense East | High | District of Odense |
|  | Odense Center | Low | District of Odense |
| Estonia | Narva area | High | Area in eastern Estonia, bordering Russia |
|  | Tartu | Low | City in central southern Estonia |
| Finland | Lieksa and Nurmes | High | Two small towns in eastern Finland |
|  | Kuopio | Low | Town in central Finland |
| Georgia | Kutaisi | High | City in western Georgia |
|  | Telavi | Low | Town, north-west of Tbilisi |
| Germany (western) | Bremen | Low | City in north-western Germany |
|  | Bremerhaven | High | The sea port that serves Bremen |
| Germany (eastern) | Jena | Low | City in south-eastern Germany |
|  | Rostock | High | City in north-eastern Germany |
| Greece | New Philadelphia | High | North-eastern district of Athens |
|  | Argyroupouli | Low | South-western district of Athens |
| Hungary | Sopron | Low | Town close to the Austrian border |
|  | Ozd | High | Town close to the Slovak border |

*(Continued)*

**Table 1:** *Continued*

| Country | Location | Hypothesized receptivity to radicalization | Geographic notes |
|---|---|---|---|
| Latvia | Agenskalns | Low | District of Riga |
| | Forstate and Jaunbuve | High | Two districts of Daugavpils, close to the Russian border |
| Portugal | Lumiar | Low | District of Lisbon in the main city area |
| | Barreiro | High | District of Lisbon on the opposite side of the river Tagus to the main city area |
| Russia | Kupchino | High | District of St Petersburg |
| | Vyborg | Low | City close to the Finnish-Russian border |
| Slovakia | Rimavska Sobota | High | Town close to the Hungarian Border |
| | Trnava | Low | City north east of Bratislava |
| Spain | Vic | High | Town around an hour from Barcelona |
| | Sant Cugat | Low | Town close to Barcelona |
| UK | Coventry | Low | City in central England |
| | Nuneaton | High | Town in central England |

*The Sociological Review*, 63:S2, pp. 1–35 (2015), DOI: 10.1111/1467-954X.12260

**Figure 1** *Research locations included in the MYPLACE project*

questionnaire concerning participation and (in)tolerance. These interviews, generally undertaken with respondents several days after the survey questionnaire, were carried out with respondents of contrasting types and intensities of political (non)engagement and levels of (in)tolerance and controlled for on key socio-demographic variables (gender, ethnicity/nationality, age and education). This design meant that all interviewees were exposed to the same sensitization to the questions in the questionnaire.[27] The follow-up interviews were undertaken using an interview scenario formulated to explore themes from the questionnaire in greater depth and with the flexibility to explore interesting topics as they emerged naturally. The common interview scenario began with a 'warm up' section designed by individual teams to maximize local sensitivity followed by six common blocks of questions on: political heritage and transmission; history and memory in everyday life; participation and understanding of 'the political'; culture and lifestyles; understanding the language of politics; and receptivity to populism/extremism. In addition to common core questions, a series of 'prompts' (including visual aids) and 'suggested additional questions' were devised by each participating team to ensure local sensitivity. A total of 901 semi-structured interviews were achieved.

*Museums and the mechanisms of memory transmission*

Further qualitative data were generated through interviews and focus groups in conjunction with the museums and other public institutions involved in memory work included in the project. The main focus of this work was on relations between social memory of problematic or 'difficult' periods of the past and young people's political and civic activism. In total, 54 focus groups with young people visiting museums and 73 interviews with experts were used to explore the role of memory in particular problematic periods of the past and how it shapes young people's attitudes, values and activities, through which populist, authoritarian and extremist ideas are reproduced or opposed. The research also explored how young people are socialized in mnemonic communities and how memories of the problematic pasts are interpreted and enacted by young people through their (non-)participation in political/civic activities. In this part of the research intergenerational interviews (with two–three generations of a single family) were conducted with a total of 180 respondents across the 14 MYPLACE countries. Ethnographic observation was conducted in a total of 18 sites of memory: 13 museums; three NGOs; one archive; and one public law institution. The contribution to this volume by Sik explores these phenomena from the perspective of the study of two contrasting Hungarian museums while Popov and Deák undertake a comprehensive cross-country analysis of this material and show that there are cross-national trends in the ways that national heritage influences political socialization within the family.

*Ethnographies*

The prioritization of validity over reliability in the generation of knowledge in this element of the MYPLACE project allowed case studies in each country (target of three per country) to be selected by partners provided that they constituted an interesting, challenging or new form of activism within the overall MYPLACE project objectives and research questions. Case studies, therefore, may be unique in terms of their geographical location, substance or nature of the activism involved. However, through a bottom-up, collaborative process, each case was ascribed to a 'cluster' of similar case studies for the purpose of cross-case analysis. A total of 44 achieved case studies were assigned to one of six clusters:[28] 'Radical right and patriotic movements' (nine cases); 'Anti-capitalist /anti-racist/anti-fascist movements' (seven cases); 'Anti-austerity/Occupy movements' (seven cases); 'Gender and minority rights movements' (seven cases); 'Youth sections of political, labour and state-sponsored organizations' (eight cases); and 'Faith based organizations' (six cases). Ethnographic studies were conducted according to guidelines identifying the distinguishing feature of the ethnographic approach as a sustained involvement in the lives of others although recognizing that fieldwork may take a variety of forms from classic 'participant observation', in which the researcher is routinely engaged in activities, communication and daily lives of respondents, to virtual or social media-based communication and engagement. In practice the fieldwork for case studies lasted from several months to more than two years. Articles in this volume by Mizen and by Koronaiou *et al.* are based on ethnographic case studies of the Occupy movement in the UK and of Golden Dawn in Greece respectively while the article by Grimm and Pilkington includes data from ethnographic studies of the English Defence League and Russian Run movement.

## Qualitative data analysis

While the sources of qualitative data are varied the project consortium employed a common approach to the coding and analysis of material. The MYPLACE qualitative data analytic strategy is based on an inductive approach but one that recognizes that such an approach is never pre-theoretical. Drawing on Goldkuhl and Cronholm (2010) and Burawoy (1998), the strategy employs inductive coding at the early stages of analysis (to maximize the opportunity for theoretical imagination) whilst undertaking a conscious process of 'theoretical matching' and validation against both data and existing theoretical frameworks at the third or interpretative level. To this end, all partners employed NVivo 9.2 software to code qualitative data, following protocols and guidelines for coding at three levels, where Level 1 nodes provide the closest, descriptive, representation of the phenomenon, Level 2 nodes group 'families' of Level 1 nodes while Level 3 nodes take the form of themes or metaphors drawing not only on the data analysed but also on relevant theoretical writing. Through the synthesis of these higher level 'nodes' at cross-case or cross-national level, micro empirical data are placed within current theoretical context as well as extending this theory on the basis of the research findings.

## Triangulation

Empirical triangulation is realized both nationally and cross-nationally. The articles by Busse *et al.* and Levinsen and Yndigegn, include data from the survey as well as from the qualitative data collection and show that the analysis of survey data benefits from the understandings gained from the interview data when it comes to explanations of *why* young people are as (in)active as they are and *why* it is that fathers tend to be the most important familial agent of influence.

Perhaps uniquely, the qualitative MYPLACE data were not translated but coded in the original language while researchers provided detailed node summaries ('node memos') in English. It is these memos that are synthesized at the cross-case or cross-national level of analysis in an adaptation of the 'meta-ethnography' method for the synthesis of qualitative empirical data (Noblit and Hare, 1988). This approach works through the principle of the 'reciprocal translations' of the meanings of one case into the meanings of another through which overarching themes, concepts or 'metaphors' evolve. The article by Grimm and Pilkington in this volume is an example of how this approach can be used also in the process of triangulation of data (in this case from the survey, semi-structured interviews and ethnographies) and cross-national qualitative data analysis (Russia, Germany and the UK). The 'loud and proud' metaphor is developed in relation to one ethnographic case study, explored and then validated through an analysis of the survey data and further qualitative material in all three countries.

## Structure of the volume

This collection of early findings of the project (which is still ongoing) reflects the three-way gaze of the MYPLACE project, considering first the importance of memory transmission and political socialization of young people, then turning to young people's current engagement with 'the political' and finally considering the potential for receptivity to and activism in 'far right' movements and organizations by young Europeans.

Articles in Part I of the volume, 'Footprints: political heritage and political socialization', consider how attitudes and practices among the current generation of 16–25 year olds are formed and shaped. Contributions explore how the internalization of political heritage by young people is accomplished via mnemonic socialization within families and peer group communication. Taking a broad overview of such socialization in the 14 European countries studied, the article by Popov and Deák demonstrates how socialization into mnemonic communities is an intersubjective and selective process. On the one hand it is conditioned by the discourses on past(s) available to young people, while, on the other, young people tend to internalize and reproduce those elements of discourse relevant to their own experience of the present. In the article by Sik, a more detailed elaboration of the conditioning of this 'political socialization' is presented in a single national context (Hungary). Here it is shown how competing national political discourses are transmitted through two specific sites of memory transmission (*lieux de mémoire*). The lack of minimal consensus on key 20th-century Hungarian political traumas – the Holocaust and state socialist terror – it is argued creates a 'memory vacuum', which has contributed to recent antidemocratic transformations in Hungarian political culture. Finally, Levinsen and Yndigegn draw on survey and interview data from Denmark to show that a significant component of the political socialization process is young people's engagement in political discussions with parents and friends. The article explores how young people experience political discussions in their everyday life and suggests that such discussion is important in the acquisition of basic democratic skills although there remains a tendency to avoid social situations where political disagreements are likely to appear.

Part II of the volume, 'The end of politics? Rethinking youth activism', considers youth and the realm of politics. Contributions employ the comparative survey data set to consider how political strategies – participation through formal institutions, engagement in political protest or political inactivity – adopted by young people across Europe are shaped by structural conditions – in particular the youth transition regime (Soler-i-Martí and Ferrer-Fons). Drawing on qualitative as well as survey data, articles in this section consider different responses to existing political culture that promotes the professionalization of participation and offers little space for integrating non-conventional engagement in decision-making processes. On the basis of a case study of young people in Germany the contribution by Busse *et al.* suggests that 'parallel worlds' are created in the form of: state-approved regulated and traditional forms of engagement (inhabited by the professionals); and forms of self-organization via projects and informal movements, engaged in by young people. One possible outcome of this is a drift towards de-democratization as politics as an 'elite project' becomes increasingly detached from everyday lives. Possible responses to

28

such a scenario are considered in contributions exploring young people's propensity to populist/authoritarian political agendas (Pollock *et al.*) and, in contrast, their participation in attempts to enact direct democracy through the Occupy movement (Mizen).

In Part III of the volume, 'A turn to the radical right?', contributions consider in more detail one specific response to frustration with the formal political realm, that is, a turn to far right and populist radical right ideologies and movements. Contributions consider evidence from MYPLACE survey data on the extent of young people's support for nationalist and far right ideology and explore which individual or contextual factors are associated with a higher propensity of young people to support such ideologies (Mieriņa and Koroļeva). The particular resonance of far right ideology among youth, and the symbolic importance of 'youth' for far right ideology, is explored in relation to youth support for Golden Dawn (Koronaiou *et al.*). Finally, taking up arguments in the second section of the volume – considering populism as radical critique of current enactments of liberal democracy – the participation of young people in ultra-patriotic movements is considered as a response to an external political environment experienced as hypocritical in its claims to openness and democracy while, in practice, silencing the discussion of uncomfortable issues that affect young people's everyday lives (Grimm and Pilkington). Drawing on data from the UK, eastern Germany and Russia, the authors argue that evidence suggests that such perceptions and experiences of 'politics' need to be viewed not as pertaining to a pathological fringe but as residing on a continuum with those of mainstream youth.

## Notes

1  The research was funded under the European Union Seventh Framework Programme (Grant Agreement number FP7–266831).
2  The methodological approach and research instruments employed are discussed in detail below.
3  The working definition of 'populism' determined at the start of the MYPLACE project was that populism can be conceptualized as a discursive pattern comprising: a diffused pattern of political communication aimed at mobilizing support and social consensus by appealing to a homogenized and unmediated notion of 'the people' and related notions (eg citizens, society, nation etc.); and an ideological pattern emanating from the tension between the political abstraction of 'the people' (and related notions) and specific social interests struggling for their preferential representation. In its ideological manifestation populism tends towards a homogenization of these concepts and their application in an exclusivist way within political struggles against internal and external opponents. Claiming an 'authentic' and/or 'direct' relation of the 'people' with political power and/or contrasting 'the people's interests' to those of other homogenized groups (eg elites, immigrants, welfare beneficiaries, trade unions etc.) are also common to populist discourses. Definitions of populism, however, are contested and competing understandings and measurements of 'populist beliefs' are explored directly in the contribution by Pollock *et al.* in this volume.
4  The authors would like to thank members of the MYPLACE research team and contributors to the volume – especially Anton Popov, Mariona Ferrer-Fons, Renata Franc, Florian Sipos and Tom Brock – whose ideas and reflections have informed this introductory article.
5  Respondents cited here participated in qualitative research elements of the MYPLACE project (interviews, focus groups or ethnographic case studies) and are referred to by pseudonym, location (or movement they participate in) and country.

6  Table 1 shows the analysis, by the authors, of rounds 1 to 6 of the ESS (2002 to 2012), which was undertaken on 14 countries with complete data on the measures used. The data were weighted for both design effects and population differences.

7  Recognizing the range of terms employed in the existing literature to describe different forms of more or less formal and 'traditional' politics, the MYPLACE project used the following working definitions of these concepts:

'Institutional politics' reflects the struggle for resources through institutions of the state and civil government and takes place at local, national and supra-national levels.

'Informal politics' describes the means of managing and regulating relations of political power and their social construction, political behaviour, policy formulation and application through non-traditional, sometimes publicly unseen, structures such as community associations, local self-help groups and online media.

'Conventional/mainstream/formal politics' describes the means of managing and regulating relations of political power and their social construction, political behaviour, policy formulation and application through traditional, highly visible political structures such as parties, elected assemblies, government, pressure groups and through processes such as elections, lobbying, rallies etc.

'Unconventional/alternative politics' describes the means of challenging or disrupting established political structures, processes and state policies and is often conducted through processes such as occupations/sit-ins, graffiti, urban riots and through new social media activism including flash mobs.

8  Included in this category were the following forms of participation: volunteered in an election campaign; contacted a politician; collected signatures; gave a political speech; or distributed leaflets with political content.

9  Included in this category were the following forms of participation: attended a public meeting dealing with political issues; signed a petition; boycotted and/or bought certain products for political, ethical or environmental reasons; wrote an article (for example, in an organization journal or a blog); wrote or forwarded a letter/email with political content; or uploaded political material to the Internet.

10 Included in this category were the following forms of participation: participated in a demonstration; participated in a strike; participated in a violent political event; occupied buildings or blocked streets/railways; wrote political messages or graffiti on walls; or participated in a flash mob.

11 Gaining publicity through media exposure was second with a mean of 5.93.

12 The text is unaltered here from the source and reflects responses given by young people online.

13 The two Greek locations showed the most negative attitudes to politics and politicians, the lowest score of the two is cited here. The two Danish locations demonstrated the most positive attitudes, the highest score is taken here.

14 Respondents were asked to rate their satisfaction with democracy in their country of residence, thus the object of satisfaction varies according to the very different constitutions of democracy across the 14 countries participating in the MYPLACE project.

15 At the time of research, however, three of the participating countries in the MYPLACE project (Russia, Georgia and Croatia) remained on the outside of this process, and the first two remain so.

16 Eurosceptics from the far Left also made their presence felt; in Greece Syriza won the elections (26 per cent).

17 These are defined as parties that: oppose immigration and ethnic and cultural diversity; have a populist 'anti-establishment' strategy; attack mainstream parties; and are ambivalent if not hostile towards liberal representative democracy (Goodwin, 2011b: x).

18 The National Front (NF) is a far-right 'whites only' political party founded in 1967 and most active during the 1970s, when it secured just over 3 per cent of the vote in those seats contested in the 1974 General Elections, but splintered over the course of the 1980s following a decline in electoral success after the first Thatcher government came to power in 1979 (Allen, 2011; Solomos, 2013; Goodwin *et al.*, 2010).

*The Sociological Review*, 63:S2, pp. 1–35 (2015), DOI: 10.1111/1467-954X.12260

19  The British National Party (BNP), founded in 1982 as an outcome of one of the splits in the NF (see above), is a formally registered political party and has had more success than any other party of the far right in Britain (Goodwin, 2011a). Although it has never secured representation at national parliamentary level, it polled 6.2 per cent of the vote in the 2010 General Election and gained two seats in European Parliament elections in 2009.

20  This study was based on a sample of 270 NF supporters generated by aggregating 22 voter intention surveys from October 1977 to April 1978.

21  Goodwin *et al.*'s study is based on aggregated omnibus data gathered in the period 2002–2006. Face-to-face interviews were conducted as part of the Ipsos MORI twice-monthly regular omnibus survey which is based on a representative quota sample. A total of 190,882 adults were interviewed of whom 1,001 respondents stated either that they had voted for the BNP, or modern-day NF, or that they would consider doing so, representing 0.5 per cent of the total sample.

22  The questionnaire was drafted in English and translated using the TRAPD methodology (Harkness, 2003).

23  Each country developed its own sampling plan for a specified geographical area using the best available list data where that was available or an alternative such as a random walk or a full census. All data collection was undertaken using face-to-face interviews with the exception of Nurmes and Lieksa in Finland where, due to the sparse population it was necessary to use some telephone interviews and self-complete forms. The age range for eligibility was to be at least 16 or less than 26 at the time of the interview.

24  Thirteen of the thirty locations exceeded this target and only five (both Danish and Finnish locations as well as Bremerhaven in Germany) managed 10 per cent less than the target sample.

25  Some variables in the data were harmonized to facilitate comparative analysis. ISCED 2011 was used for the level of education, a common parental social class variable was developed taking into account parents' educational and occupational outcomes, different conceptions of religiosity and denomination were produced to reflect comparable features in the pooled data, and notions of citizenship, ethnicity and national identity were all captured in order to articulate the concept of being part of a national majority or minority. In addition there were a number of locally specific variables some of which were used in the pooled data set such as the simple scale of political knowledge which was developed using locally specific knowledge questions, generally centred upon the current head of government, ruling party, and one other variable such as the foreign minister. Local teams were able to include specific questions from a national perspective, hence in Croatia the 'homeland war' was asked about.

26  As with all survey data there were some missing values on many variables. In a bid to reduce the extent of this the data policy was to have a code for each item for each respondent so that each 'gap' was explained at least in a technical way. Missing values are cumulative and were closely analysed along with any geographic pattern in them when statistical models were tested.

27  In a small number of research locations the target number of follow-up interviews could not be achieved from the survey sample due to low volunteer rates. In these cases, teams followed a supplementary protocol and recruited volunteers based on the same criteria as for eligibility for the survey and respondents were asked to complete the questionnaire prior to follow-up interview to ensure consistency in sensitization although the questionnaires were not included in the survey data set.

28  A small number of cases straddled clusters and were assigned a primary location but also included in the cross-case analysis of a secondary cluster.

# References

Allen, C., (2011), 'Opposing Islamification or promoting Islamophobia? Understanding the English Defence League', *Patterns of Prejudice*, 45 (4): 279–294.

Arzheimer, K., (2009), 'Contextual factors and the extreme right vote in Western Europe 1980–2002', *American Journal of Political Science*, 53 (2): 259–275.

Assmann, A. and Shortt, L., (2012), 'Memory and political change: introduction', in A. Assmann and L. Shortt (eds), *Memory and Political Change*, 1–14, London: Palgrave Macmillan.

Bakić, J., (2009), 'Extreme-right ideology, practice and supporters: case study of the Serbian Radical Party', *Journal of Contemporary European Studies*, 17 (2): 193–207.

Bartlett, J. and Littler, M., (2011), *Inside the EDL: Populist Politics in a Digital Age*, London: Demos.

Beck, U., (1986), *Risikogesellschaft. Auf dem Weg in eine andere Moderne* (Risk Society: Towards a New Modernity), Frankfurt am Main: Suhrkamp Verlag.

Beck, U. and Beck-Gernsheim, E., (2002), *Individualization: Institutionalized Individualism and its Social and Political Consequences*, London: Sage.

Birth, K., (2006), 'Past times: temporal structuring of history and memory', *Ethos*, 34 (2): 192–210.

Blais, A., E. Gindegil and N. Nevitte (2004), 'Where does turnout decline come from?', *European Journal of Political Research*, 43 (2): 221–236.

Bourdieu, P., (1979), *La distinction (Distinction)*, Paris: Editions du Minuit.

Bourdieu, P., (1985), 'Social space and the genesis of groups', *Theory and Society*, 14 (6): 723–744.

Bourdieu, P., (1989), 'Social space and symbolic power', *Sociological Theory*, 7 (1): 14–25.

Brooks, R. and Hodkinson, P., (2008), 'Introduction' (Special Issue: Young People, New Technologies and Political Engagement), *Journal of Youth Studies*, 11 (5): 473–479.

Burawoy, M., (1998), 'The extended case method', *Sociological Theory*, 16 (1): 4–33.

Castells, M., (2012), *Networks of Outrage and Hope: Social Movements in the Internet Age*, Cambridge: Polity Press.

CivicWeb, (2009), *CivicWeb: Young People, the Internet and Civic Participation – Final Policy Brief*, available at: http://www.civicweb.eu/images/stories/reports/finalpercent20_policypercent20briefper cent20final_.pdf (accessed 15 April 2014).

Cohen, C. J. and Kahne, J., (2012), *Participatory Politics: New Media and Youth Political Action*, available at: http://ypp.dmlcentral.net/sites/all/files/publications/YPP_Survey_Report_FULL.pdf (accessed 1 April 2014).

Copsey, N., (2010), *The English Defence League: A challenge to our Country and our Values of Social Inclusion, Fairness and Equality*, London: Faith Matters.

Crossley, N., (2002), *Making Sense of Social Movements*, Buckingham: Open University Press.

Dalton, R. and Wattenberg, M. P. (eds), (2000), *Parties without Partisans: Political Change in Advanced Industrial Democracies*, Oxford: Oxford University Press.

Della Porta, D., (2013), *Can Democracy Be Saved?* Cambridge: Polity Press.

Edwards, G., (2014), *Social Movements and Protest*, Cambridge: Cambridge University Press.

ESS Round 6 (2012) *European Social Survey Round 6 Data*, Data file edition 2.0. Norwegian Social Science Data Services, Norway.

Extremis Project, (2012), 'Under the microscope: public attitudes toward the English Defence League (EDL)', 8 October, available at: http://extremisproject.org/2012/10/the-english-defence-league-edl-what-do-people-think/ (accessed 5 May 2014).

Farthing, R., (2010), 'The politics of youthful antipolitics: representing the "issue" of youth participation in politics', *Journal of Youth Studies*, 13 (2): 181–195.

Fielding, N., (1981), *The National Front*, London: Routledge and Kegan Paul.

Flyvbjerg, B., (2006), 'Five misunderstandings about case-study research', *Qualitative Inquiry*, 12 (2): 219–245.

Furedi, F., (2005), *Politics of Fear: Beyond Left or Right*, London and New York: Continuum.

Furlong, A. and Cartmel, F., (1997), *Young People and Social Change: Individualization and Risk in Late Modernity*, Buckingham and Philadelphia: Open University Press.

Goodwin, M., (2011a), *New British Fascism: Rise of the British National Party*, London and New York: Routledge.

Goodwin, M., (2011b), *Right Response: Understanding and Countering Populist Extremism in Europe*, A Chatham House Report, London: Royal Institute of International Affairs (Chatham House).

Goodwin, M., Ford, R., Duffy, B. and Robey, R., (2010), 'Who votes extreme right in twenty-first-century Britain? The social bases of support for the National Front and British National Party' in R. Eatwell and M. Goodwin (eds), *The New Extremism in 21st Century Britain*, 191–210, London and New York: Routledge.

*The Sociological Review*, 63:S2, pp. 1–35 (2015), DOI: 10.1111/1467-954X.12260

Goldkuhl, G. and Cronholm, S., (2010), 'adding theoretical grounding to grounded theory: toward multi-grounded theory', *International Journal of Qualitative Methods* 9 (2), available at: http://ejour nals.library.ualberta.ca/index.php/IJQM/article/viewFile/6784/7027 (accessed 16 May 2013.

Gudkov, L., (2004), *Negativnaya Identichnost' (Negative Identity)*, Moscow: Novoe Literaturnoe Obozrenie – VTsIOM-A.

Habermas, J., (1976), *Legitimation Crisis* (trans. Thomas McCarthy), Boston: Beacon Press.

Habermas, J., (1984), *The Theory of Communicative Action* (trans. Thomas McCarthy), Boston: Beacon Press.

Habermas, J., (1991), *The Structural Transformation of the Public Sphere*, Cambridge, MA: MIT Press.

Habermas, J., (1996), *Between Facts and Norms: Contributions to a Discourse Theory of Law and Democracy* (trans. William Rehg), Cambridge, MA: The MIT Press.

Harkness, J. A. (2003), 'Questionnaire translation', in J. A. Harkness, F. van de Vijver and P. Ph. Mohler (eds), *Cross-cultural Survey Methods*, 35–56, Hoboken, NJ: John Wiley & Sons.

Henn, M. and Foard, N., (2014), 'Social differentiation in young people's political participation: the impact of social and educational factors on youth political engagement in Britain', *Journal of Youth Studies*, 17 (3): 360–380.

Henn, M., Weinstein, M. and Forrest, S., (2005), 'Uninterested youth? Young people's attitudes towards party politics in Britain', *Political Studies*, 53 (3): 556–578.

Herring, S., (2001), 'Computer-mediated discourse', in D. Schiffrin, D. Tannen and H. Hamilton (eds), *Handbook of Discourse Analysis*, Oxford: Blackwell.

Hirsch, M., (1999), 'Projected memory: Holocaust photographs in personal and public fantasy', in M. Bal, J. Crewe and L. Spitzer (eds), *Acts of Memory: Cultural Recall in the Present*, 3–23, Hanover: University Press of New England.

Hox, J., (2010), *Multilevel Analysis, Techniques and Applications*, 2nd edn, New York: Routledge.

Hulme, M., (2009), 'Life support: young people's needs in a digital age', Youthnet, available at: http://www.youthnet.org/wp-content/uploads/2011/05/Life-Support-Report.pdf (accessed 15 April 2014).

Ignazi, P., (2003), *Extreme Right Parties in Western Europe*, Oxford: Oxford University Press.

Jennings, M. K., Stoker, L. and Bowers, J., (2009), 'Politics across generations: family transmission reexamined', *The Journal of Politics*, 71 (3): 782–799.

Kääriäinen, J. and Lehtonen, H., (2006), 'The variety of social capital in welfare state regimes – a comparative study of 21 countries', *European Societies*, 8 (1): 27–57.

Keightley, E. and Pickering, M., (2012), *The Mnemonic Imagination: Remembering as Creative Practice*, Basingstoke: Palgrave Macmillan.

Kimberlee, R. H., (2002), 'Why don't British young people vote at general elections?', *Journal of Youth Studies*, 5 (1): 86–98.

Kimmel, M., (2007), 'Racism as adolescent male rite of passage: ex-Nazis in Scandinavia', *Journal of Contemporary Ethnography*, 36 (2): 202–218.

Kitschelt, H., (2007), 'Growth and persistence of the radical right in postindustrial democracies: advances and challenges in comparative research', *West European Politics*, 20 (5): 1176–1206.

Klingemann, H.-D. and Fuchs, D. (eds), (1995), *Citizens and the State*, Oxford: Oxford University Press.

Kovacs, A., (2013), 'The post-Communist extreme right: the Jobbik Party in Hungary', in R. Wodak, M. KhosraviNik, and B. Mral (eds), *Right-Wing Populism in Europe: Politics and Discourse*, 223–233, London: Bloomsbury.

Leonova, A., (2009), 'Electoral choice, cultural capital, and xenophobic attitudes in Russia, 1994–2006', in M. Laruelle (ed.), *Russian Nationalism and the National Reassertion of Russia*, 145–184, London and New York: Routledge.

Levinsen, K., (2012), 'Ethnic intolerance in Europe', unpublished paper presented at FP7 MY-PLACE Project meeting, Riga, 24 May.

LSE, (2013), 'Youth Participation in Democratic Life – Final Report', London School of Economics, available at: http://www.lse.ac.uk/businessAndConsultancy/LSEEnterprise/pdf/YouthParticipation DemocraticLife.pdf (accessed 15 April 2014).

Mah, A., (2010), 'Memory, uncertainty and industrial ruination: Walker Riverside, Newcastle upon Tyne', *International Journal of Urban and Regional Research*, 34 (2): 398–413.

Mair, P., and van Biezen, I., (2001), 'Party membership in twenty European democracies, 1980–2000', *Party Politics*, 7 (1): 5–21.

Marien, S., Hooghe, M. and Quintellier, E., (2010), 'Inequalities in non-institutionalized forms of political participation: a multi-level analysis of 25 countries', *Political Studies*, 58: 187–121.

Marsh, D., O'Toole, T., and Jones, S., (2007), *Young People and Politics in the UK: Apathy or Alienation?* New York: Palgrave Macmillan.

Mouffe, C., (2005), *On the Political*, London and New York: Routledge.

Mudde, C., (2007), *Populist Radical Right Parties in Europe*, Cambridge: Cambridge University Press.

Mudde, C., (2014), 'Introduction: youth and the extreme right: explanations, issues, and solutions', in C. Mudde (ed.), *Youth and the Extreme Right*, 1–18, New York: IDebate Press.

Muranyi, I. and Berenyi, Z., (2014), 'History and memory', in M. Ellison and G. Pollock (eds), *MYPLACE WP4 report Measuring Participation, Deliverable 4.6 Europe-wide thematic report*, available at: http://www.fp7-myplace.eu/documents/D4_6/MYPLACE_d4_6.pdf (accessed 8 December 2014).

Nestlé Family Monitor, (2003), *Young People's Attitudes towards Politics*, Nestle Family Monitor no. 16, available at: http://www.ipsos-mori.com/Assets/Docs/Archive/Polls/nfm16.pdf (accessed 12 August 2014).

Noblit, G. W. and Dwight Hare, R., (1988), *Meta-Ethnography: Synthesizing Qualitative Studies*, Newbury Park: Sage.

Norris, P. (ed.), (2001), *Digital Divide: Civic Engagement, Information Poverty, and the Internet Worldwide*, Cambridge: Cambridge University Press.

Norris, P., (2002), *Democratic Phoenix: Reinventing Political Activism*, Cambridge: Cambridge University Press.

Norris, P., (2003), 'Young people and political activism: from the politics of loyalties to the politics of choice?', presentation in Strasbourg, Council of Europe Symposium, 'Young People and democratic institutions: from disillusionment to participation'.

Norris, P., (2005), *Radical Right: Voters and Parties in the Electoral Market*, Cambridge: Cambridge University Press.

Pilkington, H., (2014), ' "Loud and proud": youth activism in the English Defence League', WP7: Interpreting Activism (Ethnographies). Deliverable 7.1: Ethnographic Case Studies of Youth Activism', *MYPLACE Deliverable Report, available* at: http://www.fp7-myplace.eu/deliverables.php

Pine, F., Kaneff, D. and Haukanes, H., (2004), 'Introduction. Memory, politics and religion: a perspective on Europe', in F. Pine, D. Kaneff and H. Haukanes (eds), *Memory, Politics and Religion: The Past Meets the Present in Europe*, 1–29, Münster: Lit Verlag.

Ragin, C. C., (1992), 'Introduction: cases of "what is a case?" ' in C. C. Ragin and H. S. Becker (eds), *What Is a Case?*, 1–17, Cambridge: Cambridge University Press.

Riley, S., Griffin, C. and Morey, Y., (2010), 'The case for "everyday politics": evaluating neo-tribal theory as a way to understand alternative forms of political participation, using electronic dance music culture as an example', *Sociology*, 44 (2): 345–363.

Schellenberg, B., (2013), 'Developments within the radical right in Germany: discourses, attitudes and actors', in R. Wodak, M. KhosraviNik and B. Mral (eds), *Right-Wing Populism in Europe: Politics and Discourse*, 149–162, London: Bloomsbury.

Sky News, (2011), 'Poll: half could vote for a far-right party', 27 February, available at: http://news.sky.com/home/politics/article/15941796 (accessed 12 August 2014).

Soler-i-Martí, R., Ferrer-Fons, M., Correia, A., de Almeida Alves, N., and Cairns, D., (2014), 'Political activism', in M. Ellison and G. Pollock (eds), *MYPLACE WP4 report Measuring Participation, Deliverable 4.6 Europe-wide thematic report*, available at: http://www.fp7-myplace.eu/documents/D4_6/MYPLACE_d4_6.pdf (accessed 8 December 2014).

Solomos, J., (2013), 'Contemporary forms of racist movements and mobilisation in Britain', in R. Wodak, M. KhosraviNik and B. Ral (eds), *Right-wing Populism in Europe*, 121–134, London: Bloomsbury Press.

*The Sociological Review*, 63:S2, pp. 1–35 (2015), DOI: 10.1111/1467-954X.12260

Stolle, D., Hooghe, M. and Micheletti, M., (2005), 'Politics in the supermarket: political consumerism as a form of political participation', *International Political Science Review*, 26 (3): 245–269.
Sudman, S., (1976), *Applied Sampling*, New York and London: Academic Press.
Wattenberg, M. P., (2006), *Is Voting for Young People?* New York: Pearson Longman.

# Appendix

**Table A1** *ESS data on levels of political activity in 14 countries\* of those aged 15–25*

|  | 2002 | 2004 | 2006 | 2008 | 2010 | 2012 |
|---|---|---|---|---|---|---|
| Member of party | 1.2 | 1.3 | 1.3 | 1.3 | 1.0 | N/A |
| Voted in last election (if eligible) | 52.6 | 53.9 | 55.0 | 58.1 | 58.6 | 58.2 |
| Contacted politician or government official in the last 12 months | 8.7 | 6.3 | 7.5 | 7.2 | 8.4 | 6.5 |
| Worked in political party or action group in the last 12 months | 4.0 | 2.9 | 2.1 | 2.3 | 2.5 | 3.1 |
| Wore or displayed campaign badge/sticker in the last 12 months | 11.6 | 10.2 | 9.5 | 9.5 | 9.4 | 8.8 |
| Signed petition in the last 12 months | 27.1 | 25.7 | 23.9 | 23.4 | 23.0 | 24.0 |
| Took part in a lawful public demonstration in the last 12 months | 14.6 | 14.3 | 12.8 | 10.6 | 11.1 | 12.4 |
| Boycotted certain products in the past 12 months | 14.8 | 12.2 | 13.0 | 12.5 | 12.1 | 14.4 |

\* Belgium, Switzerland, Germany, Denmark, Spain, Finland, France, United Kingdom, Hungary, Ireland, the Netherlands, Norway, Poland, Portugal.

Part One: Footprints: political heritage and political socialization

# Making sense of the 'difficult' past: transmission of political heritage and memory-work among young people across Europe

*Anton Popov and Dušan Deák*

**Abstract:** This article considers young people's socialization into mnemonic communities in 14 European countries. It argues that such socialization is an intersubjective and selective process that, to a great degree, depends on the particular social environment that conditions the discourses on pasts available to young people. Drawing on memory studies, it recognizes memory as a valid alternative to the institutionalized past (history) but envisages the two as inextricably connected. Given this, it identifies several strategies adopted by young people in order to socialize understandings of the past. While these strategies vary, some reveal receptivity to populist and far right ideologies. Our study demonstrates how internalization of political heritage via mnemonic socialization within families is conditioned by both the national political agenda and socio-economic situation experienced across Europe.

**Keywords:** young people, history, memory, political heritage, Europe

## Introduction

This article presents a transnational comparison of how European young people's social memories about problematic periods in their national pasts (such as coups, wars or periods of social dislocation or economic depression) are shared, produced, and used. It discusses the intersubjective processes that shape young people's socialization into mnemonic communities, that is, communities that remember and produce the past (Cappelletto, 2003). Such socialization is multidimensional and extends well beyond the understanding of the past represented by formal historical knowledge. It is the complex engagement of young people with societal knowledges and practices that forms young people's ability to understand, interpret and act out society's past. Understanding it, therefore, involves investigating how a particular society's articulations of the past form young people's current political, civic and social attitudes as well as exploring the extent

*The Sociological Review*, 63:S2, pp. 36–52 (2015), DOI: 10.1111/1467-954X.12261

of what is remembered and how (see Dechezelles, 2008; Jennings *et al.*, 2009). If we want to understand the rise of far right and populist ideologies among young people in contemporary Europe it is important to recognize and analyse this engagement.[1]

We argue that representations of the past impact on how young people see the present and position themselves in relation to political discourses that employ these representations. Moreover, our analysis shows that young people are not just passive recipients of historical discourses; they are actively involved in the interpretation and production of the past. From this follows that historical narratives are not accepted unchallenged by younger generations. Young people are in fact exposed to political struggle over the representations of the past which they often challenge in different ways. In this challenge they use the past as a resource for their political action. We show that mnemonic socialization is a selective process – drawing from both institutionalized historical narratives and family memories, young people produce their own political identity. This article extends the existing debates about political heritage in Europe that we understand as a *process* of transmission, reshaping, re-interpretation and internalization of political memories among young people.

Arguably, youth's internalization of political values and ideas is historically and culturally conditioned and is a result of its (dis-)engagement with various national pasts. Our analysis of pan-European case studies maps common and different features in the transmission of political heritages that share the ascription of being 'traumatic' or 'problematic' and evaluates the various mediums of transmission (eg museums, archives, family memorial practices, school curriculums, etc.). This study is based on young people's experiences of historical discourses as these are manifested in 'sites of memory' as well as in public institutions (such as schools), families and societal groups in which young people participate. We draw on transnational qualitative data that are derived from a common methodological approach (ethnography and discourse analysis) and theoretical framework (memory studies).[2]

In this article the concept of 'difficult past' is employed as an attempt to avoid more politically loaded categories like 'totalitarian' or 'authoritarian' past since they may enact the 'stigmatization' of already historically stigmatized European people (Buchowski, 2006). The attribute 'difficult' makes the focus of our research more inclusive – even in old democracies such as the UK people experience 'difficult times'. Seeing the past as 'difficult' or 'problematic' recognizes the experiences and interpretations of those who do not primarily, let alone professionally, engage in the production of historical discourse and in its politicization. It allows a more bottom-up re-evaluation of historical legacies.

Coups, wars, periods of social dislocation or economic depression often extend beyond political and regime boundaries. Thematically such 'difficult' periods might be grouped around the socio-political expressions of national/ethnic collectiveness and territorial claims, dictatorship, one-party regimes and governments with radical political agendas, or struggles for liberal society. In all cases these 'difficult' times must be contextualized within the economic situations faced

*The Sociological Review*, 63:S2, pp. 36–52 (2015), DOI: 10.1111/1467-954X.12261
© 2015 The Authors. Editorial organisation © 2015 The Editorial Board of the Sociological Review

locally, nationally or regionally. However, the ways in which such periods are incorporated into particular histories and the ways in which they are remembered differ due to regional, local and individual case specifics.

Our materials map young people's take on the difficult past in 14 European countries ranging from Northern Europe across the Iberian Peninsula, Western, Central and Eastern Europe, the Balkans, the Baltics up to Russia and the South Caucasus. World War II, its regimes and post-war developments (National-Socialist regime in Germany, Stalinist rule in Russia, Nazi collaborationism in Latvia, Estonia, Slovakia, Hungary and Croatia, struggles over Finland's territory, Civil war in Greece) dominate the traumas from the past in a great number of countries that constituted our case studies. After World War II come Communist regimes in the central and eastern parts of Europe and the periods of strong political figures and dictators that may, but also may not, overlap with the war period (Stalin, Hitler, Franco, the Colonels in Portugal, various Communist 'strong men', and Margaret Thatcher in Britain). Finally, a significant part in the constitution of the difficult past for the contemporary generation of young people is played by more recent wars such as those experienced in Croatia or Georgia.

The concept 'difficult past', moreover, has an ontological value in itself. The past, as a category of social practice, is manifest in the dynamic between the written, academically sanctioned (history), and the lived (memory). This is clearly seen when fundamentally different interpretations are produced; often when a society's past is contested by different opinions about what society should learn from the past and how. Although competing opinions form the common ground for societal debates on the past, agents in these debates take stances on how the past is written down, interpreted, remembered and learnt. This also gives the past the attribute of 'difficult'. Thus it is the social fact of the immanence of the past (Birth, 2006) that is disputed and not the past per se.

## Transmission of the past

Socialization into mnemonic communities involves transmission of past into present. To learn from the past, to transmit the past intelligibly to the present, entails some form of social engagement that inevitably produces a social individual with a particular social identity. Drawing on Halbwachs' (1992) conception of 'collective memory', Boyarin (1994: 23) argues that since both identity and memory are the product and manifestation of power relations at work within society they 'are virtually the same'. Further, memories are intersubjective because they are selected in order to constitute group membership and individual identity and are constantly reshaped, reinvented and reinforced as 'members contest and create the boundaries and links among themselves' (Boyarin, 1994: 26). The process of selecting memories is equally important. This is because what is remembered is also constituted by what was, or was made to be, forgotten.

Anthropological studies of memory often pay significant attention to conflicting memories as sites of the politics of identity (Pine *et al.*, 2004). The linkage between the two is hardly accidental. Memory, as an important resource employed

*The Sociological Review*, 63:S2, pp. 36–52 (2015), DOI: 10.1111/1467-954X.12261

to question the authority of established historiography, often, but not exclusively, emerges in societies living through transition, in order to revisit a nation's political heritage, and to renegotiate meanings of national identity (Assmann and Shortt, 2012: 4). Citing Maier's argument that memory is appealing because of its articulation of ethno-racial nationalism that silences the cosmopolitan discourses of history, Klein (2000: 143–145) claims that the use of memory as a 're-placement for history' is often a result and indication of the historiographic crisis currently experienced in the social sciences and humanities. Thus, what members of a particular society remember, or learn to remember, or write to remember, is not a purely individual or psychological phenomenon but the product of the relationship between politics, as a realm of power, and the social construction of meanings of the past. Here memories 'always represent at least a potential source of power and tool of opposition' (Pine *et al.*, 2004: 4). Sturkin (1997) recognizes the potential of 'cultural memory' – memories outside formal historical discourse yet rooted in cultural products and imbued with meaning – to generate alternative visions of the past (Olick and Robbins, 1998: 111).

A further aspect of memory concerns the role of experiences of the past across generations. Family, friendship groups, local and professional communities (sometimes represented through local museums, festivals, commemoration events) constitute environments for mnemonic socialization, and by extension, embodiment of political heritage (Keightley and Pickering, 2012). In practice, young people are socialized into mnemonic discourses and practices through the internalization of knowledge of their predecessors. Keightley and Pickering (2012) call this process 'mnemonic imagination', because it involves more than mere transmission of knowledge. The past shared by older generations, apart from being experienced, is also learnt and interpreted.

In this article we examine, on the basis of concrete examples from across Europe, the processes whereby the dynamics of the interactions between history (in its institutionalized forms) and social remembering/forgetting is articulated. History and memory are not mutually exclusive monoliths and the interactions between them are not unidirectional. As Eyal (2004: 8) points out, 'on the one hand, history opened itself up to the subaltern and popular ...; on the other hand, memory too opened itself up to history, and historians and intellectuals began to construe their work as an "art of memory"'. Thus, since every historian is to a considerable extent part of the mnemonic community (Birth, 2006), or has his/her own habitus (Bourdieu, 2005) and since the non-historian also learns to view the past from the books on history, both memory and historiography inevitably form contemporary historical discourse (Klein, 2000).

## Sites of memory as fieldwork sites: observing memory work

The analysis presented here draws on discourses about the past accessed mainly via 'sites of memory' (*lieux de mémoire*; Nora, 1989) – broadly understood as places where memory production can be observed and documented. Nora contrasts *milieux de mémoire*, real environments that embody memory as lived experience, and *lieux de mémoire*, sites of memory where memory is socially articulated. As Radley argues, monuments and museum collections invite and provoke people to elaborate meanings of the past making historical memory a 'collective affair' (Radley, 1990: 57).

The data drawn on here was collected at public, mainly non-academic institutions identified as important 'sites of memory' in as much as they were sites of historical discourse production.[3] These included 13 museums, one archive, one public-law institution, two NGOs, and several memorial sites.[4] Insights into construction and representation of historical narratives at the sites of memory were gathered via participant observation in public institutional settings and expert interviews with the institutions' staff members.[5]

The approach adopted here does not see young people as passive recipients of historical narratives but rather as active participants in the process of their production and interpretation. For example, official visions of history presented at commemorative sites are often challenged and interrogated by 'mass personal memory', that is, 'personal recollections held by enough individuals to have national significance' (Snider, in Ochman, 2009: 419). Making sense of present conditions through active engagement with the past therefore involves 'memory-work' (Hamilakis and Labanyi, 2008: 12). For this reason, focus groups were conducted with young people who had visited the 'sites of memory'.[6] Moreover, since of particular concern is the role which mnemonic socialization plays in political and civic activism, recruitment to focus groups included both young people who visited the museums only as part of their school/college curriculum and young activists. The local issues and themes which centred on the 'problematic' periods of the national and local history constituted the core of focus group discussions, expert interviews, production of ethnographic field notes and visual documentations at the sites of memory to different degrees across all case studies. At the same time, in all sites we attempted to access young people's views on the ways in which these memories impact on their perceptions of contemporary society and politics.

Young people's narratives demonstrate that historical discourses provide them with the means to negotiate and interpret contemporary society. These discourses also make an impact on the production of social memories and transmission of political heritage across generations. Socialization into diverse mnemonic communities displays itself in several focal points around which young people's narratives and practices are woven. These points include: trust in, or challenging of, official narratives; family memories; nostalgic attitudes and dissatisfaction with the present; and the use of the past in order to justify or condemn nationalist and xenophobic views.

## Trust in official historical narrative?

In those countries that have faced radical transformations of their political system recently, or where memories of the difficult past still linger, historical discourses have become an important field of political struggle and for the

*The Sociological Review*, 63:S2, pp. 36–52 (2015), DOI: 10.1111/1467-954X.12261

rearticulation of national identity (Assmann and Shortt, 2012). This study showed that young people participate in the societal debates around these issues and engage with the institutionalized historical narratives (eg school text books, museum exhibitions, academic publications etc.).

Uncritical attitudes were expressed mostly by non-activist participants of the focus groups, as illustrated by the following quote from the Georgian case study. 'Official [history] is history that should be known to everyone, and unofficial [history] is history that is closed [in the archives], and very few people know about it' [GEOFG3][7] (Zurabishvili and Khoshtaria, 2013: 31). In the same vein historical narratives about the Stalinist period from textbooks were reproduced by the Russian non-activist participants (Safonova *et al.*, 2013).

However, more critical or sceptical references by respondents to the official historical narratives do not necessarily correlate with a higher level of political engagement. Rather, such lack of trust in institutionalized historiography implies cynical attitudes towards those who are in power and distancing from politics. Thus, the argument that history is written by 'the winners' is put forward by respondents in the Hungarian study: 'The winner's and the loser's side. They will tell the story in a completely different way' [HFG3R4]. 'First comes the ideology, history is matched to it' [HFG1R2] (Sik, 2013: 106). This resonates with the distrust in official historiography expressed in a Slovak focus group: 'history is 100 per cent manipulated' [SKFG2R8] (Deák, 2013: 41). A similar sense of the 'dominant' and 'official' interpretation of the Soviet period as being imposed and manipulated by authorities was articulated in an Estonian focus group:

> I think that in connection with the Soviet period [...] Estonians have a feeling that there is a quite unified interpretation that they have to follow or obey [...] well, it [the Soviet period] has to be presented in as bad a light as possible [...] [ESTFG4R6]. (Nugin *et al.*, 2013: 44)

Young people in all case studies identified the education system as an institutional environment where they encountered 'official' representations of the difficult pasts. However, historical knowledge mediated by history teachers and textbooks is referred to in focus group interviews as the most untrustworthy: '[...] and all these narrations and the things that they teach us now, may not be true, at least some of them. Or maybe most of what we hear' [GRFG4R5] (Koronaiou *et al.*, 2013: 35). 'The same history can be taught many ways, while being more or less faithful to the fact' [HFG2R3] (Sik, 2013: 106).

In several case studies none of the discourses of the past connected to the sites of memory could be unambiguously defined as 'mainstream' or 'dominant'. This situation might be experienced by people as a perceived absence of consensus on national historical narratives (Eyal, 2004). It implies that citizens (including young people) are not only invited to take sides in the discursive struggle over the interpretation of the past, but that they accept the invitation. Sik (2013) suggests that strong associations of different interpretations with often opposed political ideologies might create space for the propagation of radical and politically extreme interpretations of the past. Thus both in post-socialist and south

European countries (experiencing economic recession) we observe 'historical nihilism' based on the lack of trust in institutionalized representations of the national past. This seems to be caused mainly by the over-politicization of historical discourses and effects of socio-economic and political transformations.

Other possible reasons for lack of trust and/or disinterest in history might be the decline in standards of education (especially in post-socialist countries), and current global challenges. Keightly and Pickering (2012: 104) argue that with the advance of digital and Internet technologies and relative increases in geographic mobility the mnemonic imagination stretches beyond the national past. The growth of historical nihilism, then, might also be connected with new cyber-modernity that challenges state institutions' authority and control over the representation of the past (examples of this include Wikipedia and the Anonymous movement) (see Pentzold, 2009; Ferron and Massa, 2014). However, despite the fact that the media are often mentioned as main sources of information about the past (Garder-Hansen *et al.*, 2009; Holdsworth, 2011; Keightley and Pickering, 2012) they are also named by respondents as powerful institutions that might be interested in manipulating historical representations for political or economic gains: 'I believe it's whoever has the power, and right now that's the media. They sell us a story and we're so [ . . . ] I'm not saying everyone, but we're morons in the proper sense of the word, and we believe it all [ . . . ].' [SPFG3R1] (Ferrer-Fons *et al.*, 2013: 70).

### Family memories and transmission of political heritage

The family, apart from its indisputable role in young people's socialization, provides one of the most common domains for the transmission of collective memories. Cappelletto (2003) suggests that the process of listening to memories becomes an event that contributes to the reproduction of a mnemonic community while Hirsch (1999) talks about 'postmemory' to express how the children of trauma-survivors relate to the experience of their parents, which they 'remember' only as stories (Pine *et al.*, 2004: 16). In our findings, young people both embrace family memories and distance themselves from how the past is remembered in their families. Respondents often refer to their family histories to support their disagreement with the interpretations of the past prevalent in public discourses, '[ . . . ] it's better to listen to them than to search on the Internet, because maybe that isn't true [ . . . ] Your grandparents' experience is better' [SPFG1R3] (Ferrer-Fons *et al.*, 2013: 66).

The Croatian case study, however, provides completely the opposite example of socialization into family mnemonic community. Although many respondents emphasized the importance of older generation as a source of knowledge about the past, they also talked about the importance of distancing themselves from their parents' memories, which are charged with nationalist feelings:

> Because of my opinions about the relations between Croats and Serbs I ended up in a conflict with my parents. Every time the topic is brought up, which is unfortunately

*The Sociological Review*, 63:S2, pp. 36–52 (2015), DOI: 10.1111/1467-954X.12261

very often at home, they always have the same argument – 'you weren't alive then and you have no idea what they did to us, you don't know that they butchered, exiled' and then I say, 'OK Mum, but that does not mean that some Serbian would do that to me now, I have Serbian friends, that does not mean they would do that to me [...]' I feel pressure from the older generation, as if they are angry because we want to move on, because, even though the younger generation has respect for our homeland, and I can say for myself that I am a patriot, that does not mean that I want to stay inside that same old frame of mind [CRFG2]. (Perasović and Vojak, 2013: 39)

Collective forgetting or social amnesia are also important for intergenerational transmission of political views and values. 'Collective forgetting', has been considered as part of the same social process as remembering (Narskii, 2004). Shotter (1990: 131), for example, maintains that 'social amnesia' is a process of forgetting the events that do not fit into the framework of the mnemonic community into which one has been socialised. Since collective memory is socially constructed and intersubjective in its nature, it is also selective. Shotter's understanding of this selectivity implies that in discussion about our experiences the latter are represented in 'such a way as to constitute and sustain one or another kind of social order' (Shotter, 1990: 122). In the case of families, untold stories and apparently forgotten pasts are therefore equally important for understanding the process of memory construction, transmission and interpretation among youth. This quote from Greece provides an example of how the silencing of memories of the Civil War and dictatorship is transmitted across generations as a particular political position in agreement with mainstream political discourses:

Because there may be family members who have been killed in that period, there may be disagreements [about the period] among members of the family, without anyone ever explaining why they disagree [...] some things are discussed and some are not, some things are mentioned and some are not. [GRFG1R5]. (Koronaiou *et al.*, 2013: 39)

In stark contrast to such silencing, the multi-vocality in interpretations of the past can lead to confusion of the younger generation, as in the Slovak case:

In our family it was always said, from my father's side, that everybody had a good life during the Communist regime. Conversely, from my mother's side, there [...] my great grandfather was a landowner [...] they [the Communists] came to hang him only because he was rich [...] they sent him to the uranium mines, jailed him and left only a hut for the family [...] so what am I supposed to think about it? [SKFG2R3] (Deák, 2013: 39)

Confirming Boyarin's point about the politics of memory being at the core of the construction of collective identities, in the examples cited above, the memories passed from the older generation are seen as important for young people's sense of continuity and change between their own and their parents' national identities and political position. Thus, family is an important source for discussion of political heritage but does not necessarily lead to the direct transmission of values but, on the contrary, might result in resistance to them.

## Political activism and mnemonic socialization

Whether family memories are opposed or embraced, intergenerational transmission operates in a much wider discursive field that stretches well beyond family members. In this respect it is important to turn to external political discourses and see how they interact with political heritage transmitted through the family environment. Jennings *et al.* (2009) suggest that, in general, children from highly politicized families demonstrate continuity in political partisanship with the older generations.

The ongoing public debates on the 'difficult past' may indeed catalyse the strong sense of political identity that has been shaped by historical memories passed within family:

> At school we discussed some things [...] in the previous semester I wrote an essay about oral history, about that period [he is referring to the Polytechnic uprising[8]], [...] I think that the fact that my father had told me all about it [...] prompted me to be one of those that supported the whole venture, as opposed to the others who were saying that nobody had been killed etc. Eventually, I could say that it helped me create a more 'revolutionary' identity, so to speak. [GRFG1R3] (Koronaiou *et al.,* 2013: 35–36)

Unlike the Greek respondent who opposed his 'revolutionary identity' to the political mainstream, young activists talk about the family transmission of views that are widespread in society. For instance, in two excerpts cited below, a British activist respondent attributes the origin of her left-wing anti-Thatcherism to views passed to her by her parents; similarly a left-wing activist from eastern Germany talks about being socialized into her values by her parents who were opposed to the totalitarian regime of the GDR:

> I always find my memory, like, if I were to think about the eighties and stuff, I just think 'Oh it must have been horrible then,' because my mum's like a massive socialist and she's always like, 'Oh, that bloody Thatcher' and things like that. [UKFG2R10] (Popov, 2013: 41)

> It was clearly influenced by my parents. I always remember them as rebellious. In particular, when they talk about the GDR. They were people who took to the street against injustice. And therefore, naturally, we became self-confident and rebellious too. [EGR1] (Bescherer *et al.,* 2013: 28)

However, a politicized family background also attunes children to the external political influences that in periods of upheaval 'when the political environment contains forces antithetical to parental inclinations [...] may work against within-family congruence' (Jennings *et al.*, 2009: 796). Hence, young people may distance themselves from the political views of the older generation that are considered to be 'extreme' and rather 'marginal' to the political mainstream:

> Well, when they just said that not everything was bad in those times, then it often is the case that people were taught that Jews are bad people and that fascism is a good thing and that you have to be Aryan and so on. And they were not converted to other perceptions afterwards and also [...] those are also the people who attack foreigners or take

*The Sociological Review*, 63:S2, pp. 36–52 (2015), DOI: 10.1111/1467-954X.12261

part in demonstrations against foreigners. This is alarming to me [ . . . ] [WGFG2R2].
(Hashem-Wangler *et al.*, 2013: 29)

My father was extremely active, a Member of Parliament in its first session, and he is
active again. Do we talk? Christ, no, that's a disaster. Our discussions are about why
I lean towards the left while he is more radical, I must say. I'm actually the only one
in my family with a kind of leftist view, left-centre if you like. And the others are more
right wing, so whenever we have Sunday lunches together, it is like a battleground over
political views. And it's still like that. Anyway, we don't talk about politics anymore
because it's just impossible. He calls me a Communist; I call him a right-wing extremist
and so on. Just no, it's enough. Not anymore. [CRFG1] (Perasović and Vojak, 2013:
52)

Importantly, as in the Croatian example, although the nationalist views of the father are not supported by the respondent, the active engagement with politics and
the articulated (left-wing) political position are apparently transmitted across at
least two generations of this family.

Thus, even when young people seem to be sometimes frustrated by conflicting and confusing interpretations of the past, they manifest continuities with, or
breaks in, political views of the older generation. Their reflections on the older
generation's memories of the 'difficult past' create an environment for internalization of political values and views that maintain their relevance for the young
people's own experiences. Importantly, however, past events are evaluated and
interpreted by respondents from their current position in relation to the socio-
economic conditions and political situation in their countries.

## Nostalgic memories: the 'depressing present' and 'difficult past'

As people live through socio-economic transformations they continue to express
their present concerns by referring to the past; this is interpreted by some authors
as 'nostalgia' (Davis, 1979; Shaw and Chase, 1989). Nostalgia tells us more about
the present than the past and it emerged in this study as one of the important
mechanisms conditioning how young people are socialized into the pasts of their
elders. The active phase of research for this study, 2011–2012, coincided with the
peak of economic crisis in a number of our focal countries. This clearly impacted
on respondents' reflections on the problematic or traumatic events of the past
they discussed. Although their reflections can be called nostalgic, however, that
nostalgia is articulated and rationalized in different ways.

In the British case study, respondents from different socio-economic backgrounds bring the past into their evaluations of the present in contrasting ways.
On the one hand, young people from more affluent families counterpose the 'depressing present' to a nostalgic image of their town when it held a sense of community. They associate this 'better past' with working-class council estates that
they now see as ghettos for a marginalized population (see also Hanley, 2007):

In the seventies and eighties I feel it was a lot more acceptable, because such a large,
I don't know what percentage it was, but such a large amount of the population did

live in council provided housing, and it wasn't seen as a bad thing, I think. But also the sense of community was a lot greater, which meant, sort of more, even if there was negative connotations from other classes or other cultures towards a certain community, it would be more a feeling of, 'Oh, we're all in this, like, together', all kind of, a lot more communal spirit, which I think's really important. [UKFG2R9] (Popov, 2013: 76)

On the other hand, the term 'community' is conspicuously absent in the narratives of working-class youth (Popov, 2013) and any nostalgic interpretations of the council estates are dismissed because they do not match their experiences of places where they grew up or are still living. Ironically, some British council estates sank into ghettos of the poor during the 1970s–80s under the conditions of recession, economic restructuring and political unrests of the Thatcher era. Thus, while embodied signs of urban decline are 'fragments evoking absences and loss' (Hamilakis and Labanyi, 2008: 12) for some they are representations of a harsher reality than for others. This is an example of how the past might be differently interpreted by different social groups within the same society.

In the post-socialist context, although creating nostalgic narratives, respondents rarely refer to current conditions in terms of 'economic crises' but rather see the entire 'transition period' as a time of the deterioration of living standards, economic hardship and political upheavals and loss of the moral compass of an egalitarian and fair society associated with state socialism.[9] In Croatia only one respondent mentioned the current times as a 'difficult period' in her life (Perasović and Vojak, 2013: 38) whereas another summed up the situation in a manner often observable in other post-communist countries:

I wouldn't single out any concrete event, rather the whole process of privatisation and transition. That is the thing that definitely has marked us for the next, I don't know, 500 years I guess, until some new communism and nationalisation comes around and everything starts again. This, of course, does not have to happen. But our society really has been incredibly impoverished. Not only by privatization in the 90s, but also in the last few years with all these robberies which resulted in the trials of that former political leadership. That is something that definitely has an influence on our life today. [CRFG1] (Perasović and Vojak, 2013: 48)

The present here is perceived in continuity with the difficult past – the Croatian 1990s – and interpreted as depressing and frustrating. What is important is that the difficult past is located within the 'living memory' of respondents; something Mah (2010: 402) rightly characterizes as the lack of closure between the past and present. For example, in the Georgian case study, young people's living memories of military conflicts (the Russo-Georgian war in August 2008) are linked with family memories of the early 1990s – the time after the break of the USSR – as the most difficult period when their parents lived on the brink of starvation, being unemployed or forced to search for work abroad:

The earlier wars [in the early 1990s] happened when we were not born yet, while at the time when this one [2008] happened, we were here, following the events. [...] This made this war the most difficult for us, [...] and the most difficult event in the recent history of Georgia. [GEOFG1] (Zurabishvili and Khoshtaria, 2013: 39)

*The Sociological Review*, 63:S2, pp. 36–52 (2015), DOI: 10.1111/1467-954X.12261

Nostalgia, then, needs to be interpreted in relation to living memories of the 'difficult past' and as an example of how the past is seen in order to convey dissatisfaction with current conditions. Rather than being an accurate recollection of the past, nostalgic narratives represent concerns with the problematic present which are often seen in terms of 'broken' or fragmented communities, declining living standards and social security, economic recession, collective underachievement as a nation, etc.

## Reference to the past as an expression of nationalist and xenophobic attitudes

The subject of the 'difficult' past is strongly associated with notions of nation, national identity or inter-ethnic relations that are also part of mnemonic socialization processes. As noted earlier the connection between national identity and collective memory has been observed by a number of commentators. Eyal (2004) also sees the construction of national collective identity as one of the 'goals' ascribed by society to memory. Yet, when it is necessary to 'come to terms with the past', especially the difficult past, it is required to acknowledge, remember and condemn the crimes of the past that lie at the core of collective trauma (Eyal, 2004: 24). As seen below, young people's responses indeed indicate tension around the issues of national (collective) identity and also the role of ethnic Others in their country's past.

Some focus groups saw the difficult past as 'shameful' whereas other young people refused to talk about it in terms of 'shame' implying their refusal of collective responsibility for events in history (in Germany and Russia in particular). For instance, instead of talking about the 'duty to remember' the Holocaust, western German participants emphasized that 'this must not happen again'. Their accent is on the future rather than the past. Rejecting the discourse of collective guilt also means that young people do not call it *shameful* anymore (Hashem-Wangler *et al.*, 2013: 30). This was further reflected in young people's narratives about German national identity being affected by memories of National Socialism and World War II:

> Yes, above all, Germany is labelled that way. When you go abroad as a German and you meet people there and talk to them and you tell them that you come from Germany, then very often you get confronted with remarks on Hitler or something like that. Or someone says, 'Oh, I'm a Jew, I have to be careful now' [ ... ] that has happened several times to me [others express approval]. My sister once was in Denmark and there they played a game called 'Who am I?', where you get a note on your forehead. And she immediately knew who she was [ ... ] [Adolf Hitler], yes. Such things happen all the time, Germany is always connected with this. [WGFG1R1] (Hashem-Wangler *et al.*, 2013: 33)

Russian political activists with liberal right-wing views[10] also refuse to take collective responsibility for the crimes of Stalinism which is seen as a regime alien to Russians as a nation (Safonova *et al.*, 2013: 55). At the same time the activists who are ideologically within the pro-Communist patriotic political spectrum, link anti-Stalinist discourse with pro-Western rhetoric and, therefore, view it as non-patriotic or anti-Russian. They criticized the museum's representation of de-Stalinization during the Khrushchev thaw as, 'an intelligentsia complex about the eternal guilt of the country. But only own guilt. Abroad everything is always good and perfect' [RUSFG4] (Safonova *et al.*, 2013: 49). Latvian youth considered collaboration with the Nazis in the Holocaust as a shameful past (Saleniece *et al.*, 2013: 35). However, in some narratives, similarly to the Russian participants cited above, young people blame foreign powers for apparently isolated events and suggest that collaborationism was something associated not only with Latvians as a nation:

> I think that 'shameful' is a bit strong for Latvia. Perhaps, there are events about which it would be 'uncomfortable' to speak. If you take collaborationism, we are not the only ones in this respect; in other countries there might be much more to speak about. [LTFG1R1] (Saleniece *et al.*, 2013: 36)

The term 'shameful' is used, nevertheless, in relation to the Russian speaking population's claims to the status of the Russian language in Latvia. This is closely linked to the denial of any legitimacy to the Soviet (and by extension Russian) political and cultural legacy in the country: 'Perhaps, what is [shameful] is that in our own country we couldn't use the Latvian language' [LTFG4R13] (Saleniece *et al.*, 2013: 36).

The Slovak participants expressed their dissatisfaction with policies towards ethnic minorities (Hungarians and Roma), by equating the government's support of minorities to betrayal of national interests. Here xenophobic (if not racist) sentiments are sometimes framed in nostalgic references to the Communist past:

> In those times [Communism], whites were united, and when they walked the streets, the Roma were scared. Now, it is the opposite. When a white man walks the street, he is afraid a Roma might beat him. [SKFG1R1] (Deák, 2013: 48)

In the UK case study, xenophobia and nationalism were also tied to the past, but differently. Young people associated xenophobic attitudes with the older generation socialized into a much more homogeneous society than that of their own multicultural present. Some commented that the current popularity of far right organizations (eg British National Party or English Defence League) is on the rise mostly among older people 'who actually remember the time when British traditions were there' (Popov, 2013: 58). Other research participants sympathized with the BNP's idea of preserving 'British traditions' but, nevertheless, abhorred all anti-migrant rhetoric from the far right (Popov, 2013).

## Conclusions

This article demonstrates the role that history and collective memory play in the processes of socialization of young people into mnemonic communities. It discusses this socialization in the context of pasts labelled, for different reasons, as

*The Sociological Review*, 63:S2, pp. 36–52 (2015), DOI: 10.1111/1467-954X.12261

'difficult'. Building on this the article also discusses how memory and history form the transmission of political heritage across Europe.

In the conditions of significant regime-change and socio-economic transformation, social agents including young people become sensitive to competing interpretations of the past. It is evident from our materials that young people are socialized into communities where the past is not divided into monolithic and mutually exclusive discourses of historiography and living memories. The past receives its attribute of 'difficult' when interpretations of past events are disputed, current identities renegotiated and future trajectories are uncertain. Thus, socialization into the past, being very much the product of the present, mobilizes the past in battles over the future.

In our approach to mnemonic socialization – a process that might lead to the politicization of youth – we argue that young people are far from being passive recipients of historical narratives. They are sensitive to over-politicization of historical discourses that manipulate the past in the interests of current political agendas. They also develop different strategies in interpreting past events as important for their present experiences and actions. These strategies range from a disinterest in the past, resulting in 'historical nihilism', to active engagement, where the past is a resource for their political stance. However, while over-politicization of historical discourses may lead to 'historical nihilism', it might create also the space for radical and extreme interpretations of the past that are nurtured by actors on current political scenes.

The article also demonstrates the indispensable role of family in mnemonic socialization and politicization of the younger generation (Pine *et al.*, 2004; Hirsch, 1999; Jennings *et al.*, 2009; Keightley and Pickering, 2012). It is an important channel for the transmission of memories that are opposed to more institutionalized and politically dominant historical discourses. Although in the course of intergenerational interactions the family political heritage is often passed down to the younger generation, at the same time, it might be challenged or dismissed as inappropriate to their present-day conditions. This confirms the active approach of youth to the past. Cherishing nostalgic memories is another identified strategy of approaching the past, whether that past is associated with a lost sense of community, degradation of living standards and feeling of social insecurity or collective underachievement as a nation. The 'difficult' (sometimes termed as 'shameful') past features in young people's narratives also as a reference point for justifying or rejecting growing xenophobia and nationalistic attitudes in society. In sum, the documented politicization of past, accompanied by different experiences of present socio-economic conditions, should be seen as a point from where young people's interpretations of socializing discourses on the past start and which lead them to concrete political positions.

To conclude, just as memory and history are mutually engaged with each other, so too the past and present cannot be uncoupled. In the same vein, socialization into mnemonic communities includes both the active agency of the youth in engaging with the past and its interpretations as well as internalization of historical discourses. In the course of this socialization not only the meanings of the past but also identities that embed them are negotiated and sometimes radically shifted.

## Notes

1 There is a growing body of literature dedicated to these developments. See: Miller-Idriss (2009), Shoshan (2008), Lubbers and Scheepers (2002), Leonova (2009), Dechezelles (2008), Rhodes (2009) and Mudde (2007).
2 See reports from the UK, Denmark, Finland, Germany, Russia, Estonia, Latvia, Slovakia, Hungary, Georgia, Croatia, Greece, Spain and Portugal under 'Deliverable 2.1' at http://www.fp7-myplace.eu/deliverable_21.php.
3 The article draws on case studies that are not national, but rather regionally specific (depending on the locations of sites of memory).
4 Further details are available at: http://www.fp7-myplace.eu/deliverable_21.php.
5 In some cases (eg Georgia, Russia) expert interviewees included secondary school teachers. Altogether 73 expert interviews were conducted.
6 In each case study there were three to five (altogether 54) focus group discussions with young people aged between 16 and 25.
7 Reference to focus group discussions use a code consisting of three parts: name of the country (eg GEO, for Georgia or WG for western Germany); focus group number (eg FG1 for the focus group number 1); and individual respondent number (eg R1).
8 The uprising of the Polytechnic School of Athens against the Colonels' Junta took place in November 1973. However, in collective memory, the event is associated with the fall of the military dictatorship in July 1974 (Koronaiou *et al.*, 2013: 32).
9 In the German case, so-called 'Ostalgia' is similar to the nostalgic memories of socialism in other Central and East European countries but the older generation's nostalgic recollections of the National-Socialist past are criticized and rejected by young people.
10 The focus group was conducted with a group that defined themselves as Russian National Democrats – a liberal right-wing organization that participated in the Spring protests of 2012, and participated as observers during the parliamentary (2011) and presidential (2012) elections in Russia (Safonova *et al.*, 2013: 10).

## References

Assmann, A. and Shortt, L., (2012), 'Memory and political change: introduction', in A. Assmann and L. Shortt (eds), *Memory and Political Change*, 1–14, London: Palgrave Macmillan.
Bescherer, P., Liebig, S. and Brüdern, U., (2013), *MYPLACE Deliverable 2.1: Country based reports on historical discourse production as manifested in sites of memory (Germany – Jena)*, available at: http://www.fp7-myplace.eu/documents/Partner%206%20-%20Germany%20 (Jena)%20deliverable_2_1_submission.pdf (accessed 23 June 2013).
Birth, K., (2006), 'Past times: temporal structuring of history and memory', *Ethos*, 34 (2): 192–210.
Bourdieu, P., (2005), 'Outline of the theory of practice: structures and the habitus', in G. M. Spiegel (ed.), *Practicing History: New Directions in Historical Writing after the Linguistic Turn*, 179–198, New York: Routledge.
Boyarin, J., (1994), 'Space, time, and the politics of memory', in J. Boyarin (ed.), *Remapping Memory: The Politics of TimeSpace*, 1–37, Minneapolis: University of Minnesota Press.
Buchowski, M., (2006), 'The specter of orientalism in Europe: from exotic other to stigmatized brother', *Anthropology Quarterly*, 79 (3): 463–482.
Cappelletto, F., (2003), 'Long-term memory of extreme events: from autobiography to history', *Journal of the Royal Anthropological Institute*, 9: 241–260.
Davis, F., (1979), *Yearning for Yesterday: A Sociology of Nostalgia*, New York: Free Press.

*The Sociological Review*, 63:S2, pp. 36–52 (2015), DOI: 10.1111/1467-954X.12261

Deák, D., (2013), *Addressing the 'Difficult Past': Competing Historical Narratives and the Slovak Social Memory. MYPLACE Deliverable 2.1: Country based reports on historical discourse production as manifested in sites of memory (Slovakia)*, available at: http://www.fp7-myplace.eu/documents/Partner%204%20-%20Slovakia_deliverable_2_1_submission.pdf (accessed 23 June 2013).

Dechezelles, S., (2008), 'The cultural basis of youth involvement in Italian extreme right-wing organisations', *Journal of Contemporary European Studies*, 16 (3): 363–375.

Eyal, G., (2004), 'Identity and trauma: two forms of the will to memory', *History and Memory*, 16 (1): 5–36.

Ferrer-Fons, M., Rovira, M. and Saurí, E., (2013), *MYPLACE Deliverable 2.1: Country based reports on historical discourse production as manifested in sites of memory (Spain)*, available at: http://www.fp7-myplace.eu/documents/Partner%2014%20-%20Spain_deliverable_2_1_submission.pdf (accessed 23 June 2013).

Ferron, M. and Massa, P., (2014), 'Beyond the encyclopedia: collective memories in Wikipedia', *Memory Studies*, 7 (1): 22–45.

Garder-Hansen, J., Hoskins, A. and Reading, A., (2009), *Save As … Digital Memories*, Basingstoke: Palgrave Macmillan.

Halbwachs, M., (1992), *On Collective Memory*, Chicago: University of Chicago Press.

Hamilakis, Y. and Labanyi, J., (2008), 'Introduction: time, materiality, and the work of memory', *History and Memory*, 20 (2): 5–17.

Hanley, L., (2007), *Estates: An Intimate History*, London: Granta Books.

Hashem-Wangler, A., Busse, B. and Tholen, J., (2013), *MYPLACE Deliverable 2.1: Country based reports on historical discourse production as manifested in sites of memory (Germany – Bremen)*, available at: http://www.fp7-myplace.eu/documents/Partner%205%20-%20Germany%20(Bremen)%20deliverable_2_1_submission.pdf (accessed 23 June 2013).

Hirsch, M., (1999), 'Projected memory: Holocaust photographs in personal and public fantasy', in M. Bal, J. Crewe and L. Spitzer (eds), *Acts of Memory: Cultural Recall in the Present*, 3–23, Hanover: University Press of New England.

Holdsworth, A., (2011), *Television, Memory and Nostalgia*, Basingstoke: Palgrave Macmillan.

Jennings, M. K., Stoker, L. and Bowers, J., (2009), 'Politics across generations: family transmission reexamined', *The Journal of Politics*, 71 (3): 782–799.

Keightley, E. and Pickering, M., (2012), *The Mnemonic Imagination: Remembering as Creative Practice*, Basingstoke: Palgrave Macmillan.

Klein, K. L., (2000), 'On the emergence of memory in historical discourse', *Representations*, 69: 127–150.

Koronaiou, A., Mantoglou, A., Chiotaki-Poulou, I., Kymionis, S., Lagos, E., Sakellariou, A. and Zachariadis, A., (2013), *MYPLACE Deliverable 2.1: Country based reports on historical discourse production as manifested in sites of memory (Greece)*, available at: http://www.fp7-myplace.eu/documents/Partner%2016%20-%20Greece_deliverable_2_1_submission.pdf (accessed 23 June 2013).

Leonova, A., (2009), 'Electoral choice, cultural capital, and xenophobic attitudes in Russia, 1994–2006', in M. Laruelle (ed.), *Russian Nationalism and the National Reassertion of Russia*, 145–184, London and New York: Routledge.

Lubbers, M. and Scheepers, P., (2002), 'French *Front National* voting: a micro and macro perspective', *Ethnic and Racial Studies*, 25: 120–149.

Mah, A., (2010), 'Memory, uncertainty and industrial ruination: Walker Riverside, Newcastle upon Tyne', *International Journal of Urban and Regional Research*, 34 (2): 398–413.

Miller-Idriss, C., (2009), *Blood and Culture: Youth, Right-Wing Extremism, and National Belonging in Contemporary Germany*, Durham, NC: Duke University Press.

Mudde, C., (2007), *Populist Radical Right Parties in Europe*, Cambridge: Cambridge University Press.

Narskii, I., (2004,) 'Konstruirovanie mifa o grazhdanskoi voine i osobennosti kollektivnogo zabyvaniia na Urale v 1917–1922 gg.', *Ab Imperio*, 2: 211–236.

Nora, P., (1989), 'Between memory and history: *Les Leux de mémoire*', *Representations*, 26: 7–24.

Nugin, R., Pirk, R. and Allaste, A.-A., (2013), *MYPLACE Deliverable 2.1: Country based reports on historical discourse production as manifested in sites of memory (Estonia)*, available at: http://www.fp7-myplace.eu/documents/Partner%203%20-%20Estonia_deliverable2_1 _submission.pdf (accessed 23 June 2013).

Ochman, E., (2009), 'Municipalities and the search for the local past: fragmented memory of the Red Army in Upper Silesia', *East European Politics and Society*, 23 (3): 392–420.

Olick, J. and Robbins, J., (1998), 'Social memory studies: from "collective memory" to the historical sociology of mnemonic practices', *Annual Review of Sociology*, 24: 105–140.

Pentzold, C., (2009), 'Fixing the floating gap: the online encyclopaedia Wikipedia as a global place', *Memory Studies*, 2 (2): 255–272.

Perasović, B. and Vojak, D., (2013), *MYPLACE Deliverable 2.1: Country based reports on historical discourse production as manifested in sites of memory (Croatia)*, available at: http://www.fp7-myplace.eu/documents/Partner%2013%20-%20Croatia_deliverable_2_1_submission.pdf (accessed 23 June 2013).

Pine, F., Kaneff, D. and Haukanes, H., (2004), 'Introduction. Memory, politics and religion: a perspective on Europe', in F. Pine, D. Kaneff and H. Haukanes (eds), *Memory, Politics and Religion: The Past Meets the Present in Europe*, 1–29, Münster: Lit Verlag.

Popov, A., (2013), *MYPLACE Deliverable 2.1: Country based reports on historical discourse production as manifested in sites of memory (United Kingdom)*, available at: http://www.fp7-myplace.eu/documents/Partner%201%20and%202%20-%20UK_Deliverable_2_1_submission.pdf (accessed 23 June 2013).

Radley, A., (1990), 'Artefacts, memory and a sense of the past', in D. Middleton and D. Edwards (eds), *Collective Remembering*, 46–59, London: Sage Publications.

Rhodes, J., (2009), 'The political breakthrough of the BNP: the case of Burnley', *British Politics*, 4 (1): 22–46.

Safonova, M., Fomina, A. and Krivonos, D., (2013), *MYPLACE Deliverable 2.1: Country based reports on historical discourse production as manifested in sites of memory (Russia)*, available at: http://www.fp7-myplace.eu/documents/Partner%2010%20-%20Russia_deliverable_2_1 _submission.pdf (accessed 23 June 2013).

Saleniece, I., Stasulane, A. and Dura, D., (2013), *MYPLACE Deliverable 2.1: Country based reports on historical discourse production as manifested in sites of memory (Latvia)*, available at: http://www.fp7-myplace.eu/documents/Partner%2011%20Latvia_deliverable_2_1 _submission.pdf (accessed 23 June 2013).

Shaw, C. and Chase, M. (eds), (1989), *The Imagined Past: History and Nostalgia*, Manchester: Manchester University Press.

Shoshan, N., (2008), 'Placing the extremes: cityscape, ethnic "others" and young right extremists in East Berlin', *Journal of Contemporary European Studies*, 16 (3): 377–391.

Shotter, J., (1990), 'The social construction of remembering and forgetting', in D. Middleton and D. Edwards (eds), *Collective Remembering*, 120–138, London: Sage Publications.

Sik, D., (2013), *The Dual Memory of the Holocaust and the State Socialism: the Case of Hungary. MYPLACE Deliverable 2.1: Country based reports on historical discourse production as manifested in sites of memory (Hungary)*, available at: http://www.fp7-myplace.eu/documents/Partner%2015%20-%20Hungary_deliverable_2_1_submission.pdf (accessed 23 June 2013).

Sturkin, M., (1997), *Tangled Memories: The Vietnam War, the Aids Epidemic, and the Politics of Remembering*, Berkeley, CA: University of California Press.

Zurabishvili, T. and Khoshtaria, T., (2013), *MYPLACE Deliverable 2.1: Country based reports on historical discourse production as manifested in sites of memory (Georgia)*, available at: http://www.fp7-myplace.eu/documents/Partner%2012%20-%20Georgia_deliverable_2_1_submission.pdf (accessed 23 June 2013).

*The Sociological Review*, 63:S2, pp. 36–52 (2015), DOI: 10.1111/1467-954X.12261

# Memory transmission and political socialization in post-socialist Hungary

*Domonkos Sik*

**Abstract:** This article examines and critically evaluates the processes of institutional memory transmission and political formation in post-socialist Hungary utilizing the critical theories of Habermas, Giddens and Bourdieu. In the first part of the article, a discourse analysis of the public debates about two distinctive 'lieux de mémoires' – the House of Terror and the Holocaust Memorial Center – is elaborated. The concept of 'memory vacuum' is introduced to express the lack of minimal consensus between political actors about distinctive 20th-century Hungarian political traumas: the Holocaust and state socialist terror. In the second part of the article, focus groups conducted with high school visitors ($n = 49$) to these museums are analysed to explore the relationship between their interpretations of the past and evaluations of current political issues. In the final section of the article, an attempt is made to elaborate ideal typical patterns of collective memories and ensuing political cultures. It is concluded that the recent antidemocratic transformations in Hungarian political culture might be explained as a failure of both institutional and family transmission of collective memories to embed democratic principles.

**Keywords:** collective memory, political socialization, post-socialism

## Introduction

More than 20 years after the transition, Hungarian democracy is in crisis; not only is the extreme right one of the strongest in Europe, but also the governing central right parties are dismantling democratic institutions (Tóth, 2012). The fact that the vast majority of voters support these parties notwithstanding their antidemocratic tendencies indicates that democratic principles, which were in the spotlight during the transition, have lost their attractiveness and have been replaced by politically indifferent materialism, nationalism or populist radicalism. These tendencies, it would seem, indicate a significant restructuring of Hungarian political culture. The aim of this article is to understand this process by mapping the transforming patterns of young people's political engagement in the context of the public reproduction of collective memory.

*The Sociological Review*, 63:S2, pp. 53–71 (2015), DOI: 10.1111/1467-954X.12262

The notion of political culture is a genuinely phenomenological concept. It explains political behaviour by the attitudes shaped in the process of socialization (Almond and Verba, 1963). The notion of political culture is closely related also to the concept of collective memory (Halbwachs, 1992; Nora, 1989). Political attitudes are never decontextualized, which means that political culture is always embedded within politically constructed collective interpretations of the past. From this perspective we may argue that political culture is formed by parallel processes of political socialization and memory transmission. When talking about democratic and antidemocratic patterns of political socialization and memory transmission, one inevitably steps onto normative ground, which requires critical reflection. As middle-range theories – such as Almond and Verba's or Halbwachs' theory – rarely attempt to clarify their normative basis, here we turn to theoretically more elaborated approaches such as the critical social theories of Bourdieu, Habermas and Giddens. These critical theories help illuminate various dimensions of the reconfiguration of political culture. Accordingly, in this article, middle-range theoretical frames of political culture and collective memory are complemented with the normative clarifications of critical social theories.

Based on Habermas's theory of communicative rationalization, the processes of memory transmission and political socialization can be understood as an aspect of the communicative reproduction of lifeworld. The quality of everyday interactions and debates in the public sphere are crucial for the formation of political culture since the most basic democratic competence, the capability of participating in an argumentative debate between equals (Habermas, 1984: 289-95), can be acquired only in these situations (Habermas, 1990: 166-7). The lack of such experience may result in the emergence of dogmatic interpretations of the past and indifferent or antidemocratic attitudes. A political culture based on the lack of communicative rationality is incapable of maintaining strong civil society and an active public sphere, which are the birthplaces of legitimacy in complex societies (Habermas, 1996: 360-7).

Drawing on Giddens' theory of late modernity, the processes of memory transmission and political socialization can be understood in the context of new challenges of identity formation and the emergence of life politics. While late modernity is characterized by the increase of ontological insecurity caused by the questionable status of expert institutions (Giddens, 1990: 53-4) and the emergence of risk society, it also holds new emancipatory potentials in the form of increased reflexivity and politics focusing on these challenges (Giddens, 1991: 210-23). If the formation of a reflexive identity is blocked in the course of interpersonal and institutional interactions, then regressive interpretations of the past (eg romanticized nationalism) are strengthened, which may result in intolerant, fundamentalist political reactions (Giddens, 1991: 189-91).

Based on Bourdieu's theory, memory transmission and political socialization can be understood in the context of field struggles and symbolic violence. Just as social practices as a whole are driven by habitus, that is, the incorporated structural position (Bourdieu, 1990: 53) and illusions, which are the rules of acquiring material and symbolic capitals (Bourdieu, 1998: 75-9), so, too, interpretations of

*The Sociological Review*, 63:S2, pp. 53–71 (2015), DOI: 10.1111/1467-954X.12262

the past and the horizon of political action depend on the logic of fields. If the structural inequalities between fields are extreme (eg political or economic logic controls the institutional process of memory transmission), then dominant fields prevent the autonomy of the others. If inequalities within the most significant fields are high, while mobility is hindered, then the habitus of the subordinated is either based on resigned hopelessness or frustrated radicalism. In both cases the interpretation of the past and the horizon of political action become susceptible to antidemocratic influences.[1]

These critical theories help to illuminate the various difficulties and limitations of democratic culture appearing on the level of macro structures, identities and interactions. In the first part of the article, the processes of public memory transmission are analysed in order to identify the specific Hungarian challenges. Recent intellectual debates following the opening of two *lieux de mémoire* in Budapest – the House of Terror and the Holocaust Memorial Center – are analysed employing discourse analysis, along with interviews conducted with historians attached to the museums (*n* = 6). In the second part, the consequences of the ambivalent processes of public memory transmission for political socialization are analysed with the help of focus groups conducted with high school visitors (*n* = 49) to these museums. Based on these data those family factors are identified, which are either capable of counterbalancing the ambivalences of public memory transmission, or which further increase the chances of antidemocratic political socialization.[2]

## Difficulties of post-transition memory transmission

During the decades of state socialism, the public sphere was greatly distorted by the ideological directives of the party state. Therefore, after the transition in 1989, an exceptional need for memory work arose because neither the interwar era, the Holocaust, nor the decades of state socialism had been discussed properly before. More than ten years after the transition, the opening of the House of Terror and the Holocaust Memorial Center was supposed to fill this vacuum. Accordingly, they generated ongoing widespread debates, which outline different approaches to these traumatic periods of the 20th century.[3]

The House of Terror sets out to introduce visitors to the experience of the 20th century Hungarian dictatorships, namely the Szálasi (1944–1945) and the Rákosi era (1947–1956). Although it became almost instantly one of the most popular museums in the country, both the concept and its realization were widely criticized. Many critics note that by introducing the totalitarian dictatorships as the consequences of the Nazi and Soviet occupations, the museum constructs a victimizing narrative. In this narrative the Hungarians are responsible neither for the sins of the Holocaust nor those of state socialism but are considered as the victims of occupying, foreign, totalitarian states. This narrative is criticized mainly for two reasons. In the case of the Holocaust there is a clear consensus amongst experts of the period that – as the SS officer Adolf Eichmann arrived in Hungary with no more than 200 to 300 soldiers – the participation of the

Hungarian authorities was indispensable to the deportation of almost half a million Jewish citizens. Also, the existence of an anti-Semitic consensus shared by citizens and the political elite of the interwar era is well known, which resulted in the willingness to – actively or indirectly – participate in the persecution of the Jews. In the light of this, the victimization narrative is inadequate in relation to understanding the Holocaust (Donáth, 2003; Varga, 2002; Ungváry, 2003).

In the case of state socialism the question of responsibility is more complex. As proven most clearly by the revolution of 1956, Soviet military intervention was a constant threat in the Cold War setting. In this sense, the people lost their sovereignty and could not change the political setting on their own. On the other hand, much of the population became more or less corrupted by the state socialist system as time passed. This could mean anything from small-scale exchanges of favours or backroom deals to cooperation with the secret police. These corrupted relationships, following from the logic of an enduring totalitarian system still haunt public life; this is expressed in the debates around the still non-public lists of secret police agents.

Obviously these criticisms, which appear mostly in the liberal-left media, have not gone unanswered by right-wing public intellectuals. From their point of view the most important function of the museum is the reconstruction of a positive national identity. This, they argue, requires a narrative capable of dealing with the Hungarian responsibility for the Holocaust as well as doing justice to the victims of state socialism. According to the defenders of the concept of the House of Terror these two burdens prevent the birth of a positive Hungarian identity. On the one hand the accusation of Hungarian participation in the Holocaust continuously emphasized by the liberal-left media maintains a permanently guilty conscience. On the other hand the lack of naming and punishing those who are responsible for the sins of state socialism prevents the healing of old wounds and the restoration of national pride. The key element of a narrative of 20th-century Hungarian history, which is capable of integrating these two functions, is equating Nazi and Soviet terror. This creates an abstract notion of 'totalitarian terror', which becomes an independent entity. This entity can be blamed for the sins of the Holocaust, which means that not the Hungarians as such, but only those few madmen who served the – originally Nazi – totalitarian system are responsible for it. This perspective is counterbalanced by an interpretation of communism as a Hungarian historical trauma comparable to – as Bauman puts it (1989) – the darkest moment of modernity, the Holocaust.

These narratives are the primary tools for identity politics; they help to ground a positive national identity and produce an oversimplified but acceptable interpretation of the two major traumas of the 20th century. They explain the Holocaust as something that happened to the Hungarians and not as something that was committed partially by them. They explain state socialism as a collective trauma. The focus on identity politics explains the incomprehension of right-wing intellectuals concerning criticisms of the victimizing narrative represented by the museum. For them, the goal of grounding a positive national identity is evidently legitimate, therefore those who oppose it are necessarily motivated

*The Sociological Review*, 63:S2, pp. 53–71 (2015), DOI: 10.1111/1467-954X.12262

by malevolent or 'foreign' interests. Some of them accuse opposing intellectuals of being simply politically biased (Sümegi, 2003; Schmidt, 2003), others accuse them of being the inheritors of the state socialist system (Molnár, 2002). For obvious reasons these heated debates cannot move towards a consensus; opposing opinions become entrenched and the different interpretations of the past do not meet.

The debates concerning the Holocaust Memorial Center are constituted according to the same logic of the political field; what the liberal-left intellectuals praise, the right-wing intellectuals criticize. One of the key points of debate concerns the evaluation of Miklós Horthy, who governed Hungary during the interwar period. While he cooperated with Nazi Germany in many ways, he refused the deportation of the Jews until the spring of 1944, when he finally yielded to the demands of Germany, which resulted in the fastest mass deportation in Europe. According to the narrative of the Holocaust Memorial Center, Horthy is personally responsible for these acts, as he knew the destination of the deportations, and was not forced to support the Nazi demands, especially not at this tempo. According to the right-wing narrative, the question of Horthy's responsibility is more complex as it was also he who stopped the deportations on 26 June, which resulted in the saving of the Jewish community in Budapest. The Memorial Center argues that the very fact that the process was halted is proof of Horthy's responsibility as it demonstrates that he was not controlled by the Nazi state but maintained his freedom to act. This debate goes on even today especially since the start of a controversial rehabilitation of Miklós Horthy which has seen squares being named after him and symbolically adorned with public sculptures of him, often resulting in emotionally charged protests.

Even though Horthy is not included in the narrow themes of the House of Terror, one of their historians gives a precise summary of the right-wing interpretation of his historical role:

> It is always mentioned that the Horthy era is half-fascist and stuff like that, while everybody forgets that in fact it is a tradition in Hungarian parliamentarianism, which had of course its shady side, but it was also one of the most successful attempts at modernisation, second right after the Monarchy, especially in comparison with the following decades. (János, Hungary)

A representative of the opposing discursive position, a historian of the Holocaust Memorial Center, however, criticizes both the right-wing evaluation of Horthy and its indirect representation in the House of Terror:

> Of course I could also emphasise that in 1944 we lost our independence and many other things, but then why don't we emphasise the question: why couldn't Horthy stop the transportations earlier, for example on 2 June, when Budapest was already bombed? [...] I don't understand why it is necessary, for example in the House of Terror, it's amongst the first things you face when you enter, I don't understand why it is necessary to try to justify what happened then. I think it would be much healthier to confront what happened in Hungary, what Hungarian people did to Hungarian people, and

understand how dangerous it is today, if somebody starts to say 'bastard Gipsy'. Because we've seen where it may lead. (Pál, Hungary)

The other debated point is the lack of attention devoted to those who stood up for the Jews and tried to save them through various actions. These heroes called 'life rescuers' are at the centre of the right-wing interpretation of the Holocaust. According to this, the real moral lesson of the Holocaust is not the responsibility of society and the political elite for the Holocaust, but the self-sacrifice of these people:

> Look, I think that they have a really distinctive interpretation. Unfortunately, I think that they approach from the perspective that since Adam and Eve, anti-Semitism has been a poison. I don't know [...] A few years ago the Wiesenthal Center announced the operation 'Last chance' [to call to account still living Nazi war criminals], as I remember in cooperation with the Holocaust Memorial Center, but I am not a hundred percent sure. Anyway, we announced our version of the operation 'Last chance', we searched for those who saved Jewish lives. So I think that their context is a little bit of a negative one. We try to emphasise the constructive aspects, which determine the cooperation. (János, Hungary)

The debates on Horthy and the Jew rescuers are all centred on the question of Hungarian responsibility or victimhood. In this sense the narratives of the Holocaust and communism are part of the same discursive field, dominated by the logic of party rivalry. This means that fundamentally political distinctions mark the most important reference points of collective memory formation. In this sense the narratives of the two museums are rivals in memory politics influenced by party interests. From the perspective of Bourdieu's theory, this means that, in post-transition Hungary, the political field dominates the field of memory construction. The lack of an autonomous field of memory transmission results in the subordination of the interest of understanding the past to the interests of party struggles, which prevents the grounding of collective identity on the basis of critically reflecting on historical traumas.

This political embeddedness limits the discourse on the past, as it unintentionally leads to a polarization and dogmatization of the points of view and disables the creation of an overlapping interpretation incorporating both traumas. The logic of party politics is a competing one, in Schmittian terms it divides the world into friends and enemies (Schmitt, 2007), while excluding communication oriented to mutual understanding. Of course, a perfect consensus about the interpretation of the traumas of the 20th century is hardly possible; however, the complete lack of any kind of consensus undermines a democratic political culture.[4] Without a minimal agreement about the role the Hungarian state and Hungarians played in the Holocaust and during state socialism, a collective memory capable of grounding a democratic political culture is missing. From the perspective of Habermas's theory, this means that the party narratives function as obstacles to a rational debate oriented towards mutual understanding. Instead, they conserve the tensions caused by the difficult past and maintain a disunited, suspicious, hostile climate in the public sphere, which undermines not only unbiased memory work, but any constructive political debate.

The lack of such consensus opens the space for indifferent or radical interpretations of 20th-century traumas, which may become fertile soil for antidemocratic political cultures in the present. The 'original sin' in the radical historical narrative is the Trianon Treaty closing World War I. As it resulted in the dissolution of the historical Kingdom of Hungary (which lost 72 per cent of its territory), it is interpreted as an unjust peace-dictat forced upon Hungary by the Western countries. The radical vision of the Trianon Treaty implies first of all a revisionist view, which is expressed directly in symbolic acts of visiting territories formerly belonging to Hungary (eg Transylvania), participating in charity movements aimed at people living in these areas in order to prevent their assimilation, wearing Greater Hungary maps on clothes and cars. Secondly, it implies nostalgia towards the interwar period, when revisionism was the official state ideology. This nostalgia has two implications originating from the characteristics of the interwar era. The first is the ignorance of the dangers of anti-Semitism and racism, or, in many cases, open identification with them. The second is a strong anti-leftism. Thirdly, Trianon implies anti-Western sentiments, which include hostile feelings towards the most visible characteristics of Western culture (eg consumerism, individualization), towards its economic-political institutions (global market, representative democracy) and the EU as well.[5] From the perspective of Giddens' theory, the extreme right interpretation of the 20th century represents a regressive, fundamentalist political identity. It is based on limited reflexivity and the complete rejection of expert knowledge about the past, while it is emotionally fuelled by the difficulties of late modernity including increased risks, uncertainty and ontological insecurity.

To summarize, it seems that a minimal consensus concerning the interpretation of 20th-century traumas is missing. In this sense we can talk about a 'memory vacuum', which prevents the emergence of a democratic political culture in many ways. The domination of the field of memory transmission by party politics results in constant confrontation; a 'cold civil war'. The dogmatic, uncriticizable character of the interpretations of the past distorts the public sphere and limits communicative rationality. The emergence of regressive, fundamentalist identities hinders reflexivity while generating frustration and, in some instances, actual conflict. Overall, the public processes of memory transmission in post-transition Hungary seem to provide the basis for the emergence of an antidemocratic political culture. Of course these processes are not the only factors in political socialization. They interact with the effects of other socialization agents, amongst which the family plays a key role. While public actors such as schools or the media do not have any other option but to act upon the same dividedness characterizing the museums, memories transmitted within families might provide alternative interpretations of the past. Therefore they may either strengthen or weaken the anti-democratic tendencies of political socialization originating from the memory vacuum of the public sphere. In the following section these questions are explored.

## Grappling with the past and the present

The public processes of memory transmission are institutionalized in cultural and media products, school curricula and museums. In order to grasp their effect, the functioning of these institutions needs to be observed. In what follows, the responses of museum visitors are analysed in order to describe memory transmission in action. By entering the House of Terror or the Holocaust Memorial Center the frames described above are evoked and the consequent mechanisms are set in motion, provoking reactions from visitors. As these reactions are affected by public and family memories at the same time, memory transmission must be analysed in a comprehensive way. Focus groups aimed at mapping narratives of the 20th century and their political semantics provide the opportunity for these analyses.

While earlier periods are too distant to evoke family memories, World War II and the Holocaust are close enough to do so. Different family memories of these periods are expressed by many students highlighting a wide range of potential relations to the past. One student, for example, explains how a family member was saved from labour service: 'Well, my grandmother could escape from labour service because her father was a doctor and plastered the hands or feet of all of his children' (Olga, Hungary). Another talks about the family tensions caused by their different views of the Holocaust:

> Sometimes I quarrel with my dad, which easily ends up in huge arguments. In fact we usually talk about Hitler, who I don't find a positive figure, unlike Dad. [...] My grandma lived through World War II and she usually gets up and leaves the room, and we are just left there. (Laura, Hungary)

For others it is the source of untold responsibilities:

> Well, my grandma survived World War II and we have talked about it like two times [...] about the deportation of the Jews. She lived in Derecske, and she told me how bad it was to see that they were taken in large masses, how cruelly they were treated. (Péter, Hungary)

Family memories about the state socialist dictatorship of Rákosi are also present in many students' narratives. The stories appearing in these narratives are often attached to imprisonments: 'My grandma's father was taken and they couldn't see each other for more than ten years, and didn't know anything about each other. In the end it turned out that he was in prison and was tortured continuously' (Olga, Hungary); or 'My grandfather's brother was captured by the Russians and was held as a prisoner for 5 or 6 years. These issues were not really discussed at home' (János, Hungary). Other students explain the sufferings of the inhabitants of the countryside:

> My grandmother told me stories; they dug a hole beneath the cannons and there they hid the sugar, the flour and stuff like that. When it was time to slaughter the pig, they didn't want to give it to the state, so they bought a thin one and gave that to the Russians

and hid their own in a stack of straw but the Russians started to argue and they were afraid of being taken away or shot. (Pál, Hungary)

These traumas of the early state socialist dictatorship are similar to the traumas of the Holocaust in as much as both underpin an emotionally charged view of the past. As they concentrate on unsettling 'fateful events' (Tengelyi, 2004), they ground the narratives of the past and the present. The living memory of a historical trauma transmitted by a close relative plays an exceptional role in political socialization. Personally experienced suffering holds the potential of learning the historical lessons of dictatorships, thus grounding a democratic political culture. Many young people who reported family traumas also participated in different civic actions, such as political demonstrations, charity or non-governmental organizations. One particularly active student mentions participation in human rights, anti-government demonstrations motivated by family memories of the Holocaust:

> In our school, in the 12th grade there is a huge presentation. Mine was about my grandmother, who was in Auschwitz. I conducted an interview with her, and we also had a lot of conversations. And I think I know quite a lot about this part. The others already know that this has really shaken me [...] what my grandma and my family had to go through. I think we have to talk to each other [...] that's why I went to the demonstration against the new Constitution (Ilona, Hungary).

Traumatic family memories have the power to overwrite public memories. Through the empathy originating from family relationships they can transmit a tangible experience of suffering caused by totalitarian regimes. Such experiences may provide an unquestionable reference point in the process of identity construction resulting not only in strong anti-totalitarian attitudes, but also in motivation for activism. In the Giddensian sense these factors indicate the democratic potential of family memories; the formation of a reflexive actor potentially involved in 'life politics'.

Hurt that is personally experienced, however, also holds the potential for the transmission of unresolvable conflicts thus providing the basis for a less democratic political culture. In some cases the original traumas are aggravated by the feeling of improper treatment in the present:

> My grandma felt a bit offended because her father was a colonel and her family was relocated during World War II [...] and then she felt a little bit offended because the Jews were so much in the spotlight while cases like hers were not. So this is quite a sensitive topic at home. (Olga, Hungary)

As similar narratives indicate, the discourses of the Holocaust and state socialist terror may compete not only in public debates, but also in private memories. This potential is continuously exploited by the parties, whose interest is to strengthen the binary logic of politics. Their influence is expressed in the unreflected identification with party narratives. Some students emphasize Hungarian responsibility for what happened in the Holocaust:

> I think that even if it had a great influence, politics should not tell the people what they can do. There are still millions of people. [ . . . ] And also in the end Horthy succeeded in stopping the deportations, and if it could happen once, it could have happened earlier as well. (Lilla, Hungary)

Other students criticize the one-sidedness of the Holocaust Memorial Center because it over-emphasizes the guilt of the majority: 'There was a part when they showed posters and it seemed to me a bit like they were implying that every Hungarian was posting such things and every Hungarian would agree with their content. I don't believe that this would be so simple' (Lajos, Hungary). The identification with the liberal-left or right-wing version of the past expresses an adaptation to party logic, which implies giving up reflective remembering and the acceptance of dogmatisms. These patterns exemplify what happens if the memory vacuum originating from the public sphere is not countered by credible counternarratives. In a Bourdieuian sense a habitus emerges, which is based on the acceptance of the predominance of party politics (Bourdieu, 1998: 16-17). From this perspective, the universal moral principles are overwritten by party interest, which may result in an instrumentally narrowed, antidemocratic political culture.

Unlike the Holocaust and the Rákosi-dictatorship, which has a traumatic, but unambiguous memory, the Kádár era (1956–1989) has a more controversial memory. Many students emphasize the importance of the sense of stability and security: 'My step-grandma told me that it was a bad system, but still she felt safe in it. In this sense it was a positive thing for her' (Laura, Hungary). The counterpart to this basic experience is the limitation of freedom:

> My parents have fundamentally bad memories. Because of the limitation of freedom. My grandparents would also agree with this, that even if it was economically good and everyone had good living conditions, it was still bad because of the limitation of freedom. I mean that you couldn't leave the country and stuff like that. (Ferenc, Hungary)

These nostalgic or anti-nostalgic experiences highlight the parameters of the controversial, 'deal' struck during the Kádár era whereby basic material well-being and the potential for slow progress were exchanged for the limitation of freedom. After the transition, this agreement was turned upside down in the sense that freedom was no longer limited while material security was replaced by extreme economic contingency.

Accordingly, emphasizing either freedom or security in the past is connected to one's present position. Families that were unable to handle the contingencies of capitalism, tend to refer to stability as a key characteristic of state socialism, while those that profited from the newly gained freedom, refer to the limitations of state socialism. In this sense the interpretation of the Kádár era in family discourses expresses the present political culture as well. In those families where the narrative of security is emphasized in a nostalgic manner, the Kádárian 'deal' is implicitly still accepted. This means that in exchange for material stability, giving up democratic rights is potentially negotiable. These sentiments could easily become dangerous for democratic culture, as they may imply the support of autocratic, antidemocratic political forces and movements. This is expressed in the conclusion of one student that: 'The old system was good, because there was only one candidate, who you could vote for [...]' (Pál, Hungary). Family identification with the politics of opportunism rests on a fundamentally antidemocratic perspective based on the giving up of the right of participating in the political public sphere. In a Habermasian sense such actors are incapable of democratic communication, as their perspective is limited to personal interest and they lack the capacity to ground legitimacy in public processes of mutual understanding.

The opposite of the willingness to give up democratic principles is based on the rejection of the Kádárian agreement. Such an interpretation of the Kádár era supports democratic political culture, as it expresses respect for democratic principles. In this approach the claim for justice and liberty is just as important as material security, which prevents susceptibility to populist ideas: 'Even if it was good in the economic sense for everyone and everyone lived well, it still remains negative because of the limitation of freedom' (János, Hungary). In a Habermasian sense actors whose family reject the corrupted past, experience a sense of standing up for political freedom. Such experiences potentially increase commitment to a free public sphere and a civil society capable of controlling party politics (Habermas, 1996: 107-9).

The last twenty years since the transition are particularly pertinent to this discussion because young people have their own memories of it. In this sense their interpretation of the post-transition era intermeshes with their interpretation of the present political situation. Interpretations of the transition link most clearly narratives of the past with opinions about politics. These narratives are usually very critical and emotionally charged:

> Probably if the politicians had a different attitude and didn't steal everything they see, it could have been better [...] If you take Gyurcsány [former prime minister], who said himself that he lied and after that he governed the country for I don't know how many years, well that's ridiculous. [...] That's why this whole thing is fucked up, the same man who is guilty himself tries to prohibit stealing. (Lajos, Hungary)

The lack of positive narratives about the transition is a general tendency. Young people's general attitude towards the last twenty years and the present is almost exclusively disappointed. They have memories about the post-transition era as both an economically and morally failed period. They do not compare it to the previous century full of suffering and traumas; instead they compare it to global standards, which makes them feel underdeveloped or deprived. Such a historical diagnosis on the one hand expresses that for many young people the collective memory of previous generations is not really relevant. In this sense there is a sign of a discontinuity in the historical consciousness. Such a one-sided, negative perspective results in basically two different types of political culture: a passive, apolitical, indifferent civic attitude; or the identification with populist, radical views (Sik, 2014c).

The passive behavioural pattern is often grounded in a relativist view of the past, referring to the impossibility of remembering: 'No one can know for sure, what happened! [...] It's not at all sure if it was as we know it. The point is that it's completely uncertain how things happened' (András, Hungary). These relativist thoughts are often complemented by orientalizing, self-colonizing narratives (Melegh, 2006), or feelings expressing the lack of real voice in politics:

> We always thought of ourselves as part of Western Europe, but we will never become that. A litre of petrol costs 450 Forints and the average salary is 60,000 Forints. [ . . . ] But we see that Europe is already divided. There is East and West Europe. The western people live well, they are the leaders, they export the goods and we pay for them. (Károly, Hungary)

> It's not us who determine the decisions of the parties in power, but they determine our fates and there is nothing we can do. (Pál, Hungary)

Both of these narratives refer to a feeling that action is futile. Relativism and defeatism result in many cases in suspicion and distancing from the whole sphere of party politics: 'That whole period, the Kádár era was built upon lies. And today it is still the same; politicians promise many things and they don't fulfill even half of them' (Olga, Hungary). Depending on the cultural capital of the students, these anti-political narratives may take a more or less reflective and elaborated form. They are all, nonetheless, 'rationalizations' of a passive, indifferent civic culture. Even though these experiences are clearly not nurturing a democratic political culture, they may still reduce the antidemocratic potential of the public memory vacuum. Since they express a distancing from the political field, they also imply an indirect criticism of the predominance of the political field and thus contain the potential for the emergence of autonomous semantics in a Bourdieuian sense.

The radical behavioural pattern is usually grounded in extreme right narratives of the past. One of the key elements of this narrative is implicit anti-Semitism, which is often expressed in a criticism of the narratives of the Holocaust:

> This Holocaust topic is quite complex due to political reasons and financial ones as well, obviously. [ . . . ] I don't want to go into details here, but the more they advertise this whole thing, the more attention they get and the more money as well. (Aranka, Hungary)

Anti-Semitism is complemented in many cases with xenophobia and racism:

> I can't explain it, and I don't know who educated me this way, but I hate the Romanians. [ . . . ] Probably I started to hate them because here in Budapest, not the downtown but the outskirts are full of Romanians, who walk in their disgusting clothes and sell their miserable stuff. (Lörinc, Hungary)

In the case of the Roma, the situation is even more grave:

> Well, okay, the Jews are more or less accepted, because the Jewish is a religion not a race, but the Gypsies, I think they are hated by everyone. [ . . . ] Those Gypsies who think of themselves as Gypsies and are proud of being one and have a culture, that's a different thing. [ . . . ] But the Hungarian Gypsies [ . . . ] well, they are miserable things, I could barely call them humans. (Nándor, Hungary)

Another important element of the political behaviour of the radicals is economic chauvinism and a negative attitude towards anything foreign: 'We can't find Hungarian paprika in the shops. All of them are mixed with Spanish or I don't know what. There is simply no pure Hungarian' (Aranka, Hungary). The general antipathy towards foreign things is specified in many cases by clearly identifiable actors, such as the EU or multinational companies: 'Through taxes, there is much more money leaving the country than coming in, because of the multinational companies' (Lőrinc, Hungary).

Alternative narratives about the past and the present are constructed in an alternative public sphere, accessible only to insiders: 'There are trustworthy opinions, only they must be bought as a book [...] and also they are probably banned. [...] These are not only more trustworthy, but also more logical as well. [...] They can be bought from under the counter' (Nándor, Hungary). These sources provide an oversimplifying, but seemingly coherent world view. They question common knowledge and replace it with conspiracy theories, which supposedly unveil the lies:

> Well, I think that if somebody looks into these matters from many sources and not only those which are usually presented everywhere, they can put together the big picture. They can look up the Jewish websites, what they are all about. [...] I mean, where the money comes from. There is so much money in it, it's terrible. (Aranka, Hungary)

These young people are politically more active than the average. This can be detected first of all in their peer-group relationships. While most of the non-radical students said that they usually do not discuss the past and politics with friends, the radicals mention that these topics are central: 'My friends, who were involved in the political life and try to establish a local platform, we usually have 2 to 3 hour long political discussions and we usually end up in historical questions' (Nándor, Hungary). These discussions play a key role in the formation of an alternative public sphere, where the alternative interpretations of the past and present can be discussed without the danger of confrontation with mainstream ones. However, private discussions are not the only form of political activism; it also includes involvement in party politics. The radical students participating in the research all support the extreme right party, Jobbik; they identify with their interpretation of the past and diagnosis of the present and plan to vote for them in the next elections. In this sense they expressed an identity, which attempts to deal with insecurity by turning to uncriticizable, fixed 'truths'. In a Giddensian sense, such a reaction can be understood as a regressive answer to the experienced uncertainties and disappointments, which relies on an oversimplifying, unambiguous interpretation of the world, instead of a reflexive engagement with it (Giddens, 1991: 192-196).

## From collective memory to political culture

These aspects of democratic culture allow us to analytically distinguish the different roles played by various types of memory patterns. The memories of

**Table 1:** *The effect of collective memory on the democratic character of the horizon of expectations*

| Interpretation of the past | Effect on political culture |
| --- | --- |
| Traumatic family memory of Holocaust/ state socialist terror (Rákosi era) | The emotionally charged experience of totalitarianism strengthens anti-totalitarian identity (in Giddensian sense) |
| Memory of Holocaust/ state socialist terror (Rákosi era) inserted into the frames of party narratives | The mediatized experience of totalitarianism reproduces 'memory vacuum', while weakening a critical attitude towards the political field (in Bourdieuian sense) |
| Anti-nostalgic memory of consolidated state socialism (Kádár era) | The example of a corrupt, manipulative oppression raises awareness of the importance of moral elements of democracy (civil society, critical public sphere), thus strengthens communicative-cognitive democratic values (in Habermasian sense) |
| Nostalgic memory of consolidated state socialism (Kádár era) | The identification with the agreement of giving up political freedom for material security lowers awareness of the importance of moral elements of democracy, thus weakens communicative-cognitive democratic values (in Habermasian sense) |
| Negative experiences of post-transition era | The experience of the predominance of the political field strengthens the critical attitude towards political actors (in Bourdieuian sense) |
| Negative experiences of post-transition era inserted into the frames of radical narratives | The complete disappointment in multiparty democracy strengthens a fundamentalist, anti-establishment identity (in Giddensian sense) |

different periods transmitted via various channels affect each aspect of democratic culture in a different manner. However, based on the focus groups it seems that there are unique correspondences between particular memory patterns and aspects of political culture. Accordingly, the following ideal typical relation of memory patterns and aspects of democratic cultures might be constructed (Table 1).

*The Sociological Review*, 63:S2, pp. 53–71 (2015), DOI: 10.1111/1467-954X.12262

**Table 2:** *Ideal types of political culture constructed from memory patterns*

| Ideal types of political culture | Patterns of interpretation of the past |
|---|---|
| **Coherent democrat** (anti-totalitarian identity, democratic values and critical towards the political field) | Traumatic family memory of the Holocaust/ state socialist terror (Rákosi era) + anti-nostalgic memory of consolidated state socialism (Kádár era) + negative experiences of the post-transition era |
| **Emotionally motivated democrat** (only anti-totalitarian identity) | Traumatic family memory of the Holocaust/ state socialist terror (Rákosi era) |
| **Cognitively motivated democrat** (only democratic values and critical towards political field) | Anti-nostalgic memory of consolidated state socialism (Kádár era) + negative experiences of post-transition era |
| **Coherent radical** (acceptance of the political field logic, antidemocratic values and totalitarian identity) | Family memory of the Holocaust/ state socialist terror (Rákosi era) inserted into the frames of party narratives + nostalgic memory of consolidated state socialism (Kádár era) + negative experiences of the post-transition era inserted into the frames of radical narratives |
| **Frustrated radical** (only totalitarian identity) | Negative experiences of the post-transition era inserted into the frames of radical narratives |
| **Indifferent antidemocrat** (only antidemocratic values and lack of criticism of the political field) | Family memory of Holocaust/ state socialist terror (Rákosi era) inserted into the frames of party narratives + nostalgic memory of consolidated state socialism (Kádár era) |
| **Ahistorical sceptic** (only criticism of the political field) | Negative experiences of post-transition era |
| **Coherent apolitical** (ignores the past and the present) | – |

The actual space of experience and the horizon of expectations of young people are constituted from the combination of these patterns. Based on them, several ideal types of political culture can be constructed (Table 2). These ideal types are not constituted as the result of the mere mathematical combination of the memory patterns and the consequent aspects of democratic culture. Instead, they are constructed according to the patterns experienced in the focus groups.

Those young people in the first row not only have a traumatic memory of totalitarianism but are also critical of the anti-democratic tendencies of state socialism and the predominance of the political field in the present. Such a pattern of memory implies a democratic political culture grounded at the level of identity, values and critical potential, as it contains personal motivation to resist extreme ideologies and to be aware of the dangers of the lack of checks and balances. In a certain sense these young people are the examples of how the memory vacuum generated in the public sphere can be completely overcome with the help of family memories; they replace the predominance of party logic by autonomous interpretation of the past, stand up for an uncorrupted public sphere and actively reject antidemocratic semantics.

The second and the third rows represent narrower versions of the coherent democratic memory structure. In the second row the living family memory provides an anti-totalitarian identity without being complemented by reflection on the less obvious distortions of democracy. Thus the second pattern of memory implies a perspective, which is motivated to protest against obvious injustices, but unaware of the less obvious corruptions of democratic institutions. Contrarily, young people belonging to the third row reflect on these potentials, while lacking the living memory of totalitarianism. Thus the third pattern of memory implies a critical perspective, which, however, lacks the potential of motivating action, as it is not complemented by an anti-totalitarian identity. These young people show how the distortions caused by memory vacuum can be partially handled. They either refuse intolerant semantics without being aware of the predominance of party politics and the quality of the public sphere or they are aware of these stakes without being sensitive to the antidemocratic threats.

Those young people in the fourth row not only interpret their traumatic memories of totalitarianism according to the divided political logic but also tend to emphasize the material security of state socialism over its antidemocratic tendencies, while being open to explaining the current problems through reference to oversimplifying and populist narratives. Such a pattern of memory implies an emotionally and cognitively grounded antidemocratic political culture including not only indifference to democratic values but also a totalitarian identity. In a certain sense this ideal type reveals the real danger of the 'memory vacuum', as these young people show how the distortions caused by memory vacuum can be exacerbated by family socialization: they adopt the structural predominance of party politics over collective memory in a habitus relativizing totalitarianism; they give up the claim of an undistorted public sphere producing non-dogmatic discourses; and develop a regressive, unreflected identity potentially grounding extremist, antidemocratic political action.

The fifth and the sixth rows represent two different variants of the coherently radical memory structure. In the fifth row, instead of the difficult past, unresolved personal problems organize the identity. As they cannot be handled, the tension caused by them is projected onto social problems, resulting in the blaming of virtual or actual (often ethnic) social groups for personal difficulties. In this sense the fifth pattern of memory implies a perspective, which, because of

*The Sociological Review*, 63:S2, pp. 53–71 (2015), DOI: 10.1111/1467-954X.12262
© 2015 The Author. Editorial organisation © 2015 The Editorial Board of the Sociological Review

the lack of memories capable of preventing the susceptibility to radical narratives, transforms the helpless anger into radical views. Contrary to this, in the sixth row, antidemocratic culture is not the consequence of unresolvable problems of the present, but the uncritical identification with biased interpretations of 20th-century traumas. Young people interpreting state socialism in a nostalgic manner, while accepting the parties' interpretation of historical traumas are not necessarily identifying with radical views; they are only unaware of their political consequences. Thus the sixth pattern of memory implies a perspective which transforms a lack of awareness into an antidemocratic indifference. These young people exemplify the partial actualization of the antidemocratic potential of the memory vacuum. They either develop a regressive identity suffering from limited reflexivity, ontological insecurity and unmanaged risks, without being aware of the potential dangers of intolerance arising from historical traumas, or they identify with the party logic resulting in dogmatic political views and a distorted public sphere, without being motivated to any sort of action.

The last two rows refer to spaces of experience detached from the past. In both cases young people are alienated from the collective memory, which is a third potential answer to the challenges of memory vacuum that is turning away from the difficult past. The only difference between the two cases is the reflection on the present. While in the case of the seventh row young people express critical personal narratives about the post-transition era, in the case of the eighth row they ignore the present as well. These patterns of memory vacuum may imply a passive, indifferent, cynical or sceptical political culture, which is undetermined by the collective past, instead centred on strictly private, individual goals.

## Conclusion

After outlining these ideal types, we may return to our original question concerning the emergence of antidemocratic political climate in Hungary. As the analysis of the focus groups show, various narratives of 20th-century political traumas underpin different political cultures. In this sense the emergence of an antidemocratic political climate may be understood from the perspective of the failure of memory transmission on both institutional and family levels. As public processes of memory transmission in the last twenty years have been colonized by political parties, institutional actors have failed to elaborate a non-dogmatic narrative capable of grounding a democratic political culture and a reflexive identity. It seems that this distortive effect of the memory vacuum might be overcome only by transmitting reflexive family memories of 20th-century political traumas. However, as other research focusing on these processes indicates, families are rarely capable of such a task (Szabó, 2009; Csákó, 2014). In a representative survey conducted in 2011, 18 to 19-year-old Hungarian students were asked how often they talk about the Holocaust or the state socialist dictatorship. More than 75 per cent answered 'never', another 10 per cent answered 'I don't participate in such discussions' or 'I'm not allowed to participate' meaning that only in 15 per cent of Hungarian families does the process of memory transmission take place.[6] These data indicate that not only institutions, but also families fail to ground or mediate the lessons of 20th-century political traumas, which could ground a democratic political culture. The worrisome consequences of this failure are already visible, as the majority of young people in Hungary either, by identifying with extreme semantics, actively or, by focusing on their private life, indifferently turn their backs on democratic values.

## Notes

1  For a more detailed analysis of political socialization and the critical theories of Habermas, Bourdieu and Giddens, see Sik (2014a).
2  The empirical databases used for the discourse analysis were constructed from the articles of the two leading political daily papers (*Magyar Nemzet* and *Népszabadság*), plus the two most popular political-cultural magazines (*Élet és Irodalom* and *Heti Válasz*) between 2002 and 2010. The key words for the search were 'Holokauszt Emlékközpont' and 'Terror Háza'. The participants in expert interviews were recruited from the historians and teachers working in the museums. The participant observation of young people's reception of the exhibitions took around 30 hours in each museum. The participants in focus groups were recruited during this phase, from diverse social backgrounds (eg both Budapest and the countryside, high schools and vocational schools were represented). For further methodological details see Sik (2012).
3  For a summary of Hungarian memory studies, see Laczó and Zombory (2012). For a regional analysis of memory work in post-communist countries see Apor and Sariskova (2008) and Mark (2010). For a broader European perspective see Pakier and Stråth (2010) and Blaive *et al.* (2011).
4  It is important to emphasize that a 'minimal consensus concerning the past' does not imply solely the agreement on those basic facts of the past, which are agreed by historians (eg the participation of the Hungarian authorities in the Holocaust or the clear differentiation between the totalitarian and consolidated periods of state socialism). It also means a basic historical reflexivity, that is, a mutual respect for controversial interpretations. Only such consensus – including the element of substantive agreement and reflexivity – is capable of grounding a democratic collective identity, which understands its past and present in a non-dogmatic way.
5  On the political culture of extreme right nationalism in Hungary, see Feischmidt *et al.* (2014) and Sik (2014b).
6  The survey was supported by the Hungarian Research Fund (project number: OTKA-K78579). For a detailed description of the research, see Sik (2014c).

## References

Almond, G. A. and Verba, S., (1963), *The Civic Culture: Political Attitudes and Democracy in Five Nations*, Princeton, NJ: Princeton University Press.
Apor, P. and Sariskova, O. (eds.), (2008), *Past for the Eyes: East-European Representations of Communism in Cinema and Museums after 1989*, New York and Budapest: CEU Press.
Bauman, Z., (1989), *Modernity and The Holocaust*, Ithaca, NY: Cornell University Press.
Blaive, M., Gerbel, C. and Lindernberger, Th. (eds.), (2011), *Clashes in European Memory: The Case of Communist Repression and the Holocaust*. Innsbruck, Wien and Bozen: Studien Verlag.
Bourdieu, P., (1990) *The Logic of Practice* (trans. R. Nice), Cambridge: Polity Press.
Bourdieu, P., (1998), *Practical Reason: On the Theory of Action* (trans. Randal Johnson), Stanford, CA: Stanford University Press.
Csákó, M., (2014), 'Családi emlékezet és történelem', *socio.hu*, 4 (1): 81–107.
Donáth, F., (2003), '(T)error iratok', *Élet és Irodalom*, 47 (12).
Feischmidt, M., Glózer, R., Ilyés, Z., Kasznár, V. and Zakariás, I., (2014), *Nemzet a mindennapokban – Az újnacionalizmus populáris kultúrája*, Budapest: L'Harmattan.

*The Sociological Review*, 63:S2, pp. 53–71 (2015), DOI: 10.1111/1467-954X.12262

Giddens, A., (1990), *The Consequences of Modernity*, Cambridge: Polity Press.

Giddens, A., (1991), *Modernity and Self-Identity: Self and Society in the Late Modern Age*, Cambridge: Polity Press.

Habermas, J., (1984), *The Theory of Communicative Action* (trans. M. Thomas), Boston, MA: Beacon Press.

Habermas, J., (1990), *Moral Consciousness and Communicative Action* (trans. Ch. Lenhardt and S. N. Weber), Cambridge: Polity Press.

Habermas, J., (1996), *Between Facts and Norms: Contributions to a Discourse Theory of Law and Democracy* (trans. R. William), Cambridge, MA: MIT Press.

Halbwachs, M., (1992), *On Collective Memory* (trans./ed. L. A. Coser), Chicago: University of Chicago Press.

Laczó, F. and Zombory, M., (2012), 'Between transnational embeddedness and relative isolation. the moderate rise of memory studies in Hungary', *Acta Poloniae Historica*, 106: 99–125.

Mark, J., (2010), *The Unfinished Revolution: Making Sense of the Communist Past in Central-Eastern Europe*, New Haven and London: Yale University Press.

Melegh, A., (2006), *On the East/West Slope: Globalization, Nationalism, Racism and Discourses on Eastern Europe*, Budapest: Central European University Press.

Molnár, T., (2002), 'Terror Háza: A jelképek egyenlösége', *Magyar Nemzet*, available at: http://mno.hu/velemeny/terror-haza-jelkepek-egyenlosege-798395 (accessed 27 September 2014).

Nora, P., (1989), 'Between memory and history: les lieux de mémoire', *Representations*, 26 (Special issue): 7–25.

Pakier, M. and Stråth, B. (eds), (2010), *A European Memory? Contested Histories and Politics of Remembrance*, Brooklyn, NY: Berghahn Books.

Schmidt M., (2003), 'Egy történ(elmietlen)ész kritikája', *Népszabadság*, available at: http://nol.hu/archivum/archiv-121902-102886 (accessed 27 September 2014).

Schmitt, C., (2007), *The Concept of the Political* (trans. G. Schwab), Chicago: University of Chicago Press.

Sik, D. (2012), 'The dual memory of Holocaust and state socialism: the case of Hungary', MYPLACE report deliverable 2.1., available at: http://www.fp7-myplace.eu/documents/Partner%2015%20-%20Hungary_deliverable_2_1_submission.pdf (accessed 27 September 2014).

Sik, D., (2014a), 'Critical theory and political socialisation', *Belvedere Meridionale*, 8 (4).

Sik, D., (2014b), 'The imitated public sphere: the case of Hungary's far right', in H. Druxes and P. Simpson (eds), *Far Right Media Strategies Across Europe and North America: Extreme Persuasion*, New York: Lexington Books (forthcoming).

Sik, D., (2014c), *Demokratikus kultúra és modernizáció: Állampolgári szocializáció 20 évvel a rendszerváltás után*, Budapest: L'Harmattan.

Sümegi, N., (2003), 'Össztüz a Terror Házára', *Heti Válasz*, available at: http://valasz.hu/reflektor/ossztuz-a-terror-hazara-6481 (accessed 27 September 2014).

Szabó, I., (2009), *Nemzet és szocializáció. A politika szerepe az identitások alakulásában Magyarországon 1867–2006*, Budapest: L'Harmattan Kiadó.

Tengelyi, L., (2004), *The Wild Region in Life-History*, Evanston, IL: Northwestern University Press.

Tóth, G. A. (eds), (2012), *Constitution for a Disunited Nation: On Hungary's 2011 Fundamental Law*, Budapest and New York: CEU Press.

Ungváry K., (2003), 'A pártmúzeum', *Népszabadság*, available at: http://nol.hu/archivum/archiv-327882-146316 (accessed 27 September 2014).

Varga, L., (2002), 'A kommunizmus áldozatai', *Élet és Irodalom* 46 (10).

# Political discussions with family and friends: exploring the impact of political distance

## Klaus Levinsen and Carsten Yndigegn

**Abstract:** Young people's engagement in political discussions with parents and friends represents a significant component of the political socialization process and can be seen as an activity where they learn some very basic democratic skills. Based on data from qualitative interviews and a questionnaire survey, this article explores how young people experience political discussions in their everyday life. Our data indicate that young people who feel that their father, mother or friends, respectively, hold more distant political views are less likely to engage in political discussions with each of them. These findings support previous studies in political communication suggesting that people tend to avoid social situations where political disagreements are likely to appear. Furthermore, the results show that there are significant gender differences when analysing the role of the parents as political discussion partners.

**Keywords:** political socialization, political discussion, political distance, generations, family, youth

## Introduction

With a few exceptions (Jennings, 1983; Bloemraad and Trost, 2008; Quintelier, 2011), political socialization research has focused almost exclusively on the generational transfer of political attitudes, values and party identification from parents to their offspring, typically measured as the statistical correlation between parents' and children's political views (Hyman, 1959; Greenstein, 1965; Hess and Torney, 1967; Jennings and Niemi, 1968; Easton and Dennis, 1969). This intergenerational transmission perspective has led to a number of interesting results, indicating that family influence is continual and that parents' socio-economic background and political attitudes are significant predictors of the attitudes of their children (Jennings and Langton, 1969; Jennings and Niemi, 1968, 1971; Beck and Jennings, 1975; McGlenn, 1980; Nieuwbeerta and Wittebrood, 1995; Jennings, 2007; Jennings et al., 2009) and also intentions to vote (Hooghe and Boonen, 2013).

*The Sociological Review*, 63:S2, pp. 72–91 (2015), DOI: 10.1111/1467-954X.12263
© 2015 The Authors. Editorial organisation © 2015 The Editorial Board of the Sociological Review. Published by John Wiley & Sons Ltd, 9600 Garsington Road, Oxford OX4 2DQ, UK and 350 Main Street, Malden, MA 02148, USA

However, less attention has been paid to those aspects of political socialization that relate to political engagement within the family and everyday relations with friends. Young people's engagement in political discussions with parents and friends represents a significant component of the political socialization process and can be seen as an activity where they learn some very basic democratic skills. People who engage in political discussions with family and friends tend to be more engaged in other forms of political participation. This applies to voting at elections and participation in extra-parliamentary activities such as petitions and participation in demonstrations (Gundelach and Levinsen, 2011), and also on measures of civic behaviour, attitudes and skills. McIntosh *et al.* (2007) suggest that face-to-face discussion is important for the development of civic competencies. They found that adolescents who discuss politics and current events with their parents, peers or teachers tend to score higher on measures of civic behaviour, attitudes and skills. In addition, previous qualitative studies of political mobilization emphasize the positive role of political discussion between generations and propose that family members provide direct political stimulation through discussions (Bloemraad and Trost, 2008). Jennings *et al.* (2009) notes that the character of family discussions and political conversation determines parents' influence on their children. In families with high levels of political engagement and political discussion, there is more consonance between parent and child regarding important controversial political issues as well as preferences for political parties and presidential candidates (Jennings *et al.*, 2009).

Few studies have investigated the consequences of political discussions among peers (Amnå, 2009). Quintelier (2011) finds that peers, together with family and voluntary engagement, are the most important predictors of political participation. She finds that the more young people discuss politics with their peers, the more likely they will engage in politics. Ekström and Östman (2013) find that civic talk with peers is more strongly correlated with young people's civic orientation than civic talk with parents, and Quintelier (2015) finds that discussion among peers has a higher positive effect on political engagement than discussion in the family.

This article explores how young people experience political discussions in their everyday lives and how perceived political distance between respondents and their family members and their friends affects the level of political discussion. We find this perspective particularly interesting as it may also help clarify whether attitudinal factors affect the level of engagement in political discussions. In a questionnaire survey of young Danes and a number of qualitative face-to-face interviews, we asked respondents how they experience engagement in political discussions with family and friends, and how close or distant their own political views are to the views of their discussion partners. This means that we are able to explore to what extent political differences, as perceived by respondents, shape the pattern and frequency of political discussions. Our study also provides an opportunity to critically examine whether perceived political distance plays a role for engagement in political discussions among people who basically have close relationships – namely, young people, their parents and friends.

Previous studies show that citizens' engagement in political discussion is affected by the social and attitudinal similarities of their potential discussion partners. In many ways participation in political discussions constitutes the essence of the democratic citizen. Discussion develops individuals' ability to clarify their own attitudes towards others, listen to others' political views and arrive at new insights and perhaps joint decisions. Political discussions typically differ from other types of social communication in that they focus on public issues and involve the exchange of ideological views. In addition, political discussions reflect that the partners may have different interests. Thus, disagreement is typically both a condition and a challenge, which, according to deliberative democrats, requires that partners listen to each other and adjust their own views after listening to other arguments (Conover *et al.*, 2002; Gutmann and Thompson, 2004; Esterling *et al.*, 2010). Seen from a participatory and deliberative point of view, we should expect that political disagreement between individuals nurtures political discussions and promotes further democratic engagement.

Research in political psychology and communication, however, seems to indicate that this is not necessarily the case. Most people find it uncomfortable to encounter political disagreements when they discuss politics with other people. Thus, generally speaking, people are likely to avoid social settings and situations where political disagreements occur. A number of studies have confirmed these findings, which basically support the thesis of 'enclave deliberation' and 'political homophily' suggesting that people typically engage in discussions with like-minded people (Mutz, 2002, 2006; Mutz and Martin, 2001; Morrell, 2005; Huber and Malhotra, 2013). However, none of these studies have explored these mechanisms in the family sphere and in close social relationships. This is the intention in this article.

There are a number of reasons why family and friendships are interesting contexts to explore. In contrast to political discussions in the public sphere, family and friendships are characterized by stronger emotional ties, and, in many cases, young people are still financially dependent on their parents. This may have implications for involvement in political discussions, because the discussion partners are more attentive to protecting the social order and stability of the social relations. On the other hand, the family especially can be seen as the 'natural' arena of intergenerational conflicts between parents and children, which is likely to be reflected in political discussions.

Based on the literature we expect that the tendency to avoid political disagreements will also exist in close social relationships; between young people and their parents and between young people and their friends. Aware of the fact that it is usually very difficult to determine the causal directions in these social mechanisms, we hope to shed light on this problem by also exploring qualitatively how young people describe situations where they disagree with political discussion partners.

74

## Data and methods

Our analyses are based on two different sources of data assembled by the Danish part of the European FP7 research project MYPLACE: a questionnaire survey data set, involving a sample of 936 young Danes;[1] and 60 qualitative individual interviews with respondents drawn from the list of survey participants. The survey sample was generated from populations of young citizens from two different areas of Odense, the third largest city in Denmark (193,370 inhabitants). The Danish National Register of Persons provided us with a list of the total population (age 16–25) for each of the two areas, and a random sample was drawn from each of these lists. The response rate, measured by the proportion of full face-to-face interviews by successful contacts (phone or face-to-face) was 34 per cent for the Odense East sample and 55 per cent for Odense Centre sample. The two different city areas were chosen in order to compare variations in political engagement across different socio-geographical settings. In order to establish a sound statistical basis for our analysis, we have pooled our data from the two areas into a single data file. Therefore our statistical analyses are based on the total number of respondents, adding a control for city area.[2]

The analyses of survey data include variables measuring the frequency of respondents' involvement in political discussions with family members and friends, perceived political distance to these persons, respondents' ideological orientation and political engagement and relevant socio-demographic variables (see Appendix, Table A1).

Respondents in the qualitative study were selected in accordance with a maximum variation principle, based on two criteria: the prospective respondent's score on the political participation scale, and their scores on the tolerance scale used in the survey questionnaire. Our selection also ensured variation in terms of age, gender, education, ethnicity, citizenship and nationality in each subsample. Hence, our respondents in the qualitative interviews cover activity levels from very active to passive and tolerance levels from very tolerant to very intolerant.[3]

The interviews were semi-structured and we asked questions about respondents' social and political engagement and their political attitudes to a number of different issues (for example, welfare, immigration and environmental issues). The data originates from the early part of the interview, where respondents were asked about what was currently going on that really affected people in the country, and whether this affected them or their family personally. This was the opportunity to explore whether the respondents talked to other people, such as friends or members of their family, about such issues, and to further inquire with whom and what about they had the most recent discussions. The interview sequence was concluded with a reflexive question asking about whom they considered to have been particularly influential in terms of the impact of their views upon them.[4]

The purpose of the qualitative interviews was to obtain a deeper insight and understanding of young people's political communication patterns. By adopting a mixed methods approach, we engage both quantitative and qualitative data in a parallel analytical process. Our two different types of data allow for analytical triangulation.[5] The qualitative interviews provided contextualized 'thick descriptions' of how young people themselves experience the social and political climate in their everyday lives and in their familial context; and our survey data made it possible to analyse the impact of multiple underlying variables.

In the following analyses we present our findings in thematic sections. First, using the results of the semi-structured interviews, we provide an insight into how young people themselves experience political discussions with their parents and friends. Secondly, we examine the questionnaire survey data to analyse how often young people are engaged in political discussions and who are the most prominent discussion partners. The finding that fathers are the preferred discussion partner is further analysed by means of scrutinizing the qualitative interview data. Thirdly, we explore the complex relationship between perceived political distance and engagement in political discussions by use of multivariate statistics and qualitative inquiry.

## Political discussion with family and friends

In general, politics is given limited attention by young people. Typically, other things seem to be much more relevant and urgent; challenges related to their education, finding a place to live and, especially, staying connected with friends and partners. That said, our experience was that young people – especially in the context of high unemployment – seem to be very concerned about their own prospects in the labour market and also how the political challenges of, for example, increasing unemployment, climate change and immigration are handled by politicians.

Most of the politically active young people in our qualitative sample describe their family and peers as the main actors in discussions about current social issues and politics. Almost consistently, those of our respondents who express high levels of political engagement in the local and national societal environment see the family as a 'natural' social arena for discussions about society and politics. These respondents typically had grown up in families with a vibrant culture of debating political issues, while the politically inactive came from families where political discussions were almost completely absent.

Several of the politically engaged young people recount how political discussions in the family have had an impact on the development of their own political identity and parents are often credited with having fostered political thinking. It is characteristic for this kind of interaction that most discussions with parents are seen as enriching and enjoyable, especially when they are able to manage disagreements and establish discussions based on mutual respect:

> My father might have influenced me by pushing me to think about things. I may not always agree with him, but he had me think about things. (Brian, Centre)

> We have always discussed a lot, and we have always challenged each other very much at home, so I have really got a pretty good base to form my own opinions, and I do

*The Sociological Review*, 63:S2, pp. 72–91 (2015), DOI: 10.1111/1467-954X.12263

not always agree with my [parents], but I have to give a lot of credit to my mum and her husband. That is because they have – what can I say? – they have encouraged me to take a position on what is happening in society. So they have not consciously foisted any position on me, but they have certainly helped me to shape and develop one. [ ... ] We have always discussed a lot, and it has meant that I have been forced to take a position on it because I could not just come with empty arguments. (Ann, Centre)

Although there are exceptions, politically inactive respondents typically come from families where politics were not part of the everyday conversations. Many of these young people describe a family life where almost no political and societal discussions take place:

*Interviewer*: Through your childhood and until you left home, did you discuss politics and things like that?
*Sanne*: No, we have never done that, we watched the news while we ate, but there was never really any discussion of what was said. (Sanne, East)

It is not that we sat and discussed over the dinner table. It has been more like this: 'What did you do today?' 'And what have you achieved today?' More practical things, you know. [ ... ] That is how we do it. (Gurli, Centre)

For politically inactive respondents societal and political issues outside the family sphere and everyday life are rarely the subject of discussion, and politics is considered to be somewhat distant and irrelevant to daily life. However, some respondents from families where no political discussions took place have gained inspiration from outside their own family. Such an example is given by a young woman, who experienced the 'world of politics' when she met her boyfriend's family:

Yes, I did actually [take an interest in politics] when I got together with my boyfriend because his family talked a lot about politics and expressed political opinions. [ ... ] I began, suddenly, to think that this was really an exciting issue, which I certainly could be interested in too. Then I started to keep up with politics [ ... ] because there was someone to talk to about it. (Doris, Centre)

This illustrates that inspiration to engage in political discussions also comes from outside the family. Discussions with peers are the second main arena in which young people engage in informal political discussions. Most of the respondents seem to have a quite tolerant relationship to their friends where politics is concerned and many refer to their friends and partners when talking about political issues and how they discuss politics.

It is perhaps not surprising that politically active respondents are also more involved in political discussions with family and friends than those who are politically inactive. However, it is worth noting that most of the active respondents seem to be very much aware of the role of parents and friends in shaping their political skills and identity, and during the qualitative interviews they provided a number of interesting and detailed descriptions of how they themselves experienced political communication with family and friends. Before continuing with the interpretation of these issues, however, the survey data provide an

**Table 1:** *Political discussion with family and friends*

|  | Always | Often | Sometimes | Rarely | Never | N |
|---|---|---|---|---|---|---|
| Father | 4.1 | 24.0 | 35.8 | 22.8 | 13.2 | 894 |
| Mother | 1.6 | 13.5 | 34.9 | 33.3 | 16.6 | 925 |
| Brother/sister | 2.0 | 8.6 | 24.9 | 33.9 | 30.4 | 887 |
| Grandparent | 2.2 | 6.2 | 15.1 | 29.9 | 46.3 | 769 |
| Partner | 2.2 | 25.6 | 39.3 | 22.4 | 10.3 | 544 |
| Best friend | 3.4 | 20.9 | 32.8 | 29.5 | 13.3 | 932 |

*Note.* Survey question: 'How often do you discuss political issues when you get together with the following people?'
*Source*: MYPLACE survey, 2012–13.

opportunity to analyse how often young people engage in political discussions and the frequency of discussion with different partners.

Our findings are in line with previous research indicating a significant gender difference between the roles of the parents; within the family, fathers appear to be the most frequent political discussion partners. As shown in Table 1, 28 per cent of the respondents indicate that they 'always' or 'often' talk about political issues with their father, while only 15 per cent of respondents talk politics with their mother. The reason that there are slightly fewer respondents who answered the question on political discussion with their father is that some respondents have grown up in single parent families.

Partners and best friends are also reported to be political discussion partners. Among respondents in a relationship, 28 per cent responded that he/she always or often discusses politics with their partner. Best friends are also relatively frequent discussion partners (24 per cent), while siblings and grandparents are significantly less prominent.

Evidently, the items measuring political discussion with different persons are positively correlated, especially when it comes to political discussion with parents. Thus, for example, young people who frequently engage in political discussions with their father will be more likely to discuss politics with their mother etc. (see Appendix, Table A2). However, instead of constructing a single variable measuring the overall level of political discussion, we are more interested in looking at the different patterns of discussion related to each of the discussion partners, especially the father, mother and best friend.

The dominance of the father as the most frequent political discussion partner in the family is also expressed by several of the respondents in our qualitative studies. When it comes to involvement in political discussions with fathers, two types of experiences are found: those based on basic political agreement; and those characterized by a serious disagreement. Examples of engaged fathers who

*The Sociological Review*, 63:S2, pp. 72–91 (2015), DOI: 10.1111/1467-954X.12263

feed into political discussions are typically found among respondents coming from well-educated middle-class families:

> If we hear something on television, read something in the newspaper, or just pick it up somewhere, then we discuss it. My father knows a lot. Then he asks questions – 'How is it that ...?' [ ... ] – and then the discussion gets going. (Bente, East)

> I am very much in agreement with my father, because of the examples he provides. [ ... ] It is mostly my father and I [that discuss things]. Because of his working hours, 3–11pm, we do not watch television much together but we can sit together and talk about, for example, that I think we might need a new government. 'Why is that? I think things are going well'. So, we may sit and talk about the things that crop up. [ ... ] I would say that my father and I can discuss politics no matter what. I think every time I get hold of my dad on the phone [ ... ] half of the conversation concerns politics. (Freja, East)

There are also several examples of discussions where the father and son/daughter disagree. The picture is drawn of fathers being more engaged but, in some cases, also more patronizing. One respondent characterizes her father as very eager to debate things. However, when he speaks, it often turns into a polemical speech:

> With my father, it is more factual, but [he] is also more loud-mouthed and passionate; to put it in a nice way, it is very passionate. Sometimes, it gets a bit blunt, the way things are said, but discussions develop in different ways. (Elin, Centre)

In sum, our analysis of the qualitative interviews as well as the survey data shows that the father is the dominant political discussion partner in the family. This also indicates a possible source of a continuing gender bias in the political socialization process, which obviously requires further examination.

## Perceived political distance and political discussion

The respondents in our qualitative interviews seem to engage in discussion with parents, and predominantly with their fathers, when they feel they are respected and 'stand on common ground'. However, findings also indicate that young people tend to avoid discussions with their parents when this is not the case. An extreme case is captured in the following example where a young woman reacts against a dogmatic left-wing father:

> I think perhaps that when I was 16–17 years old, I rebelled a little against my father, because he is [supporting a left-wing party]. It is the workers, etc. I thought this is nonsense. [ ... ] We do not discuss it in my family because it ends in a fight and my mum crying, because he is convinced that it is the workers that make all the difference for Denmark. (Britt, Centrum)

The behaviour adopted by this respondent is typical within family situations where parents and offspring disagree. This constellation is also found in an example provided by another respondent, where the father has not stopped disagreeing but has accepted that he cannot influence his daughter:

*The Sociological Review*, 63:S2, pp. 72–91 (2015), DOI: 10.1111/1467-954X.12263

My father, he might get mad because I have opinions of my own. Then he can be a little more, 'Then let's talk about something else' or turn on the TV. Then we do not need to discuss anymore and can just be good friends and not talk [laughs]. [ . . . ] When my father gets angry, he closes up. It's not that we are screaming. [ . . . ] He has his own way which is slightly less constructive perhaps than to sit and argue his point. (Ida, East)

Parents' behavioural and communicative style might be influenced by the gender of the young people and the parents but this cannot be concluded from the qualitative interviews. Despite a tendency for young people to avoid conflicts when they engage in political discussions with parents, the relationship need not become antagonistic. Despite the difficulties, openings still exist. As one respondent reports, he often talks politics with his mother and with friends. However 'my father tends to disagree with me, but I try [to discuss with the father] sometimes, when I have the courage to do it' (Brian, Centre). This happens when they sit at the dinner table, where the father comments upon the news and is provoked by what he has heard.

A similar example of conflict avoidance is reported by this male respondent who supports a neo-liberal political viewpoint, while his mother's political attitude is more to the left. The young man supports Liberal Alliance (neo-liberal) although he had previously supported Venstre (centre-right), which is the party his father supports. The women in the family, his mother and sister, support Socialdemokraterne (the Social Democrats):

*Chris*: My father and I have a lot [ . . . ] we share the same opinion. However, with my mother I do not share as many opinions. Not that I do not love her, but we just do not agree on things. My father and I always [ . . . ] It's probably my dad I've got my thoughts and ideologies from.
*Interviewer*: You go to your dad when you need to talk. When you talk to your mother, you end up arguing once in a while?
*Chris*: No, there are no arguments. I'm fine with her, but we just do not talk about our thoughts and what we think in political terms. [ . . . ] It's mostly with my dad that I talk about these things. (Chris, Centre)

Political disagreement does not necessarily lead to family problems. However, as in these cases it seems that some young people tend to avoid political discussions with their parents when they do not agree politically. As mentioned in the introduction this perspective calls for further investigation.

According to the literature we should expect that people usually prefer to discuss politics with people with whom they know they agree while avoiding situations where they are likely to face political disagreement (Mutz, 2002, 2006; Morrell, 2005). The question posed here is whether this is also a general social mechanism in young people's communication with their family and friends?

In order to further investigate this we continue our analysis drawing on the survey data. We apply a multivariate regression analysis which tests the statistical relationships between perceived political distance and engagement in political discussions with father, mother and friends respectively. Furthermore, the

*The Sociological Review*, 63:S2, pp. 72–91 (2015), DOI: 10.1111/1467-954X.12263

statistical analysis also gives us the opportunity to explore potential social and gendered patterns in political discussions with parents and friends.

The main explanatory variable, 'perceived political distance', is measured by asking the respondents how close or distant their political views are to the views of family members, partners and friends, respectively. Answers were given on a 10-point scale, where 0 is close and 10 is distant (see Appendix, Table A1). Research into political socialization and participation shows that various kinds of formal and informal social networks in which children and young citizens are involved – parents, friends, educational environment, as well as the media – play an important role (McLeod, 2000; McLeod *et al.*, 2010). Therefore the statistical analysis includes a number of variables, which, typically, are positively correlated with the levels of political engagement. Based on the literature on gender socialization, we should expect male respondents to be more frequently engaged in discussions than female respondents (Jennings and Niemi, 1971; Jennings, 1983; Verba *et al.*, 1997; Burns *et al.*, 2001; Coffé and Bolzendahl, 2010). We are also aware that there may prove to be gender-specific patterns in respondents' discussions with mothers and fathers, respectively. Previous studies have shown that daughters often use their mothers as role models when it comes to political engagement (Gidengil *et al.*, 2011).

Furthermore, in the statistical analysis we include relevant socio demographic variables: respondents' age, as we expect that the level of political discussion increases as people grow older; respondents' and parents' level of education, because higher education usually strengthens rhetorical skills and knowledge on societal and political issues. Typically, better educated parents will encourage their children to express opinions freely, thereby also being more likely to motivate their children to read newspapers, gain knowledge, form opinions and take part in political discussions. Furthermore, as proxies for social class we included variables on mothers' and fathers' occupations.

The majority of respondents below the age of 20 are still living together with their parents. For this reason we have applied a variable measuring whether respondents are living together with their parents or not. We expect that living together with parents will increase the frequency of political discussions with one or both of them. Furthermore, we have applied ethnicity (Danish/not Danish), regious orientation and area of residence (Centre/East) as control variables.

As shown in Table 2, we have chosen to conduct the analyses in three separate models, because we want to examine whether there are different patterns across the different discussion partners. Furthermore, it should be noted that results presented in this table are based first on a series of stepwise regressions and backward elimination of statistically insignificant variables. Full models are shown in Appendix (Table A3). Altogether, we should also note that the variance explained by the variables included in the three models is quite modest (Adj. $R^2$ = 0.155–0.185), indicating that the models far from explain a high proportion of the variation in the frequency of political discussion among respondents.

Our multivariate analyses reveal that not all of our initial expectations are confirmed. First, statistically significant gender differences are absent in the

**Table 2:** *Political distance and political discussion with father, mother and best friend, respectively*

| | Father | | Mother | | Best friend | |
|---|---|---|---|---|---|---|
| | B | SE | B | SE | B | SE |
| (Constant) | 0.348 | 0.328 | 1.170 | 0.465 | −0.415 | 0.432 |
| Gender (male) | −0.121 | 0.071 | −0.105 | 0.064 | 0.250*** | 0.070 |
| Age | 0.019 | 0.013 | −0.020 | 0.012 | 0.045** | 0.017 |
| High school education | 0.216** | 0.083 | 0.022 | 0.074 | 0.130 | 0.078 |
| Father high school education | 0.321*** | 0.094 | – | – | – | – |
| Mother high school education | −0.061 | 0.087 | 0.230** | 0.073 | 0.109 | 0.087 |
| Father higher occupation | 0.036 | 0.093 | – | – | 0.117 | 0.076 |
| Mother higher occupation | 0.047 | 0.091 | 0.284*** | 0.079 | 0.117 | 0.094 |
| Religion Muslim | – | – | – | – | 0.503*** | 126 |
| Following politics in media | 0.847*** | 0.205 | 0.577** | 0.184 | 0.587** | 0.194 |
| Political interest | 1.149*** | 0.148 | 0.914*** | 0.133 | 1.104*** | 0.141 |
| Political distance: father | −0.358** | 0.129 | | | | |
| Political distance: mother | – | – | −0.261* | 0.118 | | |
| Political distance: friend | – | – | | | −0.232* | 0.118 |
| $R^2$ | 0.196 | | 0.164 | | 0.189 | |
| Adj. $R^2$ | 0.185 | | 0.155 | | 0.179 | |

*Note.* OLS regression: $*p < 0.05$, $**p < 0.01$, $***p < 0.001$.
*Source*: MYPLACE survey, 2012–13.

frequency of discussions with both parents when controlling for the impact of a number of other individual and social background variables. It is interesting to note, however, that male respondents are more engaged in political discussions with their best friends than females. Age is not associated with frequency of political discussions with parents, possibly due to a quite narrow age span in our sample (16–25 years). We do find, however, a minor age effect in discussions with friends.

Respondents with higher education tend to engage more frequently in political discussions with their father; however, the effect is not statistically significant for discussion with mother and best friend. The most significant background variable affecting the level of political discussion with mothers is the reported level of mothers' education. As expected, we also find a relatively strong correlation between political interest, use of media for political information and the level

*The Sociological Review*, 63:S2, pp. 72–91 (2015), DOI: 10.1111/1467-954X.12263

of engagement in political discussion. This is consistent with the results of the qualitative interviews, where several respondents said that political issues in the media often lead to political discussions with parents and friends. Quite surprisingly there are no effects for ethnicity in discussing politics with parents but we do find a slight negative effect for friends; Muslim respondents tend to be more involved in political discussions with their friends than the Christian and non-religious majority.

The main question in this part of the analysis is how far perceived political distance affects the level of engagement in political discussions with parents and friends? As expected, our results reveal negative associations of perceived political distance for all models, indicating that respondents who feel that their father, mother or friends, respectively, hold more distant political views are less likely to engage in political discussions with each of them. This is an interesting finding, especially when we consider that these effects seem to be stronger in the analysis of political discussion with the father. We think this possibly also reflects that political socialization within the family is gendered, not only regarding how much young people discuss politics with parents and friends, but also when considering the consequences of perceived political distance.

The cross-sectional survey data do not allow the definitive determination of the causal mechanisms behind these negative relationships; however, the qualitative data can give us a hint as to what is at stake here. As mentioned earlier some of the young people in the qualitative interviews say that they prefer to stay out of political discussions because they want to avoid further disagreements. In some cases they do this because they are looking after their own feelings and well-being, and the general atmosphere in the family. In most of the qualitative interviews this seems to be a social behaviour chosen by the young people themselves; however, in some cases it is also one of the parents (typically the mother) who abstains from engaging in political discussions.

On the one hand this type of social behaviour can be seen as a considerate way to avoid conflicts within the family and with friends. But seen from a deliberative democratic point of view, it is a rather problematic way of handling political disagreements. Not only because it may reflect a lack of recognition and respect for others' individual political views, but also in a wider perspective because patterns of communication in the family may influence social and political behaviour later in young peoples' life. Although our design and data do not allow further analysis of socialization effects over time, we do believe that it is likely that tendencies of public 'enclave deliberation' and 'political homophily' found in previous studies (Mutz, 2002, 2006; Mutz and Martin, 2001; Morrell, 2005; Huber and Malhotra, 2013) may be rooted in familial socialization patterns.

## Conclusion

In this paper we have explored the political socialization of young people by looking at patterns in young people's political discussion with their parents and friends. The analysis of our survey data revealed that young people with high (perceived) political distance to their father, mother and/or friend discuss politics less frequently. However, the impact of political distance is strongest in discussions with fathers. Judging from what our respondents told us in the qualitative interviews, this seems to be a consequence of negative experiences from prior discussions; when political discussions with parents turn into a fixed pattern of disagreement, there is a tendency to withdraw from the discussion.

Despite the fact that Denmark is usually regarded as a country with a fairly high degree of gender equality in social as well as in political life, our study has shown that gender-based differences in parental political communication processes still exist. We can conclude that the father remains the most frequent discussion partner. Friends and partners are also frequent discussion partners and young men discuss politics more frequently with their friends than do young women. Based on the qualitative data, it seems that parental political socialization, to some extent, is rooted in traditional gender roles where fathers are more likely to be a source of information about societal issues while mothers tend towards giving advice on personal matters.

Whether these gendered patterns of political discussion with parents are established by the parents or their children is a moot point, although it is to be expected that children respond to parental behaviour. Gender differences within the family mainly exist among the parents as discussion partners and not the respondents. This might indicate that gender differences in political engagement are significantly less pronounced among the younger generations. This said, however, we do find that the young men are more involved in political discussions with their friends than the young women.

Not surprisingly, the respondents' own interest in politics influences how much they engage in political discussions. Our respondents' level of education pulls in the same direction. This is, however, only the case for discussions with fathers. Among the parents, only the mothers' level of education influences levels of political discussion with respondents. Furthermore, our analyses suggest that the influence of the media on engagement in political discussions with parents and friends should not be underestimated. We found a relatively strong correlation between political media use and the level of engagement in political discussions. In the qualitative interviews, there are indications that several patterns of use are in play. Some people use the media in the classic way, that is, as sources of information, while many others use the media as an initiator and extension of face-to-face political discussions.

Finally, returning to the main question of distance and engagement in political discussions, this study has shown that perceived political distance matters. Previous studies in political psychology and communication suggested that people tend to avoid social situations where political disagreements are likely to appear. We have explored whether these mechanisms exists in the family sphere and in close social relationships with friends, and our findings support this thesis: perceived political distance tends to reduce the likelihood of engagement in political discussions. However, so far our studies have focused on young people's political orientation and involvement in political discussions at a very general level. We suggest that further studies are needed with regard to the question of how specific policy issues, political events and conflicts affect political discussions and political engagement and with regard to the impact of different types of communication patterns in the family.

## Acknowledgements

We thank Gary Pollock (Manchester Metropolitan University), Hilary Pilkington (University of Manchester), David Nicolas Hopmann (University of Southern Denmark) and Sebastián Valenzuela (Pontificia Universidad Católica de Chile) for helpful and constructive feedback on earlier drafts of this article. This research received funding from the The European Commission *7th Framework Programme for Research and Technological Development.*

## Notes

1 The Danish survey data set includes 109 respondents, who are 26–28 years old, who were included in the statistical analyses for this article but who were removed from the merged data set in order to ensure conformity to the MYPLACE project research design (see the article by Pilkington and Pollock in this volume).

2 A more detailed report on sampling procedures, characteristics of the test population and the various questionnaire items can be found in the Danish part of MYPLACE Work Package 4: Measuring participation report (http://www.fp7-myplace.eu/deliverables.php).

3 The distinction between politically active and inactive has been measured as the level of activity within a range of items within the last 12 months before the interview. The ordinal measurement scale was divided into the levels 'never', 'once', 'twice', and 'three times or more'. The distinction of active and inactive was relative within the sample; it distinguished between those who scored highest and those who scored lowest. Political activity was an aggregated measure of twenty types of political activity: volunteering in election campaigns, contacting politicians, attending meetings, signing petitions or collecting signatures, voting for student councils, giving speeches, distributing leaflets, making consumer boycotts, writing graffiti, wearing badges, participating in demonstrations or strikes, donating money, writing articles or emails, uploading on the Internet, participating in violent events, occupying buildings or blocking streets, or participating in flash mobs.

4 All qualitative interviews were recorded, transcribed, anonymized and imported into the data analysis software, NVIVO 9.2, and coded by three coders.

5 Contemporary, state-of-the-art mixed methods research highlights four approaches: a sequential explanatory; an exploratory design; a parallel design (triangulation); and an embedded design (Bryman, 2007; Plano Clark *et al.,* 2008, Creswell, 2009). Due to the origin of data established in parallel, we have adopted triangulation as the appropriate method of data analysis (Greene, 2008; Creswell and Plano Clark, 2007; Plano Clark *et al.,* 2008; Creswell, 2009).

## References

Amnå, E., Ekström, M., Kerr, M. and Stattin, H., (2009), 'Political socialization and human agency: the development of civic engagement from adolescence to adulthood', *Statsvetenskaplig Tidskrift,* 111 (1): 27–39.

Beck, P. A. and Jennings, M. K., (1975), 'Parents as "middlepersons" in political socialization', *Journal of Politics,* 37: 83–107.

Bloemraad, I. and Trost, C., (2008), 'It's a family affair: intergenerational mobilization in the spring 2006 protests', *American Behavioral Scientist,* 52 (4): 507–532.

Bryman, A., (2007), 'Barriers to integrating quantitative and qualitative research', *Journal of Mixed Methods Research*, 1 (1): 8–22.

Burns, N., Schlozman, K. L. and Verba, S., (2001), *The Private Roots of Public Action: Gender, Quality, and Political Participation*, Cambridge, MA: Harvard University Press.

Coffé, H. and Bolzendahl, C., (2010), 'Same game, different rules? Gender differences in political participation', *Sex Roles*, 62: 318–333.

Conover, P. J., Searing, D. D, and Crewe, I. M., (2002), 'The deliberative potential of political discussion', *British Journal of Political Science*, 32 (1): 21–62.

Creswell, J. W., (2009), *Research Design: Qualitative, Quantitative, and Mixed Methods Approaches*, Thousand Oaks, CA: Sage Publications.

Creswell, J. W. and Plano Clark, V. L., (2007), *Designing and Conducting Mixed Methods Research*, Thousand Oaks, CA: Sage.

Easton, D. and Dennis, J., (1969), *Children in the Political System: Origins of Political Legitimacy*, Chicago: University of Chicago Press.

Ekström, M. and Östman, J., (2013), 'Family talk, peer talk and young people's civic orientation', *European Journal of Communication*, 28 (3): 294–308.

Esterling, K. M., Fung, A. and Lee, T., (2010). 'How much disagreement is good for democratic deliberation? The CaliforniaSpeaks Health Care Reform Experiment', Working Paper.

Gidengil, E., O'Neill, B. and Young, L., (2011), 'Her mother's daughter? The influence of childhood socialization on women's political engagement', *Journal of Women, Politics and Policy*, 31: 334–355.

Greene, J. C., (2008), 'Is mixed methods social inquiry a distinctive methodology?', *Journal of Mixed Methods Research*, 2 (1): 7–22.

Greenstein, F. I., (1965), *Children and Politics*, New Haven and London: Yale University Press.

Gundelach, P. and Levinsen, K., (2011), *Gender and Parental Political in Europe*, ECPR General Conference, Reykjavik, Iceland, 25–27 November.

Gutmann, A. and Thompson, D., (2004), *Why Deliberative Democracy?*, Princeton, NJ: Princeton University Press.

Hess, R. and Torney, J., (1967), *The Development of Political Attitudes in Children*, Chicago: Aldine Transaction Publishers.

Hooghe, M. and Boonen, J., (2013), 'The intergenerational transmission of voting intentions in a multiparty setting: an analysis of voting intentions and political discussion among 15-year-old adolescents and their parents in Belgium', *Youth & Society* (published online, printed version forthcoming), doi: 10.1177/0044118x13496826.

Huber, G. A. and Malhotra, N., (2013), 'Dimensions of political homophily: isolating choice homophily along political characteristics', Working Paper.

Hyman, H., (1959), *Political Socialization: A Study in the Psychology of Political Behaviour*, Toronto: Collier-MacMillan.

Jennings, M. K., (1983), 'Gender roles and inequalities in political participation: results from an eight-nation study', *Political Research Quarterly*, 36 (3): 364–385.

Jennings, M. K., (2007), 'Political socialization', in R. J. Dalton and H.-D. Klingemann (eds), *The Oxford Handbook of Political Behavior*, 29–44, New York: Oxford University Press.

Jennings, M. K. and Langton, K. P., (1969), 'Mothers versus fathers: the formation of political orientations among young Americans', *The Journal of Politics*, 31 (2): 329–358.

Jennings, M. K. and Niemi, R. G., (1968), 'The transmission of political values from parent to child', *The American Political Science Review*, 62 (1): 169–184.

Jennings, M. K. and Niemi, R. G., (1971), 'The division of political labour between mothers and fathers', *The American Political Science Review* 65 (1), 69–82.

Jennings, M. K., Stoker, L. and Bowers, J., (2009), 'Politics across generations: family transmission reexamined', *Journal of Politics*, 71 (3): 780–799.

McGlenn, N., (1980), 'The impact of parenthood on political participation', *Western Political Quarterly*, 33 (3): 297–313.

McLeod, J. M., (2000), 'Media and civic socialization of youth', *Journal of Adolescent Health*, 27: 45–51.

*The Sociological Review*, 63:S2, pp. 72–91 (2015), DOI: 10.1111/1467-954X.12263
© 2015 The Authors. Editorial organisation © 2015 The Editorial Board of the Sociological Review

McLeod, J. M., Shah, D., Hess, D. and Lee, N., (2010), 'Communication and education: creating competence for socialization into public life', in L. R. Sherrod, J. Torney-Purta and C. Flanagan (eds), *Handbook of Research on Civic Engagement in Youth*, 363–391, New Jersey: John Wiley and Sons.

McIntosh, H., Hart, D. and Youniss, J., (2007), 'The influence of family political discussion on youth civic development: which parent qualities matter?', *PS: Political Science and Politics*, 40 (3): 495–499.

Morrell, M. E. (2005), 'Deliberation, democratic decision-making and internal political efficacy', *Political Behavior*, 27 (1): 49–69.

Mutz, D., (2002), 'Cross-cutting social networks: testing democratic theory in practice', *American Political Science Review*, 96 (2): 111–126.

Mutz, D., (2006), *Hearing the Other Side: Deliberative versus Participatory Democracy*, New York: Cambridge University Press.

Mutz, D. C. and Martin, P. S., (2001), 'Facilitating communication across lines of political difference: the role of mass media', *American Political Science Review*, 95 (1): 97–114.

Nieuwbeerta, P., and Wittebrood, K., (1995), 'Intergenerational transmission of political party preference in the Netherlands', *Social Science Research*, 24: 243–261.

Plano Clark, V. L., Creswell, J. W., Green, D. O. N. and Shope, R. J., (2008), 'Mixing quantitative and qualitative approaches: an introduction to emergent mixed methods research', in S. N. Hesse-Biber and P. Leavy (eds), *Handbook of Emergent Methods*, New York: Guilford Press.

Quintelier, E., (2011), 'Political socialization among young people: evidence from a two-year panel study', *Politics, Culture and Socialization*, 2 (2): 193–206.

Quintelier, E., (2015), 'Engaging adolescents in politics: the longitudinal effect of political socialization agents', *Youth & Society*, 47 (1): 51–69.

Verba, S., Burns, N. and Schlozman, K. L., (1997), 'Knowing and caring about politics: gender and political engagement', *Journal of Politics*, 59: 1051–1072.

# Appendix

**Table A1** *Variables and survey items*

| Variables | Questions, answer categories/scales, and coding |
|---|---|
| Political discussion: Separate variables for: 'Your father', 'Your mother', 'The brother or sister that you are closest to' 'The grandparent that you are closest to', 'Your boyfriend/girlfriend/ partner', 'Your best friend' | Q4: How often do you discuss political issues when you get together with the following people? Answer: Always (1), Often (2), Sometimes (3), Rarely (4), Never (5), Don't know (-1). Recoded: Always (4), Often (3), Sometimes (2), Rarely (1), Never (0), |

## Continued

| Variables | Questions, answer categories/scales, and coding |
| --- | --- |
| Perceived political distance: Separate variables for: 'Your father', 'Your mother', 'The brother or sister that you are closest to' 'The grandparent that you are closest to', 'Your boyfriend/girlfriend/ partner', 'Your best friend' | Q20: On a scale of 0 to 10 where 0 is close and 10 is distant, how close or distant are your political views to the views of the following people? Transformed into a 0–1 scale |
| Gender (male) | Q54: Interviewer assessed: Male (1), Female (2). Recoded: Male (1), Female (0) |
| Respondent's age | In years |
| Respondents high school education | What is the highest level of qualification that you have received from school, college or since leaving school? 17 categories recoded into high school (1) or not (0) |
| Father high school education | Q73: What is the highest level of qualification that your father received from school/college or university? 17 categories recoded into high school (1) or not (0) |
| Mother high school education | Q77: What is the highest level of qualification that your mother received from school/college or university? 17 categories recoded into high school (1) or not (0) |
| Father higher occupation | Q76: Professional and technical occupations (1); Higher administrator occupations (2); Clerical occupations (3); Sales occupations (4); Service occupations (5); Skilled worker (6); Semi-skilled worker (7); Unskilled worker (8); Farm worker (9); 'Other' (10). Recoded: Higher occupation = (1) and (2) into (1); Else (0). |

88

*Continued*

| Variables | Questions, answer categories/scales, and coding |
|---|---|
| Mother higher occupation | Q80: Professional and technical occupations (1); Higher administrator occupations (2); Clerical occupations (3); Sales occupations (4); Service occupations (5); Skilled worker (6); Semi-skilled worker (7); Unskilled worker (8); Farm worker (9); 'Other' (10). Recoded: Higher occupation = (1) and (2) into (1); Else (0). |
| Following politics in the media | On an average day, how much time do you spend keeping yourself informed about politics and current affairs using the following media? The radio (Q3_1); The Internet (Q3_2), TV (Q3_3), Newspapers (Q3_4). Additive index variable: Q3_1 + Q3_2 + Q3_3 + Q3_4. |
| Living with parents | Q70_3: Who, apart from you, is living in this household? Parents Recoded: Yes (1) No (0) |
| Residential area (centre) | Recoded Area centre: Centre (1); East (0) |
| Danish ethnicity | Q58: What is your ethnic group? Choose one option that best describes your ethnic group or background. Recoded: Danish (1); Else (0) |
| Religion | Recoded into dummy categories: Not religious (1); Else (0) Christian (1); Else (0) Muslim (1); Else (0) Other (1); Else (0) |
| Political left-right orientation | Q21: In politics people sometimes talk of 'left' and 'right'. On a scale of 0 to 10, where 0 is left and 10 is right, would you say that you personally are left- or right-wing? Transformed into a 0–1 scale |

*Source*: MYPLACE survey, 2012–13.

**Table A2** *Correlation matrix for political discussion*

|  | (1) | (2) | (3) | (4) | (5) | (6) |
|---|---|---|---|---|---|---|
| (1) Father | 1.000 |  |  |  |  |  |
| (2) Mother | 0.428 | 1.000 |  |  |  |  |
| (3) Brother/sister | 0.291 | 0.238 | 1.000 |  |  |  |
| (4) Grandparent | 0.223 | 0.293 | 0.179 | 1.000 |  |  |
| (5) Partner | 0.280 | 0.225 | 0.240 | 0.126 | 1.000 |  |
| (6) Best friend | 0.254 | 0.214 | 0.211 | 0.147 | 0.286 | 1.000 |

*Notes.* Survey question: 'How often do you discuss political issues when you get together with the following people? All correlations are significant at the 0.01 level (2-tailed).

*Source*: MYPLACE survey, 2012–13.

**Table A3** *Political distance and political discussion with father, mother and best friend, respectively (Full model)*

|  | Father | | Mother | | Best friend | |
|---|---|---|---|---|---|---|
|  | B | SE | B | SE | B | SE |
| (Constant) | 0.427 | 0.500 | 0.730 | 0.465 | −0.601 | 0.481 |
| Gender (male) | −0.116 | 0.075 | −0.149* | 0.070 | 0.214** | 0.073 |
| Age | 0.014 | 0.019 | −0.004 | 0.017 | 0.057** | 0.018 |
| High school education | 0.223** | 0.086 | 0.073 | 0.080 | 0.069 | 0.083 |
| Father high school education | 0.301*** | 0.100 | 0.051 | 0.091 | −0.028 | 0.095 |
| Mother high school education | −0.077 | 0.090 | 0.206* | 0.084 | 0.089 | 0.087 |
| Father higher occupation | 0.029 | 0.098 | −0.012 | 0.089 | 0.130 | 0.094 |
| Mother higher occupation | 0.097 | 0.097 | 0.247** | 0.090 | 0.017 | 0.094 |
| Living with parents | −0.061 | 0.123 | 0.147 | 0.115 | 0.143 | 0.120 |
| Area (Centre) | 0.052 | 0.076 | 0.024 | 0.071 | 0.061 | 0.074 |
| Religion (ref = Christian) |  |  |  |  |  |  |
| Not religious | −0.018 | 0.093 | 0.029 | 0.087 | 0.053 | 0.090 |
| Muslim | 0.111 | 0.184 | −0.080 | 0.171 | 0.479** | 0.177 |
| Other religion | 0.151 | 0.151 | 0.147 | 0.177 | 0.006 | 0.183 |
| Ethnicity (Danish) | −0.051 | 0.135 | 0.030 | 0.127 | −0.074 | 0.131 |

*The Sociological Review*, 63:S2, pp. 72–91 (2015), DOI: 10.1111/1467-954X.12263

*Continued*

| | Father | | Mother | | Best friend | |
|---|---|---|---|---|---|---|
| | B | SE | B | SE | B | SE |
| Following politics in media | 0.800*** | 0.215 | 0.508** | 0.200 | 0.514* | 0.208 |
| Political interest | 1.099*** | 0.154 | 0.899*** | 0.143 | 1.087*** | 0.150 |
| Political left-right orientation | 0.208 | 0.159 | 0.044 | 0.148 | −0.025 | 0.152 |
| Political distance: father | −0.364** | 0.135 | | | | |
| Political distance: mother | | | −0.217 | 0.129 | | |
| Political distance: friend | | | | | −0.172 | 0.125 |
| $R^2$ | 0.192 | | 0.159 | | 0.180 | |
| Adj. $R^2$ | 0.172 | | 0.138 | | 0.160 | |

*Note.* OLS regression: *$p < 0.05$, **$p < 0.01$, ***$p < 0.001$.
*Source*: MYPLACE survey, 2012–13.

# Youth participation in context: the impact of youth transition regimes on political action strategies in Europe

## *Roger Soler-i-Martí and Mariona Ferrer-Fons*

**Abstract:** This article examines the impact of youth transition regimes (YTR) on the political participation strategies of young people from 26 locations in 12 European countries. The central hypothesis is that the way that youth transitions take place in different European contexts determines the position of youth as a group in the system of social relations that Bourdieu calls the 'social space'. Depending upon this position, young people may be more inclined to participation through institutional channels or political protest, or, in contrast, remain inactive. Thus, the specific context of youth in each society (measured through the exposure to risk and vulnerability, the length of the pathway to adulthood and the role of the welfare state) plays a crucial role in defining young people's political action strategies. Multilevel logistic regression analysis using the MYPLACE survey, the specific operationalization of the YTR and other aggregate control variables reveal that YTR centrality is a very important contextual predictor for explaining different forms of political participation among young people in Europe.

**Keywords:** youth, political participation, youth transition regimes, social space, contextual effects

## Introduction

Recent research on youth political participation has been shaped by empirical evidence of a decline in institutional political involvement and the emergence of other forms of participation such as protest and political consumerism. This has led scholars to focus on identifying generational change (see Dalton, 2007; Zukin *et al.*, 2006; Norris, 2004; Franklin *et al.*, 2004; Putnam, 2000) and on how young people understand politics in post-industrial societies (see Manning, 2013, 2010; Rossi, 2009; O'Toole, 2003; Henn *et al.*, 2002). However, rarely has this literature taken into consideration the cross-national variation in participation patterns among young people; this has resulted in a variety of differing conclusions about their preferred forms of political participation (García-Albacete, 2014). When

*The Sociological Review*, 63:S2, pp. 92–117 (2015), DOI: 10.1111/1467-954X.12264
© 2015 The Authors. Editorial organisation © 2015 The Editorial Board of the Sociological Review. Published by John Wiley & Sons Ltd, 9600 Garsington Road, Oxford OX4 2DQ, UK and 350 Main Street, Malden, MA 02148, USA

we examine young people's levels of institutional participation and protest, as we do below, we see that there is a significant divide in Europe; while, in Southern Europe, young people tend to protest as the dominant mechanism of participation, preferring it over more institutionalized forms, in certain parts of Northern Europe we find the opposite pattern. Moreover, in the new democracies of Eastern Europe, we generally find low levels of participation regardless of the type of participation that we are analysing.

Thus, while the data show contextual differences in participation strategies to be highly relevant, the influence of contextual elements (particularly those specific to young people) on youth participation has gone unnoticed.

In this article, we focus on the effect of youth transition systems or regimes on the variation in political participation patterns of young people in Europe. Youth trajectories are shaped by a system of socio-economic structures, institutional arrangements and cultural patterns referred to as 'regimes of youth transitions' (Walther, 2006) or 'transition systems' (Smyth *et al.*, 2001; Niemeyer, 2007). The sociology of youth has devoted much effort to the comparative analysis of transition models including when young people leave the parental home, form new families or pass from education to the job market (Bynner and Roberts, 1991; Holdsworth and Morgan, 2005; Jurado, 2001) and also to the public policies that shape these pathways to adulthood (Harsløf, 2005; Ertl, 2006; Niemeyer, 2007).We know that the way that transitions take place and the role of the welfare state in different national contexts determines a certain way of 'becoming an adult' in each society (Van de Velde, 2008). Thus, youth transition regimes have a crucial role in defining the position that young people as a group play in the system of social relations in each society (or, employing Bourdieu's terminology, in defining the different positions that youth takes in the 'social space'). Young people's position in the social space determines their opportunities and expectations and shapes their practices. However, even if we know that in different European countries youth transitions follow different paths, these transitions have rarely been taken into account as a contextual variable in empirical models of youth political participation.[1]

The central hypothesis of this article is that young people's dominant strategies of participation in society are shaped by youth transition regimes that determine the position of youth as a group in the social space and the individual and social resources available to them. Thus, the specific context of youth plays an important role in defining the opportunities for young people to choose to participate through institutional channels or political protest, or to remain inactive.

To confirm these arguments empirically, we use data on patterns of political participation among young people (understood as individuals between 16 and 25 years of age) in 26 locations in 12 European countries collected from a survey carried out as part of the European FP7 MYPLACE project[2] and various secondary statistical sources from these countries. In the first part of this article, we develop an analytical framework by exploring how different youth transition regimes place young people in different positions in the social space according to each country and how this shapes their participation patterns. We then

explain our empirical strategy and present the data and key variables. In the subsequent section, we discuss the results of a multilevel analysis conducted in order
to determine the influence of individual and contextual factors on participation
strategies. Finally, we present our key conclusions.

## Theoretical discussion: youth transition regimes and the position of young people in the social space

In order to understand the mechanism by which the model of youth transitions
in a given society influences youth participation strategies, we borrow a basic
idea from Bourdieu's groundbreaking work: the social space. Bourdieu (1979,
1985, 1989) used the idea of social space to represent the system of economic,
social, cultural and symbolic relationships established in a society. The position
that agents (individuals and groups) take in this space is determined by the distribution of resources; specifically, by the volume of economic, cultural, social
and symbolic capital available and by each agent's share of these forms of capital (Bourdieu, 1989). As such, their position in the social space is determined by
the accumulation of material and subjective resources, which they use to occupy
more central, important or powerful places within this space, on the one hand,
or more peripheral and unprotected positions on the other (Bourdieu, 1985). According to this perspective, the position that young people as a group occupy in
the system of relationships of a given society forms the basis for their options
for feeling more or less integrated and, as such, for seeing themselves as more
important, or more peripheral, political players in their social systems.

Youth is a time when individuals undergo a process of integration into the
system of social relationships that constitutes the social space. Achieving independence from the family, joining the labour market and assuming the life of an
adult in general should be accompanied by incorporation into spaces of greater
social centrality and importance. In fact, traditional explanations of young people's patterns of participation are closely linked to the gradual adoption of roles
of greater integration in the social space that come with age; as individuals take
on adult roles, they gain civic skills and experiences that make them more interested in public matters and in developing the skills necessary for participating
in them (Strate *et al.*, 1989; Milbrath and Goel, 1977). The work, family and
home-related aspects of transitions from youth to adulthood cause individuals
to integrate into the central spaces of social life and arouse their interest in how
society and politics work (Benedicto and Moran, 2007).

However, the road to adulthood has undergone significant changes that can
affect how young adults integrate into the social and public space. In recent
decades, the sociology of youth has emphasized increased flexibility and less stan-
dardization in young people's trajectories (Stauber and Walther, 2006; Serracant,
2012). Situations of reversibility and breaking with linearity foster the growth of
uncertainty and vulnerability and make it hard for young people to attain a solid
place to collectively build their social position and their identity (Furlong and
Cartmel, 1997; Mills *et al.*, 2005). The prolongation of these transitions makes

*The Sociological Review*, 63:S2, pp. 92–117 (2015), DOI: 10.1111/1467-954X.12264

youth itself longer. As a result, this peripheral social position is considered increasingly to be a fixed situation rather than a transitory stage. Young people are creating their social and political identity in a context of greater fragmentation and uncertainty and with less collective points of reference (Benedicto, 2013). However, these changes have different effects on young people in different countries (Nico, 2014). As we show below, there are significant differences between countries regarding the level of vulnerability and lengthening of youth transitions and the role played in both by the welfare state. It seems, therefore, that this gradual process of incorporating young people into more central and important positions in the social space has been shaped in different ways according to the youth transition regimes in each country. This has an impact on patterns of political participation for young people.

The following sections provide evidence on the existence of different youth transition regimes across Europe and develop the theoretical framework of our hypothesis discussing how this can explain differences in the positions of youth in the social space and their participation patterns. Here, we consider two dimensions of youth transition systems (the way that youth transitions occur and the role of welfare states) to see their impact on the position of youth in the social space and how it shapes participation strategies.

## Youth transition regimes: vulnerability and length

Here we examine how youth transitions take place in different European countries. To do so we consider crucial aspects that affect young people's perception of their own role in society: exposure to risk and vulnerability; and the length of the pathway to adulthood.

The different transition regime models are key mechanisms for distributing resources and exposing young people to situations of risk and vulnerability (Alegre, 2010). In countries with universalistic welfare regimes, the individualization and de-standardization of trajectories to adulthood is accompanied by training opportunities and an effective system of social protection. Thus, situations of risk are minimized and uncertainty does not necessarily lead to vulnerabilization. In corporatist systems, there is also an effective system of protection more linked to education and especially to 'finding one's place' in the job market (Van de Velde, 2008). In transition regimes with welfare models with less government influence, opportunities for transition and security depend more on the market and on the family (Alegre, 2010; Moreno and Marí-Klose, 2014). This makes young people more subject to situations of risk, uncertainty and marginality throughout the paths they take to adulthood. The experience of structural vulnerability may cause apathy to increase and even stoke mistrust towards social and political institutions (Benedicto, 2013). Thus, it can be expected that in transition regimes that foster situations of vulnerability, young people are perceived to have a less central position in the social space, whereas in countries where transitions have more protection and security mechanisms, young people feel more integrated and identify more with the institutions.

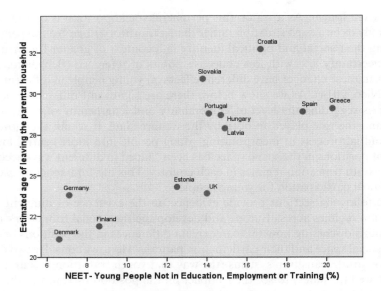

**Figure 1** *Vulnerability and length of youth transitions in Europe*
Source: *Metadata in Euro SDMX Metadata Structure (ESMS) and Labour Force Survey, Eurostat.*

Transition regimes mark the tempo of young people's life stories. Even though transitions have become longer everywhere in recent decades, there are significant differences according to country. There is a clear relationship between exposure to risk and how quickly transitions are completed. For example, the decision to leave the parental home is closely linked to having one's own income and a certain feeling of security in being able to maintain that status (Aassve *et al.*, 2001; Iacovou, 2011). The lengthening of these transitions in some countries may mean that circumstances associated with youth are not experienced as transitory aspects, but structural ones. Indeed, García-Albacete (2014) suggests that transformations in patterns of youth participation in Western Europe may arise more from the lengthening of youth than from any generational change. What is clear is that in contexts where transitions take place later, young people have more time to internalize the position associated with youth in the social space and make it their own.

To show how young people are situated with regard to youth transitions in the countries studied, we chose two indicators represented in Figure 1. To capture the different incidence of vulnerability in young people's pathways to adulthood, the NEET indicator was used. And to demonstrate the lengthening of transitions, the estimated average age that young people leave their parental home was used. It is important to note that one of the changes to youth transitions in recent years consists precisely in the fact that there is no clear border marking the end of transitions such as leaving the parental home (Machado, 2000; EGRIS, 2001).

*The Sociological Review*, 63:S2, pp. 92–117 (2015), DOI: 10.1111/1467-954X.12264

Many young people leave home for studies or work and return later. However, the indicator of the estimated average age is still valid for our purpose as it does not identify the exact moment of the 'final' transition but instead differentiates the different rhythms of transitions across European countries.

As seen in Figure 1, there is a certain linearity in the relationship between vulnerability and the lengthening of transitions, which is that leaving the parental home is closely linked to the achievement of a certain degree of financial security (Aassve *et al.*, 2001; Iacovou, 2011). Therefore, societies that offer more security to youth transitions are also societies where they happen sooner. In Denmark, Finland and Germany, transitions happen quickly and situations of vulnerability are less common. In Estonia and the United Kingdom, the age that young people leave home is low, but levels of vulnerability, expressed by youth in NEET situations, are rather high. The rest of the countries have young people leaving home later combined with high levels of vulnerability. There are especially high levels of youth in NEET situations in Greece and Spain. In these last two countries, the perception of vulnerability and uncertainty combines with a longer youth to encourage the idea that the precarious social situation of young people is in fact structural (Serracant and Fabra, 2013). Following the rationale of our hypothesis, in these countries the peripheral position in social space should lead young people to lower levels of activism – particularly institutional participation – compared to countries where young people live in more stable contexts.

*Youth transition regimes: generosity and age-orientation of the welfare state*

The role of the welfare state is crucial in framing the opportunities and expectations of young people in their transitions. In this section, we discuss how the characteristics of different welfare states in Europe shape youth transitions and situate young citizens with regard to the social space and how they adopt different forms of political participation. We know that social policies can be thought of as lines of action pursued by states that may have potential effects on the political scene. Some authors have referred to this potential effect in politics as 'policy feedback' (Skocpol and Amenta, 1986). Public policies not only affect citizens' political predispositions, but also their political actions (Mettler and Soss, 2004).

We can find two arguments to explain the association between the generosity of welfare states and political participation (Ferrer-Fons, 2005). First, social policies create beneficiaries interested in maintaining and expanding these policies (Taylor-Gooby, 2001). Citizens living in welfare states that provide a high level of de-commodification (Esping-Andersen, 1990)[3] may collaborate with political institutions to a greater extent than their counterparts in residual welfare states. A generous welfare state may give incentives to its beneficiaries to participate to defend their interests in a political system that is open and permeable to its demands. The second argument is related to the values and expectations that citizens internalize under the umbrella of the welfare state's public policies. Policy designs shape citizens' personal experiences with government and therefore influence processes of political learning and patterns of political belief (Mettler,

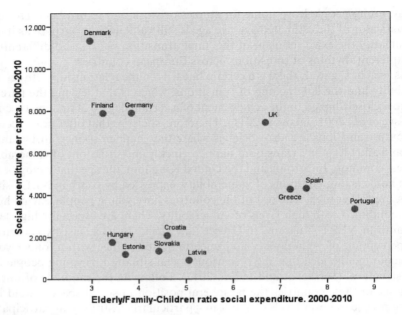

**Figure 2** *Generosity and age-orientation of social expenditure in Europe*
Source: *Metadata in Euro SDMX Metadata Structure (ESMS), Eurostat.*

2002; Mettler and Soss, 2004). Rothstein and Stolle (2003) argue that in welfare states where most programmes are universalistic, citizens tend to share a perception of more impartial institutions, which may produce high levels of external political efficacy and institutional and social trust among people.

Granted, the generosity of the welfare state is not enjoyed by different social groups in the same way. Some studies have shown how different welfare models in Europe have specific types of impact on youth transitions (Walther, 2006; Van de Velde, 2008; Harsløf, 2005). Specifically, Julia Lynch (2001, 2006) has measured how different countries of the OECD distribute their social spending based on age, demonstrating a great variability among countries. In the different forms of measurement that Lynch proposes, Mediterranean welfare states always appear as countries where spending is targeted more at older people. However, universalistic welfare regimes are where spending is most balanced among different age groups. This breakdown does not appear spontaneously but, as Mari-Klose (2012) demonstrates in the case of Spain, is closely linked to political factors and specifically to the political system's permeability to the interests of young people.

Therefore, when weighing the influence of the welfare state, and specifically of its generosity, on youth participation strategies, we must take two dimensions into account: the development and generosity of the welfare regime itself; and the age-orientation of this generosity. Figure 2 uses the indicator of per capita social expenditure to show the generosity of welfare regimes. In order to measure the

*The Sociological Review*, 63:S2, pp. 92–117 (2015), DOI: 10.1111/1467-954X.12264

age-orientation of the welfare regime, an indicator was created from Eurostat social expenditure data inspired by Lynch's 'elderly/non-elderly spending ratio' (Lynch, 2001).[4] The indicator uses Eurostat social protection data and compares social spending on 'Old-age' and 'Survivors' programmes with that on 'Family-children'; countries with a higher ratio are those where expenditure is targeted more towards the elderly while countries closer to value 1 have more balanced spending with regard to age.

Figure 2 shows clear patterns that correspond to the different welfare regimes identified in the literature (see, eg, Esping-Andersen, 1990; Gallie and Paugam, 2000). The countries of southern Europe (Spain, Portugal and Greece) have a medium–low level of expenditure overall but are distinguished by being where spending is most geared towards the elderly. The expenditure of the United Kingdom is also rather elderly-oriented, although with significantly greater spending per capita. However, the countries of northern Europe, and Denmark in particular, are where social expenditure is greatest and more oriented to programmes that benefit younger age groups. The post-communist democracies of Eastern Europe have the lowest expenditure, though they also have a balanced age-orientation. In countries where the state plays an important role in providing welfare, and where social policies are also aimed at the young, the state sends youth a message of integration into the system. Therefore our hypothesis holds that in these contexts, young people identify more with institutions and, as a result, tend to participate through the mechanisms they offer. In contexts where the state is less present, or where public expenditure is clearly geared towards other age groups, young people are positioned further from the institutional system and will be inclined to choose strategies of inactivity or protest.

Having explained the mechanisms that make the different youth transition regimes situate young people in positions of greater or lesser centrality in the social space, we now test the hypothesis that these different positions have an impact on patterns of political participation of youth through empirical analysis. In the following section we present the analytical strategy and specify how the different dimensions of political participation and the centrality of young people in youth transition regimes are operationalized before presenting a discussion of the findings.

## Research design: data and empirical strategy

In this paper we use individual and aggregate data. The individual data used for the analysis come from the survey of the FP7 MYPLACE project. This survey is an ideal source of information for several reasons. First, it is a survey aimed at young people from 16 to 25 years of age that collects information particularly adapted to this cohort. Secondly, it contains questions that measure a very broad range of political action that improves the operationalization of our dependent variables. Finally, its multilevel structure provides a good opportunity for analysing contextual factors. The survey was carried out at two contrasting locations in 14 different European countries (four in the case of Germany, with two in former East Germany and two in former West Germany) with approximately 600 individuals.[5] The structure of the individual data from the different locations allows the inclusion of local contextual variables that comparative country-based studies usually cannot address and that we know can be useful in the more immediate context of individuals explaining their predispositions for participating.

In terms of context, the data emanates from two different sources. The location data comes from the MYPLACE project. However, we have included also national indicators in our analysis that primarily come from Eurostat and other aggregate databases. The variables used and their sources are described in detail below.

Multilevel estimates are used since the structure of the data of the MYPLACE survey allows individual and contextual factors to be included in the same model. This type of analysis is appropriate for data when observations of the sample are not independent; in our case, the survey respondents are nested within 26 localities and we assume that a significant part of the different patterns of political participation are explained by contextual factors associated with these locations. These 26 locations are also nested within 12 countries. This could justify a three-level analysis, with the understanding that the observations among locations are not independent from each other either, but grouped into countries. However, the number of countries is too small for this type of study (Maas and Hox, 2005; Bell *et al.*, 2010) and the structure of the data has characteristics that minimize the possible problems stemming from not taking this third level of country into account. A failure to consider the grouping of the localities into countries could cause the results to underestimate the standard errors, especially when the number of units in a cluster is significantly higher than others or when the units within each cluster are very similar (Hox, 2010). None of these conditions occur in the MYPLACE data; there are always two locations per country (except in the case of Germany, where there are four). Regarding the similarity of the locations, the criterion for choosing the locations was that they contrasted in terms of socioeconomic conditions.[6] Therefore, we opted for a two-level analysis with 26 locations and approximately 600 individuals in each location. As we explain below, the multilevel models use logistic regression due to the dichotomic nature of the dependent variables. Here we explain the operationalization of the different variables that we use in the empirical analysis and show the descriptive findings.

*Dependent variables: political action strategies*

Until the 1970s, studies of political participation using individual survey data, focused almost exclusively on electoral behaviour, but following Verba and Nie's (1972) broadening of the definition of political participation, many approaches to categorizing different forms of political participation have appeared. Although expressed in different ways, a persistent criterion for categorizing types of participation relates to the level of integration of forms of participation in the institutional political system (see, eg, Barnes and Kaase, 1979; Teorell *et al.*, 2007).

Some recent research into youth participation uses this same criterion to explain the evolution of forms of participation. Norris (2004), for example, distinguishes between citizen-oriented actions, linked to institutional politics, and cause-oriented ones, aimed directly at social and political issues of interest. In general, the studies indicate that the vast majority of young people feel a certain degree of alienation from institutional politics, while more direct forms of social and political involvement such as protest and political consumerism are growing (O'Toole, 2003; Zukin *et al.*, 2006; Dalton, 2008; Manning, 2013).

For our purposes, while using the same criterion, we distinguish between (1) institutional participation, grouping different actions of participation aimed at institutions and integrated into the system and (2) protest, which contains more forms of participation that, on the contrary, aim to challenge the institutional system and does not use channels of political representation. We explicitly included (3) passivity in the study as a way for young people to relate to politics because we are interested in discovering the individual and contextual mechanisms that favour political inactivity. We are especially interested in seeing how youth transition regimes may or may not favour greater contexts of passivity.

The MYPLACE survey contains a range of political actions that we could include in our categories of participation. However, for the purpose of our research we have opted to select only those actions that better differentiate between institutional participation and protest. In our analysis we are more interested in differentiating different strategies of political action rather than focusing on global levels of participation. Barnes and Kaase (1979) differentiate between conventional and unconventional participation and the majority of classifications in political participation have followed a similar method, distinguishing between those forms that are more integrated in the formal political system and those that are developed outside the formal political system and which usually challenge it.[7] Here this distinction is particularly useful as we expect young people living in more integrated contexts to be more prone to participate through institutional forms while protest has a more complex relation to youth transition regimes. As Painter-Main (2014) emphasizes, protest can be an expression for challenging elites but also a consequence of a growing repertoire of participation for integrated citizens. In the first case, we would expect more protest in contexts where youth transition regimes lead young people to peripheral positions and, in the second, protest should complement other forms of participation in contexts where young people have a central position in the social space.

These participation strategies are employed here through the three following dummy variables: (1) institutional participation refers to young people who claim to participate in at least one political party or union or who have participated as volunteers in an electoral campaign or contacted a politician or local councillor in the last 12 months;[8] (2) protest refers to young people who have participated in at least one demonstration or a strike or who have occupied buildings or blocked streets or railways; and (3) the indicator of inactivity refers to young people who claim they have not performed any of the aforementioned actions.

**Table 1:**  *Political action strategies of youth per location*

|  |  | Institutional participation | Protest | Inactivity |
|---|---|---|---|---|
| Croatia | Podsljeme (Zagreb) | 18.9 | 23.0 | 66.4 |
|  | Pescenica Zitnjak (Zagreb) | 13.0 | 19.6 | 72.1 |
| Denmark | Odense East | 52.1 | 28.6 | 36.6 |
|  | Odense Centre | 54.2 | 21.6 | 36.3 |
| Estonia | Narva area | 20.3 | 9.1 | 75.0 |
|  | Tartu | 24.0 | 20.5 | 63.4 |
| Finland | Lieksa and Nurmes | 23.7 | 7.7 | 71.0 |
|  | Kuopio | 46.3 | 9.8 | 49.8 |
| Germany (western) | Bremen | 27.5 | 48.0 | 41.4 |
|  | Bremerhaven | 21.4 | 38.6 | 53.9 |
| Germany (eastern) | Jena | 28.6 | 41.8 | 47.5 |
|  | Rostock | 29.6 | 39.6 | 47.5 |
| Greece | New Philadelphia (Athens) | 9.5 | 40.2 | 58.0 |
|  | Argyroupouli (Athens) | 13.1 | 38.5 | 57.0 |
| Hungary | Downtown Sopron | 2.2 | 1.3 | 97.2 |
|  | Downtown Ozd | 3.2 | 0.8 | 96.3 |
| Latvia | Agenskalns (Riga) | 14.5 | 10.5 | 80.2 |
|  | Forstate & Jaunbuve (Daugavpils) | 6.5 | 4.2 | 91.0 |
| Portugal | Lumiar (Lisbon) | 14.1 | 26.8 | 65.1 |
|  | Barreiro | 6.1 | 18.4 | 79.8 |
| Slovakia | Rimavska Sobota | 11.8 | 5.7 | 84.5 |
|  | Trnava | 13.7 | 14.5 | 78.3 |
| Spain | Vic | 17.8 | 75.5 | 22.8 |
|  | Sant Cugat del Vallès | 19.3 | 74.3 | 23.6 |
| United Kingdom | Coventry | 27.5 | 23.1 | 61.6 |
|  | Nuneaton | 19.6 | 14.0 | 71.5 |
| Average locations |  | 20.6 | 23.5 | 64.2 |

*Source*: MYPLACE survey, 2012–13.

In Table 1, we show how these forms of political involvement are broken down as a percentage of overall youth in each location ordered by country.[9]

The data on different forms of participation indicates the diversity of participatory strategies according to the locations studied. There are some locations in the study with very high levels of all forms of political activism, especially the four German cities. In the locations in the Mediterranean countries, especially in

Spain and Greece, participation through protest clearly dominates, while young people who participate institutionally are nearly insignificant. At the other extreme, in the city of Kuopio, in Finland, there is practically no political protest, whereas half the young population participates institutionally. There are quite a few locations where the majority strategy is inactivity. Prominent in this regard are the cases of Sopron and Ozd in Hungary and of Daugavpils in Latvia, where the level of inactivity is over 90 per cent. Therefore, when we examine patterns of participation in different places in Europe, we see great variation.

*Independent variable: centrality of young people in youth transition regimes (YTRs)*

We discussed above how different aspects that characterize youth transition regimes (YTRs) affect the position that young people have as a group in the social space. Our thesis is that this position shapes their patterns of political participation since it defines their material and psychological distance from spaces of social and political importance. Therefore, our independent variable is not just the type of youth transition regime but the centrality of this position in the social space that these regimes reserve for youth.

Studies of transition regimes usually take countries as a unit of analysis (Raffe, 2014). The form that YTRs adopt is obviously closely tied to state-linked welfare models, public policies and political traditions (Niemeyer, 2007; Alegre, 2010). However, by framing a young individual's opportunities and expectations, the effect that the YTR has may also be influenced by the local context. The criterion for selecting the two locations in each country of the MYPLACE project (while trying to capture contrasting socioeconomic situations, among other factors) makes it an especially good idea to measure the location-level variation of some characteristics of the YTR.

To do so, a synthesis variable was created that includes the four key national-level indicators described above and three new aggregate location-level indicators taken from the MYPLACE survey. The different indicators, which appear in Table 2, correspond to the YTR dimensions defined above: length and vulnerability in youth transitions; and welfare state generosity and age-orientation. The variation in terms of location is included in dimensions of length and vulnerability in the transitions since the characteristics of welfare state generosity and age-orientation are invariably shared by the locations of a single country. To create the resulting variable 'centrality of young people in YTRs', the dimensions of the seven indicators were standardized; the minimum value was assigned to situations with longer or more vulnerable transitions, less welfare state generosity and social spending more oriented towards the elderly; the maximum value was assigned to contrary situations.[10] The resulting variable is a scale from 0 to 10, in which 0 indicates a transition system that puts young people in a position of maximum distance from spaces of social centrality and 10 represents the position of greatest centrality.

*The Sociological Review*, 63:S2, pp. 92–117 (2015), DOI: 10.1111/1467-954X.12264
© 2015 The Authors. Editorial organisation © 2015 The Editorial Board of the Sociological Review

**Table 2:** *Dimensions and indicators of centrality of young people in YTRs*

| | Length of youth transitions | | Vulnerability in youth transitions | | | Welfare state | | Centrality of young people in YTRs (0–10 scale) |
|---|---|---|---|---|---|---|---|---|
| | (L) Young people living out of parental household (%) | (C) Estimated age of leaving the parental household (years) | (L) Youth unemployment (%) | (C) NEET (%) | (L) Households with financial difficulties (%) | Generosity (C) Social expenditure per capita. 2000–2010 (€) | Age-orientation (C) Elderly/Family-Children ratio social expenditure. 2000–2010 | |
| Odense Centre (DK) | 77.8 | 21.1 | 4.8 | 6.6 | 6.0 | 11,334 | 2.97 | 9.76 |
| Odense East (DK) | 69.3 | 21.1 | 8.3 | 6.6 | 7.6 | 11,334 | 2.97 | 9.40 |
| Jena (GER) | 82.8 | 23.8 | 1.6 | 7.1 | 8.7 | 7,900 | 3.85 | 8.86 |
| Rostock (GER) | 78.0 | 23.8 | 2.8 | 7.1 | 10.5 | 7,900 | 3.85 | 8.69 |
| Kuopio (FI) | 75.7 | 21.9 | 4.1 | 8.6 | 18.5 | 7,888 | 3.24 | 8.65 |
| Bremen (GER) | 44.0 | 23.8 | 3.6 | 7.1 | 8.7 | 7,900 | 3.85 | 8.07 |
| Lieksa & Nurmes (FI) | 33.0 | 21.9 | 4.2 | 8.6 | 13.6 | 7,888 | 3.24 | 7.97 |
| Bremerhaven (GER) | 47.8 | 23.8 | 7.8 | 7.1 | 13.5 | 7,900 | 3.85 | 7.84 |
| Coventry (UK) | 63.7 | 23.9 | 11.6 | 14.0 | 20.6 | 7,422 | 6.70 | 6.28 |
| Tartu (ES) | 35.2 | 24.3 | 4.1 | 12.5 | 19.6 | 1,181 | 3.71 | 6.16 |
| Nuneaton (UK) | 30.5 | 23.9 | 17.5 | 14 | 21.0 | 7,422 | 6.70 | 5.39 |
| Narva area (ES) | 25.6 | 24.3 | 15.4 | 12.5 | 36.4 | 1,181 | 3.71 | 5.10 |
| Sopron (HU) | 8.6 | 28.7 | 3.9 | 14.7 | 24.9 | 1,763 | 3.43 | 4.96 |

(Continued)

*The Sociological Review*, 63:S2, pp. 92–117 (2015), DOI: 10.1111/1467-954X.12264

**Table 2:** *Continued*

| | Length of youth transitions | | Vulnerability in youth transitions | | | Welfare state | | Centrality of young people in YTRs (0–10 scale) |
|---|---|---|---|---|---|---|---|---|
| | (L) Young people living out of parental household (%) | (C) Estimated age of leaving the parental household (years) | (L) Youth unemployment (%) | (C) NEET (%) | (L) Households with financial difficulties (%) | Generosity (C) Social expenditure per capita. 2000–2010 (€) | Age-orientation (C) Elderly/Family-Children ratio social expenditure. 2000–2010 | |
| Agenskalns (LAT) | 39.7 | 27.9 | 4.2 | 14.9 | 33.9 | 892 | 5.06 | 4.87 |
| Trnava (SK) | 11.9 | 30.9 | 8.2 | 13.8 | 35.2 | 1,337 | 4.42 | 4.11 |
| Forstate & Jaunbuve (LAT) | 29.8 | 27.9 | 10.0 | 14.9 | 50.0 | 892 | 5.06 | 4.08 |
| St. Cugat (SP) | 7.9 | 28.9 | 3.9 | 18.8 | 17.4 | 4,280 | 7.56 | 3.94 |
| Ozd (HU) | 18.4 | 28.7 | 13.9 | 14.7 | 62.9 | 1,763 | 3.43 | 3.88 |
| Vic (SP) | 20.9 | 28.9 | 10.7 | 18.8 | 20.2 | 4,280 | 7.56 | 3.79 |
| Lumiar (POR) | 20.9 | 28.8 | 11.7 | 14.1 | 23.8 | 3,295 | 8.59 | 3.78 |
| Podsljeme (CR) | 3.5 | 32.7 | 12.0 | 16.7 | 13.8 | 2,078 | 4.60 | 3.75 |
| Pescenica (CR) | 7.9 | 32.7 | 16.9 | 16.7 | 20.3 | 2,078 | 4.60 | 3.46 |
| Barreiro (POR) | 17.3 | 28.8 | 12.4 | 14.1 | 42.1 | 3,295 | 8.59 | 3.31 |
| Rimavska Sobota (SK) | 13.0 | 30.9 | 21.4 | 13.8 | 57.8 | 1,337 | 4.42 | 3.04 |
| New Philadelphia (GR) | 10.8 | 29.1 | 16.0 | 20.3 | 76.1 | 4,244 | 7.22 | 2.11 |
| Argyroupouli (GR) | 7.6 | 29.1 | 19.2 | 20.3 | 67.1 | 4,244 | 7.22 | 2.09 |

*Notes.* (L) Location indicator // (C) Country indicator.
*Source:* MYPLACE survey, 2012–2013 for location indicators and Eurostat for national indicators.

The findings portray a spectrum of different situations regarding the position of centrality in the social space of young people in the various YTRs at each location. As expected, the countries' locations have very similar positions even though we also see significant differences coming particularly from local vulnerability indicators. The locations are ordered from more to less centrality. Roughly speaking, the locations of the Scandinavian countries and Germany present the highest levels of centrality, followed by the locations in the UK and, though with more variation, in the Baltic countries. Next come most of the locations in Eastern Europe, while Mediterranean locations are those scoring the least centrality with our indicator.

*Control variables*

Other independent variables are added to the model that the literature has identified as important for explaining patterns of participation (especially among the general population) and serve a control function. On the individual level, we control for socio-demographic variables such as age and sex, as well as key variables for participation including the level of education (having completed secondary school) and the social class of family of origin (a variable with eight values that we treat as continuous and that shows the level of education and professional status of the mother and father). We include variables that reflect the individual situation with regard to youth transitions; whether individuals live independently of the parental household and their activity status (studying, working, inactive or unemployed). We collect two political attitudes: being interested in politics (dummy variable); and the level of satisfaction with how democracy works (on a scale of 0 to 10). Finally, we also add the variable of participating in formal or issue-oriented organizations.[11]

With regard to the variables of context, we include the total population of the location's surrounding urban area[12] to consider the rural/urban effect. A dummy variable is added that shows if any type of election was held in the year prior to the survey in order to bear in mind the mobilizing effect of electoral processes and if the city has a university.[13] The overall percentage of young people that participate in formal political and issue-oriented organizations is also collected as a contextual variable indicating the level of association density in the location.[14] The impact of the crisis on the young people of each country is observed through the indicator of growth in long-term youth unemployment in 2007–2012.[15] Finally, an indicator of the years that the country has been a democracy[16] is added to gain a measure of the level of democratic tradition, which may also have an impact on participatory practices.

**Empirical discussion**

Table 3 presents, first, the variance components to see how the logistic regression models of the three participation variables evolve as we introduce new elements. The empty model is a regression with random intercept that we use only to show

*The Sociological Review*, 63:S2, pp. 92–117 (2015), DOI: 10.1111/1467-954X.12264
© 2015 The Authors. Editorial organisation © 2015 The Editorial Board of the Sociological Review

**Table 3:** *Variance components of regression models explaining participation strategies*

| | Empty model | With individual level variables | With individual and location level variables | | |
| --- | --- | --- | --- | --- | --- |
| | | | Without YTR centrality | With YTR centrality | With YTR centrality and interactions |
| **Institutional participation** | | | | | |
| σ (location level) | 0.830 | 0.495 | 0.240 | 0.166 | 0.778 |
| -loglikelihood | 62824 | 64920.2 | 65004.2 | 64999.1 | 65131,207 |
| Intra-class correlation | 0.201 | 0.131 | 0.068 | 0.048 | 0.191 |
| **Protest** | | | | | |
| σ (location level) | 1.806 | 1.518 | 1.015 | 0.792 | |
| -loglikelihood | 63275.7 | 64874.4 | 65096.7 | 65099.8 | |
| Intra-class correlation | 0.354 | 0.316 | 0.236 | 0.194 | |
| **Passivity** | | | | | |
| σ (location level) | 1.284 | 0.986 | 0.640 | 0.339 | |
| -loglikelihood | 58787.3 | 60532.4 | 60649.8 | 60627.2 | |
| Intra-class correlation | 0.281 | 0.231 | 0.163 | 0.093 | |

*Source:* MYPLACE survey, 2012–2013 for individual and location variables and Eurostat for national variables.

that there is a significant part of the variance (above 20 per cent in all three cases) that is explained by differences of location. As such, it confirms that it is important to take both individual and contextual factors into account. The next models show the variance components when we introduce individual variables. The fact that some high levels of variance attributed to the location are maintained (see intra-class correlation) indicates that contextual differences continue to be important, especially when we consider the composition effect. This means that the variance between locations is not due to the different characteristics of the individuals in each location, but to factors linked to the location itself. At this point, we note that the intra-class correlation remains much higher in the case of protest than in the case of institutional participation. This leads us to the idea that protest is more linked to contextual factors while institutional activism is a form of involvement with more similar patterns across the different European locations. Furthermore, compared to the empty model, by introducing the individual variables, the variance attributed to locations dropped by 40.3 per cent for institutional participation and only 15.9 per cent for protest. This means that the different individual characteristics of young people based on their location explain the different levels of institutional participation much better than protest, which must be attributed overwhelmingly to genuinely contextual elements.

The next models, in Table 3, include the contextual variables and we can see how the explained variance improves. We present a model without the variable of centrality of young people in YTRs to discover its impact on residual variance according to location. The findings indicate that the variable of centrality greatly helps to explain the differences between locations regarding participation strategies; it lowers residual variance by 30.8 per cent for institutional participation, 22 per cent for protest and 47 per cent in the case of passivity.

Finally, Table 4 presents the substantive findings of the final multilevel logistic regression models. With regard to the influence of the individual variables, in general predictable results appear, such as the positive influence on participation arising from the level of education and the social position of the family, interest in politics and participation in organizations. The variables associated with the personal situation in youth transitions give mixed results. It seems that situations of greater dependency (like living with one's parents or being a student) favour participation in protest, while those of greater independence (like living on one's own and working) tend towards institutional participation. Moreover, being inactive or unemployed favours passivity. Finally, it should be stressed that the feeling of dissatisfaction with how democracy works favours all forms of activism. Satisfaction with democracy and one's relationship to participation has been interpreted variously based on the context (Canache et al., 2001). In some cases, satisfaction with democracy has been associated with a greater predisposition to vote (Kopp, 2001), while in others a critical attitude towards the system is considered to increase political protest (Kaase and Marsh, 1979; Fuchs and Klingemann, 1995). Our findings show that dissatisfaction with how democracy works favours participation in its different forms. The context of the economic

**Table 4:** *Individual and contextual determinants of participation strategies of youth*

| | Institutional participation Model 1 | Protest Model 2 | Passivity Model 3 | Protest (with interactions) Model 4 |
|---|---|---|---|---|
| Intercept | $-5.344^{***}$ | $-7.660^{***}$ | $7.052^{***}$ | $-7.833^{***}$ |
| ***Individual variables*** | | | | |
| Age | $0.040^{***}$ | $-0.006$ | $-0.029^{***}$ | $-0.005$ |
| Sex (female) | $-0.189^{***}$ | $-0.103^{**}$ | $0.131^{***}$ | $-0.107^{**}$ |
| Secondary education | $0.179^{***}$ | $0.188^{***}$ | $-0.225^{***}$ | $0.185^{***}$ |
| Social class of origin | $0.086^{*}$ | $0.305^{***}$ | $-0.241^{***}$ | $0.304^{***}$ |
| Living out parental home | $0.138^{**}$ | $-0.232^{***}$ | $0.070$ | $-0.23^{***}$ |
| Activity | | | | |
|   Studying | $-0.303^{***}$ | $0.123^{*}$ | $0.081$ | $0.126^{*}$ |
|   Unemployed or inactive | $-0.348^{***}$ | $-0.037$ | $0.270$ | $-0.033$ |
|   Working (ref.) | ref. | ref. | ref. | ref. |
| Political interest | $0.877^{***}$ | $0.626^{***}$ | $-0.743^{***}$ | $0.818^{***}$ |
| Satisfaction with democracy | $-0.023^{**}$ | $-0.102^{***}$ | $0.065^{***}$ | $0.098^{***}$ |
| Participation in formal org. | $0.811^{***}$ | $0.461^{***}$ | $-0.695^{***}$ | $0.728^{***}$ |
| Participation in issue-oriented org. | $0.873^{***}$ | $1.025^{***}$ | $-1.022^{***}$ | $0.877^{***}$ |
| ***Contextual variables*** | | | | |
| Population of the urban area | $0.000$ | $0.000$ | $0.000$ | $0.000$ |
| Elections in the last year | $-0.007$ | $0.915^{*}$ | $-0.518$ | $0.916^{*}$ |
| University in the location | $-0.204$ | $0.387$ | $0.064$ | $0.378$ |
| % of formal political org. in the location | $0.019^{*}$ | $-0.042^{*}$ | $0.009$ | $-0.042^{*}$ |
| % of issue-oriented org. in the location | $-0.021$ | $0.047^{*}$ | $-0.004$ | $0.047^{*}$ |

*(Continued)*

**Table 4:** *Continued*

|  | Institutional participation Model 1 | Protest Model 2 | Passivity Model 3 | Protest (with interactions) Model 4 |
|---|---|---|---|---|
| Crisis impact (long-term unemployment 07-12) | 0.058** | 0.231*** | −0.204*** | 0.232*** |
| Democratic tradition (years of democracy) | 0.001 | 0.001 | 0.000 | 0.001 |
| YTR centrality | 0.330*** | 0.613** | −0.661*** | 0.649*** |
| *Cross-level interactions* |  |  |  |  |
| Political interest * YTR centrality |  |  |  | −0.037* |
| Satisfaction dem. * YTR centrality |  |  |  | 0.001 |
| Part. formal org. * YTR centrality |  |  |  | −0.047** |
| Part. issue-oriented org. * YTR centrality |  |  |  | 0.025 |

$n$ level1 = 12.843 // $n$ level2 = 26.
Sig. *$p < 0.1$, **$p < 0.05$, ***$p < 0.01$
*Source*: MYPLACE survey, 2012–2013 for individual and location variables and Eurostat for national variables.

recession probably strengthens the link between critical attitudes and participation among young people.

With regard to the contextual variables, neither the size of the population, the existence of a university in the town or city nor the democratic tradition is significant once the other variables have been controlled for. However, if some kind of election was held, there is a statistically significant coefficient in the protest model. Organizational density also has an impact on young people's propensity to participate; this indicates the importance of access to the collective resources of the social environment such as social networks and organizational resources (Huckfeldt, 1979; Knoke, 1990; Rosenstone and Hansen, 1993; Putnam, 1994). Even so, the types of groups must be differentiated; where there are more issue-oriented organizations and movements, young people tend to use political protest. The presence of formal associations favours institutional participation, but at the expense of protest. The impact of the crisis, measured through a rise in

110

long-term youth unemployment, is revealed as one of the most decisive contextual variables. The effect is significant and positive when referring to institutional participation, but especially so for political protest. It seems that young people in the environments most affected by the crisis have reacted with more mobilization. This corresponds to the individual effect of satisfaction with democracy; it seems that mobilization strategies are favoured in contexts where the crisis has had a greater impact and where attitudes are more critical of how the system works.

In relation to our key variable, the effect of young people's position in the social space based on the transitions system, the variable of YTR centrality appears significant in all models. The YTR contexts where young people have more peripheral positions, with longer and more vulnerable transitions and less support from the welfare state, favour the strategy of passivity. However, social contexts in which young people have positions of greater centrality favour participation through both institutional forms and political protest. Models 1 and 3 indicate that the effect of centrality in YTRs for institutional participation and passivity is quite clear. In both cases, the intra-class correlation (0.048 and 0.093, respectively) indicates that the models explain a significant part of the variance in contextual terms. In the case of protest, however, it is easy to think that the relation with centrality in YTRs is not so linear. In fact, protest is a form of participation associated with circumstances of greater confrontation with the political and social system than institutional participation (Marsh, 1977; Dalton, 2002) and, as a result, is closer to groups less integrated into the system. As such, we should expect the positive relation between centrality in YTRs and protest given in model 2 to be more complex. For this reason we ran another multilevel regression (model 4) for protest which includes variables of interaction between YTR centrality and a range of individual level variables.

In particular, we present the interaction of centrality with the individual variables in the model that have a political nature: two political attitudes (political interest and satisfaction with democracy); and two variables of collaboration with political organizations (participation in formal organizations and participation in issue-oriented organizations). The reason for including these interactions is to see if these different indicators of individual political involvement have different effects on protest according to the nature of YTR. The interaction of the YTR centrality indicator with satisfaction with democracy and with participation in issue-oriented organizations does not seem significant. However, political interest and involvement in formal organizations does have a differentiated effect on political protest, depending on centrality in the YTRs. The negative coefficient in both interaction variables indicates that the more central the position of young people in YTR, the less influence both interest in politics and participation in formal organizations have. In other words, in contexts where young people have a peripheral position in social space the fact of being individually involved in the political life (through showing interest in politics or participation in formal organizations) is more important for explaining participation in protest actions. In these contexts of the greater precariousness of youth, the fact of being involved in formal politics also leads to more confrontational political action, while in contexts where young people feel more integrated in spaces of centrality, protest is less associated with being politically involved.

Nevertheless, coefficients indicate that even if these interaction effects exist, they are not very powerful. In fact, Table 3 shows that even in the model with interactions, the residual variance for protest continues to be much higher than in the other participation strategies. This leads us to understand that unlike the other participation strategies, protest is a type of activism that is much more affected by very specific contextual circumstances (such as agents' strategies, the response of the elites, cycles of temporary mobilization, etc.) that are more difficult to collect with extensive research strategies than with case studies (Ferrer-Fons, 2005). However, the introduction of interaction variables provides better understanding of the complexity of factors that intervene in protest strategies.

## Conclusions

Youth transition regimes not only define the framework of material opportunities in which young people undertake their school-work transitions or the process of leaving their parents' home and living on their own. The different patterns of youth transition regimes set up cultural models of normalcy that frame their psychological orientations (Walther, 2006). For Bourdieu (1979, 1985, 1989), the position that individuals and groups occupy in the social space determines their material, cultural and symbolic resources, which they use to participate in the system of social relations.

In this article, we have seen how there is great diversity in the transition systems in Europe(based on elements such as exposure to risk, the length of young people's pathways to adulthood and welfare state generosity and age-orientation) that put young people in a position that is relatively integrated into the system of social relations. Based on estimates of multilevel models that take individual and contextual factors into consideration, we have demonstrated empirically also how this position of greater or lesser centrality in the social space is an important factor for defining young people's strategies of political participation. Specifically, societies where YTRs give young people positions of greater centrality tend to favour participation (and particularly institutional participation). However, in contexts where YTRs place young people in more peripheral positions, passivity is usually the dominant strategy. Political protest has a more complex relation to YTRs: on the one hand, the most integrated YTRs favour protest like any form of participation; on the other hand, it seems that in more precarious YTR contexts, the fact of being politically involved is a more determining factor for protest as, probably in these contexts, political involvement is more associated to feelings of grievance. In any case, our analysis also showed the limitation of extensive research strategies for analysing protest since compared to other forms of political action, it is a type of participation closely linked to highly specific and variable contextual circumstances where the temporary perspective is also very relevant.

*The Sociological Review*, 63:S2, pp. 92–117 (2015), DOI: 10.1111/1467-954X.12264

The link that this paper establishes between the discipline of comparative youth transition studies and the literature of political participation is a key and novel contribution to understanding young people's relationship to politics. Recent research has sought explanations of generational change in young people's forms of political participation (see Dalton, 2007; Zukin *et al.*, 2006; Norris, 2004; Franklin *et al.*, 2004). Studies have also stressed how changes in post-industrial societies, individualization and the information society are changing young people's understanding of politics (see Benedicto, 2013; Manning, 2013, 2010; Rossi, 2009; O'Toole, 2003; Henn *et al.*, 2002), but the influence of contextual elements specific to young people on their participation has gone unnoticed. The data, however, show that the differences in participation strategies according to the country and location in question are highly relevant. Taking YTRs into account as a priority contextual factor complements other contributions in the literature on the effects of context on participation, which usually refer to the whole population.

Europe is experiencing a period in which economic crisis has heightened de-standardization, exposure to risk and uncertainty in young people's pathways to adulthood (Cairns *et al.*, 2014; Dietrich, 2012). Economic and political reforms stemming from the crisis also have an impact on the response that welfare states give to the needs of youth transitions. Therefore, it must be borne in mind that one of the consequences of the youth transition models emerging in this period of change may clearly affect the political strategies of young people and how they participate with regard to democracy.

## Notes

1 Some recent studies have addressed the issue of the influence of destandardization and lengthening of youth transitions on youth political attitudes and participation at the individual level. See, for example, García-Albacete (2014), Benedicto (2013), Soler-i-Martí and Sánchez (2013) and Smets (2010).
2 MYPLACE data from the following countries are drawn on in this article: Croatia, Denmark, Estonia, Finland, Germany, Greece, Hungary, Latvia, Portugal, Slovakia, Spain and the United Kingdom.
3 Decommodification takes place 'when a service is rendered as a matter of right, and when a person can maintain a livelihood without reliance on the market' (Esping-Andersen, 1990: 21–22).
4 Lynch (2001, 2006) proposes several more complex indicators that include other types of social expenditure aimed at unemployment, housing, education or healthcare. The results of these indicators keep the order of the countries mostly unchanged after considering the age-orientation of their social expenditure.
5 For our analysis, we do not use surveys in Russia and Georgia. We opted for including only European Union countries in order to reduce variation in the macro-political context and to ensure comparability of national data that mainly come from Eurostat. Bearing this in mind, our study is based on approximately 15,000 surveys conducted in 26 different locations in 12 countries.
6 A comparison of the differences between locations in each country based on the survey can be found in an overview report from the project, available at: http://www.fp7-myplace.eu/documents/WP4D4-5overviewreportv1.pdf.

7  See, for example, the distinction between representational and extra-representational participation in Teorell *et al.* (2007) or citizen-oriented and cause-oriented in Norris (2004) or elite-directed and elite-challenging participation in Inglehart and Welzel (2005).

8  We have chosen not to include voting in the institutional participation indicator because we would lose many cases as our sample begins at 16 years old. In addition voting is influenced by some legal and institutional factors (such as compulsory voting, electoral system, etc.) that would distract from the focus of analysis.

9  The percentages of each row do not add up to 100 per cent because there are individuals that can be included in both dimensions of activity: institutional participation and protest. This group of individuals ranges from 0.3 per cent in Ozd (Hungary) to 17.9 per cent in Jena (Germany).

10  In order to measure the statistical reliability of the new indicator, we calculated Cronbach's alpha of the seven items once they were standardized. The result ($\alpha = 0.902$) shows strong internal consistency.

11  Participation in formal organizations includes participating or cooperating in religious or church organizations, national or local youth parliaments or councils, national cultural organizations, student unions or local or neighbourhood associations. It does not include political parties or trade unions because they are part of the dependent variable. Issue-oriented organizations refer to environmental organizations, animal welfare groups, peace organizations, human rights organizations, women's organizations and anti-globalization movements.

12  In some cases, locations correspond to whole urban centres, but in others they are neighbourhoods or districts of larger cities.

13  The information for these three contextual variables comes from a database created as part of the MYPLACE project with demographic and socio-political information on the locations.

14  To obtain these data, we take the aggregate data by location from the same MYPLACE survey.

15  Taken from the Labour Force Survey, Eurostat.

16  The 'years of democracy' variable is taken from the following database: https://sites.google.com/site/joseantoniocheibub/datasets/democracy-and-dictatorship-revisited. For a discussion of the same, see Cheibub *et al.* (2010).

# References

Aassve, A., Billari, F. C. and Ongaro, F., (2001), 'The impact of income and employment status on leaving home: evidence from the Italian ECHP sample', *Labour: Review of Labour Economics and Industrial Relations*, 15 (3): 501–529.

Alegre, M. A., (2010), 'El règim de benestar juvenil a Catalunya. Fonts de benestar i oportunitats transicionals dels joves catalans', in Secretaria de Joventut, *Pla Nacional de Joventut 2010–2020. Síntesi dels estudis d'avaluació realitzats per la Secretaria de Joventut*, Barcelona: Secretaria de Joventut.

Barnes, S. and Kaase, M., (1979), *Political Action: Mass Participation in Five Democracies*, Beverly Hills, CA: Sage Publications.

Bell, B., Morgan, G., Kromrey, J. and Ferron, J., (2010), 'The impact of small cluster size on multilevel models: a Monte Carlo examination of two-level models with binary and continuous predictors', in *JSM Proceedings, Section on Survey Research Methods*, Vancouver, BC: American Statistical Association.

Benedicto, J., (2013), 'The political cultures of young people: an uncertain and unstable combinatorial logic', *Journal of Youth Studies*, 16 (6): 712–729.

Benedicto, J. and Morán, M. L., (2007), 'Becoming a citizen: analysing the social representations of citizenship among young people', *European Societies*, 9 (4): 601–622.

Bourdieu, P., (1979), *La distinction*, Paris: Editions du Minuit.

Bourdieu, P., (1985), 'Social space and the genesis of groups', *Theory and Society*, 14 (6): 723–744.

Bourdieu, P., (1989), 'Social space and symbolic power', *Sociological Theory*, 7 (1): 14–25.

Bynner, J. and Roberts, K., (1991), *Youth and Work: Transition to Employment in England and Germany*, London: Anglo-German Foundation.

*The Sociological Review*, 63:S2, pp. 92–117 (2015), DOI: 10.1111/1467-954X.12264

Cairns, D., Growiec, K. and Alves, N. A., (2014), 'Another "missing middle"? The marginalised majority of tertiary-educated youth in Portugal during the economic crisis', *Journal of Youth Studies*, DOI: 10.1080/13676261.2013.878789.

Canache, D., Mondak, J. and Seligson, M. A., (2001), 'Meaning and measurement in cross-national research on satisfaction with democracy', *Public Opinion Quarterly*, 65: 506–528.

Cheibub, J. A., Gandhi, J. and Vreeland, J. R., (2010), 'Democracy and dictatorship revisited', *Public Choice*, 143 (2-1): 67–101.

Dalton, R., (2002), *Citizen Politics: Public Opinion and Political Parties in Advanced Industrial Democracies*, London: Chatham House.

Dalton, R., (2007), *The Good Citizen. How a Younger Generation Is Reshaping American Politics*, Washington: CQ Press.

Dalton, R., (2008), 'Citizenship norms and the expansion of political participation', *Political Studies*, 56 (1): 76–98.

Dietrich, H., (2012), *Youth Unemployment in Europe: Theoretical Considerations and Empirical Findings*, Berlin: International Policy Analysis (IPA) Friedrich-Ebert-Stiftung.

EGRIS, (2001), 'Misleading trajectories: transition dilemmas for young adults in Europe', *Journal of Youth Studies*, 4 (1): 101–118.

Ertl, H., (2006), 'European Union policies in education and training: the Lisbon agenda as a turning point?', *Comparative Education*, 42: 5–27.

Esping-Andersen, G., (1990), *The Three Words of Welfare Capitalism*, Cambridge: Polity Press.

Ferrer-Fons, M., (2005), 'Inequality in access to political action: determinants of political membership and protest in Western Europe', PhD thesis, Florence: European University Institute.

Franklin, M. N., Lyons, P. and Marsh, M., (2004), 'Generational basis of turnout decline in established democracies', *Acta Politica*, 39 (2): 115–151.

Fuchs, D. and Klingemann, H. D., (1995), 'Citizens and the state: a changing relationship', in H. D. Klingemann and D. Fuchs (eds), *Citizens and the State*, Oxford: Oxford University Press.

Furlong, A. and Cartmel, F., (1997), *Young People and Social Change: Individualisation and Risk in Late Modernity*, Buckingham: Open University Press.

Gallie, D. and Paugam, S. (eds), (2000), *Welfare Regimes and the Experience of Unemployment in Europe*, Oxford: Oxford University Press.

García-Albacete, G., (2014), *Young People's Political Participation in Western Europe: Continuity or Generational Change?*, Basingstoke: Palgrave Macmillan.

Harsløf, I., (2005), '"Integrative" or "defensive" youth activation in nine welfare states', *Journal of Youth Studies*, 8 (4): 461–481.

Henn, M., Weinstein, M. and Wring, D., (2002), 'A generation apart? Youth and political participation in Britain', *The British Journal of Politics and International Relations*, 4 (2): 167–192.

Holdsworth, C. and Morgan, D. H. J., (2005), *Transitions in Context: Leaving Home, Independence and Adulthood*, Maidenhead: Open University Press.

Hox, J., (2010), *Multilevel Analysis, Techniques and Applications*, New York: Routledge.

Huckfeldt, R. R., (1979), 'Political participation and the neighbourhood social context', *American Journal of Political Science*, 23: 579–592.

Iacovou, M., (2011), 'Leaving home: independence, togetherness and income in Europe', Population Division Expert Paper No 2011/10, New York: United Nations.

Inglehart, R., and Welzel, C., (2005), *Modernization, Cultural Change and Democracy: The Human Development Sequence*, Cambridge: Cambridge University Press.

Jurado, T., (2001), *Youth in Transition: Housing, Employment, Social Policies and Families in France and Spain*, Aldershot: Ashgate.

Kaase, M. and Marsh, A., (1979), 'Political action: a theoretical perspective', in S. Barnes and M. Kaase, *Political Action: Mass Participation in Five Western Democracies*, Beverly Hills, CA: Sage.

Knoke, D., (1990), *Political Networks: The Structural Perspective*, Cambridge: Cambridge University Press.

Kopp, K. D., (2001), 'Why do people vote? The cognitive-illusion proposition and its test', *Kyklos*, 54: 355–378.

Lynch, J., (2001), 'The age-orientation of social policy regimes in OECD countries', *Journal of Social Policy*, 30: 411–436.

Lynch, J., (2006), *Age in the Welfare State*, Cambridge: Cambridge University Press.

Maas, C. and Hox, J., (2005), 'Sufficient sample sizes for multilevel modeling', *Methodology: European Journal of Research Methods for the Behavioral and Social Sciences*, 1 (3): 86–92.

Machado, J., (2000), 'Transitions and youth cultures', *International Social Science Journal*, 164: 219–232.

Manning, N., (2010), 'Tensions in young people's conceptualisation and practice of politics', *Sociological Research Online*, 15 (4).

Manning, N., (2013), '"I mainly look at things on an issue by issue basis": reflexivity and *phronêsis* in young people's political engagements', *Journal of Youth Studies*, 16 (1): 17–33.

Mari-Klose, P., (2012), 'Prioridades poco prioritarias. Jóvenes en la agenda gubernamental en España (1982–1996)', *Revista Española de Investigaciones Sociológicas*, 140: 69–88.

Marsh, A., (1977), *Protest and Political Consciousness*, London: Sage.

Mettler, S., (2002), 'Bringing the state back in to civic engagement: policy feedback effects of the G.I. Bill for World War II Veterans', *American Political Science Review*, 96: 351–365.

Mettler, S. and Soss, J., (2004), 'The consequences of public policy for democratic citizenship: bridging policy studies and mass politics', *Perspective on Politics*, 2 (1): 55–73.

Milbrath, L. and Goel, M., (1977), *Political Participation: How and Why Do People Get Involved in Politics*, Lanham, MD: University Press of America.

Mills, M., Blossfeld, H. P. and Klijzing, E., (2005), 'Becoming an adult in uncertain times', in M. Mills and K. Kurz (eds), *Globalization, Uncertainty and Youth in Society*, London: Routledge.

Moreno, L. and Mari-Klose, P., (2013), 'Youth, family change and welfare arrangements: is the South still so different?', *European Societies*, 15 (4): 493–513.

Nico, M., (2014), 'Variability in the transitions to adulthood in Europe: a critical approach to de-standardization of the life course', *Journal of Youth Studies*, 17 (2): 166–182.

Niemeyer, B., (2007), 'Between school and work: dilemmas in European comparative transition research', *European Journal of Vocational Training*, 41: 116–136.

Norris, P., (2004), 'Young people and political activism: from the politics of loyalties to the politics of choice', Report for the Council of Europe Symposium 'Young people and democratic institutions: from disillusionment to participation', Strasbourg, 27–28 November 2003.

O'Toole, T., (2003), 'Engaging with young people's conceptions of the political', *Children's Geographies*, 1 (1): 71–90.

Painter-Main, M., (2014), 'Repertoire-building or elite-challenging? Understanding political engagement in Canada', in E. Gidengil and H. Bastedo (eds), *Canadian Democracy from the Ground Up*, Toronto: University of British Columbia Press.

Putnam, R., (1994), *Making Democracy Work: Civic Traditions in Modern Italy*, Princeton, NJ: Princeton University Press.

Putnam, R., (2000), *Bowling Alone: The Collapse and Revival of American Community*, New York: Simon & Schuster.

Raffe, D., (2014), 'Explaining national differences in education-work transitions', *European Societies*, 16 (2): 175–193.

Rosenstone, S. J. and Hansen, J. M., (1993), *Mobilization, Participation and Democracy in America*, New York: Macmillan.

Rossi, F., (2009), 'Youth political participation: is this the end of generational cleavage?', *International Sociology*, 24 (4): 467–497.

Rothstein, B. and Stolle, D., (2003), 'Social capital, impartiality and the welfare state: an institutional approach', in M. Hooghe and D. Stolle (eds), *Generating Social Capital: Civil Society and Institutions in Comparative Perspective*, New York: Palgrave Macmillan.

Serracant, P., (2012), 'Changing youth? Continuities and ruptures in transitions into adulthood among Catalan young people', *Journal of Youth Studies*, 15 (2): 161–176.

*The Sociological Review*, 63:S2, pp. 92–117 (2015), DOI: 10.1111/1467-954X.12264

Serracant, P. and Fabra, S., (2013), 'La joventut en temps de crisi. Una mirada global a l'evolució de les trajectòries juvenils', in P. Serracant (ed.), *Enquesta a la joventut de Catalunya 2012*, Barcelona: Direcció General de Joventut.

Skocpol, T. and Amenta, E., (1986), 'States and social policies', *Annual Review of Sociology*, 12: 131–157.

Smets, K., (2010), 'A widening generational divide? Assessing the age gap in voter turnout between younger and older citizens', PhD thesis, Florence: European University Institute.

Smyth, E., Gangl, M., Raffe, D., Hannan, D. and McCoy, S., (2001), *A Comparative Analysis of Transitions from Education to Work in Europe (CATEWE): Final Report*, Dublin: ESRI.

Soler-i-Martí, R. and Sánchez, E., (2013), 'Participació i política. Les persones joves davant l'esfera pública', in P. Serracant (ed.), *Enquesta a la Joventut de Catalunya*, Barcelona: Direcció General de Joventut.

Stauber, B. and Walther, A., (2006), 'De-standardised pathways to adulthood: European perspectives on informal learning in informal networks', *Papers*, 79: 241–262.

Strate, J., Parrish, C., Elder, C. and Ford, C., (1989), 'Life span, civic development and voting participation', *American Political Science Review*, 83 (2): 443–464.

Taylor-Gooby, P., (2001), 'Sustaining state welfare in hard times: who will pay for the bill?', *Journal of European Social Policy*, 11 (2): 133–147.

Teorell, J., Torcal, M. and Montero, J. R., (2007), 'Political participation: mapping the terrain', in J. van Deth, J. R. Montero and A. Westhlom (eds), *Citizenship and Involvement in European Democracies: A Comparative Analysis*, New York: Routledge.

Van de Velde, C., (2008), *Devenir adulte. Sociologie comparée de la jeunesse en Europe*, Paris: Presses Universitaires de France.

Verba, S. and Nie, N., (1972), *Participation in America: Political Democracy and Social Equality*, New York: Harper & Row.

Walther, A., (2006), 'Regimes of youth transitions: choice, flexibility and security in young people's experiences across different European contexts', *Young*, 14 (2): 119–139.

Zukin, C., Keeter, S., Andolina, M., Jenkins, K. and DelliCarpini, M. X., (2006), *A New Engagement? Political Participation, Civic Life, and the Changing American Citizen*, New York: Oxford University Press.

# Two worlds of participation: young people and politics in Germany

*Britta Busse, Alexandra Hashem-Wangler and Jochen Tholen*

**Abstract:** Germany's political system is, in large part, based on John Stuart Mill's (1958) idea of a representative democracy, which aims to involve people in policy-forming processes. However, the constitution of a parliamentary democracy fosters tendencies towards a *professionalization* of participation, which leads to a strong cleavage between elites and other citizens. Drawing on original, quantitative and qualitative, empirical data we seek to show that this political culture fosters the existence of two *parallel worlds*: one is characterized by statutory regulated forms of engagement and qualified members; the other is inhabited by young people who engage rather in self-organized projects and institutions distant from patterns of conventional political engagement. There is, moreover, relatively little mutual exchange between these two worlds, which potentially endangers the essence of democracy. In this article a typology of different forms of political engagement is developed in order to better explain such parallel worlds and their consequences.

**Keywords:** political participation, professionalization of political participation, decision-making processes, non-formal participation

## Introduction

Declining electoral participation and declining membership of political parties, especially among young people, together with the growing complexity of politics, point to the fact that citizens' involvement in political processes is changing. This seems far from the optimal shape of a representative democracy, which aims at involving people in policy-forming processes and promoting civic competencies (Mill, 2008 [1861]). The acceleration of economic development as a result of globalization and the digital revolution, as well as an increasing lack of democratic legitimization of major political decision-making institutions (European Central Bank etc.) have led to doubts about a sustainable future for democracy. As a result, academic literature, discussing everything from the 'crisis of democracy' to

*The Sociological Review*, 63:S2, pp. 118–140 (2015), DOI: 10.1111/1467-954X.12265
© 2015 The Authors. Editorial organisation © 2015 The Editorial Board of the Sociological Review. Published by John Wiley & Sons Ltd, 9600 Garsington Road, Oxford OX4 2DQ, UK and 350 Main Street, Malden, MA 02148, USA

the promise of new forms of democracy in a third stage of modernity, is filling the shelves of libraries worldwide.

Among those who express a pessimistic view on the fate of democracy, Croizier *et al.* (1975) argue that democratic governments in the industrial world have lost their ability to operate, overwhelmed by the problems they confront. Nearly 40 years later this pessimistic view has been reiterated by Zakaria (2013), who states that the last four decades have been lost to the challenge of adapting Western democracies to the demands of reflexive modernity. In this regard, the danger to Western democracies would not be sudden death but sclerosis. Crouch (2004) takes up Habermas's (1973) discussion of problems of legitimation in the era of late capitalism through a focus on the growing power of global business. He sees post-democracy as characterized by disinterest in widespread citizen involvement in politics. Streek (2013) strengthens this line of argument by pointing to the failure of democracy in the global financial crisis from 2008, which he sees as an outcome of economic neo-liberalism, accompanied by a growing gap between rich and poor. As a result, the 'emergence of political authority beyond the nation state led to a shift in the set of established justifications of legitimate authority' (Zürn, 2013: 10). In other words, more and more democracies empower political institutions which are not truly democratic (like, for instance, the European Commission or the European Council).

Another argument within this strand of discussion highlights a 'democratic paradox' (Blühdorn, 2013). On the one hand, the process of modernity promotes the individualization and emancipation of subjects and, in this respect, satisfies citizens' demands for freedom, self-determination and self-realization. On the other hand, 'reflexive modernity' (Beck *et al.*, 1996) is undermining the principles of democracy; international integration and complex procedures increasingly render democratic procedures ineffective and even counter-productive. According to Embacher (2009) all these trends lead not only to annoyance with politics but have far-reaching consequences for general perceptions of democratic systems and public policy.

Notwithstanding such observations, however, a rather idealized understanding of democracy prevails in much public and academic discussion. Throughout history, democracy has been considered an ideal, uniting those who govern with those who are governed (Rosanvallon, 2008). Here, the natural distance between the two has been overlooked often and leads to misunderstandings and disappointments. Considering the history of democracy, Nolte (2011: 8) argues that democracy 'has always questioned itself, reinvented itself and creatively extended itself'. A more realistic discussion about the opportunities and limits of liberal democracy is thus necessary.

Countering any wholesale adoption of the 'crisis thesis', a growing number of scholars emphasize that today's democracy offers many more tools and possible forms of intervention than traditional representative democracy. During the last decades, for a limited number of politically active citizens, opportunities to be politically engaged *beyond* political parties have widened. This is a product of a network society (Castells, 1997) and is deepened by the digital revolution.

The sociology of modernization (Smith *et al.*, 2013), drawing on Bakhtin's concept of dialogism (1981) and Habermas's theory of communicative action (1981), describes more options for political participation by non-elites. This bottom-up approach also includes the concept of liberal democracy as driven and organized by social movements (Hardt and Negri, 2013).

Bearing in mind both these sets of arguments, we might anticipate that decreasing engagement in traditional political organizations, and young people's indifference towards political parties, is not indicative of a 'freezing' of the system of parliamentary democracy, but is more likely to activate its dynamics and its further development *beyond* the area of institutional participation, resulting in a 'multiple democracy' (Nolte, 2011). This would include all so-called 'alternative' forms of engagement, voluntary work in social and political matters and citizens' action groups, that is, organizations and groups operating outside the area of direct political institutions.

However, within these two strands of 'post-democracy' discourse a third scenario of political (dis)engagement becomes apparent. The constitution of a parliamentary democracy fosters 'two worlds of participation'. There are tendencies towards favouring *professionalized* participation by citizens. In this context, the existing political system, the authorities and the state, face the challenge of involving young people with all their *diverse forms* of engagement into decision-making processes. This task is difficult as the characteristics of a functioning parliamentary governmental system – the relatively well-organized parties, qualified political representatives and disciplined party fractions within the parliament – differ considerably from (not only) young people's understandings of politics and political engagement as practised in alternative and less hierarchical forms.

Here a limitation of our arguments emerges: only a minority of young people are politically active, and an even smaller number of young people are involved in new social movements (della Porta and Rucht, 2013). Even during the zenith of spectacular political activities, for example the 'Außerparlamentarische Opposition-APO' (extra-parliamentary opposition) from 1968 and the then successive waves of social movements in West Germany, only 10 per cent or fewer students in West Germany participated in the demonstrations (Rucht, 2008). Generally, only 10–15 per cent of a cohort of young people develop a political group identity which, in turn, shapes the identity of another 40 to 50 per cent of this cohort. The remaining 40 per cent are not influenced (Hurrelmann and Albrecht, 2014). Examining different intensities of participation is important as it allows us to estimate whether the parliamentary governmental system can strengthen its existing (weak) ties to the 'second world' of *alternative* political participation or whether the current system of political participation will develop further towards an elite project.

In Germany's history, liberal democracy has lasted no more than two generations. Introduced by the Western allies after 1945 in the Western part of the country and enlarged after 1990 to the Eastern part, democracy has become a major foundation of German policy and society. Thus, although the process of democratization in Germany is viewed widely as a success story, this article suggests

*The Sociological Review*, 63:S2, pp. 118–140 (2015), DOI: 10.1111/1467-954X.12265

**Table 1:** *General political interest: high*

| Year | Young people between 15 and 24 years (%) |
|---|---|
| 1984 | 55 |
| 1991 | 57 |
| 1996 | 47 |
| 1999 | 43 |
| 2002 | 34 |
| 2006 | 39 |
| 2010 | 40 |

*Source*: Shell Deutschland Holding, 2010: 138

that the existing German political culture in practice fosters 'parallel worlds'. On the one hand there is a world of state regulated, traditional forms of engagement undertaken by qualified members, while, in parallel to this world, young people engage in projects and institutions that display a form of self-organization that is distant from conventional political engagement. This suggests that (especially young) people, at least a considerable part of the age cohort, are demanding a participatory democracy rather than the representative one, which has been determined and managed since 1945 by the country's elites.

Moreover, despite the availability of many state-sponsored service points in Germany that offer information, advice and qualifications for young people's alternative project ideas,[1] our results show that there is a discrepancy between the *reach* and thus the effect in political matters of alternative forms of participation and forms of engagement undertaken by qualified members in Germany.

## Traditional and alternative forms of engagement: interdependency and integration

Recent debate among German political scientists and sociologists reflects the concern that young people tend increasingly to distance themselves from politics. Surveys show that their interest in politics has decreased. The longitudinal Shell Youth Study, for example, demonstrates the change in 'political interest' among young people over the last 30 years (Shell Deutschland Holding, 2010). Table 1 shows that the relatively high interest in politics during the 1980s declined steadily until the first years of the new century; its decline amounts to more than one-third of the starting figure.

Although in the last decade (since 2002) interest in politics has slightly increased, and appears to have stabilized, the fact that not even half of young people are interested in politics demands an explanation by both politicians and political scientists. Is it symptomatic of a generation of young people who have little engagement with politics?

*The Sociological Review*, 63:S2, pp. 118–140 (2015), DOI: 10.1111/1467-954X.12265
© 2015 The Authors. Editorial organisation © 2015 The Editorial Board of the Sociological Review

**Table 2:** *Development of political interest – young people between 12 and 25*

| Percentage of each group showing 'high' political interest | 2002 | 2006 | 2010 |
|---|---|---|---|
| *Political interest related to gender* | | | |
| Male | 37 | 40 | 42 |
| Female | 23 | 30 | 31 |
| *Political interest related to age groups* | | | |
| 12–14 | 11 | 15 | 21 |
| 15–17 | 20 | 26 | 33 |
| 18–21 | 38 | 42 | 38 |
| 22–25 | 44 | 48 | 47 |
| *Political interest related to parental social status (class)* | | | |
| Underclass | 16 | 23 | 16 |
| Lower middle class | 24 | 29 | 26 |
| Middle class | 32 | 32 | 36 |
| Upper middle class | 34 | 43 | 48 |
| Upper class | 43 | 50 | 51 |

*Source*: Shell Deutschland Holding (2010: 130).

While Table 2 indicates that both gender and parental social status have an impact on young people's interest in political issues, it is the age cohort that proves to be the most significant for the purposes of our discussion; interest in politics increases with age.

Similarly, research on the voting behaviour of young people in Germany demonstrates that voter turnout increases with age (Schäfer, 2013). Typically, voting behaviour appears as an S-shaped profile in the life cycle. First-time voters use the newly gained right to vote relatively often but during the second and third election, thus in their mid-20s, the participation rate decreases (Schäfer, 2013). The reasons for this are explained often by family situations and increased geographical mobility during the education and training life-phase (Eilfort, 1994). German general elections in 2009 confirmed this trend; young people aged 21 to 24 had the lowest turnout (59 per cent). Similarly, for young people between 25 and 29, voter turnout (61 per cent) was significantly below the average.[2]

The notion of youth apathy and disengagement is strengthened by recent research on forms of popular engagement. The EUYOUPART youth survey 2004 shows that alternative forms of participation are more attractive to young people than traditional formal political engagement in organizations that are characterized by clear hierarchical structures and exclusive membership (such as a youth section of a party or a trade union group). Almost half of all young people interviewed (49 per cent) had been or were members of a sports club, followed by

*The Sociological Review*, 63:S2, pp. 118–140 (2015), DOI: 10.1111/1467-954X.12265

cultural associations (25 per cent) and religious/church-related organizations (17 per cent). However, only 9 per cent were members of the youth organization of a political party or trade union. In line with this turn away from formal membership in traditional organizations, participation in protest events has gained increasing popularity among young people (Rucht, 2011). In Germany this form of engagement is transmitted to children already in school, where classes are regularly encouraged by their teachers to take part in protests against cutbacks in education or in protests relating to other local matters. The Shell Youth Study 2010 confirms this trend: 44 per cent of all young people (12–25 years) were at least 'probably willing' to take part in a protest meeting and 45 per cent of these respondents said that they had already taken part in such meetings (Shell Deutschland Holding, 2010).

However, the discourse of youth apathy and disengagement from politics typically relies on 'quantitative methodologies and orthodox hegemonic notions of politics' (Manning, 2010: 2). This conceptualization has been described by Henn *et al.* (2002: 170) as 'conventional political science' that equates interest in electoral politics with knowledge and interest in politics in general. It is a model that privileges political institutions and implies that engagement in traditional political organizations is the 'real politics'.

There is a vibrant scientific discourse dealing with these hegemonic notions of politics and analysing alternative forms of engagement. Gaiser *et al.* (2010), for instance, refer to data from the DJI Youth Survey 2003 and distinguish three forms of participation: traditional clubs, associations and organizations; other formal groups (NGOs); and activities that are temporary and/or situational. These more detailed classifications contribute to a broadening of the term 'political activity', so that even sporadic or situational youth engagement can be seen in their political context. Harris *et al.* (2010) also address the changing nature of participation for young people and stress that growing engagement in alternative forms is the result of barriers (perceiving politicians as reluctant to listen to youth, inappropriate political language, political structures that marginalize young people) that hinder young people from taking part in formal politics. Similarly, Riley *et al.* (2010) criticize top-down models of political participation that fail to reflect the diverse ways that young people act upon social and political issues and argue that 'partying' constitutes a form of political consumerism.

However, while these studies seek to uncover emerging forms of public and private engagement and emphasize the political character of alternative forms of engagement, they fail to consider the interdependencies between these two forms of engagement. Recognition of the existence of informal or alternative forms of political engagement, moreover, tells us neither whether or not they are actually integrated into democratic processes, nor, indeed, whether or not they *are* political. Furthermore, there is little research on the exchange or cooperation between young people who are active in an alternative group and those engaged in more traditional formal organizations. Thus, drawing on new empirical data, in the next section we ask: what is political engagement?; and can any form of social participation be considered 'political'?

## Methodological aspects of the MYPLACE study in Germany: Bremen and Bremerhaven

In this paper we use complementary data sources from the MYPLACE project carried out in north-western Germany. Between September 2012 and March 2013, 936 questionnaire interviews with 16 to 25 year olds were conducted with CAPI[3] technology in Bremen and Bremerhaven.[4] The survey asked respondents, *inter alia*, about their political interest, participation and civic engagement, social networks, understanding of democracy, attitudes to violence and human rights. Respondents were chosen by a list-based[5] random selection procedure. At the end of each survey interview, respondents were asked to participate in qualitative follow-up interviews. From the survey respondents, 60 volunteers for the in-depth interviews were selected following the criteria elaborated for the MYPLACE project (see Pilkington and Pollock in this volume). The interviews were conducted at the respondents' homes following a schedule which focused on the inter-generational transfer of historical and political knowledge, interest and attitudes, experiences with diverse forms of political participation, populist opinions, evaluations of EU politics and migration to Germany.

In addition to survey and interview data, field research – 2012–2014 – was conducted with two groups of politically active young people as part of the ethnographic research for MYPLACE. One group, the Bremen youth section of the German Metalworkers Union (IGM Youth), engages young people politically in a more or less formal way. Hierarchical structures and formal decision-making processes underpin this labour union youth section. In contrast, the second group (AntiDis AG) is characterized by its alternative forms of political engagement and independent organizational structure. Attached to a Bundesliga football club in Northern Germany, AntiDis AG brings together young football fans and ultras to oppose discrimination against women, migrants, LGBT and disabled people. Its activism takes the form of distributing flyers in front of the football stadium and the organization of choreographed performances during matches. Through participant observation and conducting semi-structured interviews for these two ethnographic case studies, we gained insight into the group members' perceptions and evaluations of politics.

This triangulation of survey and interview data with field research represents an innovative approach to research on youth engagement. Other existing studies provide insight into young people's disenchantment with politics (Gaiser *et al.*, 2010) or show that alternative ways of participation are gaining ground among young people (Bakker and de Vreese, 2011; Stolle *et al.*, 2005). Our results suggest that there is a discrepancy between the *reach* of alternative forms and forms of engagement undertaken by qualified members in Germany – a result emanating from triangulating the MYPLACE data.

*The Sociological Review*, 63:S2, pp. 118–140 (2015), DOI: 10.1111/1467-954X.12265

**Table 3:** *Distribution of engagement in organizations and political activities done*

| Engagement in organizations | Frequency % (n) | Political activities done | Frequency % (n) |
|---|---|---|---|
| Active in political organization | 8.5 (80) | Formal political activities | 3.6 (33) |
| Active in alternative social/cultural organization | 34.6 (324) | Non-formal political activities | 39.8 (365) |
| Active in political and alternative organization | 13.8 (129) | Formal and non-formal political activities | 39.5 (362) |
| Not active in any organization | 43.1 (403) | No activities at all | 17.1 (157) |
| Total | 100 (936) | | 100 (917) |

*Source*: MYPLACE survey, two locations in western Germany 2012–13.

## MYPLACE: results

*Survey data: formal versus informal participation*

To capture the forms of engagement in which interviewees in the survey were involved, we divided the respondents into four groups: survey respondents who had been engaged in traditional political organizations;[6] respondents engaged in alternative organizations;[7] respondents involved in both kinds of organizations; and respondents who had not been engaged in any organization at all during the last 12 months. To include engaged young people who were not members of any organization, but nevertheless active, we included membership, participation in an organization's activity and having done voluntary work for the organization, as engagement in an organization. Additionally, we classified single activities young people might have done during the last 12 months into: formal political activities;[8] non-formal political activities;[9] both formal and non-formal political activities; and neither formal nor informal political activities. By distinguishing between traditional and alternative political activities and support for traditional and alternative political organizations, we aimed to capture two worlds of political participation that young people are offered today. In the following discussion we demonstrate differences between those participating in these two worlds.

Table 3 demonstrates that traditional political organizations are less attractive to young people than alternative forms of engagement. Furthermore, more than 40 per cent of respondents were not engaged in any organization. Similarly, formal political activities were less popular among our respondents than

**Table 4:** *Share of eligible voters in the 2009 national election among organization and activity cluster members*

| Engagement in organizations | Voted % (n) | Political activities done | Voted % (n) |
|---|---|---|---|
| Active in political organization | 73.1[a,b,c] (38) | Formal political activities | 78.9[a,b,c] (15) |
| Active in alternative social/cultural organization | 69.2[c] (108) | Non-formal political activities | 64.1[c] (123) |
| Active in political and alternative organization | 88.6[b] (62) | Formal and non-formal political activities | 83.4[b] (171) |
| Not active in any organization | 63.8[a,c] (146) | No activities at all | 50.0[a,c] (45) |
| Total | 69.8** (354) | | 70.0*** (354) |

***$p < 0.001$; **$p < 0.01$; different letters denote significant differences at the $p < 0.05$ level between groups.
*Source*: MYPLACE survey, two locations in western Germany 2012–13.

non-formal activities. Even though in Germany a demonstration culture is transmitted to young people at schools and thus probably all respondents had been asked to participate in a demonstration,[10] 17 per cent had not participated in any political activity, not even in a single demonstration.

Arguably, the central pillar of a parliamentary democracy, and the main involvement in decision-making that it offers, are elections. To examine the extent to which our respondents were making use of this opportunity, we compared participation or abstention in the 2009 general elections (*Bundestagswahl*) in our organizational and activity clusters. Respondents who were not eligible to vote in that election were excluded from the analysis.

With one exception all the clusters contain more voters than non-voters (overall differences are significant at the $p < 0.01$ level for members of organizational clusters and on a $p < 0.001$ level for other political activists). Only the cluster of respondents who did not participate in any political activity during the last 12 months had an equal share of voters and non-voters (see Table 4). Thus, participating in elections is a form of political engagement which is largely accepted by young people. However, we found significant differences between voters and non-voters belonging to the different clusters. The highest voter rates are found among young people engaged in formal political organizations (either only in formal or in formal as well as alternative ones). Interestingly, the most pronounced differences were between the respondents involved in formal and alternative organizations compared to the non-active and those active only in alternative organizations. The voter distribution among the political action clusters shows similar results. Among the eligible respondents who reported an involvement in a formal political activity, about 80 per cent voted in the 2009 election; among the interviewees involved in only non-formal political activities it was about 64 per cent and among the non-active it was 50 per cent. These results indicate that actual engagement in elections is higher among young people who are part of formal political organizations. We will return to this finding later.

To find out more about the characteristics of the cluster members, we analysed the clusters with respect to socio-demographic variables: gender, age group (16–19 years and 20–25 years) and level of education (A-levels+; lower education). Table 5 displays the socio-demographic distribution of cluster members. Considering gender, overall significant differences for the distribution among organizational clusters are revealed at $p < 0.05$. While men prefer formal political organizations, women favour alternative organizations. Significantly more women than men participate in non-formal political activities, while young men take more part in formal and alternative activities.

In relation to different age groups, young people between 16 and 19 years of age were significantly more represented in alternative organizations whereas older respondents were more often attracted by formal organizations (only formal as well as formal and alternative). Concerning single political activities, one significant difference was found between the age groups; younger respondents preferred alternative activities only. Overall, differences in the cluster distribution are significant at $p < 0.001$ for organizational affiliations.

Finally, we found significantly more individuals with higher education among the respondents who were involved in traditional political organizations. Interviewees with a lower level of education preferred to support only alternative organizations. The overall difference in the distribution of educational levels among the organizational clusters is highly significant ($p < 0.001$). The same is true for the educational level difference between participants in different activities. The combination of formal and alternative activities was practised significantly more often by higher than by lower educated young people. Furthermore, significant differences between educational levels and political activities can be found; the higher educated were less often absent from all kinds of activities.

## Implications of survey data findings

In sum, the survey data indicate that formal political organizations engage more males than females, young people in older age groups, and the higher educated. Individual political activities that are non-formal are preferred mainly by women and younger respondents, while formal and non-formal activities attract more highly educated men. Respondents with a low level of education are less active than the more highly educated. However, it should be noted that age interacts with level of education. When controlling for age, significant differences between the higher and the lower educated in the cluster engaging in both kinds of

**Table 5:** *Socio-demographic distribution among organizations and activity cluster members*

| Engagement in organizations | | | Political activities done | | |
|---|---|---|---|---|---|
| | | Gender | | | |
| | Male % (n) | Female % (n) | | Male % (n) | Female % (n) |
| Active in political organization | 11.1[a] (53) | 6.1[b] (27) | Formal political activities | 3.3[a] (16) | 3.9[a] (17) |
| Active in alternative social/cultural organization | 31.7[a] (152) | 38.3[b] (170) | Non-formal political activities | 36.6[a] (175) | 43.3[b] (190) |
| Active in political and alternative organization | 14.8[a] (71) | 12.4[a] (55) | Formal and non-formal political activities | 43.7[a] (209) | 34.9[b] (153) |
| Not active in any organization | 42.4[a] (203) | 43.2[a] (192) | No activities at all | 16.3[a] (78) | 18.0[a] (79) |
| Total | 100* (479) | 100* (444) | | 100 (478) | 100 (439) |
| | | Age | | | |
| | 16–19 % (n) | 20–25 % (n) | | 16–19 % (n) | 20–25 % (n) |
| Active in political organization | 5.7[a] (25) | 11.3[b] (55) | Formal political activities | 2.8[a] (12) | 4.3[a] (21) |
| Active in alternative social/cultural organization | 42.2[a] (184) | 28.3[b] (138) | Non-formal political activities | 43.4[a] (185) | 36.7[b] (180) |
| Active in political and alternative organization | 11.2[a] (49) | 15.8[b] (77) | Formal and non-formal political activities | 38.5[a] (164) | 40.3[a] (198) |
| Not active in any organization | 40.8[a] (178) | 44.6[a] (217) | No activities at all | 15.3[a] (65) | 18.7[a] (92) |
| Total | 100*** (436) | 100*** (487) | | 100 (426) | 100 (491) |

*(Continued)*

*The Sociological Review*, 63:S2, pp. 118–140 (2015), DOI: 10.1111/1467-954X.12265
© 2015 The Authors. Editorial organisation © 2015 The Editorial Board of the Sociological Review

**Table 5:** *Continued*

| Engagement in organizations | Level of education | | Political activities done | Level of education | |
|---|---|---|---|---|---|
| | Low % (n) | High % (n) | | Low % (n) | High % (n) |
| Active in political organization | 5.7[a] (30) | 12.7[b] (50) | Formal political activities | 3.8[a] (20) | 3.4[a] (13) |
| Active in alternative social/cultural organization | 39.6[a] (210) | 28.5[b] (112) | Non-formal political activities | 42.5[a] (225) | 36.2[a] (140) |
| Active in political and alternative organization | 11.9[a] (63) | 16.0[a] (63) | Formal and non-formal political activities | 33.4[a] (177) | 47.8[b] (185) |
| Not active in any organization | 42.8[a] (227) | 42.7[a] (168) | No activities at all | 20.4[a] (108) | 12.7[b] (49) |
| Total | 100*** (530) | 100*** (393) | | 100*** (530) | 100*** (387) |

***$p < 0.001$; *$p < 0.05$; different letters denote significant differences at the $p < 0.05$ level between groups.

Source: Calculated from data from MYPLACE survey, western Germany 2012–13.

organizations disappear. Only within the older age group are significant differences between higher and lower educated detectable in the cluster for engagement in traditional political organizations. Accordingly, only slightly significant differences ($p < 0.1$) remain for the young people aged 20 years and over. For political activities also, the significant differences between the two levels of education interact with age. Differences remain only for the higher age group, when age is controlled for.

These results raise questions about what explains the differences identified. Why is it that formal organizations and activities are more attractive for older and highly educated males? Do the differences regarding engagement in elections (a form of formal politics) stem from young people's own involvement in different forms of organizations and activities? What are the advantages perceived by young people who are not engaged in formal political structures but in alternative forms of engagement? We seek to answer these questions by drawing on qualitative material from in-depth interviews and ethnographic case studies.

## Qualitative interviews: formal versus informal participation

The interviewees were asked about their engagement in alternative, informal political associations, such as politically oriented youth clubs or school/university project groups. Only a few of them were engaged in political, cultural or religious groups. More interest was expressed in youth clubs and single activities like demonstrations and many respondents described themselves as critical consumers. These forms of engagement seem to mesh with the everyday experiences of today's youth. Demonstrations were mentioned most often; almost every interviewee had participated in a demonstration. However, this does not mean that every respondent was convinced of the effectiveness of demonstrations. Some respondents (12 out of 60), who supported formal and alternative organizations and activities, explicitly expressed scepticism towards the effectiveness of demonstrations and partly corroborated this with their own experiences:

> *Interviewer*: What impressions did you get when demonstrating?
> *Benediktus*: Well, it is definitely kind of frustrating, because my impression is that it is never very successful. But I think it is still better to demonstrate than do nothing. [ ... ]
> *Interviewer*: What do you think are the reasons for demonstrations' lack of success?
> *Benediktus*: I guess there are different factors, but in educational politics, for instance, a demonstration of a few hundred or thousand people does not impress politicians too much, so they do not want to change anything. Or 'Stuttgart 21'[11] – that didn't bring the expected success because there are simply things or economic interests which are more important for politicians than people's opinions. (Benediktus, HB)

In this respect, many interviewees agreed on two points; namely that demonstrations did not influence politicians and thus were deemed to be ineffective. Nevertheless, they were considered to be a way of expressing one's opinions and thus respondents stressed that people should participate whenever a cause associated with a demonstration was important. Nonetheless, nine respondents (out of sixty) reported that they believed in the possibility of changing things by demonstrating. All these respondents were engaged in alternative organizations or activities, in most cases supplemented by formal activities.

Another topic of interest for young people is critical consumer behaviour. Forty of the sixty respondents were critical consumers when it came to buying food or clothing. Several factors were named as triggers for buying or boycotting certain products: supporting socially fair payment for regional farmers or workers in developing countries; concerns about health (for example, when preferring to buy organic fruit) and observing 'political correctness'. However, since fair trade products are generally more expensive than the alternatives, many potential critical consumers could not afford to support this kind of political activity. Twenty two respondents (members of all organizational and activity clusters) admitted to not being critical consumers for financial reasons, personal convenience or ignorance.

Hence, among the alternative, informal ways of expressing political opinions there were two that captured the interviewees' interest: demonstrations; and

*The Sociological Review*, 63:S2, pp. 118–140 (2015), DOI: 10.1111/1467-954X.12265

consumer behaviour. Interestingly, many young people participated in demonstrations even though they were not convinced of their effectiveness. In contrast, consumer boycotts and buycotts were perceived to be effective by most respondents and were practised by two-thirds of the in-depth interviewees.

As far as traditional forms of engagement are concerned, most of the interviewees talked about elections in a positive manner; they enjoyed participating in elections as they perceived them to be an effective way of influencing politics. This was especially true when the elections they reported on were regional elections involving familiar politicians elected by a smaller number of voters than in general elections. In these cases, the interviewees felt able to make a real difference by voting. Similarly, participating in national or EU elections was evaluated positively, though many stated that their single vote would disappear in the mass of voters. However, many interviewees emphasized that it was not acceptable to them when people who did not participate in elections complained about the outcome afterwards. Moreover, participating in elections was considered important because voting for any (moderate) party decreased the share of votes for extremist parties:

> *Interviewer*: What was it like for you [participating in an election]?
> *Jennifer*: I liked it because many people say that they don't vote, which I don't understand, because at the end of the day they complain about politics, about what they [politicians] do wrong. I think it is important to participate in elections to prevent the wrong parties from getting into power. So you can say, 'I played my part in establishing the government as we have it now'. (Jennifer, BHV)

Nevertheless, a range of reasons for not voting were cited by six respondents: none of the political parties fully represents the respondent's personal interests (four respondents); lack of interest in elections (one respondent); and a lack of trust in the election process (one respondent). With one exception (a person engaged in formal and alternative organizations), none of these six respondents who stayed away from the ballot box supported any form of political organization. All in all, the in-depth interviews revealed a high level of conviction that voting was effective. This result is supported by the quantitative data demonstrating that 64 per cent of respondents chose one of the three highest trust values on an 11-point-scale when it comes to evaluating the efficacy of voting (84 per cent chose a value higher than 5, which was a neutral value).

Finally, we analysed respondents' opinions towards party membership as a stand-in for their attitudes towards traditionally organized political engagement. According to Table 3, and other studies including the Shell Youth Study (Shell Deutschland Holding, 2010), only a minority of young people were engaged in traditional political organizations. None of the in-depth interviewees was a party member at the time of the interview, nor had they been at any time in the past. However, at least 11 interviewees out of 60 said that they could imagine future party membership and highlighted positive aspects connected with it, above all, having the chance to directly advance their own views:

*The Sociological Review*, 63:S2, pp. 118–140 (2015), DOI: 10.1111/1467-954X.12265

> Well, for me personally it is not always enough to talk about it [politics] with friends. I would like to participate and be a part of expressing and forming a party's opinion. (Ronny, BHV)

This statement illustrates that some young people believe in the effectiveness of traditional political organizations. Nevertheless, there are factors that keep the majority from becoming a member of a party's youth section. Fourteen of our interviewees, for instance, argued that party membership would be too time consuming and they would feel obliged to be always informed about current political discussions. A further 16 respondents said that they could not join a party as there was no party that they fully agreed with:

> Well, yes [...] parties are somehow [...] I cannot identify with any party one hundred per cent. I think you would do better to become a member of an organisation, the trade union or whatever, if you have specific interests. In my view, parties are much too abstract and extensive. (Elisabeth, HB)

Some respondents also remarked that they were not sufficiently interested in politics to join a party. In total, 45 respondents gave arguments *against* becoming a party member, while only 11 respondents cited positive aspects of party membership.

A further reason for withdrawing from traditional politics – given by more than one-third of the interviewees – was that they did not perceive any differences between the governing parties. Thus, when considering the obstacles to young people's engagement in traditional party politics, the MYPLACE results point towards a perception that politics fails to represent youth interests. Other reasons for the low proportion of young party members include lack of time or lack of interest in intensive engagement.

When young people turn away from traditional political engagement, while still wanting to be politically involved, what makes them feel more comfortable in joining alternative organizations like youth clubs? We conducted two ethnographic case studies to explore the differences between traditional (relatively unpopular) and alternative (relatively popular) forms of engagement.

Comparing the ethnographic case studies with the findings from the qualitative interviews, quite similar narratives about politicians and political parties emerge. Members from the alternative football fan group AntiDis AG and the trade union IGM Youth displayed a general disenchantment with formal politics and distance from politicians. They explained this with the same reasoning as described in the previous passages. In each group, by far the majority of the respondents complained about the lack of credibility of political parties and politicians. This lack of credibility was explained by the power-obsessed behaviour widespread among politicians who were first and foremost concerned with winning votes and, to achieve this, they gave empty promises.

Narratives about their own engagement and positive experiences in their groups shed light on the (imagined) shortcomings of political party youth sections. For instance, one respondent noted that the absence of hierarchical

132

structures was one of the most positive features of working in the alternative group AntiDis AG. In line with this, almost half of the AntiDis AG members stated that it was the system of authority, with its pressure to adapt to rigid political programmes, that prevented politicians from taking effective and innovative action.

> Basically, it is democratic but I find it quite [...] it is kind of an authoritarian system, where one quickly gets excluded if you question things – also from the leadership. [...] Following in such an unquestioning fashion is just the wrong way. One must be able to question things at any time. (Paul, AGF)

The aversion to strict hierarchical decision-making was not limited to alternative youth groups. IGM members too continuously highlighted the leeway that they had in their engagement both within the structures of the IGM (implementation of 'modern' ideas with regard to demonstrations) and within the structures of the companies. Despite their trainee positions, they stressed that they had considerable scope for action as active trade union members in their companies' structures (for example, the right to say something critical in front of the training officer, influence decisions concerning trainees, etc.). Thus, even in associations with seemingly strict hierarchical structures young people appreciated their freedom of action and were motivated by this independence from hierarchical constraints.

To understand the factors that render traditional trade union youth sections more attractive for their members than political organizations, we might consider the ways in which young people from both groups began their engagement in the groups. In most cases, the interviewees reported 'having been found by the group' rather than having been on the search for it themselves. In the AntiDis AG, nearly all members stated that they joined the group after they heard about it from friends or other fans. Similarly, the IGM Youth members said that other trainees or direct trade union campaigns had attracted them to become members of the group. Political parties had failed to do this for respondents. One interviewee was once '[...] asking for information about what was going on in my neighbourhood. But there was nobody who would say, 'Just drop by and join us' or something like that' (Danny, IGM). This suggests that young people are looking for more professionalism combined with personal attention: 'Maybe the parties should really try to approach young people' (Richard, IGM).

It was not only the failed or missed approach by politicians to young people that was criticized. Another respondent referred to the protracted political processes and the delayed results: 'Politics is a field that does not necessarily fit young people. Because young people do not really have the calmness to sit down, to talk about something, to discuss it and, only after two years then, to have a solution' (IGM, Andree). Often, it is the endless discussions – which are *not* followed by direct activities – that demotivate young people from participating in traditional political organizations.

The interviewees from both groups explained that if engagement had a visible reference to their everyday lives and to their interests and attitudes, then they would be more inclined to engage. As one member put it: 'I mean it is also an attitude that I stand for. And if I can implement it in the group then I would actually do it with pleasure' (Luke, IGM).

Obviously, what young people liked about their engagement in the IGM Youth and AntiDis AG was the possibility of *direct* engagement in clearly structured activities where results could be perceived within a short period of time.

Not only the alternative group but also the young trade union members' ideas of democracy and decision-making appear to differ considerably from the characteristics of a functioning parliamentary government system. Thus, relatively well-organized parties, qualified political representatives and disciplined party fractions within parliament actually discourage young people from engaging.

However, despite the similarities, the ethnographic results reveal considerable differences between the two forms of engagement that indicate the existence of 'two worlds' of participation. Contrary to the alternative AntiDis AG, which displays a very low level of trust in political parties and an aversion to the perceived non-functioning of democracy, the trade union youth group presents itself as open to cooperation with political parties. Moreover, members from the IGM Youth expressed considerably more trust in the democratic system in Germany and displayed a clearer understanding of, and a greater insight into, the structures and processes of democracy because their own organizational structure resembles the formal conditions of politics.

Being against the political system, the alternative group tried to influence politics and society on a *parallel* level through their own demonstrations and activities. The trade union members, on the other hand, considered their focused engagement as *complementary* to politics. Thus, a gap between the two forms of participation becomes visible on the operational level.

The *reach* of the two forms of engagement also means they have a differential impact at the level of political processes. The groups' impact on decision-making processes at the democratic *nation-wide* level was reported only by the traditional IGM Youth. Its respondents referred more often to the nation-wide effects of their activities. In particular, they referred to the demonstration campaign 'Operation Hiring' in Cologne and its subsequent project 'Revolution Education',[12] both organized by the Youth Section and supported by the 'adult' trade union full-time officers. These campaigns were reported to be not only community-enhancing and identity-strengthening, but first and foremost effective on the nation-wide level by having a high impact on labour law and educational policy. This success was ascribed to the German-wide organization of the IGM Youth and its effective networking with diverse institutions.

The alternatively organized AntiDis AG, on the other hand, did not establish a direct link between its engagement and members' work lives or employment aspirations. A direct effect on political decision-making processes was not mentioned. Media resonance was most frequently mentioned as a marker of success. For instance, the fact that their stadium choreography against homophobia had been reported in the media was considered evidence that this had been a successful activity. However, while such action may well have an indirect impact on

*The Sociological Review*, 63:S2, pp. 118–140 (2015), DOI: 10.1111/1467-954X.12265
© 2015 The Authors. Editorial organisation © 2015 The Editorial Board of the Sociological Review

society and politics, in the sense that it transmits a political message, it lacks efficacy at the level of political decision-making.

This group had been successful in raising awareness of diverse forms of discrimination and thereby had an impact on society. The effects of the activities, however, had only a regional reach even though their network to other similar groups operated on a German-wide level. The strong non-hierarchical orientation of this kind of alternative group did not fit with the demands of the (hierarchical) structure of a parliamentary democracy with a strongly organized decision-making process.

*Combining quantitative and qualitative data: new insights*

The survey data allowed us to distinguish different preferences for political engagement available to young people in contemporary Germany's democratic structures and institutions. Respondents fell into four subgroups, which we describe as those engaged in: formal participation; alternative participation; formal *and* alternative participation; or no participation at all. Survey data also revealed that formal political participation is above all attractive to well-educated, males and young people aged 20 years and older while alternative participation attracts more females and young people aged 16 to 19.

The qualitative material employed in the analysis allowed us to explore further the reasons for these preferences. In the course of interviews and ethnographic case studies, young people expressed their views on the effectiveness and benefits of, and barriers to, different forms of engagement, lending new insight into young people's understanding of political participation in Germany. These qualitative data indicate that young people perceive different forms of participation to have different impacts on decision-making processes. While formal participation is felt to have more influence on politics, alternative participation offers greater opportunity for direct engagement although has less impact on decision-making processes. The qualitative data from the MYPLACE project thus suggest that the 'second world' of *alternative* political participation does not have the same reach as professionalized participation in traditional political organizations. Moreover, if the lack of embedding in political institutional structures is the reason for alternative groups' lower impact on political decision-making, then we might conclude that representative democracy's aim to involve people in policy-forming processes and the idea of a 'multiple democracy' (Nolte, 2011) is still to be achieved.

## Conclusions

Democracy in Germany now stands at a crossroads. It may either retain its representative shape (with some minor reforms)and risk the insidious alienation of (young) people, or it may opt for implementing substantial change to the existing structures and institutions in a way that better reflects young people's understanding of political participation.

The existing political culture favours the professionalization of participation and offers little space for integrating non-conventional engagement in decision-making processes. Both past research and our data demonstrate that young Germans are generally interested in political issues and are committed to the principles of democracy. However, their narratives on how they regard and define politics and participation, as well as how they perceive democracy and voting, show that there is a gap between their preferred modes of formal and informal engagement and the decision-making authorities. Our empirical evidence distinguishes three groups of young people with regard to political participation:

· Those who are engaged in traditional organizations and who display more insight into and understanding of democratic processes. They comprehend and accept that democratic decision-making requires time and that results cannot be achieved immediately.
· In contrast, young people engaged in alternative organizations often lack patience with traditional political structures and are less convinced of the efficacy of traditional politics.
· Finally, disengaged young people do not believe in the efficacy of any form of engagement. They participate in elections but mostly out of a sense of civic duty.

Considering these groups of (dis)engaged young people, the question arises as to how these groups will develop in the future and the significance of this for democracy. We argue that the most important function of social and political participation is social integration and social support of, and by, others. Such integration may take place through sports clubs, youth fire brigades or other organizations which have no apparent political level but which can raise awareness in society or even influence decision-making processes in the diverse spheres of society and the political system (see Gaiser *et al.*, 2010). However, it is crucial to note that the two different forms of engagement must have equal access to formal politics and decision-making institutions. If young people are confident in the efficacy of their own engagement, they are more motivated to participate in politics. Moreover, young people need some sense that their political activities have a tangible connection to their everyday lives and to their interests and attitudes in order to be actively engaged.

Currently, the requirements of representative democracy, with its party-oriented decision-making, and the forms of civic engagement favoured by (a minority of) young people, rooted in diverse youth cultures, constitute two parallel working systems. It is true that while democracy, in the context of modernity, finds itself embroiled in increasingly complex procedures that render democratic processes ineffective (Blühdorn, 2013), it also offers many more tools and possible forms of intervention than any previous traditional representative democracy (Habermas, 1981). However, the constitution of a parliamentary democracy such as that found in Germany fosters tendencies towards *professionalized* participation by its citizens. For a functioning parliamentary governmental system,

*The Sociological Review*, 63:S2, pp. 118–140 (2015), DOI: 10.1111/1467-954X.12265

relatively well-organized parties, qualified political representatives and disciplined party fractions within the parliament are essential. Our evidence demonstrates that this political culture fosters *parallel worlds* where, on the one side, there are the state-approved regulated and traditional forms of engagement, with qualified members, and, on the other side, there is a small minority of young people who actively engage, rather, in projects and institutions (and moreover a larger number of youths who passively support these kinds of participation) that display a form of self-organization that is distant from patterns of conventional political engagement. Moreover, this split between association-lobbyism and 'unprofessional activism' is currently not bridged by new elements of direct democracy.

Thus, based on the empirical data, we suggest that representative democracy needs to be more permeable in order to allow young people from all fields to have direct access to decision-making institutions. Moreover, a serious dialogue needs to be established and fostered between the 'two worlds' of formal and traditional fields of engagement by politicians themselves. Particularly at local level this venture appears to be reasonable, since on the local level it affects the needs and interests of young people more directly and effectively. These developments could lead to a 'realistic' (Rosanvallon, 2008) *modernization* of democracy that allows young people *to be part* of decision-making processes among broader forms of participation.

*Communication* (Habermas, 1981) could be a key tool to bridging the gap between these two parallel worlds. However, since communication and dialogue is always driven by an imbalance of power between participating actors (Weber, 1973), the less powerful actor (in this case, young people) should not only be guaranteed legal access to the decision-making institutions of a liberal democracy, but be given proactive encouragement by wider society (eg elites, parents, teachers). Each society should consider the significance of social inclusion, in a wider sense; this implies that social integration (of young people) is as important for a liberal democracy as the engagement of (young) people in formal political structures.

The existence of these parallel worlds of political participation (alongside the professionalization of participation) has a number of potential outcomes. The first is a scenario in which we see a subtle de-democratization of the political system; the parliamentary governmental system would survive but with weak ties to the second (alternative) world of political participation. This would eventually result in the current system of political participation developing into an elite project and contributing to a 'crisis of democracy'. The second scenario is the slow incorporation of some tools of direct democracy into the current system of parliamentary democracy *and* a fundamental change in hitherto prevailing understandings of economic growth, environment and well-being. Insofar as the outcome of communication is more than a change in the formal-structural processes of representative democracy (it involves a change in political substance as well), this would tend more towards a dynamic modernization of representative democracy.

Though the current system of political participation tends more towards an elite project, in the long run the second scenario seems more likely. There is a strong chance of modernizing liberal democracy and reconciling these parallel worlds, because – according to our empirical data – the majority of young people in Germany support the basic ideas of democracy while cross-country analysis of MYPLACE data shows respondents in German locations to be the most positively oriented to liberal democracy (see contributions to this volume by Pollock *et al.* and Grimm and Pilkington). Bridging the gap between the parallel worlds through a reasonable implementation of new forms of social and political participation by young people offers the prospect, therefore, of the dynamic modernization of democracy.

This would fit into Karl Mannheim's model of the 'generative renewal of societies' (1928), which means that processes of modernity could better be explained by referring to the generational affiliation of different social actors.

## Notes

1 For instance, the Servicestelle Jugendbeteiligung, available at: http://www.servicestelle-jugendbeteiligung.de/grundlagen/ or the Zentrum für Eigenständige Jugendpolitik, available at: http://www.allianz-fuer-jugend.de/Autorenbeitraege/Eine-Eigenstaendige-Jugendpolitik-fuer-Deutschland/461d10/ (accessed 3 December 2014).

2 The trend is not limited to Germany. Research in the UK and Australia has demonstrated that, compared to older people, young people tend to be less interested in formal politics, be less likely to vote or be a member of a political party member or to display high political knowledge (Furlong and Cartmel, 2007; Harris *et al.*, 2010).

3 CAPI stands for computer-assisted personal interview and describes a personal interview situation with an interviewer directly typing in the respondent's answers with the help of a laptop.

4 As detailed in the Introduction to this volume, locations in countries were selected on the basis of contrasting socio-demographic indicators. In this case, the more prosperous districts of the city of Bremen were chosen to contrast the city of Bremerhaven, which is characterized by a much higher rate of unemployment, poorer infrastructure and poorer living conditions.

5 The list comprised all 16–25 year olds living in city districts that were chosen in advance in order to produce a contrast between more prosperous and more socially deprived locations. The lists were focused on persons instead of households and were extracted from the official population register.

6 Traditional political organizations comprise: political parties, trade unions, youth parliaments, student unions and neighbourhood associations.

7 Alternative organizations include environmental, peace, human rights, cultural, women's, anti-globalization, religious organizations, youth fire brigade and youth clubs.

8 As formal political activities we used volunteering in an election campaign, contacting politicians, giving political speeches, donating money to a political group, and voting in student union elections.

9 Non-formal political activities comprise: attending public political/social meetings, signing petitions, collecting signatures, distributing leaflets, boycotting/buycotting products, writing messages on walls/graffiti, wearing political badges, participating in demonstrations and strikes, writing political articles, writing/forwarding political letters/emails, participating in violent events, occupying buildings/streets, participating in a flashmob, uploading political material.

10 Demonstrations by German school students are a common part of the regular curriculum and start in early years. The participation as such and the single activities and preparations for it are

*The Sociological Review*, 63:S2, pp. 118–140 (2015), DOI: 10.1111/1467-954X.12265

decided by individual teachers or by the school administration. Since pupils are released from school lessons during the demonstrations, participation is obligatory.
11 Stuttgart 21 is a railway and urban development project in Stuttgart, Germany. Since 2009, numerous protests against the disputed project have taken place. On 30 September 2010, hundreds of demonstrators were injured when the police used water cannons, pepper spray and batons against protestors.
12 The 'Operation Hiring' (Ger.: *Operation Übernahme*) was about securing the employment of apprentices after their apprenticeship by the companies. This campaign was completed successfully in 2012–13, with agreements for the employment of almost 100 per cent of young people by their training companies. In 2013–14, the so-called 'Revolution Education' (Ger.: *Revolution Bildung*) addressed the issue of the need to improve the poor educational situation at universities, colleges and in schools (see http://www.operationuebernahme.de/ and http://www.revolutionbildung.de/).

# References

Bakhtin, M., (1981), 'The dialogue imagination: four essays', in M. Holquist (ed.), *Dialogism*, Austin, TX: University of Texas Press.
Bakker, T. P. and de Vreese, C. H., (2011), 'Good news for the future? Young people, Internet use, and political participation', *Communication Research*, 38: 451–470.
Beck, U., Giddens, A. and Lash, S., (1996), *Reflexive Modernisierung. Eine Kontroverse*, Frankfurt am Main: Suhrkamp Verlag.
Blühdorn, I., (2013), *Simulative Demokratie*, Berlin: Suhrkamp Verlag.
Castells, M., (1997), *The Information Age: Economy, Society, and Culture*, 3 vols, Oxford and Malden, MA: Blackwell.
Crouch, C., (2004), *Post-democracy*, Cambridge: Polity Press.
Croizier, M., Huntington, S. and Watanuki, J., (1975), *The Crisis of Democracy. Report on the Governability of Democracies, to the Trilateral Commission*, New York: New York University Press.
della Porta, D. and Rucht, D. (eds.) (2013), *Meeting Democracy: Power and Deliberation in Global Justice Movements*, Cambridge: Cambridge University Press.
Eilfort, M., (1994), *Die Nichtwähler: Wahlenthaltung als Form des Wahlverhaltens*, Paderborn: Schöningh Verlag.
Embacher, S., (2009), *Demokratie! Nein Danke*, Bonn: Verlag J. H. W. Dietz.
Furlong, A. and Cartmel, F., (2007), *Young People and Social Change, New Perspectives*, 2nd edn, Berkshire: Open University Press.
Gaiser, W., de Rijke, J. and Spannring, R., (2010), 'Youth and political participation – empirical results for Germany within a European context', *Young*, 18 (9): 427–450.
Habermas, J., (1973), *Legitimationsprobleme im Spätkapitalismus*, Frankfurt am Main: Suhrkamp Verlag.
Habermas, J. (1981), *Theorie des kommunikativen Handelns*, Frankfurt am Main: Suhrkamp Verlag.
Hardt, M. and Negri, A., (2013), *Demokratie! Wofür wir kämpfen*, Frankfurt am Main/New York: Campus Verlag.
Harris, A., Wyn, J. and Younes, S., (2010), 'Beyond apathetic or activist youth: "ordinary"' young people and contemporary forms of participation', *Young*, 18 (1): 9–32.
Henn, M., Weinstein, M. and Wring, D., (2002), 'A generation apart? Youth and political participation in Britain', *British Journal of Politics and International Relations*, 4 (2): 167–192.
Hurrelmann, K. and Albrecht, E., (2014), *Die heimlichen Revolutionäre*, Weinheim/Basel: Beltz Verlag.
Mannheim, K., (1928), 'Das Problem der Generationen', *Kölner Vierteljahreshefte für Soziologie*, 7 (2): 157–184.
Manning, N., (2010), 'Tensions in young people's conceptualisation and practice of politics', *Sociological Research Online*, 15 (4): 11.
Mill, J., (2008 [1861]), *Considerations on Representative Government*, New York: Cosimo Classics.

Nolte, P., (2011), 'Von der repräsentativen zur multiplen Demokratie', *Aus Politik und Zeitgeschichte*, 1-2: 5–12.

Riley, S., Morey, I. and Griffin, C., (2010), 'The "pleasure citizen": analysing partying as a form of social and political participation', *Young*, 18 (1): 33–54.

Rosanvallon, P., (2008), *La Légitimité démocratique*, Paris: Éditions du Seuil.

Rucht, D. (2008), *Die sozialen Bewegungen in Deutschland seit 1945*, Frankfurt am Main and New York: Campus Verlag.

Rucht, D., (2011), *Bürgerprotest in der Parteiendemokratie*, Presentation at Akademie für Politische Bildung Tutzing (8 November, unpublished).

Schäfer, A., (2013), 'Wahlbeteiligung und Nichtwähler', *Aus Politik und Zeitgeschichte*, 63 (48-49): 39–46.

Shell Deutschland Holding, (2010), *Jugend 2010. Eine pragmatische Generation behauptet sich*, Bonn: Bundeszentrale für politische Bildung.

Smith, A., Thomas, T. and Holmwood, J., (2013), 'Sociologies of moderation', *Sociological Review*, 61: 6–17.

Stolle, D., Hooghe, M., and Micheletti, M., (2005), 'Politics in the supermarket: political consumerism as a form of political participation', *International Political Science Review*, 26: 245–269.

Streek, W., (2013), *Gekaufte Zeit. Die vertagte Krise des demokratischen Kapitalismus*, Frankfurter Adorno-Vorlesungen, Berlin: Suhrkamp Verlag.

Weber, M., (1973), *Wirtschaft und Gesellschaft*, Tübingen, J.C.P. Mohr (Paul Siebeck).

Zakaria, F., (2013), 'Can America be fixed? The new crisis of democracy', *Foreign Affairs*, January–February.

Zürn, M., (2013), 'Die schwindende Macht der Mehrheiten. Warum Legitimationskonflikte in der Demokratie zunehmen', *Wissenschaftszentrum Berlin-Mitteilungen*, 139: 10–13.

*The Sociological Review*, 63:S2, pp. 118–140 (2015), DOI: 10.1111/1467-954X.12265

# Populism, ideology and contradiction: mapping young people's political views

*Gary Pollock, Tom Brock and Mark Ellison*

**Abstract:** Forms of populism have long been a component of modern political discourse and systems where democracy relies upon popular legitimacy. There is, however, an uneasy relationship between some widely held views of 'the people' and the parties which seek to govern them. Contemporary academic and political discourse on populism often equates these views with right-wing politics, whilst some radical scholars, suggest that these views, whilst controversial, are nonetheless examples of democratic expression. Using survey evidence from 14 European countries, we show that young people take up a mixture of political positions, some of which are strongly associated with indices of populism – cynicism, authoritarianism, nativism, xenophobia – others of which do not map neatly onto the typical 'left-right' spectrum. We find evidence that some young people hold contradictory, often conflicting political viewpoints, which are reflective of the historical and cultural contexts of each location rather than of a 'populist' ideology. Where some theorists might use the term 'populism' pejoratively to denote a poorly and emotively grounded political ideology, we argue that this description denies its democratic legitimacy, as evidence suggests that young people draw on populist rhetoric to articulate views that are more reflective of local and regional concerns.

**Keywords:** populism, politics, young people, ideology, contradiction, democracy

## Introduction

The rise of political parties described as 'populist' has been widespread throughout Europe in recent years. In many countries such parties now represent a more significant force, in terms of electoral success, than at any time since the end of World War II. Over the past twenty years populism has become a structural feature of most European party political systems, arguably constituting a new party type across the political spectrum (Zaslove, 2008). As such, it has been suggested that it represents a fundamental challenge to contemporary democracy (Pinelli, 2011). Parties classified as 'populist' have been able to take significant numbers of MPs away from mainstream parties and in some countries they are able to

*The Sociological Review*, 63:S2, pp. 141–166 (2015), DOI: 10.1111/1467-954X.12266
© 2015 The Authors. Editorial organisation © 2015 The Editorial Board of the Sociological Review. Published by John Wiley & Sons Ltd, 9600 Garsington Road, Oxford OX4 2DQ, UK and 350 Main Street, Malden, MA 02148, USA

enter into ruling coalition governments such as the Freedom Party in Austria 2000 to 2005. In some cases, the effect of this has been that populist parties now influence mainstream parties in their policy programme development (Jennings, 2011). This paper does not seek to explain why this has been the case; such an explanation would require a nuanced analysis of both the supply- and demand-related factors within any local historical context. It suggests, however, that the preconditions for such shifts in the political landscape can be illuminated through the exploration of empirically demonstrable demand-related beliefs.

Much of the voluminous literature on populism discusses conceptual issues in an attempt to clarify precisely what is under analysis. Early work on populism shows a concern with a phenomenon which is regarded as orthogonal to the left-right spectrum (Worsley, 1969; Laclau, 1979). Understood thus, forms of populism have been seen as central to movements dedicated to promoting political developments that are of benefit to parts of the population in regions where large swathes feel the government is not representative of their concerns.

The extension of voting rights to wider society during the early parts of the twentieth century broadened the content of politics beyond the sectoral interests of elites in society. The roots of these changes, of course, lie in developments from the previous century such that change was gradual with no teleological trajectory (Tilly, 2004). There is no inevitable structure and trajectory for democracies, rather, they are built upon local and regional struggles, compromises and hegemonies, which means that the pace and type of politics that emerges is tied to cultural components that cannot be ignored (see, for example, Kopstein and Reilly, 2000).

Despite this local specificity, the element of populism that is most accepted as a core conceptual feature is its association with forms of anti-elitism and a cynicism towards those who are responsible for government. This can be seen in the works of Canovan (1999) and Laclau (2005), for whom, 'populism', refers to ways that *individuals* express their unfulfilled political demands *collectively* in the face of established structures of power and authority and dominant ideas and cultural values. Thus, for both, populism is intricately tied to issues of representation and democracy, as the people's concerns are a necessary part of the democratic process and must be heard. They differ on the extent to which populism is a good thing; Canovan refers to populism as the 'shadow' of democracy on more than one occasion, for example (1999: 3, 10, 16). Nonetheless, there is no pejorative connotation here; populism is still considered a legitimate component of political discourse if not its central element.

There is another tradition, however, whose tone can be said to create folk devils of those who subscribe to positions which are commonly referred to as populist. Ruzza (2009: 87), for example, suggests that the emergence of an uncivil society can be attributed to the 'anti-modern' thinking of political actors, whose 'territorial' and 'culturally exclusionist' behaviour render them populist and, ultimately, undemocratic. Other arguments that place populism in opposition to democracy can be found also in the work of Bale (2013), Baggini (2013) and Fieschi (2004).

*The Sociological Review*, 63:S2, pp. 141–166 (2015), DOI: 10.1111/1467-954X.12266

In *Hatred of Democracy*, Jaques Rancière (2006: 80) points to the potential dangers and agendas that reside behind this academic dismissal of populist views. He writes that the term 'populism' is often used as a rhetorical strategy that silences dissent in relation to the prevailing consensus; the 'oligarch', as he calls it, of social and political science, works to govern without people, that is, 'without any dividing of the people; to govern without politics'. The implication of this, for Rancière is that if science cannot impress its vision of progress upon the people, then those people are dismissed as 'ignorant', 'backward' and attached to a past that is no longer in keeping with what the experts consider to be legitimate. Indeed, it is interesting that so little of the contemporary discourse is open to the possibility of populism *as* politics where populism is a form of political praxis (Laclau, 2005; Jansen, 2011), or of populism as a phenomenon that may exist comfortably on the left as well as the right (Deiwiks, 2009; March, 2011; Moffit and Tormey, 2014).

The divergent perspectives on populism stem from uncertainties over how to define its boundaries. For example, Brett (2013) describes populism as a 'stretched concept', having been adapted by different researchers for different purposes. According to Brett (2013: 410), populism has been used by academics, policy-makers and politicians as a synonym for 'popularity' or to denote a wide range of political positions from 'violent racism to agrarian socialism'. The term has been used also to refer to 'democratic argument' (Painter, 2013) indicating the need to recognize that populism is as much a form of rhetoric, than strictly an ideological position. Indeed, populism refers to the rule of the people and, thus, implicitly acknowledges the need for democratic debate and struggle. Similarly, the literature is divided over the extent to which populism is a problem for democracy; while some see it as a destabilizing influence on political institutions others view it as a component capable of engaging the wider population in political debate (Vasilopoulou *et al.*, 2014). Arguably, understandings of populism are bound to contemporary manifestations of democracy; an 'antagonistic discontinuity' between the two renders fruitless attempts to close down populist discourse (Abts and Rummens, 2007).

We take as our starting point the need to objectively examine forms of populism as legitimate political positions within a pluralist discourse. According to Laclau and Mouffe (1985) social divisions are inherent in the very possibility of a democratic politics. One cannot simply erase from political discourse those positions or perspectives that one disagrees with. Such a move chimes with a blurring of the frontiers between left and right in recent decades, a move which has been regarded as positive (Giddens, 1994, 1998) but which has arguably undermined positive elements that radical and plural democratic forms of debate can take. Our understanding of that which is political is informed by Mouffe's work on agonism where she argues that there is a need for room within democracy for open debate where there is discursive space given to all positions within a system of broad toleration (Mouffe, 2000, 2005). Drawing on Schmitt's (1996) 'friend-foe' distinction, Mouffe argues that central to politics is the need to be able to passionately articulate *what* and *whom* you oppose with the consequence that to deny the possibility of this will on the one hand 'sanitize' politics, that is, make it dull and uninteresting and, on the other, will drive political passions elsewhere (Mouffe, 2002). Similarly, Canovan's (1999) work argues that there is a need to regard 'the people' and their concerns as legitimate. Unfortunately, she later undermines this claim, when, in her conclusion, she suggests that whilst the people's concerns are a necessary part of the democratic process, they may need to be kept in check to further the 'redemptive' character of democracy. Indeed this is something that is typical of contemporary academic discourse where the concerns of 'the people', whilst 'real' and 'legitimate' in their democratic expression, are viewed as undesirable and, ultimately, equated with right-wing politics (see Mudde, 2004, 2007).

As Laclau and Mouffe (1985) note, such political essentialism is problematic because it closes down the space to give sufficient attention to how an individual's politics reflects their struggle with structural positions that are local and specific. For Laclau and Mouffe these 'points of antagonism' take on different 'forms of struggle' as individuals develop political views that then allow them to interpret and respond to their structural positions within any given social formation. Of course, much of this thinking – about the value of autonomy and the importance of context – extends from Gramsci (1971) who suggested that counter-hegemonic forces should not concentrate their attack on a single front, against one seat of power, but, rather, should engage in a variety of progressive struggles according to its own contextually specific logic (Laclau and Mouffe, 1985). In other words, local struggles reflect contextually specific antagonisms that have provided the grounds for locally situated groups to organize into counter-hegemonic movements. For Laclau and Mouffe, the scale and scope of these struggles vary depending on whether the antagonisms are represented more broadly. Thus, a national movement may be considered 'local' in the sense that it reflects contextually specific concerns that need to be addressed. The important point of Laclau and Mouffe is that in focusing on context one reserves a space for plurality and autonomy among the elements for the creation of a counter-hegemonic bloc and this is central for the sort of innovation in tactics needed to respond effectively to the specificity of contemporary antagonisms (see Brock and Carrigan, 2014; also Smith, 2012).

This position is well supported in classical liberal texts (eg, Mill, 1972) but, more recently, in the arguments of John Keane (2009: 855), who argues that the democratic ideal is linked to an active commitment to 'pluriversality' – the need to 'empower people *everywhere*, so that they can get on with living their *diverse* lives on earth freed from the pride and prejudice of moguls, magnates, tyrants and tycoons' (emphasis added).

This is our point of departure. We look to research on young people's political views in 14 European countries to consider the important role that local and regional factors play in explaining the differences in views *between* these locales whilst also pausing to consider the contradictions that emerge *within* them. In other words, the empirical realities of young people's politics leads us to question the myth that the term 'populism' peddles: that ideology is a well-integrated

*The Sociological Review*, 63:S2, pp. 141–166 (2015), DOI: 10.1111/1467-954X.12266

system of beliefs that adequately pits the concerns of the 'ordinary people' against some other social group. Rather, we would suggest that populisms emerge to reflect the local and regional conditions that prompt young people to problematize concrete problems.

This is significant for us because we wish to challenge academic discourse that has a strong normative perspective and often denies open debate over the legitimacy of views it finds undesirable. In this discourse, it is widely understood that the propensity of the general population towards particular policies often described as populist is high but that the failure of so-called populist parties to mobilize this support is the reason why such views never actually reach the statute books (Mudde, 2007). Looking to the views of young people, we hope to show why such a conclusion necessarily implies possible power imbalances between how young people's political views are treated across Europe.

In a recent study of voters (Akkerman *et al.*, 2014), evidence suggests that populist views are associated with a propensity for voting for populist parties. While this may seem tautological, attitudes do not always translate into behaviour. The evidence examined in this paper contributes to the literature on the demand side of populism, through an engagement with individual views on four specific dimensions associated with both populism and the extreme right wing: xenophobia,[1] cynicism, authoritarianism and nativism. This four-dimensional representation of components of (right-wing) populism has been used elsewhere (Mudde, 2007; Harrison and Bruter, 2011). We argue that views expressed on these dimensions, whatever their content, are important indicators of the political concerns of these young people. We are interested in the extent to which views are independent of locale or are regionally specific and the extent to which dimensions of populism are associated with the left-right political spectrum, in particular its extremities. Finally, we are interested in the ideological coherence, or rather the lack of it, when it comes to young people's 'populist' views.

The article thus tests the following three hypotheses:

Hypothesis 1: that dimensions of populism are locally specific.
Hypothesis 2: that populist views are orthogonal to the left–right spectrum.
Hypothesis 3: that there are ideological contradictions associated with those regarded as possessing populist views.

## Data and methods

The MYPLACE questionnaire survey, explained in greater depth in the introduction to this volume is a common research instrument administered to a representative sample of 16–25 year olds in 30 separate locations in 14 different countries. The data was collected between September 2012 and April 2013, with an achieved overall sample of 16,935. Each country selected two contrasting locations (with four in Germany: two in the old East and two in the old West) where the criteria for selection was that there were a priori reasons to suggest that the attitudes, behaviour and experiences of the young people would be different. This means that we have a range of research sites, each with distinct features which are unique to themselves and which require an understanding of local as well as national contexts to fully appreciate the reasons why young people hold the attitudes that they do. It is important to reiterate that these are a series of local case studies and not nationally representative results.

Four indices representing the aforementioned dimensions of populism (xeno-phobia, cynicism, authoritarianism and nativism) are created using a range of questions from the MYPLACE survey. While our analysis is embedded within a critical engagement with previous empirical work on populism we do not reject the use of these widely accepted measures. Our aim is to better understand the dynamics which contribute to widespread support for such indices of populism and to explore the legitimacy of these beliefs in mainstream political discourse. The questions used to construct these indices are presented in the Appendix. All composite variables are justified on the basis of factor analysis, and internal relia-bility is measured using Cronbach's alpha or Pearson's $r$. All questions used were five-point Likert scales which were recoded to 0 to 4, summed and rescaled 0 to 1, with a high score representing high levels on each index (see the Appendix).

The central method used here to test the hypotheses are multilevel regression models (Hox, 2010; Heck *et al.*, 2010) as these models are best able to articulate the structure of the research design. The 30 different research sites are selected in order to maximize variability within each country and it is a reasonable assump-tion to anticipate variability between countries.

Four models are presented, one for each of the dimensions described above. Final models with a common set of individual and contextual variables are shown in order to facilitate comparability of predictor variables.

## Findings

The mean scores for each location on each of the four dimensions as well as the left–right scale are shown in Table 1 along with the overall grand mean. The dark shading indicates those locations which are in the upper quartile and the pale shading those that are in the lower quartile and thus highlight the locations where there are higher and lower average tendencies to have these views. Average levels of cynicism and nativism are high (0.692 and 0.705 respectively on a scale of 0 to 1), well above the centre of the scale, whereas the average for xenophobia (0.544) is towards the centre of the scale and for authoritarianism (0.344) it is much lower. Almost all these figures are within one standard deviation of the mean, the exceptions being both Danish sites on the cynicism index and three of the German sites (not Bremerhaven) on the xenophobia index. It is inappropriate to draw strong conclusions from these figures as they represent the mean scores for each location independent from any other variable and are therefore sensitive to the distribution of the index within the location. They are of interest, however, in terms of the magnitude of the scores on the cynicism and nativism indices, both of which are a clear indication of the general strength of views across the board on these issues. Harrison and Bruter (2011) find the same but are more

*The Sociological Review*, 63:S2, pp. 141–166 (2015), DOI: 10.1111/1467-954X.12266

**Table 1:** *Dimensions of populism by location, shaded figures are in top quartile (dark grey) and bottom quartile (light grey)*

| | Location | Xenophobia | Cynicism | Authoritarian | Nativism | Left-right |
|---|---|---|---|---|---|---|
| Croatia | Podsljeme | 0.625 | 0.740 | 0.537 | 0.711 | 0.51 |
| | Pescenica Zitnjak | 0.566 | 0.773 | 0.506 | 0.660 | 0.47 |
| Denmark | Odense East | 0.403 | 0.473 | 0.312 | 0.622 | 0.48 |
| | Odense Center | 0.391 | 0.432 | 0.249 | 0.628 | 0.48 |
| Estonia | Narva | 0.506 | 0.661 | 0.365 | 0.582 | 0.45 |
| | Tartu | 0.521 | 0.621 | 0.310 | 0.786 | 0.56 |
| Finland | Lieksa and Nurmes | 0.626 | 0.544 | 0.326 | 0.782 | 0.54 |
| | Kuopio | 0.426 | 0.481 | 0.199 | 0.670 | 0.51 |
| Georgia | Kutaisi | 0.620 | 0.607 | 0.565 | 0.807 | 0.59 |
| | Telavi | 0.627 | 0.603 | 0.486 | 0.810 | 0.62 |
| Germany (western) | Bremen | 0.296 | 0.675 | 0.114 | 0.621 | 0.38 |
| | Bremerhaven | 0.388 | 0.684 | 0.203 | 0.648 | 0.41 |
| Germany (eastern) | Jena | 0.267 | 0.656 | 0.095 | 0.595 | 0.38 |
| | Rostock | 0.312 | 0.673 | 0.143 | 0.628 | 0.39 |
| Greece | New Philadelphia | 0.671 | 0.857 | 0.296 | 0.828 | 0.45 |
| | Argyroupouli | 0.674 | 0.827 | 0.285 | 0.791 | 0.48 |
| Hungary | Sopron | 0.672 | 0.721 | 0.309 | 0.731 | 0.60 |
| | Ozd | 0.751 | 0.703 | 0.459 | 0.809 | 0.56 |
| Latvia | Agenskalns | 0.621 | 0.668 | 0.385 | 0.737 | 0.58 |
| | Forstate and Jaunbuve | 0.566 | 0.700 | 0.395 | 0.507 | 0.48 |
| Portugal | Lumiar | 0.543 | 0.747 | 0.398 | 0.771 | 0.48 |
| | Barreiro | 0.564 | 0.792 | 0.434 | 0.797 | 0.42 |
| Russia | Kupchino | 0.654 | 0.724 | 0.410 | 0.705 | 0.55 |
| | Vyborg | 0.691 | 0.730 | 0.418 | 0.806 | 0.63 |
| Slovakia | Rimavska Sobota | 0.638 | 0.745 | 0.411 | 0.697 | 0.55 |
| | Trnava | 0.702 | 0.758 | 0.345 | 0.801 | 0.55 |
| Spain | Vic | 0.470 | 0.767 | 0.193 | 0.571 | 0.32 |
| | Sant Cugat | 0.443 | 0.759 | 0.164 | 0.587 | 0.35 |
| UK | Coventry | 0.452 | 0.697 | 0.467 | 0.693 | 0.46 |
| | Nuneaton | 0.577 | 0.661 | 0.561 | 0.720 | 0.45 |
| | **grand mean** | **0.544** | **0.692** | **0.344** | **0.705** | **0.48** |
| | **SD of grand mean** | **0.231** | **0.215** | **0.259** | **0.205** | **0.23** |
| | **Upper quartile** | **0.635** | **0.747** | **0.430** | **0.790** | **0.55** |
| | **Lower quartile** | **0.445** | **0.657** | **0.258** | **0.628** | **0.45** |

*Source*: MYPLACE survey, 2012–13.

interested in regional variation as opposed to the absolute figure. Our belief is that the average magnitude is an important indicator of the breadth of populist views and as such shows that these dimensions, at least, must be regarded as central to personal political views and not some sort of aberration. It is also worth noting that all four German locations as well as both Danish ones have average scores below the grand mean on all four indices.

Each index is used as a dependent variable in a multilevel model and subject to analysis alongside a common set of independent variables. Table 2 shows that for all four models a multilevel model is justified and that in all cases there is significant improvement in the fit of the model as both individual level and location specific variables are included.

When the average location scores for authoritarianism, nativism and xenophobia are plotted alongside cynicism there is further reinforcement of the locational and regional structure of our data. While these spatial positions are insensitive to individual associations between these variables, such that no strong conclusions can be made from them, there are hints that there may be country specific averages where the paired locations are close to one another such as the locations in Greece, Spain and Portugal. On the other hand there is also evidence of significant contrast between research locations within a country such as in the UK, Croatia and Latvia. These contrasts are a function of the choice of the research location, which sought to maximize within country contrasts.

*Multilevel models*

The importance of locally specific explanations is shown in two ways. First, the intra class correlations for all four models demonstrate that it would be inappropriate to treat the data set as unstructured. The analysis must take into account that there are 30 different locations as by doing so the predictive power of the models is significantly enhanced by between 19 per cent and 31 per cent (with xenophobia,[2] 31 per cent; cynicism,[3] 22 per cent; authoritarianism,[4] 26 per cent and nativism,[5] 19 per cent respectively). Secondly, the inclusion of the country-level variable indicating welfare state type (Esping-Andersen, 1990; Kääriäinen and Lehtonen, 2006) further improves the model in all cases and brings out a contrast between post-socialist countries and Nordic locations; the latter are less likely to be xenophobic, to display cynicism and authoritarian views. Similarly, respondents from German locations (a conservative welfare state region), when contrasted with post-socialist ones, are less likely to be xenophobic and authoritarian, although there is no significant difference in terms of cynicism. There is, however, a tendency for respondents in all four German locations (including those in what used to be East Germany) to be less nativist than in post-socialist countries. On this measure, eastern Germany is an outlier compared to other post-socialist countries. The other findings of significance in terms of welfare state regions is the contrast between Mediterranean locations and post-socialist ones where the former are more likely to display cynicism but less likely than Mediterranean locations to display authoritarian tendencies. Finally, our data

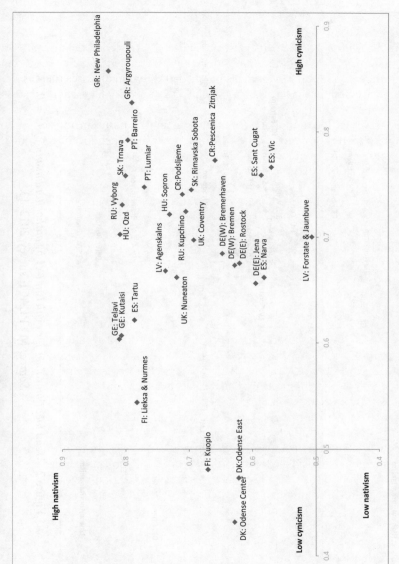

**Figure 1** *Mean location values for cynicism* $(x)$ *by nativism* $(y)$ $(r = 0.4203)$
*Source:* MYPLACE survey, 2012–13.

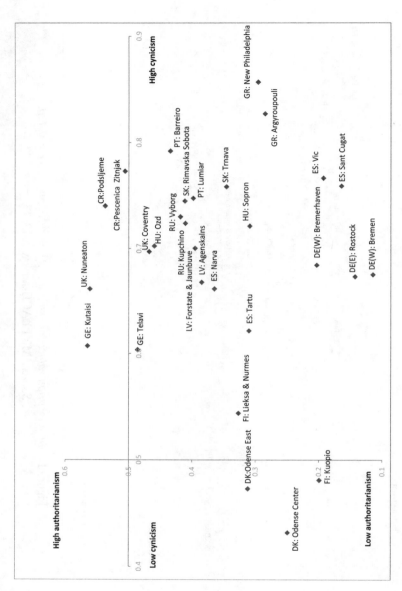

**Figure 2** *Mean location values for cynicism (x) by authoritarianism (y) (r = 0.132)*
*Source:* MYPLACE survey, 2012–13.

*The Sociological Review*, 63:S2, pp. 141–166 (2015), DOI: 10.1111/1467-954X.12266

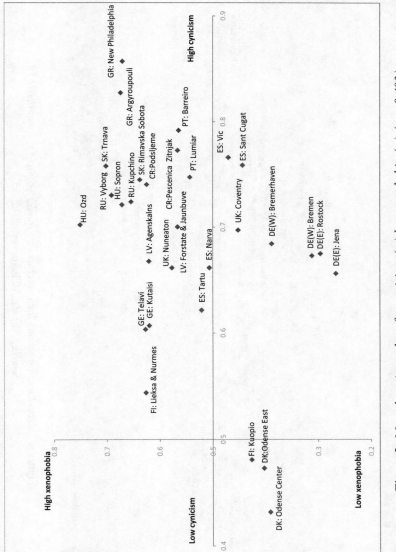

**Figure 3** *Mean location values for cynicism (x) by xenophobia (y) (r = 0.403)*
*Source:* MYPLACE survey, 2012–13.

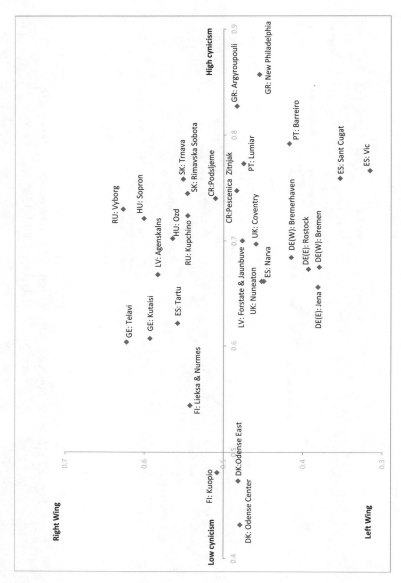

**Figure 4** *Mean location values for cynicism (x) by 'left-right' (y) (r=-0.181)*
*Source: MYPLACE survey, 2012–13.*

*The Sociological Review*, 63:S2, pp. 141–166 (2015), DOI: 10.1111/1467-954X.12266

**Table 2:** *Variance components of each model*

| | | Empty model (random intercept only) | With individual level explanatory variables | With country level explanatory variables |
|---|---|---|---|---|
| Xenophobia | $\sigma$ (individual level) | 0.0367 | 0.0339 | 0.0338 |
| | $\sigma$ (country level) | 0.0167 | 0.0105 | 0.0035 |
| | -loglikelihood | −5650.456 | −6441.071 | −6274.807 |
| Cynicism | $\sigma$ (individual level) | 0.0365 | 0.0324 | 0.0321 |
| | $\sigma$ (country level) | 0.0104 | 0.0048 | 0.0010 |
| | -loglikelihood | −5756.272 | −7073.288 | −929.860 |
| Authoritarianism | $\sigma$ (individual level) | 0.0482 | 0.0437 | 0.0429 |
| | $\sigma$ (country level) | 0.0172 | 0.0128 | 0.0072 |
| | -loglikelihood | −2242.700 | −3251.836 | −3437.508 |
| Nativism | $\sigma$ (individual level) | 0.0323 | 0.0300 | 0.0301 |
| | $\sigma$ (country level) | 0.0076 | 0.0061 | 0.0053 |
| | -loglikelihood | −7472.375 | −8208.362 | −7848.408 |

*Source*: MYPLACE survey, 2012–13.

showed no significant differences between the UK locations (liberal welfare state region) and the post-socialist ones.

Our second hypothesis, on the orthogonality between populism and the left–right spectrum, is tested using the question where respondents indicate where they are on a 0 to 10 scale. We have simplified this into four categories: 'clear[6] left' (scores 0–2); 'clear right' (scores 8–10); 'centre' (scores 3–7); and 'don't know' using the central 'between clear left and right' category as the reference. This variable is an indication of a personal position on a political scale allowing for expressions of extremity. Thirteen per cent of the distribution is 'clear left' and 11 per cent 'clear right' using this method.

The results show that there is a strong relationship between respondents' stated position on the left–right spectrum and their position on three of the four indices xenophobia, authoritarianism and nativism – with those on the clear right scoring high and the clear left scoring low. In terms of these three dimensions there is clear evidence that there is a relationship. On the third index on cynicism the findings are reversed with those on the left significantly more likely to be cynical and those on the right less likely, though this result is not significant. This complex picture can be interpreted to show that the hypothesis of independence between these four dimensions and the left–right spectrum cannot be fully supported. However, in terms of confirming or refuting a definition of populism focusing on anti-elitism – measured here by cynicism – it is possible to conclude that there is no association between those who say they are on the clear right (when compared to those in the centre of the political spectrum) and their cynicism. In fact, although the data are less clear, cynicism would appear to have the opposite political spectrum connotations compared to the other three dimensions. What it is possible to assert, therefore, is that because there is no differentiation between those on the clear right and those in the centre in terms of cynicism, equating cynicism with those on the right is incorrect.

The final hypothesis tests the extent to which we can see ideological coherence within the populism indices. This is measured using the respondents' answers to a question on different economic policies where what are traditionally understood as economically left-wing perspectives – 'Competition is harmful, it brings out the worst in people' and 'Incomes should be made more equal' – contrast with economically right-wing perspectives – 'The unemployed should have to take any job available or lose their unemployment benefits' and 'Private ownership of business and industry should be increased'. For three of the models the indices show that both the economically left- and right-wing variables are positively associated with high scores for xenophobia, authoritarianism and nativism. For all three of these models, respondents scoring highly display both left- and right-wing ideological preferences. For the cynicism index, however, there is a significant association between a high score and those supporting economically left-wing policies. We therefore feel that there is strong support for our hypothesis that when examining these four dimensions that these young people often hold positions which are contradictory in terms of traditionally understood economic ideologies.

When examining the individual level socio-demographic predictors, gender was significant, with males scoring higher than females and, therefore, more likely to display xenophobia, cynicism and authoritarianism tendencies. The age variable shows a negative significant effect; slightly older young people tend to score lower on the xenophobia, authoritarianism and nativism scales. However, the reverse is true with cynicism where the model suggests that young people at the upper end are more likely to be cynical than their younger counterparts. Parental social class is also significant; xenophobia, authoritarianism and nativism are negatively associated with higher social classes.

Respondents who are more 'pro-democratic' are less likely to display xenophobic, authoritarian and nativist views than those who are less 'pro-democratic'. However, the opposite is true with cynicism where young people who score highly on the pro-democracy index are more cynical. Young people who have higher levels of satisfaction with democracy in their country are significantly less cynical

*The Sociological Review*, 63:S2, pp. 141–166 (2015), DOI: 10.1111/1467-954X.12266
© 2015 The Authors. Editorial organisation © 2015 The Editorial Board of the Sociological Review

**Table 3:** *Multilevel models of xenophobia, cynicism, authoritarianism and nativism*

| | Model 1: Xenophobia n2 = 31, n1 = 12,435 | | Model 2: Cynicism n2 = 31, n1 = 12,484 | | Model 3: Authoritarianism n2 = 31, n1 = 12,303 | | Model 4: Nativism n2 = 31, n1 = 12,786 | |
|---|---|---|---|---|---|---|---|---|
| | B | SE | B | SE | B | SE | B | SE |
| *Individual-level predictors:* | | | | | | | | |
| Other | 0.034 | 0.093 | 0.052 | 0.060 | 0.126 | 0.070 | 0.057 | 0.115 |
| Unemployed | 0.062 | 0.078 | 0.031 | 0.051 | 0.072 | 0.059 | 0.094 | 0.098 |
| In education | −0.293*** | 0.055 | −0.019 | 0.036 | −0.366*** | 0.041 | −0.152* | 0.069 |
| Employed (Ref) | | | | | | | | |
| Male | 0.115** | 0.041 | 0.071** | 0.027 | 0.101** | 0.031 | 0.027 | 0.051 |
| Female (Ref) | | | | | | | | |
| Minority | −0.774*** | 0.062 | 0.035 | 0.040 | 0.123** | 0.046 | −0.992*** | 0.077 |
| Majority (Ref) | | | | | | | | |
| Class 0 (lowest) | 0.351*** | 0.056 | 0.038 | 0.036 | 0.273*** | 0.042 | 0.333*** | 0.070 |
| Class 1 | 0.345*** | 0.073 | 0.023 | 0.048 | 0.134* | 0.055 | 0.200* | 0.091 |
| Class 2 | 0.183* | 0.073 | 0.025 | 0.047 | 0.061 | 0.055 | 0.073 | 0.091 |
| Class 3 (highest)(Ref) | | | | | | | | |
| Left wing | −0.373*** | 0.061 | 0.157*** | 0.040 | −0.181*** | 0.046 | −0.603*** | 0.076 |
| Right wing | 0.606*** | 0.067 | −0.073 | 0.043 | 0.330*** | 0.050 | 0.646*** | 0.083 |
| Left-Right: Don't Know | 0.104 | 0.068 | 0.029 | 0.044 | 0.012 | 0.051 | −0.090 | 0.084 |
| Centre (Ref) | | | | | | | | |
| Age | −0.027** | 0.009 | 0.026*** | 0.006 | −0.048*** | 0.006 | −0.028** | 0.011 |

(*Continued*)

**Table 3:** *Continued*

| | Model 1: Xenophobia n2 = 31, n1 = 12,435 | | Model 2: Cynicism n2 = 31, n1 = 12,484 | | Model 3: Authoritarianism n2 = 31, n1 = 12,303 | | Model 4: Nativism n2 = 31, n1 = 12,786 | |
|---|---|---|---|---|---|---|---|---|
| | B | SE | B | SE | B | SE | B | SE |
| Political knowledge | -0.015 | 0.025 | 0.015 | 0.016 | -0.210*** | 0.019 | 0.050 | 0.031 |
| Satisfaction with life | -0.036** | 0.011 | -0.004 | 0.007 | -0.026** | 0.008 | 0.023~ | 0.014 |
| Trust in Parliament | -0.045*** | 0.010 | -0.140*** | 0.006 | 0.000 | 0.007 | 0.087*** | 0.012 |
| Pro-democracy index | -0.107*** | 0.015 | 0.066*** | 0.010 | -0.145*** | 0.011 | -0.051** | 0.018 |
| Satisfaction with democracy | -0.016 | 0.011 | -0.109*** | 0.007 | 0.005 | 0.008 | 0.091*** | 0.013 |
| Economically right-wing (take job) | 0.474*** | 0.044 | 0.021 | 0.028 | 0.223*** | 0.033 | 0.524*** | 0.054 |
| Economically-right wing (private ownership) | 0.204*** | 0.049 | -0.089** | 0.031 | 0.307*** | 0.036 | 0.341*** | 0.060 |
| Economically left-wing (Competition is harmful) | 0.189*** | 0.043 | 0.118*** | 0.028 | 0.395*** | 0.032 | -0.012 | 0.054 |
| Economically lef- wing (Incomes equal) | 0.228*** | 0.057 | 0.400*** | 0.037 | 0.107* | 0.043 | 0.117~ | 0.071 |
| Finding it financially difficult | 0.205*** | 0.054 | 0.104** | 0.035 | -0.027 | 0.040 | -0.005 | 0.067 |
| Interested in politics | -0.164*** | 0.044 | -0.006 | 0.029 | -0.204*** | 0.033 | -0.033 | 0.055 |
| Number of close friends from a different or minority group | -0.323*** | 0.027 | 0.029 | 0.018 | -0.019 | 0.020 | -0.243*** | 0.034 |

*(Continued)*

*The Sociological Review*, 63:S2, pp. 141–166 (2015), DOI: 10.1111/1467-954X.12266
© 2015 The Authors. Editorial organisation © 2015 The Editorial Board of the Sociological Review

**Table 3:** *Continued*

|  | Model 1: Xenophobia n2 = 31, n1 = 12,435 | | Model 2: Cynicism n2 = 31, n1 = 12,484 | | Model 3: Authoritarianism n2 = 31, n1 = 12,303 | | Model 4: Nativism n2 = 31, n1 = 12,786 | |
|---|---|---|---|---|---|---|---|---|
|  | B | SE | B | SE | B | SE | B | SE |
| *Contextual predictors:* | | | | | | | | |
| Nordic | −1.669*** | 0.409 | −1.290*** | 0.151 | −0.831* | 0.390 | −1.229~ | 0.669 |
| Conservative | −2.945*** | 0.407 | 0.049 | 0.149 | −1.646*** | 0.389 | −1.585* | 0.667 |
| Mediterranean | −0.534 | 0.350 | 0.418** | 0.128 | −0.746* | 0.334 | 0.262 | 0.574 |
| Liberal | −0.724 | 0.541 | −0.031 | 0.197 | 0.674 | 0.517 | 0.033 | 0.888 |
| Post-socialist (Ref) | | | | | | | | |
| *Constant* | 8.543*** | 0.310 | 5.369*** | 0.172 | 4.982*** | 0.258 | 10.972*** | 0.436 |

\*\*\**p* < 0.001, \*\**p* < 0.01, \**p* < 0.05, ~*p* < 0.1, two-tailed tests.
*Source:* MYPLACE survey, 2012–13.

and have higher levels of nativism. Respondents who have greater trust in parliament are significantly less likely to display xenophobia and cynicism tendencies and are also significantly more likely to display nativism tendencies.

## Discussion

This paper has begun to map out young people's political views across Europe using the MYPLACE survey data. The analysis suggests that young people take up a mixture of political positions, some of which are strongly associated with indices of 'populism' – cynicism, authoritarianism, nativism and xenophobia. What we have shown, in the first instance, is that there is a tendency for these positions to map on to locations where there are regional or political histories that support the shaping of these views. Thus, locations within western European welfare states are less likely to be authoritarian, nativist and xenophobic when compared to post-socialist countries. We find evidence to support the claim that post-socialist countries are more likely to be populist than modern welfare states.

However, we should approach the term 'populism' with some critical distance, for where research has, in the past, equated it with political extremes, we have sought to view it within the wider context of democratic struggle. We have done this by opening up the term 'populism' to explore (i) local and regional variations; (ii) the statistical independence of political cynicism; and (iii) ideological inconsistency. Rather than equate populism with either left- or right-wing ideology, we have tried to show that young people's political views are often plural and contradictory in nature. Young people's views do not always cohere into a single ideological project and this should be an understood and respected aspect of democracy (Rancière, 2006; Laclau, 2005).

While Mudde (2007) suggests that a focus on political parties is of greater importance than political attitudes in the extent to which they are able to mobilize views regarded as dangerous or inappropriate within contemporary democracy, we believe that it is important to study political views from a standpoint that accepts the legitimacy of individual viewpoints. It is arguably an indication of the failure of the contemporary democratic political system if the political views of people are regarded as secondary to an analysis of political parties. The danger here is obvious: that in focusing on political parties one closes down voices that seek to make difficult issues heard.

In mapping young people's political views, we find evidence to suggest that there is a variability/plurality of populisms that young people deploy, across Europe, to contend with social and political issues that are local and regional in scope. This makes it difficult to essentialize what populism constitutes as young people's views comprise a variety of ideological elements – often contradictory – and this is why location and regional factors must be considered. Evidence shows that there is an important macro element to the shaping of young people's political views and this should be acknowledged when describing manifestations of populism.

*The Sociological Review*, 63:S2, pp. 141–166 (2015), DOI: 10.1111/1467-954X.12266

*Why are location and regional factors important when mapping young people's political views?*

In approaching the term 'populism' from the perspective that it is a plurality, we have constructed a set of indices and tested them for local and regional variations, showing that young people's political views may be shaped by location and region. Thus, there is evidence to suggest that interesting similarities and differences occur *between* locations but also *within* locations. We would suggest that to attribute social, cultural and political contexts to explaining these differences would require further qualitative exploration. Yet, in opening up the possibility of local and regional variation, we suggest that there is evidence to support the argument that young people are voicing concerns that reflect their direct lived experiences.

This paper shows that many of the young people surveyed (indeed the majority in some regions) can be regarded as populist to the extent that there is a strong tendency to express a cynicism towards politicians and political institutions. The evidence is also clear that aggregate levels of nativism also tend to be quite high. On both dimensions, however, it is clear that there is a strong geographical pattern which must be understood within the political histories of the locations studied. At the same time we show the ways in which these young people are associated with further dimensions attributed to populism on the right wing. These often exist alongside an engagement in politics and political processes. These findings also demonstrate the importance of regional specificity; regions with similar historical trajectories and welfare regimes show similar patterns.

We believe our data supports our view that populism must be a plurality because it must recognize the many demands that popular subjects make in regard to local and regional issues. There is literature which suggests that political participation is geographically clustered and that citizens' participatory behaviour is heavily influenced by the behaviour of those who live in close proximity to them (Tam Cho and Rudolph, 2008; Kopstein and Reilly, 2000). Here, it is suggested that 'geographic diffusion' plays an important role in how norms, resources and institutions are diffused and how this leads to the construction of political democracies. Whilst it is not our intention to prove this claim, our evidence does highlight how locality influences young people's political views.

Following Laclau (2007), we suggest that until it is clear why these articulations (particular views) or representations (general positions) emerge – possibly as counter-hegemonic interventions of the right against the centre – then it is superficial to suggest that 'populism is on the rise'. In other words, our evidence suggests that such is the plurality of populist views that to grasp at an explanation of the 'rise' or 'fall' of populism requires a sophisticated analysis of the local and regional features that create the conditions for the emergence of such views. In the absence of such recognition, it is plausible that the current trend – of pathologizing populist views – will continue. 'Populism-as-radicalism' will continue as a strategy, of the Centre, that can be used to close down the conditions for the development of a specific dialectic that Mouffe sees as key to democracy – agonism.

*Why is it important that young people's views be considered orthogonal to the left-right spectrum?*

It follows that young people's locally influenced concerns might not map neatly onto the typical 'left–right'[7] spectrum given that variation between and within locations would mean that young people's views reflect a plurality that emerges to contest local and regional structures of power and authority. Thus, it makes sense that evidence shows populism to be partially independent from the left–right spectrum, as young people respond to a deep dissatisfaction with contemporary politics but in ways that mirror their local and regional concerns. In other words, it is possible to draw from the analysis the following point: cynicism is high across Europe but it is orthogonal to the left–right spectrum. This prompts questions about the failure of both left and right politics to capture the voices, concerns and imaginations of contemporary youth (see Patterson, 2014). This is important because it serves as an indication that populism is not wedded to a particular ideological project as is the case in literatures which equate it with left- or right-wing politics. If it is the case that, for some, populism is not 'aligned' to a particular ideological project, then there is scope to explore whether some individuals consider their views to be 'populist' and, reflecting on hypothesis 1, how social, cultural and political contexts shape these views.

*Why is it important that young people's views are contradictory?*

Local issues will inevitably cut across issues of ideological coherence and the results show that young people's personal viewpoints can be informed by opposing ideologies. This is supported by the data, which suggest that young people often hold positions which are contradictory in terms of traditionally understood economic ideologies. Again, it is important not to delegitimize the agent in this context by suggesting that these contradictions emerge as a result of personal confusion or a problem with accepting change. Rather, it is plausible that these contradictions are normal expressions of a range of incompatible social logics and beliefs that provide common-'sense' with elements of incoherence (Laclau and Mouffe, 1985). We would argue that these elements are a practical aspect of democratic struggle and might make it difficult for left- and right-wing ideologies to capture young people's concerns and issues. Indeed, there is a sense in which we now need to consider *how* and *why* such concerns coalesce into what Laclau and Mouffe (1985: 129–130) refer to as a 'logic of equivalence' – a representative and democratic front for young people's political views whatever they may be.

Arguably 'populism' is, at best, a misnomer or, at worse, a rhetorical device that only serves to silence the voices of politicized young people. As a misnomer, we could argue that the term 'populism' does not capture the empirical realities of young people's political concerns. Drawing on the empirical research, we have shown that we need to pluralize how political dissent/assent is expressed – as populism*s* – in order to render explicit, analytically, the geospatial-historical conditions under which such views emerge. Indeed, we would suggest that the term 'populism' is a misnomer precisely because it fails to capture the empirical complexities that exist when new belief systems emerge (or old belief systems re-emerge in new ways). If we recognize the pluralistic nature of political dissent/assent, then the term populism becomes a tool through which legitimate, democratic expressions (of concrete, local problems) become 'boxed-off' as illegitimate forms of political utterance, for example as populist attitudes which must not be platformed. In effect, such a rhetorical strategy only reifies the contradiction – of *people's concerns versus the hegemonic political centre* – without resolving its necessary conditions for existence.

One question that is now common in the literature is to ask: are these views (of youth) either *corrective* or a *threat* to democracy? (Mudde and Kaltwasser, 2012). In response to this, we might suggest that if academics and politicians are uncomfortable with the pronouncements by right-wing parties, then it may be that this discomfort should prompt the creation of a critique of the centre as part of a wider engagement with the wider crises in Western democracy that the views of these young people reflect.

## Conclusion

This paper has begun to map young people's political views across Europe by analysing survey data from locations within 14 European countries. Inspired by the argument that populist views are expressions of democratic struggle, not the views of a 'backward' or 'ignorant' people, we have tried to open up the definition of populism to the plurality that would follow should this be case. The analysis has provided evidence to this effect. There is local and regional variation in populist views and these views are themselves subject to pluralism and inconsistency. This is important because it presents a challenge to those who would use 'populism' as a convenient pejorative term to dissimulate young people's political views. Perhaps an even greater challenge is to find ways to create the conditions to accommodate ideological plurality and contradiction whilst at the same time facilitating populist perspectives as a legitimate component of mainstream discourse.

## Notes

1 See the Appendix for an explanation of how each of these dimensions is operationalized in this study.
2 Due to the high number of missing cases in some of the questions, 27 per cent of the cases were excluded from the regression analysis, leaving $n = 12,435$. The initial analysis of variance components reveals that 68.8 per cent of variance in xenophobia can be explained by differences between individuals, whereas 31.2 per cent of the variance lies at the level of localities (intra-class correlation (ICC) = 0.312) (Table 2). The substantial variation at the level of localities means that it is necessary to search for contextual variables that would help to explain it. Inclusion of the

individual level variables resulted in a 7.6 per cent decrease of residual, individual level variance, and led to an even larger – 36.7 per cent –reduction in intercept variance. This means that much of the observed differences between localities are due to the composition effect, that is, differing individual characteristics of their young residents. In the next step, we added a number of contextual variables, which helped to achieve a massive 67.1 per cent reduction of intercept variance compared to the model containing only the individual level predictors – again, an improvement that is highly significant. This means that our selected contextual variables are capable of explaining a huge portion of the unexplained variation in xenophobia between localities. Only 9.3 per cent of unexplained variance remains at the level of localities, although it is still significant (at the 0.01 level). The chi-square test of deviances ($\Delta df = 31$, $\Delta$loglikelihood $= 624.351$) confirms that it is statistically significant.

3   Again, 26.3 per cent of the cases were excluded from the regression analysis due to missing values, leaving $n = 12,484$. The initial analysis of variance components reveals that 77.8 per cent of variance in cynicism can be explained by differences between individuals, whereas 22.2 per cent of the variance lies at the level of localities (intra-class correlation (ICC) $= 0.222$) (Table 2). The substantial variation at the level of localities means that it is necessary to search for contextual variables that would help to explain it. Inclusion of the previously described individual level variables resulted in a 13 per cent decrease of residual, individual level variance, and led to an even larger – 53.6 per cent – reduction in intercept variance. It means that much of the observed differences between localities are due to the composition effect, that is, differing individual characteristics of their young residents. In the next step, we added a number of contextual variables, which helped to achieve a massive 79.8 percent reduction of intercept variance compared to the model containing only the individual level predictors – again, an improvement that is highly significant. This means that our selected contextual variables are capable of explaining a huge portion of the unexplained variation in cynicism between localities. Only 3 per cent of unexplained variance remains at the level of localities, although it is still significant (at the 0.01 level).The chi-square test of deviances ($\Delta df = 31$, $\Delta$loglikelihood $= 1173.588$) confirms that it is statistically significant.

4   There were 27.4 per cent of cases with missing values excluded from the regression analysis, leaving $n = 12,303$. The initial analysis of variance components reveals that 73.7 per cent of variance in authoritarianism can be explained by differences between individuals, whereas 26.3 per cent of the variance lies at the level of localities (intra-class correlation (ICC) $= 0.263$) (Table 2). The substantial variation at the level of localities means that it is necessary to search for contextual variables that would help to explain it. Inclusion of the previously described individual level variables resulted in a 9.3 per cent decrease of residual, individual level variance, and led to an even larger – 25.4 per cent – reduction in intercept variance. It means that much of the observed differences between localities are due to the composition effect, that is, differing individual characteristics of their young residents. In the next step, we added a number of contextual variables, which helped to achieve a 43.7 per cent reduction of intercept variance compared to the model containing only the individual level predictors – again, an improvement that is highly significant. This means that our selected contextual variables are capable of explaining a huge portion of the unexplained variation in authoritarian between localities. Only 14.4 per cent of unexplained variance remains at the level of localities, although it is still significant (at the 0.01 level). The chi-square test of deviances ($\Delta df = 31$, $\Delta$loglikelihood $= 1194.808$) confirms that it is statistically significant.

5   In this model, 24.5 per cent of the cases were excluded from the regression analysis, leaving $n = 12,768$. The initial analysis of variance components reveals that 81 per cent of variance in nativism can be explained by differences between individuals, whereas 19 per cent of the variance lies at the level of localities (intra-class correlation (ICC) $= 0.19$) (Table 2). The substantial variation at the level of localities means that it is necessary to search for contextual variables that would help to explain it. Inclusion of the previously described individual level variables resulted in a 7 per cent decrease of residual, individual level variance, and led to an even larger – 19.8 per cent – reduction in intercept variance. This means that much of the observed differences between localities are due to the composition effect, that is, differing individual characteristics of their young residents. In the next step, we added a number of contextual variables, which helped to achieve a 12.4 per cent

*The Sociological Review*, 63:S2, pp. 141–166 (2015), DOI: 10.1111/1467-954X.12266

reduction of intercept variance compared to the model containing only the individual level predictors – again, an improvement that is highly significant. This means that our selected contextual variables are capable of explaining a huge portion of the unexplained variation in nativism between localities. Only 15 per cent of unexplained variance remains at the level of localities, although it is still significant (at the 0.01 level). The chi-square test of deviances ($\Delta df = 31$, $\Delta$loglikelihood $= 376.033$) confirms that it is statistically significant.

6 The description of 'clear' left and right is used here rather than 'extreme' or 'radical' because of the way in which the spectrum variable has been recoded to include the three codes at either end of the spectrum. It seems inappropriate to use the descriptor 'extreme' as this ought to be reserved for those at the extremities but by self-assigning toward one of the far ends is, arguably, a 'clear' preference.

7 Understandings of 'left' and 'right' vary across Europe. High levels of 'don't know' responses were found in many countries, not just post-socialist, which rendered the use of the 0–10 scale problematic hence the decision to produce a categorical representation which is more robust as it captures both those with stated positions as well as those for whom the question led to uncertainty.

# References

Abts, K. and Rummens, S., (2007), 'Populism versus democracy', *Political Studies*, 55: 405–424.

Akkerman, A., Mudde, C. and Zaslove, A., (2014), 'How populist are the people? Measuring populist attitudes in voters', *Comparative Political Studies*, 47 (9): 1324–1353.

Baggini, J., (2013), *A Very British Populism*, available at: http://counterpoint.uk.com/wp-content/uploads/2013/09/507_CP_RRadical_UK_Web.pdf (accessed 20 September 2014).

Bale, T., (2013), 'Countering populism: snog, marry, avoid?', available at: http://www.policy-network.net/pno_detail.aspx?ID=4374&title=Countering-populism-Snog-Marry-Avoid (accessed 20 September 2014).

Brett, W., (2013), 'What's an elite to do? The threat of populism from left, right and centre', *The Political Quarterly*, 84 (3): 410–413.

Brock, T. and Carrigan, M., (2014), 'Realism and contingency: a relational realist analysis of the UK student protests', *Journal for the Theory of Social Behaviour*, Early View available at: http://onlinelibrary.wiley.com/doi/10.1111/jtsb.12076/abstract (accessed 6 December 2014).

Canovan, M., (1999), 'Trust the people! Populism and the two faces of democracy', *Political Studies*, 47 (1): 2–16.

Deiwiks, C., (2009), 'Populism', *Living Reviews in Democracy*, available at: http://www.living reviews.org/lrd-2009-3 (accessed 14 August 2014).

Esping-Andersen, G., (1990), *The Three Worlds of Welfare Capitalism*, Princeton, NJ: Princeton University Press.

Fieschi, F., (2004), *Fascism, Populism and the Fifth Republic: In the Shadow of Democracy*, Manchester: Manchester University Press.

Giddens, A., (1994), *Beyond Left and Right: The Future of Radical Politics*, Cambridge: Polity Press.

Giddens, A., (1998), *The Third Way: The Renewal of Social Democracy*, Cambridge: Polity Press.

Gramsci, A., (1971), *Selections from Prison Notebooks*, London: Lawrence and Wishart.

Harrison, S. and Bruter, M., (2011), *Mapping Right Wing Ideology*, Basingstoke: Palgrave.

Heck, R. H., Thomas S. L. and Tabata L. N., (2010), *Multilevel and Longitudinal Modeling with IBM SPSS*, New York: Routledge.

Hox, J., (2010), *Multilevel Analysis, Techniques and Applications*, 2nd edn. New York: Routledge.

Jansen, R. S., (2011), 'Populist mobilization: a new theoretical approach to populism', *Sociological Theory*, 29 (2): 75–96.

Jennings, C., (2011), 'The good, the bad and the populist: a model of political agency with emotional voters', *European Journal of Political Economy*, 27: 621–624.

Kääriäinen, J. and Lehtonen, H., (2006), 'The variety of social capital in welfare state regimes – a comparative study of 21 countries', *European Societies*, 8 (1): 27–57.

Keane, J., (2009), *The Life and Death of Democracy*, New York: Pocket Books.

Kopstein, J. and Reilly, D. A., (2000), 'Geographic diffusion and the transformation of the postcommunist world', *World Politics*, 53 (1): 1–37.

Laclau, E., (1979), *Politics and Ideology in Marxist Theory*, London: Verso.

Laclau, E., (2005), *On Populist Reason*, London: Verso.

Laclau, E. and Mouffe, C., (1985), *Hegemony and Socialist Strategy*, London: Verso.

March, L., (2011), *Radical Left Parties in Europe*, London: Routledge.

Mill, J. S. (1972), 'On liberty', in *Utilitarianism, Liberty, Representative Government*, New York: Dutton.

Moffitt, B. and Tormey, S., (2014), 'Rethinking populism: politics, mediatisation and political style', *Political Studies*, 62: 381–397.

Mouffe, C., (2000), *The Democratic Paradox*, London: Verso.

Mouffe, C., (2002), *Politics and Passions: The Stakes of Democracy*, London: Centre for the Study of Democracy.

Mouffe, C., (2005), *On the Political*, London: Routledge.

Mudde, C., (2004), 'The populist zeitgeist', *Government and Opposition*, 39 (4): 542–563.

Mudde, C., (2007), *Populist Radical Right Parties in Europe*, Cambridge: Cambridge University Press.

Mudde, C. and Kaltwasser, C. R., (2012), 'Exclusionary vs. inclusionary populism: comparing contemporary Europe and Latin America', *Government and Opposition*, 48: 147–174.

Painter, A., (2013), 'Democratic stress, the populist signal and extremist threat', available at: http://www.policy-network.net/publications/4357/Democratic-stress-the-populist-signal-and-extremist-threat (accessed 19 September 2014).

Patterson, C., (2014), 'Both the left and right are failing young people on jobs', *The Guardian*, available at: http://www.theguardian.com/commentisfree/2014/jan/03/right-left-failing-young-people-jobs (accessed 24 September 2014).

Pinelli, C., (2011), 'The populist challenge to constitutional democracy', *European Constitutional Law Review*, 7 (1): 5–16.

Rancière, J., (2006), *Hated of Democracy*, London: Verso.

Ruzza, C., (2009), 'Populism and euroscepticism: towards uncivil society?' *Policy and Society*, 28: 87–98.

Schmitt, C., (1996 [1932]), *The Concept of the Political*, Chicago, IL: University of Chicago Press.

Smith, A. M., (2012), *Laclau and Mouffe: The Radical Democratic Imaginary*, London: Routledge.

Tam Cho, W. K. and Rudolph, T. J., (2008), 'Emanating political participation: untangling the spatial structure behind participation', *British Journal of Political Science*, 38 (2): 273–289.

Tilly, C., (2004), *Contention and Democracy in Europe* 1650–2000, Cambridge: Cambridge University Press.

Vasilopoulou, S., Halikiopoulou, D. and Exadaktylos, T., (2014), 'Greece in crisis: austerity, populism and the politics of blame', *Journal of Common Market Studies*, 52 (2): 388–402.

Worsley, P., (1969), 'The concept of populism', in G. Ionescu and E. Gellner (eds), *Populism – Its Meanings and National Characteristics*, London: Weidenfeld and Nicolson.

Zaslove, A., (2008), 'Here to stay? Populism as a new party type', *European Review*, 16 (3): 319–336.

*The Sociological Review*, 63:S2, pp. 141–166 (2015), DOI: 10.1111/1467-954X.12266

# Appendix

**Table A1** *Dependent variable construction*

| Questions | Factor | Cronbach's alpha/Pearson's $r$ |
|---|---|---|
| Consider the following statements and indicate whether you agree or disagree: 'Foreigners should not be allowed to buy land in [COUNTRY]' | Xenophobia | Alpha = 0.658, varies from 0.330 (Georgia) to 0.710 (Finland) |
| Do you agree or disagree with the following statements? '[COUNTRY] should have stricter border controls and visa restrictions to prevent further immigration'. | | |
| 'When jobs are scarce, employers should give priority to [COUNTRY] people over foreign workers' | | |
| Five-point Likert scales 'agree' to 'Disagree', recoded 0–4, summed and rescaled 0–1 with a high score indicating xenophobia. | | |
| Do you agree or disagree? Politicians are corrupt. The rich have too much influence over politics. 1–5 Likert scale recoded to 0–4, summed and rescaled 0–1, high score indicating high cynicism. | Cynicism | $r = 0.473$, varies from 0.29 in Spain and western Germany to 0.555 in Croatia |
| I am going to describe various types of political systems and ask what you think about each as a way of governing this country. For each one, would you say it is a very good, fairly good, fairly bad or very bad way of governing the country? | Authoritarianism | $r = 0.471$, varies from 0.22 in Portugal to 0.514 in western Germany |
| Having a strong leader who is not constrained by parliament | | |
| Having the army rule | | |
| 5 point scale of 'good' to 'bad', recoded 0–4, summed and rescaled 0–1 with a high score indicating tendency to 'good' | | |

*Continued*

| Questions | Factor | Cronbach's alpha/Pearson's *r* |
|---|---|---|
| Some people say the following things are important for being a citizen of [COUNTRY]. Others say that they are not important. How important do you think each of the following is?<br>To have been born in [COUNTRY]<br>To be able to speak [THE NATIONAL LANGUAGE]<br>To have at least one [COUNTRY] parent<br>To respect [COUNTRY] political institutions and laws<br>Five-point Likert scale 'very important' to 'not important at all' recoded 0–4, summed and rescaled 0–1 with a high score indicating a tendency towards importance. | Nativism | Alpha = 0.685, Varies from 0.610 in western Germany to 0.750 in Hungary and Georgia |

*The Sociological Review*, 63:S2, pp. 141–166 (2015), DOI: 10.1111/1467-954X.12266

# The madness that is the world: young activists' emotional reasoning and their participation in a local Occupy movement

## Phil Mizen

**Abstract:** The focus of this paper is young people's participation in the Occupy protest movement that emerged in the early autumn of 2011. Its concern is with the emotional dimensions of this and in particular the significance of emotions to the reasoning of young people who came to commit significant time and energy to the movement. Its starting point is the critique of emotions as narrowly subjective, whereby the passions that events like Occupy arouse are treated as beyond the scope of human reason. The rightful rejection of this reductionist argument has given rise to an interest in understandings of the emotional content of social and political protest as normatively constituted, but this paper seeks a different perspective by arguing that the emotions of Occupy activists can be regarded as a reasonable force. It does so by discussing findings from long-term qualitative research with a Local Occupy movement somewhere in England and Wales. Using the arguments of social realists, the paper explores this data to examine why things matter sufficiently for young people to care about them and how the emotional force that this involves constitutes an indispensable source of reason in young activists' decisions to become involved in Local Occupy.

**Keywords:** young people, emotion, social movements, Occupy, reason, reasoning

In his rapid response to the international emergence of the Occupy movement, Manuel Castells (2012) begins with a lament for the categorical exclusion of individuals from studies of social movements. His concern is that to locate Occupy's origins in the humiliation precipitated by the global crisis of 2008/9 (Gitlin, 2013, 2012; Calhoun, 2013; Chomsky, 2012) is insufficient to answer questions of how its multitudinous and varied constituent parts came into being. To satisfy questions of what precisely brought hundreds of thousands of people, many of them young, to give their active support to Occupy, Castells (2012: 13) asserts that there is a need to give careful attention to the lives of those individuals ultimately responsible for its existence, to those persons who took to the streets 'in their material flesh and mind'.

*The Sociological Review*, 63:S2, pp. 167–182 (2015), DOI: 10.1111/1467-954X.12267

The precise target of Castells' vexation remains curiously unspecified, but his frustration with the neglect of the people who comprise social movements resonates with critique elsewhere. Specifically, James M. Jasper (2011, 2010, 2006) has written extensively on the limits and decline of the 'big structure' accounts of social movements and their categorical neglect of the motivations, meanings and understandings possessed by activists. In concentrating on organizational factors like staffing and fundraising, and external circumstances like resources and repression, Jasper is concerned that the study of popular protest has lost touch with those 'individuals ... along with their decisions, dilemmas, defections and so on' (Jasper, 2010: 967) who make up these movements. Echoing Castells' exasperation, his concern is that without taking seriously the 'grievances and attitudes' (2010: 966) of activists, those people ultimately responsible for creating and transforming social movements will be taken for granted as passively awaiting their mobilization, or activists *in potentia* awaiting the structural conditions necessary for their radicalism to come fully formed onto the historical stage.

Of course, neither the model of the activist as cultural dope or its flipside, qua the structurally overdetermined activist, is adequate. Both positions offer little means of understanding what connects people to the social movements in which they become involved or, indeed, why young people would want to become involved in a movement as inchoate and lacking identity as Occupy was in the late summer of 2011. It is therefore significant that both Castells and Jasper give considerable analytical significance to emotions as a way of comprehending individuals' motivations for engaging in social protest action. For Castells (2012: 13), protest movements are at root emotional movements where, '[...] the big bang of a social movement starts with the transformation of emotion into action'. For Jasper, too, not only are 'emotions [...] present in every phase and every aspect of protest' but they should play an essential part in any theory of social movement action: 'virtually all the cultural models and concepts currently in use (eg frames, identities, narratives) are mis-specified if they do not include explicit emotional causal mechanisms' (Jasper, 2011: 286).

How best, in turn, to specify these 'causal mechanisms' without returning the emotional dimension of social movement protest to associations with the irrational is less clear, however. To point to the 'untenable contrast of emotions with rationality' (Jasper, 2011: 286) is a necessary first step to take, one that allows the reason-emotion, fact-value dualities to be deconstructed in ways that show how feelings can and do exert a considerable force on how people reason about the world and how to change it. What is rarely considered, however, is the reverse of this, where facts are recognized as integral to the creation of values and evaluations, and emotions constitute a form of human reasoning (Sayer, 2011). Yet, this reciprocal deconstruction is necessary if emotions are to be regarded as having more than subjective significance; that they are something more than personal standpoints that have little to do with reason. By failing to permit emotions to enter the realm of reason(ing) the risk is that they are treated, at worst, as the preserve of an individual's irrational drives or, at best, as a source of individual taste or preference. Equating collective protest with the irrational has rightly

*The Sociological Review*, 63:S2, pp. 167–182 (2015), DOI: 10.1111/1467-954X.12267

been a long-discredited approach to understanding social movements (Le Bon, 1960); and, for similar reasons, youth studies too has done much to extricate understandings of youth from its 'bio-political' reduction to adolescent storm and stress (Cohen, 1997). Personal taste and individual preference may be the stock in trade of rational choice theorists of political action, but their crude reduction of human agency to instrumental self-interest cannot account for the substantive rationality of voluntary collective action and the conditioning influence of social values and ethical norms on political protest (Archer, 2000).

It is in recognition that modes of feeling can be culturally defined that some social movement analysts have turned their attention to the normative dimensions of emotions, but this too risks another form of subjectivism. It is clearly the case that social movements look to arouse and shape emotions 'as a way to get things done' (Jasper, 2011: 148) and that all sorts of rhetorical displays, visual tactics, modes of encouragement and persuasive techniques are arrayed to provoke and condition activists' emotions. It is also the case that 'people learn cultural norms to interpret their affective states and learn to name their feelings with specific labels' (Ruiz-Junco, 2012: 46), and that social movements too look to mediate, frame and structure feelings along these lines. 'Regardless of the stance on social constructionism that analysts [of social movements] adopt', Ruiz-Junco continues, 'they generally assume that the fluctuating, ever-shifting and heterogeneous emotional lava that we experience hardens into feelings that people interpret, name and oftentimes, subsume under normative feeling rules'. Yet, if matters are left here this argument provides little scope for comprehending why some things matter enough in the first place for people to become sufficiently emotional about them to join a political protest or, for that matter, why they would want to work on ('harden'?) their emotions by consciously 'naming' and 'interpreting' them; including accommodating their emotions to those normative patterns of feeling characteristic of political protest and social movements. Without an understanding of why young people care enough about something for it to have emotional significance, the danger is that these social constructionist accounts of human feelings will also lead to a subjectivist reading that equates activist emotions with the unthinking (and thus irrational) response to a culturally constituted emotional rulebook.

## Commentaries on concerns

To avoid these subjectivist pitfalls there is much to be gained by foregrounding the reasonable qualities of activists' emotions through treating them as a constituent of human reasoning; that is, as a fundamental part of the powers and properties of human beings that are neither solely irrational nor simply the product of normative expectations. This is a position advanced by social realists and their consideration of emotions as integral to human reasoning, rather than as marking a threat to it (Nussbaum, 2001; Williams, 2001). As 'commentaries on our concerns' (Archer, 2000: 195, 193), the contention is that emotions are among the main constituents of the rich inner lives of human beings, 'properties of people that are intertwined with their sociality, but irreducible to it'. As attributes specific to humans but nevertheless inevitably entwined with their sociality, emotions are clearly matters of culture, but it is a *non sequitur* to regard how humans feel as the bequest of society or of the specific cultures into which they enter. People may well interpret their emotions through normative frameworks, but it does not follow that what they feel is unrelated to anything independent of these. More specifically, to accept that activists may learn to name their feelings in line with the 'rules' of their movements does not mean that they cannot do anything but accept these culturally proscribed 'labels', as if the only things that mattered enough for activists to become emotional about them were the product of social conventions. It has been pointed out that people can and do find their emotional responses unhelpful or unsatisfactory, precisely because emotions have as their object things with properties and powers beyond how conventions may define them (Sayer, 2011). To think otherwise would be to entertain the absurd position that what activists become most emotional about – degradation, discrimination, inequality, abuses of power – are only conventionally defined and so are capable of being wished away.

For these reasons the realist emphasis is on the relational nature of human emotions and how they relate to objects that exist in the world, including culture and normative conventions. Clearly of subjective importance in that humans feel them in body and mind, emotions are thus treated as more than just individual standpoints; states of affect that are produced by individual humans but which are not readily susceptible to the influence of evidence and evaluation. On the contrary, 'emerging from situations to signal their import for our concerns' (Archer, 2000: 196), realists emphasize emotions as affective modes of awareness of situations, a means of identifying and selecting what it is about one's circumstances that provides the basis for one's feelings. To do so requires acknowledging distinctions between emotions *of* and *about* something, where the former points to emotions as the human experience of feelings and the latter relates these feelings to the concerns that people hold. In affording a means to identify what it is about a situation that provides the grounds for such feelings, emotions play an indispensible role in human reasoning as a 'form of evaluative judgement of matters affecting or believed to be affecting our well-being and that of others and the other things that we care about' (Sayer, 2011: 36). Without this emotional inner life constituted in and through its relation to a world of concern nothing would matter to people, certainly not the substantive issues and ideas that animate social movements but not even the normatively constituted rules and cultures that social constructionists see as defining the range of emotions accessible to political activists.

Seen in this way, emotions are not only essential to human reasoning, but they are both a requirement for human well-being and form a basis for social action. To flourish, human beings, including children and young people (Mizen and Ofosu-Kusi, 2013; Bluebond-Langner and Korbin, 2007), require the permanent monitoring that emotions provide in the form of a 'continuous running commentary (that is something we are never without) and therefore it is only in sudden or urgent contexts that we are aware of a specific emotion' (Archer, 2000: 197). The realist focus, therefore, is not the presence or absence of emotions, nor how they help or hinder human action under particular circumstances, such as participation in social movements. Rather, 'as a highly discriminating and valuable response to the flow of experience' (Sayer, 2011: 36), attention is directed to the 'emotional reasoning' and 'emotional intelligence' involved in the continual monitoring of the things that people care about. It is in these reasonable and intelligent qualities of emotions that hurt or harm may be discerned and, consequently, from which the desire to bring about change or to prevent others from doing the same may emerge. It is these qualities to emotions that may further allow nuanced assessments of situations and sources of empathy capable of leading to social critique. These reasonable and intelligent qualities of emotions are far from fallible, but then again neither is the hard-headed rationality more commonly associated with reason. Moreover, as commentaries on the things that people care most about, emotions find significance as the 'shoving power' (Archer and Tritter, 2000: 6) or 'force of ought' (Sayer, 2011: 140) capable of animating the actions of people above and beyond their normative obligations.

## Researching Local Occupy

This concern with the emotions of social movement activists was explored through case study[1] research of young people's participation in a Local Occupy[2] group. Unlike many of the high profile Occupy protest groups and encampments established in major world cities in the late summer and early autumn of 2011 – for example, New York (Gitlin, 2013, 2012; Calhoun, 2013; Chomsky, 2012), Los Angeles (Uitermark and Nicholls, 2012), Boston (Juris *et al.*, 2012), Madrid and Barcelona (Abellán *et al.,* 2012; Castells, 2012) and Amsterdam (Uitermark and Nicholls, 2012) – these smaller Occupy groups and demonstrations received little publicity and have not featured significantly in subsequent research (cf. Smith and Glidden, 2012; Smith *et al.,* 2012; Alimi, 2012). It was to address the existence of these smaller but numerically more significant Occupy groups that almost two years of fieldwork began with Local Occupy shortly after it was created on 15 October 2011, the designated Occupy global day of action.

The research was conceived of as a dialogue with a purpose, a term that borrows from Burawoy's (2007) commitment to dialogue as the basis for a reflexive ethnography. Throughout the fieldwork, attempts were made to establish and maintain an iterative relationship with participants in Local Occupy through regular visits to the camps,[3] participation in discussion and debate, and attendance at associated protests, demonstrations, workshops and other related events. During this time a significant programme of data collection took place through field observations, individual interviews and participation in group discussions, both recorded and unrecorded. Much of this research activity was based at the Local Occupy encampment, but it also continued with individual activists long after the camp was voluntarily discontinued some six months or so after it had been first established. Particular attention was given to those constituting the 'inner movement of core activists' (Gitlin, 2013: 3), people who (had) either lived at the camp for significant periods, slept there regularly or who visited on an almost daily basis while their involvement lasted.

It is this self-defined 'core' group that thus feature most significantly within an extensive and unique data set of a local Occupy movement. This comprises records of individual interviews and discussions with 36 activists, including 19 respondents who participated in a recorded interview at least once. From this figure of 19, nine respondents participated in two or more recorded sessions, four in three or more and one who participated in five. Also included in the data set are records of group discussions, a small number of which were recorded. The shortest recorded interview lasted for just under half an hour and the longest, a group session, for just under three hours, and in total they comprise approximately 290,000 words of verbatim transcripts. A field diary containing extensive observational material and notes on unrecorded interviews and discussions, of approximately 25,000 words, further supported the recorded interview data. In addition, the researcher took approximately 110 photographs and collected many others taken by participants or posted on the Internet. Further context and detail was garnered from websites and Facebook walls, including the closed Local Occupy Facebook planning group to which the researcher was given access. Also collected were examples of artwork, pamphlets and other printed material, as well as several hours of video that the group, its supporters and other casual visitors had uploaded to the Internet.

One of the rationales for identifying Local Occupy as a case study within the wider MYPLACE project was the expectation that significant numbers of young people[4] would be involved. Writing about the upsurge in political protest prior to Occupy, the journalist Paul Mason began his explanation of *Why It's Kicking Off Everywhere* by pointing out that, 'At heart of this is a new sociological type: a graduate with no future' (2011, no page number). In a similar vein, Todd Gitlin notes of his involvement in Occupy Wall Street (hereafter OWS) that, 'By inspection, they are largely young …' (2013: 15) and Castells cites research on OWS showing that, 'as in similar movements in other countries, the Occupy participants appear to be relatively young, educated people whose professional expectations are limited in the current economy' (2012: 167). It was not being claimed that Occupy was a political movement of the young, or that it lacked wider social, ethnic and gender diversity, but that young people were involved as vigorous advocates of the movement's passionate indignation.

This impression of Occupy as a relatively youthful movement was confirmed during initial fieldwork visits. Nevertheless, as the research progressed so did awareness that the composition of Local Occupy was more complex than these claims to its inherent youthfulness allowed. Young people frequenting the camps did assume significant roles and were well represented within its 'inner movement', and they were also much in evidence in more marginal roles, such as around the fringes of meetings, casual visitors to the camps and non-active supporters at demonstrations and other actions. Yet the participation of the young turned out to be only one part of what was a much more socially diverse

*The Sociological Review*, 63:S2, pp. 167–182 (2015), DOI: 10.1111/1467-954X.12267

movement in which the young took part alongside older people. This diversity was accordingly reflected in the collection of fieldwork data and will no doubt form the subject of future analysis. However, it is attention to the emotional reasoning involved in the young activists' decisions to become involved in Local Occupy that this paper is primarily concerned.

## Coming out of the concrete

But how did it spread, Phil? How did it spread from Wall Street to all these nations? Was it people communicating on the web? Err, I don't know, don't know how, how it spread, whether it was a zeitgeist feeling and everybody just turned up and went, 'well, they're in Wall Street, we're gonna turn up' and then it just spread [...] (Alex, late 20s/early 30s)[5]

Alex's surprise at how Occupy seemingly spread from nowhere is one that is shared more widely. 'Spontaneous' is Gitlin's (2013: 5) favoured description for Occupy Wall Street's sudden appearance on 17 September 2011, while Castells remarks about Occupy's global attraction that 'no one expected it [...] it just happened', (Castells, 2012). Occupy was no rootless movement, however, and its origins have been located in the great upsurge in popular discontent following the global financial crisis of 2008. However, to locate its antecedents in Tunisia, Iceland, Egypt or Spain (Mason, 2012) does not really answer questions of what brought people to the point where they were prepared to mobilize in support of something that possessed little in the way of history, definition or organization (Gitlin, 2012).

Yet people did turn out for Occupy and in numbers that were matched only by the equally unexpected breadth of its appeal. Calhoun writes of 'an extraordinary 6 weeks in 2011' (2013: 27) when at least 600 spontaneous occupations broke out in cities and other locations traversing the entire landmass of the United States following the creation of OWS. It was the October 2011 day of action when Occupy went global with spontaneous demonstrations recorded in more than 950 cities in 82 countries. In the United Kingdom, attention was focused on Occupy London Stock Exchange and its large and vibrant tented encampment outside St Paul's Cathedral. Scores of protests invoking the Occupy mantle also appeared elsewhere, most of which petered out in a matter of hours or days (Abellán *et al.,* 2012). Many of these fleeting or small-scale protests received minimal publicity and knowledge of their existence was often limited.[6] Nevertheless, one sympathetic mapping[7] of Occupy's presence conservatively estimated the creation of 52 lasting camps and demonstrations stretching the length and breadth of the United Kingdom.

Why, then, did people come out to support such a little known entity and in such large numbers? What accounts for the apparent spontaneity of Occupy's emergence? More specifically, why did, as one (middle aged) activist put it, 'people start [...] to come out of the concrete, not the woodwork, out of the concrete' (Robbie) to give their active support to Local Occupy? What brought those many

    173

young people who actively supported Local Occupy to the point where they got actively involved in something so hitherto ill defined and potentially provocative?

Spontaneity suggests impulse and whim rather than calculation and rationality and at one level this does describe the beginnings of some young activists' lengthy involvement with Local Occupy. This did sometimes involve spur of the moment decisions that had hinged on chance encounters or a precipitate response to the unexpected. For all the considerable interest generated by the popular protest in the Middle East, Southern Europe and North America, first encounters with Local Occupy could happen with little or no knowledge of these larger developments; and certainly nothing in the way of direct engagement with the Internet buzz and chatter that Occupy began to generate. Some would speak of literally stumbling upon what was then a rudimentary assembly, a curious but unanticipated break to journeys embarked upon for other reasons. Alex, for instance, had come upon Local Occupy on its first day by chance, while the then two tents and excited voices had attracted Robbie during the early hours of its second morning while making his way home from a party. Rose also spoke of knowing nothing of Occupy before her chance encounter during its first days while strolling through the area. In contrast, Heather's curiosity had been stirred sufficiently to actively seek out the camp on its second day, but only after she too had learned of its existence by chance from a fellow college student.

Chance and happenstance may thus seem appropriate explanations for how some young people came across Local Occupy, but this fails to account for why they didn't then move on. Part of the explanation for this lay in the immediate and compelling intuitive force that these first contacts with Local Occupy could generate. In Robbie's case 'optimism', 'joy' and 'beauty' combined with the serendipity of his discovery to convince him that this was where his immediate destiny lay. Alex couched his explanation in similarly fated terms, while Heather too spoke of her initial response as one of powerful and absorbing influences. 'I think it comes back to not being able to do anything else [ ... ]', was her explanation, where this 'amazing' experience exerted a natural and compelling force. As she continued, 'I had this, you know, this urge to be there, like I knew that it was the right place for me to be, like, I, I couldn't have thought of doing anything else' (late teens/early 20s).

For all the intuitive appeal, at another level the stream of emotions of excitement and necessity could also be highly discerning. Felt as much as articulated, these young people nonetheless described how their initial feelings had connected with some of their deeper concerns, 'sentiments' (Joe, late 20s/early 30s) laid down over time that could be directly related to previous situations and circumstances. Often this relation was only hinted at, like in Alex's asides to the restlessness he felt with his unsatisfying work and unfulfilling personal relationships, and how these had in turn explained his need to wander the city. Robbie too alluded to how his first experience of Local Occupy brought to mind the considerable anxieties he carried from his earlier life and how working in a cynical and exploitative profession had been responsible for the serious erosion of his self-belief and purpose. Describing her involvement as 'by chance', Rose too connected the force

*The Sociological Review*, 63:S2, pp. 167–182 (2015), DOI: 10.1111/1467-954X.12267

of her encounter to the 'proper despair' she was then feeling, a sharp sense of despondence and vulnerability that she linked to 'personal things in my life like my, my housing, money, blah, blah, blah, not having a job, all of this'. Compared to her anguish and anxiety, Local Occupy had quite literally stopped her in her tracks.

> I was walking through town really upset and I see, and, and I met Robbie and I see tents and I thought, what's going on here, what's this? He's like, ah, and he's explaining it to me about Occupy and whatever. I said, do you know what?, I'm coming, I'm staying here. Yeah. (Rose, late 20s/early 30s).

Elsewhere, the discerning force of their emotions was much more clearly apparent. Here the insights offered by their emotions related more clearly to a slowly accreted and brooding disquiet with life, and the possession of a sometimes ill-defined but keenly felt awareness of becoming progressively troubled by the world around them. The development of these perceptions could be a long and gradual process, like when Heather traced the sudden impact of Local Occupy to sets of concerns that had emerged some years earlier. In our conversations together she spoke of her agitation and anxiety and how from an early age she had been troubled by a persistent and sometimes unsettling unease. Fixing these feelings to the wars in Iraq and Afghanistan and then their disastrous aftermaths, Heather recounted her mounting discontent and alarm with the drawn-out conflicts and how this disquiet had moved her to go online in the search of more information. Then aged 13 or 14 she 'just stumbled across these forums and blogs because, well, I have no idea why, but I, I just, I was just looking into all this stuff … about war, about oil and money'. The 'conspiracy theories and all of the sort of subversive like subjects' she discovered 'sort of sparked in my mind', moments of luminosity that then faded away but which were rekindled again with far more strength. '[When] I started Occupy it started off those feelings again of, you know, the world's corrupt, um, now everybody knows [ … ] it was real [ie her former unease] but it was in the back of my mind, I was asleep.' What she felt when first attending Local Occupy had been familiar, but its force was likened to being shaken awake, '[because] when it came to Occupy it was something fierce. As soon as you find out, it's something fierce inside you and you want people to know' (Heather, late teens/early 20s).

## Learning from A to B

For other young people the paths to Local Occupy were more deliberate and calculated affairs, but ones in which their emotions played equally discerning roles. These were young people more likely to possess a history of activism or prior experience of protest. They also watched events leading up to Occupy with growing interest and excitement, and steps to become involved were actively pursued. For these young people, their emotions not only provided good reason to act but they also constituted a source of judicious reflection and re-evaluation. No less passionate or moved by what they did and the situations encountered, these young people spoke of their coming to Local Occupy as the consequence of long-term feelings and reflections, as what had once felt right no longer seemed to be the case and as previously satisfying courses of action in turn became the object of newfound discontent.

This was demonstrated in how Laura traced the possession of her long-standing concerns to her decision to turn up on the day of action. Describing herself as 'politically aware' from an early age she too linked this awareness to the alarm she felt as a teenager while watching the build up to the war in Iraq and how this then turned to anger following the invasion and its bloody after-math. Speaking with gentle eloquence and her customary understatement, she recounted her indignation at the death and suffering the war was causing, and the craven disregard for human life displayed by a self-serving elite responsible for the debacle. It was this indignation and anger that had moved Laura to protest in London alongside hundreds of thousands of others and then to focus her concerns through giving her active support to the Stop the War movement. Significantly, however, this first serious commitment to political activism had provided a salutary lesson and Laura became dissatisfied with the course of action she had undertaken. Epitomized by the proclivity of anti-war protest for what she called 'A to B marches', Laura found that her discontent only deepened. 'I always got really frustrated that it was, like, for this one day everyone cares about this stuff and you feel like you're doing something important.' She continued, 'And I've always found it frustrating that it's, you know, one day and that's it, then you've got to wait for your next protest' (early/mid 20s).

Whatever the normative force and rules of feeling that these protest movements looked to exercise upon their members, Laura's was a much more troubled experience. Instead of learning to identify her feelings within their normative framework, she found in its place an even deeper sense of disquiet. This found a particular focus on their *modus operandi* where having to wait for the 'next protest' alone was inadequate, a feeling that surfaced once again when her anger at the financial crisis of 2008 and consequent political embrace of austerity led her again to protest. Once again the object of her 'frustration' was the resort to 'A to B marches', together with the ineffectual campaigns and lobbying of the public sector trade unions that she had hoped would provide a more meaningful source of opposition. Attending sporadic and often poorly attended demonstrations, Laura also spoke of her concerns about the deadening effects of mass culture on the willingness and ability of people to offer dissent: 'When I walked, when I walked through towns like [name] or [name], it's just like consumerism, consumerism, shopping, shopping, get drunk, blah, blah, blah.' What these experiences told her was that there was pressing need for sustained and immediate action against a world that was profoundly unfair and unjust. It was for this reason that Laura became interested and then involved in the politics and practices of anarchism, to which she had come to feel a passionate commitment. It was this conviction that had also alerted her to the grassroots and popular upheavals now taking place across the world and in which she sought participation online. For her, the subsequent calls to Local Occupy marked an expression of this reason,

*The Sociological Review*, 63:S2, pp. 167–182 (2015), DOI: 10.1111/1467-954X.12267

a discerning emotionality that had culminated in her decision to become one of instigators and (to begin with) key protagonists.

Laura's example demonstrates the continuous commentary that emotions contributed to young people's reasoning about the world and their eventual decisions to commit themselves to Local Occupy. Moreover, it further shows that not only did their emotions provide a constant source of reason, but they also contributed to these young people's deliberations and reflections in sometimes complex and intricate paths to Local Occupy. This was again the case with Joe who, like Laura, felt in Occupy the expression of something that was both different and profound.

> So, I turned up on that first day and when I left the house after watching the news, sort of having this idea what was going to happen, I says, I said to my mum and dad, I took a [sleeping] bag and I said, 'I gonna, I'm going be camping out all night'. (late 20s/early 30s)

Joe's excitement and optimism thus certainly involved impulse, but it too expressed a more deeply held set of concerns. In talking at length of how he came to be involved on that first day, Joe too recounted the discontents and unease he felt about the world from a young age and how significant to these were a series of encounters with the state and its clumsy and ineffectual intrusions into the fabric of his family life. Watching with discomfort and annoyance how health and social work professionals dealt with the needs of his loved ones, Joe spoke of how he too became the object of their attentions when he dropped out of school aged 14. School for him had been unrewarding and this sense of dislocation only grew as his attempts to find meaningful work and then live independently met with limited success. For Joe it was these experiences that produced what he described as feelings of 'a raw righteousness' whose object was 'the madness that is the world'. It was this powerful indignation and sense of legitimate anger that had moved him to seek self-education in Marxist and radical socialist writings, and their associated parties and movements. Having already found the promises and practices of the social democratic left unsatisfying, Joe nevertheless became progressively disillusioned with the revolutionary left and the dissonance between its ideas of freedom and democracy and its insistence on the conformity of its activists. It was this disquiet that provided the basis of Joe's growing interest in social and community action and its seemingly more satisfying connections with the lived experiences and daily needs of his friends and family, and in its commitment to open and free association. Together with a very close friend, Joe was thus moved to begin 'several open projects', small-scale schemes and minor initiatives that also fed upon the inspiration provided by his mother and her own experiments in working class community activism. For Joe his burgeoning friendship and its associated projects were a tangible expression of his growing conviction to the intrinsic worth of self-directed activity:

> [...] the things that we used to talk about made me think that what gave us any meaning to any of our conversations or our own feelings of what life was all about was that, you

know, if you do what you're interested in … then you know, that's good enough, you become productive and we sort of, we felt like we could achieve a lot me and my friend by just, just, just working on the things that were, we felt, felt were meaningful.

These 'hobbies', as Joe termed them, expressed both his unease with the world and his corresponding belief in the necessity of alternative ways of living. For Joe, the worth of his 'hobbies' lay in their collaborative and convivial nature and the satisfaction he derived from actions whose means were as significant as their ends. Joe's good friend nevertheless died unexpectedly about a year before his involvement with Local Occupy and alongside his shock and grief, Joe grew concerned that something of greater significance might also be lost. It was this concern that Joe identified as directly instrumental in his decision to grab his sleeping bag and head for the planned Local Occupy gathering. 'What brought me to the camp was, was just a feeling that I'd been sobered by the loss of my friend, my good friend', is how he put it. 'I liked the conversations I had with [friend's name], I learnt a lot from him, he taught me a lot about the world and I just wanted to keep that reciprocal learning going'. Full of optimism and hope, as well as filled with righteous anger, it was Joe's conviction that helped

[…] creat[e] a space where people can ask questions of themselves and the world and maybe create a synthesis [ … ] whereby [ … ] they're giving something and taking something and may be helping to create a better world and that was really, really a massive thing that was central to my life after my friend died [ … ] you're better doing the things that you love and enjoy for yourself, than being a sort of a tool, or a cog in a machine.

## Fearing nothing but fear

Contained in Joe's emotional reasoning was also the presence of fear and his anxiety that his cherished values might pass along with the death of his friend. Yet fear is more likely to figure in analysis of emotions and social movements as an obstacle rather than a spur to action, where '[ … ] a key question to understand is when and how and why one person or a thousand people decide, individually, to do something they are repeatedly warned not to do because they will be punished' (Castells, 2012: 13). This fear of reprimand and possible punishment was certainly apparent in the reasoning of core Local Occupiers, but not always with the degree of salience that Castells suggests. Some protestors like Ray (late teens/early 20s), for instance, saw in their fears little reason for concern beyond the possession of mild anxiety that once elaborated and reflected upon was insufficient to muster a deterrent. 'The worst thing they could do us for was, um, aggravated trespass', was Ray's reflection, 'which when it comes to a group of say 40 people, they're not likely to take you to court'.

For others, in contrast, fear provides a much more significant source of reasoning. In these instances, it is in the intelligence of their emotions that good cause is found to overcome the dread of force and fear of repercussions that their activism may provoke. Adamant that, '[g]enerally, I don't fear things [ … ] I feared nothing', Heather too conceded her anxiety about participating in Local Occupy

*The Sociological Review*, 63:S2, pp. 167–182 (2015), DOI: 10.1111/1467-954X.12267

but the object of her fear was not so much authority, but her understanding of her own vulnerability. As one of the few young women to participate in Local Occupy's inner movement and to live at the camp for months at a time, Heather was alive to the possible perils of taking up residence in such a relatively unregulated space 'in the middle of town, in a tent, [where] anyone can walk in, anyone can take an opposing view to you [...]'. Yet importantly these fears only served to strengthen her resolve. To succumb to 'the fear of like, oh if I talk to him what if he [...] [puts her in peril]', would necessitate relinquishing some of the things that she had come to care most forcefully about. 'I've never been scared of wandering into the unknown because what, what are we here for other than to learn from each other, learn new things?' She continued, 'if you don't talk to that person, or if you don't engage with someone you don't know [...] then you're never going to know anything outside of what other people are telling you'. For Heather, the force of this reason was significant enough to overcome both her own reservations and those of her father and college teachers.

> I, I, I couldn't have, you know, cowered back, I couldn't have worn a mask [ie hidden], I couldn't have, you know, shielded [myself] because that was [...] I had this, you know, this urge to be there, I knew it was the right place for me to be, like I, I couldn't have thought of doing anything else, I couldn't have shut my mouth [...]

If Heather's fears dwelt on her understanding of her own frailty, others did locate the object of their concerns at more of a distance. In participating in radical social movements in general, and Local Occupy in particular, it was acknowledged that they would come under the scrutiny of the police and the security services. Several participants spoke of examples of attempted infiltrations of the camp but their concerns also emanated from how their own and others' previous activism had exposed them to the attention of the authorities. For Clive and Laura this meant the uneasy acceptance that their earlier activities had attracted the attention of the police and their participation in anarchist organized demonstrations had been closely monitored through the various paraphernalia of modern surveillance: afar from circling helicopters and the watchful eye of telephoto lenses, and up-close via hand-held video cameras and police spotters. They had, they insisted, found themselves literally caught in the crosshairs when protesting at a major political event, '[...] snipers trained on us as we walked past [...] the police came over with their cameras, filming our group, so we put a flag in front of their cameras and they all ran round us about to kettle us' (Laura, early/mid 20s). Both found these encounters unsettling, moments of concerns about their personal welfare and which, for Clive, had contributed to his decision to '[...] mask up quite a lot' (early/mid 20s). He continued, 'I'm not out to cause trouble but I know that, you know, our little group, when we go out on a protest, we're going to be watched [...]'. For his partner, Laura, the experience of being monitored in such a close and intrusive fashion was felt in similarly discomfiting terms, but she took from this a characteristic source of defiance. Keenly aware of how her distinctive deportment made her presence at any demonstration a conspicuous one, Laura nevertheless held her style and manner to be a visible expression of her commitment not to let the fear of authority deny her the inalienable right that 'everyone should be able to be in a protest however they want'.

In this respect, fear of one's own vulnerability in the face of power is part and parcel of the unfolding emotional reasoning that led to participation in Local Occupy. Yet, in the testimonies of Laura, Heather and the others we also find some of the answers to Castells' question of how and why activists come to commit themselves in the face of such fears. If emotions provide an intelligent commentary on well-being and the things that one values, then it is in these that young people also find good reasons to confront and then transcend their fears. This is certainly evident in Laura's defiant style of dress and refusal to succumb to what she regarded as blatant intimidation. It is also glimpsed in Heather's determined efforts to overcome her real concerns about her safety derived from the desire to know about things she cared about for herself. As she summed up during one of our lengthy conversations, '[ . . . ] with the fear thing, like I, I forget to, like, to be fearful, like I, I literally have a drive and I'll just do it.'

## Conclusion

The argument advanced in this paper is that emotions are a fruitful object of analysis in the study of young people's participation in social movements. Protest and movement activism necessarily involve an emotional dimension, not least because feelings have to be sufficiently strong for young people to become active, while the arousal and organization of feelings are a necessary activity if social movements are to form and develop. The problem, however, is that this focus on emotions can lead to subjectivist understandings of this significance. If, on the one hand, emotions are regarded as solely the instinctive preserve of individuals then they remain susceptible to equations with irrational and unreasonable behaviour, accusations that take on further significance when equated with a view of youth and adolescence as one of psychosocial turmoil. More important for sociological concerns, on the other hand, is the current importance given to the normative significance of emotions in processes of social movement formation and development. The problem here, however, is that a different form of subjectivism may be embraced. This is one that risks regarding emotions as the unthinking product of normative constraints, where young activists unthinkingly identify and interpret their emotions according to the structures of feeling put down by the movements of which they are a part. To avoid such subjectivist understandings of young activists' emotions this paper has advocated a different approach. This is one that draws upon the arguments of social realists and the stress they give to the reasonable qualities of emotions and to their objective dimensions. Thus emotions are understood here as part of young people's reasoning activities undertaken in relation to those things that they care most forcefully about.

These themes have been explored in relation to data from research with a Local Occupy movement and specifically to how young people first became involved. Tracing through in considerable detail their feelings and sentiments, it has been argued that emotions do play a clear and decisive role in these young people's evaluations of the world and their understandings of their relations to the things that they care most forcefully about. Accordingly, not only do young people care about people, places and events sufficiently enough for them to provide the 'shoving power' required to animate their participation in Local Occupy, but these processes of emotional reasoning can take complex and nuanced forms. Young Occupy activists can and do, moreover, engage in constant deliberation with the concerns that they come to hold. It is this evaluative component of their emotional reasoning that explains how courses of action first embarked upon are then found unsatisfactory and thus are modified or abandoned. In this respect Local Occupy's creation by young people was neither the product of emotional irrationality nor a normatively constituted affair. On the contrary, it has been argued here that the making of Local Occupy emerged from young people's longstanding concerns about the world, together with the emotional intelligence accumulated from the experiences of the practical successes and failures involved in trying to do something about them.

## Notes

1 This paper draws upon research undertaken as part of the MYPLACE study (www.fp7-myplace.eu), funded under the European Community's FP7 programme (FP7–266831). The author would like to thank all those involved in Local Occupy who generously contributed their time and thoughts; and to the reviewers for their comments on this paper.

2 It is recognized that the term Local Occupy may be misleading because all Occupy demonstrations were by definition locally anchored. However, Local Occupy is used simply to locate the case study within the national and international movement of which it was a part and to highlight its existence as a smaller, regionally based example. The term Local Occupy also safeguards the confidentiality and anonymity of its participants, as does the removal of all identifying names and places.

3 There were two Local Occupy camps following the voluntary relocation of the first camp to a second site.

4 The research design defined young people as those under 30 years old in line with the parameters of the MYPLACE project more generally. It must be noted that a small number of respondents who satisfied this requirement when the research began had passed the 30-year-old threshold by the time the fieldwork had been completed.

5 All quotations are verbatim and all names are pseudonyms. The ages of respondents quoted are left purposefully ambiguous to ensure anonymity and are intended to convey simply that a respondent is a younger young adult or an older young adult.

6 Occupy camps were created near to the Hinckley Point nuclear reactor in Somerset and the intelligence base at Menwith Hill, for instance, but neither achieved much publicity.

7 http://www.occupyuk.info (accessed 28 November 2013).

## References

Abellán, J., Sequera, J. and Janoschka, M., (2012), 'Occupying the Hotel Madrid: a laboratory for urban resistance', *Social Movement Studies*, 11 (3–4): 320–326.

Alimi, E. Y., (2012), ' "Occupy Israel": a tale of startling success and hopeful failure', *Social Movement Studies*, 11 (3–4): 402–407.

Archer, M. S., (2000), *Being Human: The Problem of Agency*, Cambridge: Cambridge University Press.

Archer, M. S. and Tritter, J. Q., (2000), 'Introduction', in M. S. Archer and J. Q. Tritter (eds), *Rational Choice Theory: Resisting Colonization*, London: Routledge.

Bluebond-Langner, M. and Korbin, J. E., (2007), 'Challenges and opportunities in the anthropology of childhoods: an introduction to "Children, Childhoods and Childhood Studies"', *American Anthropologist*, 109 (2): 241–246.

Burawoy, M., (2007), 'Multi-case ethnography: reflections on 20 years fieldwork in socialism', Sociology Symposium, Newcastle University.

Calhoun, C., (2013), 'Occupy Wall Street in perspective', *The British Journal of Sociology*, 64 (1): 26–38.

Castells, M., (2012), *Networks of Outrage and Hope: Social Movements in the Internet Age*, Cambridge: Polity Press.

Chomsky, N., (2012), *Occupy*, London: Penguin Books.

Cohen, P., (1997), *Rethinking the Youth Question*, Basingstoke: Macmillan.

Gitlin, T., (2012), *Occupy Nation: The Roots, Spirit and The Promise of Occupy Wall Street*, New York: It Books.

Gitlin, T., (2013), 'Occupy's predicament: the moment and the prospects for the movement', *The British Journal of Sociology*, 64 (1): 3–25.

Jasper, J. M., (2006), 'Emotions and the microfoundations of politics: rethinking ends and needs', in S. Clarke, P. Hoggett and S. Thompson (eds), *Emotion, Politics and Society*, Basingstoke: Palgrave Macmillan.

Jasper, J. M., (2010), 'Social movement theory today: towards a theory of action', *Sociology Compass*, 4 (11): 965–976.

Jasper, J. M., (2011), 'Emotions and social movements: twenty years of theory and research', *Annual Review of Sociology*, 37 (1): 285–303.

Juris, J. S., Royane, M., Shokooh-Valle, F. and Wengronowitz, R., (2012), 'Negotiating power and difference within the 99%', *Social Movement Studies*, 11 (3–4): 434–440.

Le Bon, G., (1960), *The Crowd: A Study of the Popular Mind*, New York: Viking Press.

Mason, P., (2011), 'Twenty reasons why it's kicking off everywhere', available at: http://www.bbc.co.uk/blogs/newsnight/paulmason/2011/02/twenty_reasons_why_its_kicking.html (accessed 19 December 2013).

Mason, P., (2012), *Why It's Kicking Off Everywhere*, London: Verso.

Mizen, P. and Ofosu-Kusi, Y., (2013), 'Agency as vulnerability: accounting for children's movement to the streets of Accra', *The Sociological Review*, 61 (2): 363–382.

Nussbaum, M. C., (2001), *Upheavals of Thought: The Intelligence of Emotions*, Cambridge: Cambridge University Press.

Ruiz-Junco, N., (2012), 'Feeling social movements: theoretical contributions to social movement research on emotions', *Sociology Compass*, 7 (1): 45–54.

Sayer, A., (2011), *Why Things Matter to People: Social Science, Values and Ethical Life*, Cambridge: Cambridge University Press.

Smith, C., Castañeda, E. and Heyman, J., (2012), 'The homeless and Occupy El Paso: creating community among the 99%', *Social Movement Studies*, 11 (3–4): 356–366.

Smith, J. and Glidden, B., (2012), 'Occupy Pittsburgh and the challenges of participatory democracy', *Social Movement Studies*, 11 (3–4): 288–294.

Uitermark, J. and Nicholls, W., (2012), 'How local networks shape a global movement: comparing occupy in Amsterdam and Los Angeles', *Social Movement Studies*, 11 (3–4): 295–301.

Williams, S. J., (2001), *Emotion and Social Theory*, London: Routledge.

*The Sociological Review*, 63:S2, pp. 167–182 (2015), DOI: 10.1111/1467-954X.12267
© 2015 The Author. Editorial organisation © 2015 The Editorial Board of the Sociological Review

# Part Three: A turn to the radical right?

# Support for far right ideology and anti-migrant attitudes among youth in Europe: A comparative analysis

*Inta Mieriņa and Ilze Koroļeva*

**Abstract:** The last decade has seen a notable increase in support for far right parties and an alarming rise of right-wing extremism across Europe. Drawing on a new comparative youth survey in 14 European countries, this article provides deeper insight into young people's support for nationalist and far right ideology: negative attitudes towards minorities, xenophobia, welfare chauvinism and exclusionism in relation to migrants. We first map the support for far right ideology among youth in Europe, and then use multilevel regression analysis (16,935 individuals nested in 30 locations) to investigate which individual or contextual factors are associated with a higher propensity among young people towards getting involved in far right movements.

**Keywords:** far right, ethnic nationalism, identity, migration, xenophobia

## Introduction

Since the 1980s, social scientists have increasingly voiced their concern about the re-emergence of nationalist, anti-immigrant and anti-establishment sentiments among the masses and the growth of a new populist radical right party family in Western Europe. The global recession of 2009 intensified economic grievances and helped the populist radical right such as the Danish People's Party, UK Independence Party or (True) Finns as well as extreme right parties such as Golden Dawn in Greece and Jobbik in Hungary achieve significant electoral success. Instead of countering their arguments, most mainstream parties have shifted to the right as well, in an attempt to recapture voters (Yilmaz, 2012). Immigration and integration policies have been placed at the forefront of many Western European parties' agendas, and occupy a significant place in the political landscape (Rydgren, 2005; Yilmaz, 2012).

Support for 'far' (ie extreme, populist radical or radical) right parties has recently become one of the most intensely studied topics in political science. However, analysis of voting behaviour does not provide an accurate account of how

*The Sociological Review*, 63:S2, pp. 183–205 (2015), DOI: 10.1111/1467-954X.12268
© 2015 The Authors. Editorial organisation © 2015 The Editorial Board of the Sociological Review. Published by John Wiley & Sons Ltd, 9600 Garsington Road, Oxford OX4 2DQ, UK and 350 Main Street, Malden, MA 02148, USA

widespread or strong the support for far right ideology is (Pop-Eleches, 2010), and neither does it measure the potential of far right movements to mobilize supporters (Kedar, 2005; Kitschelt, 2007). Analysis of prejudice and discriminatory attitudes towards outgroups could help to answer those questions better, yet they have so far received comparatively little attention in political science.

Moreover, studies on the far right have often led to inconsistent, even contradictory, results (Golder, 2003), which might be due to differences in data coverage. Up until now a comparative pan-European perspective has been largely missing from scholarly work; most authors concentrate either on the established democracies in Western Europe (eg Lubbers *et al.*, 2002; Arzheimer and Carter, 2006; Arzheimer, 2009; Spies and Franzmann, 2011) or East-Central Europe (Mudde, 2005; Bustikova and Kitschelt, 2009; Pop-Elches, 2010; Bustikova, 2014).[1] A significant drawback of the existing studies is that typically they explore either only individual level, or only contextual level predictors. The former are unable to explain differences across time and countries, while the latter are prone to a 'composition effect', that is, differences in far right support might stem purely from the fact that some socio-demographic groups are represented in certain research locations in larger numbers. Using multilevel models with both individual characteristics and contextual level variables is one way to solve this problem (Lubbers *et al.*, 2002; Arzheimer and Carter, 2006; Arzheimer, 2009).

Previous research in Western Europe has found that, on average, young people – along with those who are 65 or older – are most likely to support far right parties (Arzheimer and Carter, 2006; Arzheimer, 2009; Lubbers *et al.*, 2002).[2] Nevertheless, there might be considerable differences between countries that the aforementioned studies do not explore.[3] Considering that the group of young people in general surveys is typically small, reliable data on how strong the support for different populist or extreme ideas is among youth in Europe, especially its Eastern part, and what motivations drive it, is lacking. In this paper we draw on the MYPLACE dataset of 14 European countries,[4] to explore young people's support for the ideas voiced by far right parties: negative attitudes towards minorities, xenophobia, welfare chauvinism and exclusionism in relation to migrants. A multi-level regression analysis with 16,935 individuals clustered in 30 localities around Europe is used to investigate which individual or contextual level factors are associated with a higher propensity to support far right ideology and, thus, getting involved in far right movements.

The results show that ethnic nationalism, along with financial problems and economic insecurity (resource stress and perceived competition) are some of the most important factors behind xenophobia, welfare chauvinism and exclusionism, and they are at least partly responsible for the comparatively high prevalence of anti-migrant sentiments in East-Central Europe. The results also show that young people who have low interest and poor understanding of politics tend to be more receptive to far right ideology. Unfortunately the data suggest that media, instead of educating youth and dispelling prejudice, further worsen attitudes towards minorities and migrants. Perceptions of immigration and immigrants' rights are also influenced by ideology; liberal regimes such as in the UK are more

*The Sociological Review*, 63:S2, pp. 183–205 (2015), DOI: 10.1111/1467-954X.12268
© 2015 The Authors. Editorial organisation © 2015 The Editorial Board of the Sociological Review

likely than other types of welfare regime to produce xenophobic and exclusionist attitudes.

In the next section we provide an overview of the existing knowledge on the different potential sources of the support for the far right. In the light of this review, we then move to formulate our hypotheses, discuss data and methods and, finally, conduct descriptive and inferential analysis.

## The core ideology of the far right

Despite the growing prominence of research on the far right, there is still a lack of a commonly accepted definition, and quite a lot of conceptual confusion. Kai Arzheimer and Elisabeth Carter (2006) talk about 'extreme right' parties. Cas Mudde (2007) distinguishes 'populist radical right' as a separate type of party. Herbert Kitschelt (2007) argues that there is no need to qualify most current radical right parties as 'populist' and thus, like Pippa Norris (2005), he opts for 'radical right'. The word 'extreme' is avoided as it would imply rejection of democracy as a political system – a belief which is not shared by all, or even most, radical right parties of today (Kitschelt, 2007; Mudde, 2007, 2010). Often 'radical' and 'extreme' are used interchangeably, despite the fact that there are clear conceptual differences which must be recognized (Kitschelt, 2007; Mudde, 2007, 2010).

Cas Mudde's research suggests that radical right ideology typically rests on nationalism, xenophobia, welfare chauvinism, and law and order (Mudde, 2000; see also Arzheimer and Carter, 2006; Ishiyama, 2009). The ideological core of the new 'populist radical right' ideology, according to Mudde (2007), is a combination of nativism, authoritarianism and populism, of which nativism is considered as the key feature. It holds that 'states should be inhabited exclusively by members of the native group ('the nation') and that non-native elements (persons and ideas) are fundamentally threatening to the homogenous nation-state' (Mudde, 2007: 19). The myth of the homogenous nation is put before the individual and his/her civil rights (Minkenberg, 2000). Based on Carter (2005), Kitschelt (2007) conceptualizes 'radical right' parties as those that are: nationalist/xenophobic; and racist or, at least, culturally conformist. Drawing on the analysis of post-communist countries, Ishiyama (2009: 488) conceptualizes the 'extreme right wing' voter as someone who is 'highly nationalistic, hostile to minority rights and highly sceptical regarding European integration'. Whilst recognizing the nuanced differences between conceptual terms, in this article we employ a broader term 'far right' to include all categories discussed here (Mudde, 2010).

## Factors affecting support for the far right

Different disciplines propose differing explanations of the causes of support for far right parties and ideology (van der Brug *et al.*, 2005; Arzheimer, 2009). Below we explore some of the most frequently mentioned groups of explanations.

## Socio-psychological explanations

Talking about socio-psychological determinants of far right appeal, earlier post-World War II theories mainly focused on *personality traits* and *value orientations* that make a person more receptive to this kind of ideology, or blamed *social disaggregation* brought about by social change (Arzheimer, 2009).

Classical theories of scapegoating (Dollard *et al.*, 1939; Zawadzki, 1948) and Realistic Group Conflict (Sherif and Sherif, 1953) talk about g*roup conflicts* as the root cause of ethnic tensions and far right views. If scapegoating is psychologically driven and based on emotions, Realistic Group Conflict theory assumes that conflict is instrumental, and prejudice and discrimination are based on real competition over scarce resources. Esses *et al.* (1998) develop this theory further in their 'instrumental model of group conflict', arguing that resource stress over jobs, money, power and so on, combined with a presence of a relevant outgroup perceived as a competitor is an essential source of group conflicts, discrimination and xenophobia.

In some cases perceived threat to national identity and culture posed by immigration (the ideational argument) can be equally or even more important (Golder, 2003; Yilmaz, 2012; Sears and Henry, 2003). According to social identity theory (Tajfel and Turner, 1979), the conflict is about group identity and self-esteem. Blaming an unfavourable economic condition on others (outgroup) allows the preservation of a positive group image. A desire for a 'cultural nation' can also play into the hands of the far right, whereas 'political nation' is more inclusive (Hjern, 1998; Lewin-Epstein and Levanon, 2005; Ishiyama, 2009). Unlike civic identity which is voluntary and based on participation in the political community, acceptance of the prevailing culture and respect for countries' laws and institutions, national identity which is based on being born in a country and belonging to a certain ethnic group, is more exclusionist towards outsiders (foreigners) (Hjern, 1998; Lewin-Epstein and Levanon, 2005).

According to the cultural affinity thesis, those who are themselves excluded from the dominant culture, are more likely to develop feelings of acceptance and empathy towards members of other marginalized or minority groups (Espenshade and Hempstead, 1996; Fetzer, 2000; Lewin-Epstein and Levanon, 2005). Members of the dominant group may be more opposed to, for example, admitting others to citizenship, as they would lose their advantage in terms of citizenship status. According to the contact hypothesis (Allport, 1954; Fetzer, 2000) prejudice and hostility towards minorities diminishes if people have more contact and communication with members of these groups, unless there is a real group conflict for resources; in this case proximity only increases intergroup hostility (Esses *et al.*, 1998).

## Social background explanations

Sociologists have linked the increasing xenophobia, racism and support for the far right to the process of modernization (Minkenberg, 2000; Rydgren, 2005; Mudde, 2007). In times of rapid socio-economic change (globalization, risk society, post-industrialization, post-communism, deep economic recessions), or personal struggles, individuals begin feeling insecure and can become aggressive and hostile (Betz, 1998).

Young people are typically among those that suffer the effects of socio-economic transformations the most (Toots and Bachmann, 2010: 35) and their insecure situation in the labour market facilitates support for far right parties (Arzheimer and Carter, 2006).

Especially likely to support the far right are the unemployed, working class and lower-middle class citizens – in particular manual workers, petty bourgeoisie and those in routine non-manual employment, as they worry that the growing influx of migrants may undermine their social and economic position (Lubbers *et al.*, 2002; van der Brug *et al.*, 2005; Kitschelt, 2007; Arzheimer, 2009). Their views can be seen as based on self-interest and instrumental group conflict. Far right parties also get disproportionally large support from those with a lower level of education and specifically men (Lubbers *et al.*, 2002; Lewin-Epstein and Levanon, 2005; Arzheimer, 2009).

*Socio-structural explanations*

Socio-structural models try to explain support for the far right by aggregate level variables such as level of immigration, economic conditions and level of support for the political system (van der Brug *et al.*, 2005). The most commonly mentioned factor that unconditionally increases support for the far right in Western Europe is high and increasing levels of immigration (Jackman and Volpert, 1996; Golder, 2003; Arzheimer, 2009; Knigge, 1998).

Besides immigration, the majority of studies find that the number of immigrants, asylum seekers, non-EU residents, or share of foreign-born residents is positively linked with the far right vote (Lubbers *et al.*, 2002; Swank and Betz, 2003; Arzheimer 2009). Yet, there is also an indication that the association between the size of minority group and support for far right ideology could be non-linear (Bustikova, 2014).

With regard to unemployment, the conclusions are inconsistent. Some authors argue that unemployment rates have a significant effect on voting for the far right (Jackman and Volpert, 1996; Esses *et al.*, 1998; Golder, 2003; Arzheimer, 2009), while some others find that the effect is, in fact, negative (Knigge, 1998; Lubbers *et al.*, 2002; Arzheimer and Carter, 2006) or there is no effect (Bustikova, 2014). In addition, high economic volatility (Bustikova, 2014) and the unsatisfactory economic situation (Esses *et al.*, 1998) seem to increase support for the far right.

According to Kitschelt (2007), far right parties are more likely to attract votes in post-industrial economies that have encompassing welfare systems that extend substantial social benefits to everyone, even immigrants. On the other hand, low social expenditure leads to economic insecurity (Mau *et al.*, 2012) thus the liberal regime type might facilitate xenophobia and negative attitudes towards minorities more than the Nordic type that offers comprehensive social insurance coverage. Indeed, recent studies (Swank and Betz, 2003; Arzheimer, 2009) have drawn attention to the importance of welfare state institutions in mitigating the effect of liberalization, immigration and unemployment. Generous and employment-oriented welfare states have been found to reduce the risk of increasing support for the far right (Bustikova and Kitschelt, 2009).

Although xenophobia, ethno-nationalism, exclusionism and welfare chauvinism have been portrayed by the international media as more of a problem in Western Europe, emerging research on the far right in East-Central Europe (ECE) shows that as a legacy of national independence movements and nationalist sentiments during the collapse of the Soviet Union, people in this region are especially sensitive to ethnic issues (Evans and Whitefield, 1993). Although far right parties in ECE have had very different fortunes, prejudice towards certain minority groups is widespread, the level of racist extremist violence is *on average* higher than in the West, and in some countries there are still notable skinhead subcultures with links to political organizations (Mudde, 2005; Pop-Eleches, 2010). Moreover, the historical memory of the large influx of immigrants from other Soviet republics during the communist period might have contributed to xenophobia in at least some of the post-Soviet countries.

### The impact of media, information and populism

The media plays a crucial role in whether a far right party receives enough exposure to raise the prominence of their issues in the public eye (Rydgren, 2005; Boomgaarden and Vliegenthart, 2007). According to Rydgren (2005) part of the success of far right parties in countries like Denmark is that they have succeeded in shifting public attention from socio-economic issues to socio-cultural issues (such as immigration, culture, religion, law and order, abortion).

Some researchers have argued that 'extremist movements are movements of disaffection' (Lipset and Raab, 1978: 428) and resentment (Betz, 1998). Indeed, far right parties are especially likely to attract disaffected and alienated voters (Betz, 1998; Lubbers *et al.*, 2002; Rydgren, 2005), as well as those who are critical of the political system and dissatisfied with their political leaders (Knigge, 1998; Lubbers *et al.*, 2002; Arzheimer, 2009). Far right ideology seemingly provides an answer as to what to fear, and who to blame for both collective and personal failures. This is especially appealing to people who have little knowledge of politics and little trust in institutions (Rydgren, 2003).

### Hypotheses

Based on Esses *et al.*'s (1998) instrumental model of group conflict, we can expect that *H1*: those in less advantageous social-economic positions in terms of education, occupation, social class and income, are more likely to support far right ideology. Xenophobia and negative attitudes towards minorities often thrive on ignorance and irrational fear, thus we expect that *H2*: far right ideology appeals most to people who have little trust in politicians, little knowledge and information about politics, and who do not follow news in the media very often. In line

*The Sociological Review*, 63:S2, pp. 183–205 (2015), DOI: 10.1111/1467-954X.12268

with social identity theory *H3*: ethnic nationalism can be expected to facilitate xenophobia, outgroup hostility and the appeal of far right ideology.

Turning to contextual variables, we posit that welfare state type can have an effect on attitudes towards minorities and immigrants. Considering the increased economic insecurity linked to low social expenditure we expect that *H4a*: the liberal regime type facilitates xenophobia more than the Nordic type. Due to historical reasons, we expect that *H4b*: negative attitudes toward minorities and immigrants are most characteristic of youth in post-socialist countries in East-Central Europe.

## Data and method

### Data

The data we use comes from the MYPLACE project. The advantages of this data are twofold. First, the project specifically targets young people aged 16–25, thus allowing us to explore the prevalence of far right attitudes in more detail and with better statistical precision in a group that is typically at the forefront of na-tionalist extremist groups and violent racist subcultures and incidents. Second, the sample was specifically designed to suit multilevel analysis techniques. Two contrasting locations were selected in each country (including eastern and west-ern Germany) with approximately 600 respondents in one location (Appendix Table A1). Interviews were conducted as face-to-face personal interviews in re-spondents' homes, using random sampling (in some cases the full sample). The fieldwork took place between September 2012 and April 2013.

## Method

In this article we use multilevel regression analysis which allows testing simulta-neously in one model for the effect of individual and contextual level variables. Unlike the ordinary multiple regression models, multilevel analysis accounts for the fact that the observations in the sample are not independent; individuals are nested within localities, thus, it provides correct standard errors and unbiased estimates of contextual effects, reducing the possibility of Type I error.

In our sample 16,935 individuals are nested within 30 localities which are fur-ther nested within 14 countries, calling for the application of a three-level anal-ysis. As three-level analysis has certain drawbacks in terms of complexity and estimation difficulty (Hox, 2010: 32) we performed a number of tests to check the usefulness of such a strategy. Due to the specific sampling design of the MY-PLACE survey,[5] only a small proportion (2–4 per cent) of variance in our de-pendent variables can be found at the level of countries. This means that adding the third, country, level to our analysis is not justified and, due to a small num-ber of level 3 cases, not recommended. Hence, we opted for two-level analysis.[6] Since there are no strong theoretical arguments why the individual or contextual explanations of far right views should systematically vary across locations, we use random intercept models with fixed slopes.

## Indicators

### Dependent variables

The core of far right ideology is xenophobia, measured in the MYPLACE survey by '[country] should have stricter border controls and visa restrictions to prevent further immigration'. Welfare exclusionism and chauvinism is another form of negative attitude towards immigrants. It can refer to different resources such as jobs, welfare (health care, housing, education), or property such as land, thus, we use a summary index of three variables (see Appendix Table A2).

Another characteristic feature of far right ideology is negative attitudes towards minorities. Seven items were available that measure negative attitudes towards Roma, Jews and Muslims as well as towards a more general category of 'immigrants' (see Appendix Table A2). Which social group is disliked or stigmatized the most differs from country to country, thus, a summary index was created from these seven items.[7]

### Independent variables

Among the independent variables we include the following social background characteristics: education, income (how easy to cope on present household income), economic status, social class,[8] age and gender.

To test the populist thesis and importance of information in reducing support for far right ideology we include dissatisfaction with incumbent politicians index, intensity of following news in media index, along with interest in politics and political knowledge (Appendix Table A2).

To test the relationship between minority status and far right views we include country of birth, citizenship and ethnic group (majority, other). Ethnic nationalism was coded as a summary variable from how important it is, for being a citizen of [COUNTRY], 'to have been born in [country]' and 'to have at least one ethnic [country] parent)'.

Based on the contact hypothesis, we also control for generalized trust and contact with minorities (how many close friends of a different race/ethnic group the respondent has).

At the macro level we include dummy variables for welfare state type (Kääriäinen and Lehtonen, 2006). We also control for contextual characteristics such as the size of the area, immigration rates, changes in GPD during the recent economic crisis (2008–11), locality-level poverty rates,[9] as well as the percentage of young people born outside the country (as a proxy for recent immigrant population) and belonging to an ethnic minority (as a proxy for ethnic diversity). Unfortunately, no locality-level data on youth unemployment was available and aggregation of respondents' answers in this case was deemed to be not reliable.

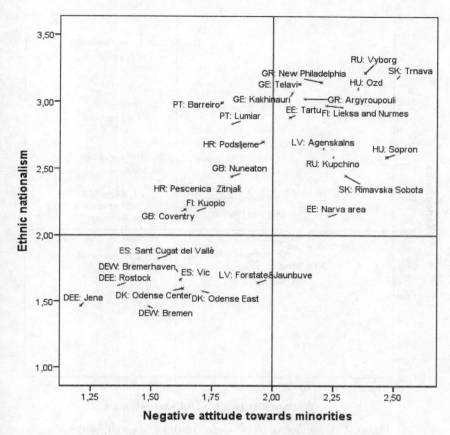

**Figure 1** *Ethnic nationalism and negative attitudes towards minorities*
*Notes:* Country names coded according to ISO 3166-1. RU – Russia, LV –
Latvia, EE – Estonia, SK – Slovakia, HR – Croatia, HU – Hungary, PT –
Portugal, ES – Spain, FI – Finland, GB – United Kingdom, DK – Denmark,
GE – Georgia, GR – Greece, DEE – East Germany, DEW – West Germany.
*Source:* MYPLACE survey, 2012–13.

Results

*Mapping the appeal of far right ideology across locations*

We begin our analysis with mapping the support for far right ideology in each of
the 30 survey locations. Figure 1 shows the mean scores for ethnic nationalism
and negative attitudes towards minority groups.

Nationalist sentiments, as well as most negative attitudes towards minorities
tend to be most widespread among youth in East-Central Europe and Greece.
Young people in Portuguese locations also support ethnic nationalism, yet
attitudes towards minorities are more positive. Similarly, in the UK and Croatian locations, despite comparatively high ethnic nationalism, minorities are

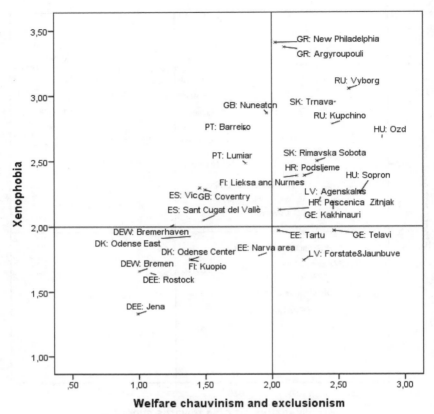

**Figure 2** *Xenophobia, welfare chauvinism and exclusionism*
*Notes:* RU – Russia, LV – Latvia, EE – Estonia, SK – Slovakia, HR – Croatia,
HU – Hungary, PT – Portugal, ES – Spain, FI – Finland, GB – United
Kingdom, DK – Denmark, GE – Georgia, GR – Greece, DEE – East Germany,
DEW – West Germany.
*Source:* MYPLACE survey, 2012–13.

perceived *on average* more positively than negatively. Attitudes towards minorities are most tolerant and inclusive and ethnic nationalism least widespread in
Denmark, Spain and Germany.

Of all surveyed young people, youth in Greek locations are most wary of immigrants; almost 90 per cent supported restrictions on further immigration. Similar attitudes are observed in both Russian locations. However, xenophobia, welfare chauvinism and exclusionism are also extremely widespread in Hungary and
Slovakia, which experience much less immigration (Figure 2). Young people in
other post-Soviet locations in Georgia, Latvia and Estonia also tend to support
exclusionism with regard to immigrants, although they do not worry as much
about limiting immigration which is currently very low. Youth in Portugal, on

*The Sociological Review*, 63:S2, pp. 183–205 (2015), DOI: 10.1111/1467-954X.12268

**Table 1:** *Variance components of regression models*

| | | Empty model (random intercept only) | With individual level explanatory variables | With country level explanatory variables |
|---|---|---|---|---|
| Negative attitudes towards minorities | σ (individual level) | 0.291 | 0.257 | 0.257 |
| | σ (country level) | 0.118 | 0.057 | 0.019 |
| | -loglikelihood | 18536.315 | 16768.540 | 16818.570 |
| Xenophobia | σ (individual level) | 1.056 | 0.971 | 0.971 |
| | σ (country level) | 0.279 | 0.162 | .052 |
| | -loglikelihood | 41859.459 | 39614.391 | 39653.719 |
| Welfare chauvinism and exclusionism | σ (individual level) | 0.537 | 0.474 | 0.474 |
| | σ (country level) | 0.278 | 0.136 | 0.022 |
| | -loglikelihood | 31571.574 | 29092.526 | 29121.193 |

*Source*: MYPLACE survey, 2012–13.

the contrary, tend to agree that it is necessary to restrict immigration, yet they mostly do not support excluding immigrants from welfare, jobs or land ownership.

Sometimes large differences can be observed between locations within a country. Respondents in Nuneaton (UK), for instance, are less tolerant towards immigrants and see ethnic and religious minorities in more negative terms than respondents in the more ethnically diverse Coventry. Youth in Germany stand out as the least xenophobic and welfare exclusionist, followed by Denmark.

*What factors drive negative attitudes towards minorities and immigrants?*

To better understand what factors are responsible for the observed differences, we now turn to the analysis of determinants of far right views.

The initial analysis of variance components (Table 1) reveals that a significant proportion – 29 per cent of variance in negative attitudes towards minorities, 21 per cent in xenophobia, and 34 per cent in welfare chauvinism and exclusionism – lies at the level of localities.

Inclusion of the individual level variables resulted in a 12 per cent decrease of residual, individual level variance of negative attitudes towards minorities, welfare chauvinism and exclusionism, 8 per cent decrease in individual level variance of xenophobia and an even larger – 40–50 per cent – reduction in intercept variance. This means that much of the observed difference between research locations is due to the composition effect, that is, differing individual characteristics among their young residents.

Adding contextual variables significantly improves the model fit, helping to achieve almost 70 per cent reduction of intercept variance in negative attitudes towards minorities and xenophobia, and 84 per cent in welfare chauvinism and exclusionism. Less than 7 per cent of unexplained variance remains at the level of localities.

Turning to the substantive results (Table 2), in line with hypothesis H2, we find that one of the strongest predictors of negative attitudes towards immigrants and minorities among youth is ethnic nationalism. A one unit increase in ethnic nationalism on a five-point scale is associated with a 0.132 unit increase in negative attitudes towards minorities, a 0.234 unit increase in xenophobia, and a 0.2 unit increase in welfare chauvinism and exclusionism measured on the same scale.

The analysis lends further support to realistic group conflict theory and the instrumental model of group conflict (H3); negative attitudes towards immigrants and minorities are more common among young people in less advantageous socio-economic positions, that is, those with less than upper secondary education, whose family is struggling financially and whose parents do not belong to the highest social class. Interestingly, though, if income is accounted for, young people who are employed tend to have more negative attitudes towards minorities and to be more xenophobic than the unemployed, whereas students tend to be the most tolerant and least chauvinistic.

As regards the cultural affinity thesis, our analysis confirms that negative attitudes towards minorities are more common among the dominant ethnic group than among those who belong to minorities themselves, regardless of citizenship status, and that negative attitudes towards immigrants are more common among citizens than those who are not citizens themselves. Interestingly, though, controlled for citizenship and ethnic group, young people born outside the country bear more negative attitudes towards minority groups than those born in the country of residence, and ethnic minorities do not demonstrate more empathy towards immigrants than the majority youth. This relationship is intriguing and requires further exploration.

Results for welfare chauvinism and exclusionism lend further support for the cultural affinity thesis: welfare chauvinism and exclusionism in relation to immigrants is less widespread among young people who belong to an ethnic minority, are born outside the country and are not citizens themselves. On the other hand, this result can be interpreted as concern about one's own situation and desire not to be excluded.

The analysis also shows that xenophobia is strongly linked to citizenship status. However, xenophobia does not depend on whether the person is a member of a majority or minority group or on his or her country of birth (Sig. < 0.05). There is no extra empathy from members of minority ethnic groups or former immigrants towards potential future immigrants.

In line with the populist thesis (H2), we find that political distrust is one of the strongest predictors of support for far right ideology. Xenophobia, anti-minority attitudes, welfare chauvinism and exclusionism are more widespread

**Table 2:** *Determinants of negative attitudes towards minorities, xenophobia, welfare chauvinism and exclusionism*

| | Negative attitudes towards minorities (n2=30, n1=11454) | | Xenophobia (n2=30, n1=14419) | | Welfare chauvinism and exclusionism (n2=30, n1=14165) | |
|---|---|---|---|---|---|---|
| | B | SE | b | SE | b | SE |
| *Individual-level predictors* | | | | | | |
| Gender (a man) | 0.074*** | 0.010 | 0.060*** | 0.017 | 0.043*** | 0.012 |
| Age | 0.002 | 0.002 | 0.000 | 0.004 | 0.008** | 0.003 |
| Tertiary education | Ref. | Ref. | Ref. | Ref. | Ref. | Ref. |
| Upper secondary education | 0.047*** | 0.014 | 0.049~ | 0.025 | 0.078*** | 0.018 |
| Less than upper secondary education | 0.085*** | 0.018 | 0.098** | 0.032 | 0.131*** | 0.022 |
| Employed | Ref. | Ref. | Ref. | Ref. | Ref. | Ref. |
| Unemployed | −0.035~ | 0.019 | −0.072* | 0.032 | 0.016 | 0.022 |
| In education | −0.065*** | 0.013 | −0.090*** | 0.023 | −0.078*** | 0.016 |
| Other | −0.032 | 0.023 | 0.003 | 0.038 | −0.061* | 0.027 |
| Class 3 | Ref. | Ref. | Ref. | Ref. | Ref. | Ref. |
| Class 2 | 0.047*** | 0.014 | 0.054~ | 0.031 | 0.017 | 0.022 |
| Class 1 | 0.085*** | 0.018 | 0.123*** | 0.031 | 0.030 | 0.022 |
| Class 0 | 0.000 | 0.000 | 0.103*** | 0.024 | 0.044** | 0.017 |
| Financial problems in the household | 0.029* | 0.012 | 0.073*** | 0.021 | 0.052*** | 0.015 |

*(Continued)*

*The Sociological Review*, 63:S2, pp. 183–205 (2015), DOI: 10.1111/1467-954X.12268

195

**Table 2:** *Continued*

| | Negative attitudes towards minorities (n2=30, n1=11454) | | Xenophobia (n2=30, n1=14419) | | Welfare chauvinism and exclusionism (n2=30, n1=14165) | |
|---|---|---|---|---|---|---|
| | B | SE | b | SE | b | SE |
| Dominant ethnicity in the country of residence | 0.039* | 0.018 | 0.044 | 0.032 | 0.076*** | 0.022 |
| Citizen of the county | 0.015 | 0.026 | 0.203*** | 0.046 | 0.164*** | 0.032 |
| Born in the county | -0.128*** | 0.025 | 0.059 | 0.043 | 0.119*** | 0.030 |
| Ethnic nationalism | 0.132*** | 0.005 | 0.234*** | 0.008 | 0.200*** | 0.006 |
| Political knowledge | -0.023*** | 0.006 | -0.024* | 0.010 | -0.006 | 0.007 |
| Interest in politics | -0.042*** | 0.006 | -0.045*** | 0.011 | -0.033*** | 0.008 |
| Media exposure | 0.014*** | 0.002 | 0.010** | 0.004 | 0.008** | 0.003 |
| Social trust | -0.018*** | 0.002 | -0.017*** | 0.004 | -0.021*** | 0.003 |
| Political trust | -0.029*** | 0.002 | -0.021*** | 0.004 | -0.025*** | 0.003 |
| Number of friends of other ethnicity/race | -0.045*** | 0.004 | -0.052*** | 0.007 | -0.060*** | 0.005 |
| *Contextual predictors:* | Ref. | | Ref. | | Ref. | |

*(Continued)*

*The Sociological Review*, 63:S2, pp. 183–205 (2015), DOI: 10.1111/1467-954X.12268
© 2015 The Authors. Editorial organisation © 2015 The Editorial Board of the Sociological Review

**Table 2:** *Continued*

| | Negative attitudes towards minorities (n2=30, n1=11454) | | Xenophobia (n2=30, n1=14419) | | Welfare chauvinism and exclusionism (n2=30, n1=14165) | |
|---|---|---|---|---|---|---|
| | B | SE | b | SE | b | SE |
| GDP growth during the crisis (2008–2011) | 0.002 | 0.004 | 0.006 | 0.007 | 0.006 | 0.004 |
| per cent of families in the area exp. fin. difficulties | 0.007** | 0.002 | 0.015*** | 0.004 | 0.003 | 0.002 |
| per cent of young people born abroad | -0.002 | 0.005 | -0.002 | 0.008 | -0.011* | 0.005 |
| per cent of young people of non-majority ethnicity | -0.002 | 0.002 | -0.006~ | 0.003 | 0.004~ | 0.002 |
| Net immigration rates | 0.007 | 0.017 | 0.083* | 0.029 | 0.032 | 0.019 |
| Size of the area (million) | 0.042 | 0.0311 | 0.135* | 0.052 | 0.033 | 0.034 |
| Liberal | Ref. | Ref. | Ref. | Ref. | Ref. | Ref. |
| Post-socialist | 0.178 | 0.154 | -0.623 | 0.257 | 0.269 | 0.169 |
| Nordic | 0.138 | 00.151 | -0.585* | 0.253 | -0.200 | 0.165 |
| Conservative | -0.167 | 00.147 | -0.634* | 0.245 | -0.552** | 0.161 |
| Mediterranean | -0.191 | 00.145 | -0.521* | 0.242 | -0.207 | 0.158 |
| Constant | 10.460*** | 00.176 | 10.585*** | 0.296 | 0.843*** | 0.196 |

*** $p < 0.001$, ** $p < 0.01$, * $p < 0.05$, ~ $p < 0.1$, two-tailed tests.
*Source:* MYPLACE survey, 2012–13.

among young people who have little interest and understanding of politics. However, contrary to our expectations, young people who watch different media channels more frequently are more – not less – likely to hold xenophobic, exclusionist views and negative attitudes towards all kinds of minorities. This result suggests that the media are at least partly responsible for the recent spread of xenophobic and far right sentiments across Europe.

Like other researchers, we find that men are more likely than women to be xenophobic, welfare chauvinist and exclusionist and to hold negative attitudes towards minorities. Another important factor is social trust; those who do not trust others in general are more likely to have negative attitudes towards minorities, and to be xenophobic and exclusionist as regards immigrants. The fact that welfare chauvinism and exclusionism is strongly linked to social and political distrust could be explained by fear that immigrants could abuse the system in a dishonest manner. Finally, as predicted by the contact hypothesis, attitudes towards all kinds of minorities and immigrants improve if people have more contact with minorities themselves.[10]

Analysis of contextual level predictors again lends support to the instrumental model of group conflict; alongside one's personal financial situation, the overall economic situation in the area is among the strongest predictors of xenophobia and negative attitudes towards minorities as it contributes to resource stress. A 20 per cent increase in the number of poor families in the area would lead to a 0.3 units increase in xenophobia and 0.14 units increase in negative attitudes towards minorities on a five-point scale.

As predicted by the theory, higher immigration rates facilitate xenophobia, that is, calls for limiting immigration. However, neither immigration rates nor the overall economic situation in the area or its development in the country affects welfare chauvinism and exclusionism. This shows that exclusionist attitudes are more a matter of ideology.

Welfare chauvinism and exclusionism depend on the welfare state model; they are less widespread in the conservative model (Germany) than in the liberal model (UK). Moreover, in accordance with hypothesis H4a, when the other factors are accounted for, the liberal welfare state type is more likely to produce xenophobia than any other type of welfare regime. Subjective socio-economic insecurity is likely to contribute to resource stress in liberal regimes (Mau *et al.*, 2012), fuelling group competition.

The analysis does not confirm hypothesis H4b regarding the importance of a country's post-socialist status for far right views. One can conclude that other factors rather than post-socialist status are responsible for comparatively high rates of xenophobia, welfare chauvinism, exclusionism and overall negative attitudes towards minorities in East-Central Europe (see Figure 1 and Figure 2).

*Robustness of results*

Given that multilevel models can sometimes provide inconsistent results (Maas and Hox, 2004), we performed a number of robustness tests. Our main concern was the high number (in some cases, more than 25 per cent) of missing values in the 'negative attitude towards minorities' scale. Hence, we conducted the analysis separately for each of the minority groups: Muslims, Jews and Roma (the group most prone to discrimination). We also estimated the models with social expenditure as a percentage of GDP instead of welfare state types. The results (available from the authors, on request) remain largely unchanged, which gives us confidence in our findings and their robustness.

## Conclusions

Using new data collected as part of the MYPLACE youth survey, in this article we have explored young people's support for far right ideology and analysed which factors are associated with holding far right views. We find that despite comparatively low immigration rates, young people in post-socialist locations, along with Greek locations, tend to have more negative predispositions and to be more xenophobic and exclusionist towards immigrants than young people in Western European locations. Moreover, we have demonstrated that young Europeans' views on immigrants vary greatly even within the boundaries of one country, thus below-national level analysis should be the preferred strategy in future studies.

Our analysis shows that negative attitudes towards minorities and immigrants are often rooted in ethnic nationalism, that is, a belief that one has to be born in a country or have at least one ethnic parent for being a citizen of a country. A more over-arching civic national identity – based on respect for countries' institutions and laws – is more likely to create an inclusive, cohesive society.

The data strongly support the instrumental model of group conflict, confirming that resource stress over money, status and, most of all, jobs is an essential source of group conflicts. Living in poverty or seeing poverty facilitates negative attitudes towards minorities and significantly increases xenophobia, welfare chauvinism and exclusionism, especially if immigration rates are high. Far right ideology is especially appealing to groups of society who experience a higher level of insecurity and perceived competition.

An essential finding of this study concerns the importance of ensuring fair and adequate information to the public, and the failure of media to accomplish that. Support for far right ideology among youth is driven by the fact that young people often have little interest in and, accordingly, not a very good understanding of politics. The analysis shows that frequent use of different media channels leads to further worsening of attitudes towards minorities, as well as an increase in xenophobia, welfare chauvinism and exclusionism. One can conclude that the media are at least partly responsible for the recent spread of populism and far right views in Europe. Negative attitudes towards minorities and immigrants are also linked to political and social distrust while more contact with representatives of minority groups can help to overcome prejudice and hostility.

Analysis of contextual factors has revealed that the high prevalence of far right views in East-Central Europe cannot be explained by the socialist past or post-socialist status as such, but rather a number of other factors such as resource stress, low social and political trust, little contact with people of different ethnic background as well as ethnic nationalism, which, historically, has been important for the self-determination of the new post-socialist nations (Ishiyama, 2009).

Liberal welfare regimes, as found in the UK, are more likely than any other type of welfare regime to produce xenophobic attitudes. In this welfare regime type young people tend to be more welfare chauvinist and exclusionist than in the conservative model. One can conclude that ideology plays an important role in the formation of young peoples' attitudes towards the rights of immigrants. This finding has powerful implications; it suggests that liberalization and retrenchment of universal welfare policies is not the right answer to immigration; by increasing economic insecurity and perceived competition for scarce resources it would rather heighten anti-immigrant sentiments. From this point-of-view the dismantling of the European Social Model observed during the recent economic crisis risks facilitating exclusionist attitudes among European youth.

# Notes

1 Two exceptions, which include post-communist countries alongside Western European countries, are Norris (2005) and Mudde (2007).

2 Possible reasons for the U-shaped support for far right parties are discussed in more detail in Arzheimer and Carter (2006).

3 For example, in the UK YouGov 'Profile of voters February 2013' reveals that 48 per cent of the potential UKIP voters were 60+, whereas only 8 per cent of their supporters were 18–29 years old.

4 The research underpinning this article was undertaken under the auspices of the MYPLACE project (FP7-266831). Financial support for writing this article was additionally provided by the ESF project 'The emigrant communities of Latvia: National identity, transnational relations, and diaspora politics' (2013/0055/1DP/1.1.1.2.0/13/APIA/VIAA/040).

5 The fact that the sample is clustered typically leads to units within one cluster (in this case, localities in a country) being more similar to one another than if they were drawn randomly from a pool of independent units. Therefore the effective sample size is in fact smaller than the number of units in the sample. Disregarding it leads to underestimating the standard errors, especially if: the number of units in one cluster is large; and units within one cluster are very similar (Hox, 2010). In our case the number of localities within a country is only two (except for Germany where it is four), and the localities have specifically been selected on the basis of their differing socio-economic characteristics (for a description of national samples, see: http://www.fp7-myplace.eu/documents/WP4D4-5overviewreportv1.pdf), ie two localities within one country might differ more than they differ from localities in other countries. Thus, one might expect that the intra-class correlation (ICC) is small.

6 Since our models do not include country dummies (in order to be able to include variables such as welfare state type which are measured at the country level), we have to assume that no country effect remains after controlling for the contextual variables. If this assumption is not true, it will result in biased results.

7 Principal Component Analysis suggested a one-factor solution, based on Eigenvalues >1, which explains 44 per cent of the variation in the data. This means that if a person has a negative attitude towards one minority group, he or she is more likely to have negative attitudes towards other groups too.

*The Sociological Review*, 63:S2, pp. 183–205 (2015), DOI: 10.1111/1467-954X.12268

8  Social class is usually calculated on the basis of occupation. Considering that many young people have not entered the labour market yet, we use parents' social class as a proxy for young people's social class (see: Appendix Table A2).
9  Percentage of families who find it very difficult to get by on present income is aggregated from the answers of respondents as this is the most precise available measure at the level of localities. One must note, however, that the answers only refer to households with at least one young person 16–25 years of age, so the variable can only be considered a crude proxy for the level of the prosperity of the area.
10 It is also possible than people who have more friends of other ethnicity do so *because* they have more positive attitudes. Nevertheless, the contact hypothesis is also supported by the fact that exclusionism is lower in localities where there are more people around who were born abroad.

# References

Allport, G. W., (1954), *The Nature of Prejudice*, Cambridge: Addison-Wesley.
Arzheimer, K., (2009), 'Contextual factors and the extreme right vote in Western Europe, 1980–2002', *American Journal of Political Science*, 53 (2): 259–275.
Arzheimer, K. and Carter, E., (2006), 'Political opportunity structures and right-wing extremist party success', *European Journal of Political Research*, 45: 419–443.
Betz, H.-G., (1998), 'Introduction', in H.-G. Betz and S. Immerfall (eds), *The New Politics of the Right: Neo-Populist Parties and Movements in Established Democracies*, 1–10, Basingstoke: Macmillan.
Boomgaarden, H. G. and Vliegenthart, R., (2007), 'Explaining the rise of anti-immigrant parties: the role of news media content', *Electoral Studies*, 26: 404–417.
Bustikova, L., (2014), 'Revenge of the radical right', *Comparative Political Studies*, 1–28, Online First, DOI: 10.1177/0010414013516069.
Bustikova, L. and Kitschelt, H., (2009), 'The radical right in post-communist Europe: Comparative perspectives on legacies and party competition', *Communist and Post-Communist Studies*, 42: 459–483.
Carter, E., (2005), *The Extreme Right in Western Europe: Success or Failure?* Manchester: Manchester University Press.
Dollard, J., Doob, L. W., Miller, N. E., Mowrer, O. H. and Sears., R. R., (1939), *Frustration and Aggression*, New Haven: Yale University Press.
Espenshade, T. J. and Hempstead, K., (1996), 'Contemporary American attitudes toward U.S. immigration', *International Migration Review*, 30 (2): 535–570.
Esses, V. M., Jackson, L. M. and Armstrong, T. L., (1998), 'Intergroup competition and attitudes towards immigrants and immigration: an instrumental model of group conflict', *Journal of Social Issues*, 54 (4): 699–724.
Evans, G. and Whitefield, S., (1993), 'Identifying the bases of party competition in Eastern Europe', *British Journal of Political Science*, 23 (4): 521–548.
Fetzer, J. S., (2000), *Public Attitudes toward Immigration in the United States, France, and Germany*, New York: Cambridge University Press.
Golder, M., (2003), 'Explaining variation in the success of extreme right parties in Western Europe', *Comparative Political Studies*, 36 (4): 432–466.
Hjern, M., (1998), 'National identities, national pride and xenophobia: a comparison of four Western countries', *Acta Sociologica*, 41: 335–347.
Hox, J., (2010), *Multilevel Analysis, Techniques and Applications*, 2nd edn, New York: Routledge.
Ishiyama, J., (2009), 'Historical legacies and the size of the red-brown vote in post-communist politics', *Communist and Post-Communist Studies*, 42: 485–504.
Jackman, R. W. and Volpert, K., (1996), 'Conditions favouring parties of the extreme right in Western Europe', *British Journal of Political Science*, 26 (4): 501–521.
Kääriäinen, J. and Lehtonen, H., (2006), 'The variety of social capital in welfare state regimes – a comparative study of 21 countries', *European Societies*, 8 (1): 27–57.

Kedar, O., (2005), 'When moderate voters prefer extreme parties: policy balancing in parliamentary elections', *The American Political Science Review*, 99 (2): 185–199.

Kitschelt, K., (2007), 'Growth and persistence of the radical right in postindustrial democracies: advances and challenges in comparative research', *West European Politics*, 30 (5): 1176–1206.

Knigge, P., (1998), 'The ecological correlates of right-wing extremism in Western Europe', *European Journal of Political Research*, 34: 249–279.

Lewin-Epstein, N. and Levanon, A., (2005), 'National identity and xenophobia in an ethnically divided society', *International Journal on Multicultural Societies*, 7 (2): 90–118.

Lipset, S. M. and Raab, E., (1978), *The Politics of Unreason: Right-wing Extremism in America, 1790–1977*, 2nd edn, Chicago: University of Chicago Press.

Lubbers, M., Gijsberts, M. and Sheepers, P., (2002), 'Extreme right-wing voting in Western Europe', *European Journal of Political Research*, 41: 345–378.

Maas, C. J. M. and Hox, J. J., (2004), 'Robustness issues in multilevel regression analysis', *Statistica Neerlandic*, 58 (2): 127–137.

Mau, S., Mewes, J. and Schöneck, M., (2012), 'What determines subjective socio-economic insecurity? Context and class in comparative perspective', *Socio-Economic Review*, 10: 655–682.

Minkenberg, M., (2000), 'The renewal of the radical right: between modernity and anti-modernity', *Government and Opposition*, 35 (2): 170-188.

Mudde, C., (2000), *The Ideology of the Extreme Right*, Manchester: Manchester University Press.

Mudde, C., (2005), 'Racist extremism in Central and Eastern Europe', *East European Politics and Societies*, 19 (2): 161–184.

Mudde, C., (2007), *Populist Radical Right Parties in Europe*, Cambridge: Cambridge University Press.

Mudde, C., (2010), 'The populist radical right: a pathological normalcy', *West European Politics*, 33(6): 1167–1186.

Norris, P., (2005), *Radical Right: Voters and Parties in the Electoral Market*, New York: Cambridge University Press.

Pop-Eleches, G., (2010), 'Throwing out the bums: protest voting and unorthodox parties after communism', *World Politics*, 62 (2): 221–260.

Rydgren, J., (2003), 'Meso-level reasons for racism and xenophobia. some converging and diverging effects of radical right populism in France and Sweden', *European Journal of Social Theory*, 6 (1): 45–68.

Rydgren, J., (2005), 'Is extreme right-wing populism contagious? Explaining the emergence of a new party family', *European Journal of Political Research*, 44: 413–437.

Sears, D. O. and Henry, P. J., (2003), 'The origins of symbolic racism', *Journal of Personality and Social Psychology*, 85 (2): 259–275.

Sherif, M. and Sherif, C. W., (1953), *Groups in Harmony and Tension: An Integration of Studies on Intergroup Relation*, New York: Harper and Brothers.

Spies, D. and Franzmann, S. T., (2011), 'A two-dimensional approach to the political opportunity structure of extreme right parties in Western Europe', *West European Politics*, 34 (5): 1044–1069.

Swank, D. and Betz, H.-G., (2003), 'Globalization, the welfare state and right-wing populism in Western Europe', *Socio-Economic Review*, 1: 215–245.

Tajfel, H. and Turner, J. C., (1979), 'An integrative theory of intergroup relations', in W. G. Austin and S. Worchel (eds), *The Social Psychology of Intergroup Relations*, 33–47, Monterey: Brooks/Cole Pub. Co.

Toots, A. and Bachmann, J., (2010), 'Contemporary welfare regimes in Baltic States: adapting post-communist conditions to post-modern challenges', *Studies of Transition States and Societies*, 2 (2): 31–44.

van der Brug, W., Fennema, M. and Tillie, J., (2005), 'Why some anti-immigrant parties fail and others succeed: a two-step model of aggregate electoral support', *Comparative Political Studies*, 38 (5): 537–573.

Yilmaz, F., (2012), 'Right-wing hegemony and immigration: how the populist far-right achieved hegemony through the immigration debate in Europe', *Current Sociology*, 60 (3): 368–381.

Zawadzki, B., (1948), 'Limitations on the scapegoat theory of justice', *Journal of Abnormal and Social Psychology*, 43: 127–141.

202

**Appendix**
**Table A1:** *Countries and localities included in the sample*

| Location | | Sample size |
| --- | --- | --- |
| Croatia | Podsljeme | 610 |
| | Pescenica Zitnjak | 606 |
| Denmark | Odense East | 413 |
| | Odense Center | 402 |
| Estonia | Narva area | 617 |
| | Tartu | 634 |
| Finland | Lieksa and Nurmes | 452 |
| | Kuopio | 430 |
| Georgia | Kakhinauri region of Kutaisi | 579 |
| | Telavi | 588 |
| Western Germany | Bremen | 604 |
| | Bremerhaven | 332 |
| Eastern Germany | Jena | 608 |
| | Rostock | 608 |
| Greece | New Philadelphia | 600 |
| | Argyroupouli | 595 |
| Hungary | Downtown area of Sopron | 597 |
| | Downtown area of Ozd | 590 |
| Latvia | Agenskalns apkaime in Riga | 600 |
| | Forstate&Jaunbuve in Daugavpils | 600 |
| Portugal | Lumiar | 596 |
| | Barreiro | 594 |
| Russia | Kupchino | 599 |
| | Part of Vyborg | 600 |
| Slovakia | Vic | 600 |
| | Sant Cugat del Vallès | 600 |
| Spain | Vic | 597 |
| | Sant Cugat del Valles | 592 |
| UK | Coventry | 542 |
| | Nuneaton | 550 |

*Source*: MYPLACE survey, 2012–13.

*The Sociological Review*, 63:S2, pp. 183–205 (2015), DOI: 10.1111/1467-954X.12268

**Table A2:** *Question wording*

| Questions | Factor | Scale reliability |
|---|---|---|
| Roma, Gypsies and travellers make a positive contribution to society (strongly agree, agree, neither agree nor disagree, disagree, strongly disagree) | Negative attitude towards minorities index | 0.73 |
| The police should be stricter with Roma / Gypsies / travellers | | |
| Jewish people talk too much about what happened to them during the Holocaust | | |
| Jewish people make an important contribution to society | | |
| Muslims make a positive contribution to society | | |
| It is right to be suspicious of Muslims | | |
| Migrants greatly contribute to national cultural diversity | | |
| [country] should have stricter border controls and visa restrictions to prevent further immigration' (strongly agree, agree, neither agree nor disagree, disagree, strongly disagree) | Xenophobia | - |
| Foreigners should not be allowed to buy land in [COUNTRY] (strongly agree, agree, neither agree nor disagree, disagree, strongly disagree) | | |
| Migrants should have the same rights to welfare (health care, housing, education) as people from [COUNTRY] | Welfare chauvinism and exclusionism | - |
| When jobs are scarce, employers should give priority to [COUNTRY] people over foreign workers | | |
| On an average day, how much time do you spend keeping yourself informed about politics and current affairs using the following media: radio, TV, Internet, newspapers (no time at all, less than 1/2 hour, 1/2 hour to 1 hour, more than 1 hour) | Media exposure index | - |

(Continued)

*The Sociological Review*, 63:S2, pp. 183–205 (2015), DOI: 10.1111/1467-954X.12268

*Continued*

| Questions | Factor | Scale reliability |
|---|---|---|
| Some people say the following things are important for being a citizen of [COUNTRY]. Others say that they are not important. How important do you think each of the following is? To have been born in [COUNTRY]; To have at least one [COUNTRY] parent (very important, important, neither important nor unimportant, not very important, not important at all) | Ethnic nationalism | Cronbach's alpha >0.7 in all countries except Estonia (0.62) |
| Which of the descriptions on this card comes closest to how you feel about your household's income today?: Living comfortably on present income, Coping on present income, Finding it difficult on present income, Finding it very difficult on present income | Income | - |
| Generally speaking, would you say that most people can be trusted, or that you can't be too careful in dealing with people? Please tell me on a score of 0 to 10, where 0 means most people can be trusted and 10 means you can't be too careful. (0–10) | Social trust | - |
| Please tell me on a scale of 0–10 how much you trust each of the following institutions and organizations. 0 means 'do not trust at all', and 10 means 'complete trust': The head of government (PM), Parliament, political parties. | Political trust index | Cronbach's alpha >0.7 in all countries except Georgia (0.65) |
| Calculated on the basis of parents' education and occupation when the respondent was 16 years of age. Parents' social class measured on 0–4 point scale, where 1 point is given for a parent having a higher education or having a professional and technical occupation (doctor, teacher, engineer, etc.) or administrator occupation (banker, high government official, etc.). | Social class | - |
| How many of your close friends are (have) … different race / ethnic or minority group to yours? | Contact with minorities | - |

*Source:* MYPLACE survey, 2012–13.

# 'Loud and proud': youth and the politics of silencing

## Robert Grimm and Hilary Pilkington

**Abstract:** This article considers negative or critical views towards democracy and politics among young people, including supporters of ultra-patriotic or populist radical right movements, in the UK, eastern Germany and Russia. These countries represent a range of political heritages and current constitutions of democracy but, in all three contexts, it is suggested, young people experience some degree of the closing down of 'legitimate' political discourse as a result of the social distance between 'politicians' and 'people like us' and the legal and cultural circumscriptions on 'acceptable' issues for discussion. The article draws on survey data, semi-structured interviews and ethnographic case studies from the MYPLACE project to show variation between young people in these three countries in their experience of formal politics as a 'politics of silencing'. Moreover, the article explores the relationship between perceived 'silencing', the expression of dissatisfaction with democracy and receptivity to populist radical right ideology.

**Keywords:** youth, political participation, democracy, anti-politics, populist radical right, Europe

## Introduction

When we first started EDL [English Defence League], [...] we always got told it would never be a politics thing. But now all of a sudden they want to be in politics [...] That'll be the day that I come out because if we're in politics it's going to look bad when we go to a demo [...] We am going to end up being peaceful. [...] You all just stand there quiet, listening. That ain't EDL. EDL's loud. (Ray, EDL, UK)[1]

This article explores the contention that participation in ultra-patriotic or populist radical right movements constitutes one end of a continuum of negative views towards 'the political' (understood as the conventional institutions of liberal democracies and the 'political class') among young people across Europe. It is prompted by the articulation by members of the English Defence League[2] of the rejection of 'politics', where the latter is understood to require of the citizen only that they 'stand there quiet, listening' and is counterposed to their own

*The Sociological Review*, 63:S2, pp. 206–230 (2015), DOI: 10.1111/1467-954X.12269

activism in a movement in which they can be 'loud and proud'. In this article we ask whether the disavowal of politics increases the propensity towards receptivity to radical right ideology. More specifically we question whether the rejection of the political as currently constituted is confined to an extremist fringe or might be more usefully understood as one end of a continuum of views and practices among young people in Europe today.

To explore this question, the political attitudes and behaviour of young people in three countries – the UK, eastern Germany and Russia – are considered. These countries were selected as they provide examples of diverse political heritages and contemporary experiences of democracy. Past experience of authoritarian modes of government are found in eastern Germany (national socialism and state socialism) and Russia (state socialism following popular revolution) while the UK provides a contrasting case where there is no authoritarian political heritage. These countries also represent different constitutions of democracy today: stable, established liberal/neo-liberal democracy (UK); rapid post-socialist transition to liberal democracy after national reunification (eastern Germany); and post-socialist 'managed democracy' characterized by constrained political expression and state condoned intolerance (Russia). Taking three contrasting contexts allows us to trace variation in attitudes to, and engagement with, 'the political' and the populist radical right but also to formulate provisional contentions based on the experience of a particular subsection of the population (youth) that speak to critical democratic theory more broadly.

## Democracy: deficit, disavowal or dissensus?

European societies are experiencing a crisis of democratic legitimacy manifest in an erosion of trust in politicians, disidentification with mainstream parties and criticism of key political institutions and actors (Hay, 2007), albeit alongside continued support for the basic principles of democracy. Norris (2011) argues that contemporary societies are characterized by a 'democratic deficit' rooted in the divergence between levels of satisfaction with the performance of democracy and public aspirations. This democratic deficit is understood to underpin surface manifestations of 'disengagement' from conventional politics and is particularly manifest among the younger generation (Sloam, 2013; Furedi, 2005).

Data from large-scale and longitudinal surveys such as the European Social Survey (ESS) confirm the decline in traditional forms of participation (voting, political party and trade union membership and allegiance), lack of interest in public affairs and absence of personal efficacy in the political process among young people that is highlighted in the published academic literature (Kimberlee, 2002; Wattenberg, 2006; Dalton and Wattenberg (eds), 2000; Blais et al., 2004). Claims that decline in traditional participation is compensated by an increase in non-conventional forms of political participation (online participation, political consumerism (Marien et al., 2010; Stolle et al., 2005) are less readily confirmed, however. Data from the last six ESS rounds in the UK between 2002 and 2012 suggest that although young people *are* more likely to engage in non-institutional than institutional forms of political activity, trends in levels of non-conventional political participation remain either stable or show a decline.[3]

To understand the complex constellation of political attitudes and behaviour of young people, we need theoretical tools predicated neither on a vision of youth as peculiarly 'apathetic' (Furedi, 2005: 40) nor on the assumption that political apathy is largely a myth and the disconnect from politics is confined to the narrow, institutional kind (Brooks and Hodkinson, 2008). We need theories, rather, that illuminate the paradox that young people display a profound disillusionment with the current democratic system, and are highly critical of political actors, yet continue to be, in principle, supportive of democratic forms of government.

The concept of 'democratic deficit' explains young people's disengagement from formal politics as an expression of the gap between expectations and experiences of contemporary democracy. It is unable to advance our understanding of young people as political actors, however, since it posits the 'critical citizen' as one who finds the current enactment of the system to be imperfect but open to institutional fixing when it is precisely with these institutions that young people have lost faith. Beck and Beck-Gernsheim's (2002: 158) understanding of youth (dis)engagement as the practice of a 'politics of youthful antipolitics' is more attentive to questions of youthful agency; antipolitics, they argue, is reflected in a refusal to care about institutionalized politics while 'unintentionally acting very politically by depriving politics of attention, labour, consent and power'. While this notion of the disavowal of the political is helpful for understanding the articulation of attitudes towards political institutions and actors (discussed below), it simplifies a more complex picture. Young people do more than 'simply stay at home' (2002: 159) and, when they do engage, they are more inclined to do so in unconventional politics – street politics, life-style politics and symbolic action – while continuing to consider traditional modes of political action, such as voting, to be more effective. Moreover, the expression of 'youthful antipolitics' is seen by Beck and Beck-Gernsheim (2002: 157) as predicated on the experience of 'living under the preconditions of internalized democracy'; yet, as will be demonstrated below, similar practices are found in countries, such as Russia, where this is not the case.

In an attempt to address these paradoxes directly, we turn to broader critiques of liberal democracy. Rancière notes that the legitimization of democracy that has followed the collapse of 'totalitarianism' in Europe has not increased attachment to the institutional mechanisms of democracy but, on the contrary, 'the victory of so-called formal democracy is accompanied by a noticeable disaffection with regard to its forms' (Rancière, 1999: 96–97). He points to the importance of contestation for the vibrancy of democracy; when the institutions of parliamentary representation were being contested by generations of militant socialists and communists, they were cherished and protected more vigilantly (1999: 97). As a consequence, Mouffe (2005: 66) argues, right-wing populism has made inroads precisely in those places where traditional democratic parties have lost their

*The Sociological Review*, 63:S2, pp. 206–230 (2015), DOI: 10.1111/1467-954X.12269

appeal to the electorate who can no longer distinguish between them in the 'stifling consensus' that has gripped the political system.

This raises fundamental questions about the importance of the process of debate and deliberation in the constitution and reclamation of democracy. On the one hand, the practice of non-conventional forms of political participation, in new social movements for example, can be understood as a radical democratic intervention; an act of reclaiming and revitalizing the political through the creation of spaces of 'autonomous communication' in which more horizontal, inclusive and substantive debate takes place (Castells, 2012: 11). In the practice of such forms of 'deliberative democracy', preferences are not aggregated and represented through democratic institutions but formed or transformed through the democratic process (Della Porta, 2013: 61). However, the valorization of the method of consensus central to deliberative democratic approaches may be experienced by some young people as equally exclusionary. For those for whom formal politics is associated with meaningless debate, the centrality of 'talk' to deliberative democratic alternatives undermines its 'alternative' status. This suggests the pertinence of a rather different radical democratic critique which questions claims that 'consensus', as the outcome of deliberation, ensures democratic inclusion. Mouffe (2005) argues that understanding politics as the search for a universal rational consensus can reduce it to attempts to design institutions capable of reconciling all conflicting interests and values, when the essence of democratic politics is, in fact, the legitimate expression of such conflict. Even more simply, Rancière (2011: 1) argues that 'dissensus', not consensus, lies at the heart of politics since 'There is politics because the common is divided'.

This raises the final theoretical issue of concern in this article; the possibility that populist radical right movements may themselves 'articulate albeit in a very problematic way, real democratic demands which are not taken into account by traditional parties' (Mouffe, 2005: 71). The suggestion that legitimate democratic demands of the population at large may be articulated through new forms of radical right movements is confirmed by Mudde (2007) who distinguishes between classic 'extreme' or 'far right' political parties, which are in essence antidemocratic, and a new populist form of the radical right which remains broadly democratic despite opposing some fundamental values of liberal democracy and promoting an ideological blend of nativism, authoritarianism, and populism. Empirical evidence from across Europe suggests that 'it makes much more sense to consider the populist radical right as a [...] radicalized version of mainstream ideas, and not as a "normal pathology" unconnected to the mainstream' (Mudde, 2007: 297).

The empirical sections of this article speak to these critical interventions into democratic theory as they consider young people's attitudes to, experience of and response to 'the political' in the three countries selected. First, we briefly consider (dis)satisfaction with democracy as expressed by 'mainstream' youth participating in survey and semi-structured interview elements of the MYPLACE project. Triangulating these data, we explore whether patterns in the institutions 'least trusted', and how respondents express their attitudes to them, confirm the 'democratic deficit' argument or suggest a more fundamental critique of consensus democracy. Secondly, we explore articulations of young people's experience of the political as an exclusionary realm, which fails to fulfil its claim to express and represent multiple, diverse voices. We consider perceptions that certain subjects, which are 'important to people like me', are considered 'unacceptable' political topics and excluded from debate, and ask how the variation in perceptions of this 'silencing' relates to the wider political and cultural context. Thirdly, we consider receptivity to populist radical right ideas and movements as one specific response to the 'stifling consensus' of the formal political realm. We explore the link between (dis)satisfaction with democracy and a rejection of political pluralism (measured through support for authoritarian rule) among the 'mainstream' youth population before employing data from ethnographic studies of young activists in radical right and patriotic movements to confirm Mudde's proposition (see above) that attitudes among the latter constitute a continuum of 'mainstream' views.

## Data sources

Data from the MYPLACE project used here emanate from three countries (UK, Russia and eastern Germany) and three data sets: survey data; semi-structured interviews; and ethnographic case studies. Triangulation of survey and qualitative data for this article was conducted in a parallel rather than sequential form, employing different data sets as a check on inference from that data and recognizing honestly where correlations between data proved coincidental, unenlightening or contradictory.

### Survey and interview data

The survey instrument and data analysis strategy are outlined in the contribution by Pilkington and Pollock to this volume. This article draws on survey data from: Jena and Rostock (eastern Germany, $n = 1,216$); Kupchino (St Petersburg) and Vyborg (Russia, $n = 1,199$); and Coventry and Nuneaton (UK, $n = 1,092$). Follow-up semi-structured interviews with a sub-sample of survey respondents were conducted in each location following the principles of recruitment and selection elaborated in Pilkington and Pollock (this volume). Approximately 60 interviews were conducted in each country and respondent sets largely reflected the survey sample in terms of socio-demographic variables (see Appendix Table A1). Notwithstanding the case study approach of the project, findings are compared in this article by country rather than location following evidence that on key hypotheses tested (eg satisfaction with the democracy, trust in the political system and political class) country-based research locations behave in a similar way.

*The Sociological Review*, 63:S2, pp. 206–230 (2015), DOI: 10.1111/1467-954X.12269

*Ethnographic case studies*

Two ethnographic case studies from the 'Radical right and patriotic' movements cluster of the MYPLACE project are drawn on in this article.[4]

The first is a study of the English Defence League (EDL), a 'feet on the street' movement founded in 2009 to protest against 'extremist Islam' and disrespect for British troops. Its leaders and mission statements distance the movement from classic far right organizations in the UK (British National Party, National Front etc.) leading it to be characterized as an 'Islamophobic new social movement' (Copsey, 2010: 11), social movement with a 'new far right' ideology (Jackson, 2011) or social movement of the populist radical right (Pilkington, 2014). Data used are from observation while attending demonstrations and other events with members of local EDL divisions (April 2012–November 2014) and semistructured interviews with 35 respondents (see Pilkington, 2014).

The second study was conducted with the St Petersburg branch of the organization Russian Run, active since January 2011. Russian Run is a sports movement which aims to promote a healthy lifestyle (especially sobriety) among young people; its primary activity is weekly mass jogs. The movement is aligned, however, with nationalist and patriotic groups as evident from the chanting of nationalist slogans and the presence of nationalist symbols on participants' clothes, flags etc. Data drawn on come from observation during participation in jogs and other events (March 2012–January 2013) and semi-structured interviews with 22 respondents (see Zinoviev, 2014).

## Rejecting the political: democratic deficit or anti-politics?

The exploration of young people's engagement with 'the political' leads us to consider, first, standard measures of (dis)satisfaction with democracy, trust in political institutions, the political class and efficacy of action among survey respondents before employing qualitative data to consider the depth and quality of the critique articulated.

*(Dis)satisfaction with democracy and trust in institutions*

The verdict that the democratic system 'could do better' is evident from MYPLACE survey findings. Asked to rate their satisfaction with the way in which democracy works in their country on a scale from 0 to 10, young people in Russia are the least satisfied (mean = 4.92). In the UK the mean is just over the mid-way point (mean = 5.28). Young eastern Germans are most satisfied with democracy (mean = 6.29). To compare, the European Social Survey (Round 6, 2012) overall mean for satisfaction with democracy on the same scale was 5.3 and, for respondents aged 16–25, 5.7.

Qualitative interview data confirm the general trust in Germany's democracy. Free elections were the most important reason for support of the political system although respondents also believed they had some control over political decisions and praised Germany's multi-party system for offering more political choice and diversity in parliament than the two-party systems of the UK and the USA (Björn, EG).

In contrast, UK respondents are much less inclined to recognize the positive aspects of democracy. A more common expression was the articulation of dissatisfaction with how it works alongside a recognition that it was 'the least bad option'.

> [...] you can never be truly democratic because [...] people who voted for Labour like at the last election aren't represented [...] are they by the government? So it's not democratic but [...] it's the lesser evil really isn't it, I think, this system. (David, UK)

Of course, responses to interview questions eliciting views on the current political system need to be read in the context of a widely accepted view that the UK is among the oldest democracies in the world as well as the absence of any experience or recent historical memory of fascist or other authoritarian systems.

Maximum scepticism about the working of democracy is found in Russia. In semi-structured interviews, while accepting that the country is more democratic than it was in Soviet times, respondents often referred to democracy as 'something we are striving for in theory' (Alla, Russia) or 'emerging gradually' (Alisa, Russia). When asked whether Russia's political scene could be described as democratic, Alina responds by characterizing the country as a terminally ill patient 'in remission' (Alina, Russia).

The Russian data must be read also in the context of the protest events of 2011–12 that followed parliamentary and presidential elections, the outcomes of which were widely perceived to have been manipulated by the governing regime. The impact of this on respondents' understandings of the current state of democracy in Russia is evident in the following response to the same question as to whether Russia's political system was democratic: 'I don't think so, no. Well, I think the elections demonstrated that. That is, everyone like voted for one lot, but the other lot won.' (Marina, Russia)

In absolute terms, trust in institutions – measured by level of trust in a variety of institutions on a scale of 0 to 10 – is low among MYPLACE survey respondents (see Figure 1). It is consistently lowest among young Russians and highest among young eastern Germans. Particularly low levels of trust are invested in *political* institutions – trust in heads of government, in parliament and in political parties – as opposed to institutions that uphold the order of the state and the rule of law (police, courts). On the measure of trust in political parties, in all three locations, young people's trust falls under the mid-way point on the scale.

The data from semi-structured interviews confirm the perceived gap between political parties and politicians and the ordinary electorate. In the UK, the most frequent spontaneous association with political parties is that they are 'all the same' (mentioned by a third of respondents) and that they 'do not keep their promises' (mentioned by one-fifth). The vast majority of attitudes expressed towards politicians by UK respondents are negative. They are perceived to be deceitful ('liars', 'hypocrites'), weak, interested in self-presentation (or image), and being 'out of touch' with 'the average person'.

*The Sociological Review*, 63:S2, pp. 206–230 (2015), DOI: 10.1111/1467-954X.12269
© 2015 The Authors. *The Sociological Review* © 2015 The Editorial Board of *The Sociological Review*

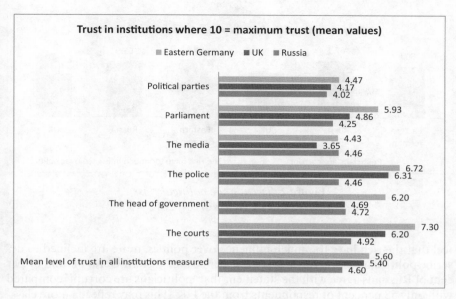

**Figure 1** *Trust in institutions*
*Source:* MYPLACE survey, 2012–13.

Among Russian interview respondents, politics, politicians and political insti-tutions are seen as one and the same and referred to as 'detached', a 'dirty thing', 'a show' or a group of 'people in suits'. Politicians and government structures are considered 'remote' from the life of ordinary people (mentioned by more than a third of respondents) (Zhelnina *et al.*, 2013: 18). This is expressed as a conscious rejection of engagement with politics:

> [...] I don't watch the news. I generally watch TV as little as possible. I try to not turn it on. [...] Well, probably these are my stereotypes, that all politicians, it's all bad. They're all terrible, they are stupid. They are thieves. (Olga, Russia)

In the UK, widespread discussion of the current coalition government being heavily dominated by those from top public schools and elite universities, also encourages a feeling that politicians are not only 'out of touch' but a class apart. This gives rise to a sense that there is no route into politics for 'someone like me':

> Because I don't, I haven't got the right blood, my blood ain't blue [...] I think that's something they need to sort out 'cause I reckon if you could get somebody in there who's been to a council estate. [...] That's lived with nothing [...] I reckon a party would go a long way, because they know what sort of things [...] really affect the poor. (Craig, UK)

This sentiment is reflected in survey responses; almost three-quarters (74 per cent) of respondents from the UK feel that the rich have too much influence over politics (see Figure 2). While fewer respondents in Russia and eastern Germany

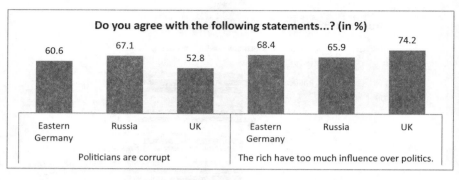

**Figure 2** *Trust in the political class*
*Source:* MYPLACE survey, 2012–13.

feel that the rich have too much influence over politics, more are inclined to describe politicians as 'corrupt'. Sixty-one per cent of eastern Germans and 67 per cent of Russians agree with the statement that 'politicians are corrupt' compared with only 53 per cent of respondents from the UK. This may reflect a more class-based articulation among British respondents of more widely shared sentiments and finds some confirmation from qualitative data.

Although, as Figure 2 shows, trust in institutions is persistently higher among eastern German respondents than among their Russian and UK counterparts, respondents in the eastern German research sites shared the perception of the existence of a gap between the population and its representatives. They found it difficult to align themselves with specific parties and felt that the political agendas of the main parties were increasingly converging without offering clear alternatives for tackling economic and social challenges. Parties were seen as too rigid in their structures and too driven by the constant need to win elections; for some, only the Pirate Party offered 'a small ray of hope' (Oliver, EG). Respondents in eastern Germany were also sceptical about the integrity of political actors. There was a general acceptance that politicians are dishonest and make false promises for strategic reasons, particularly in the run-up to elections. The influence of business lobbyists on political decisions and party donations from businesses was a particular object of criticism: 'I think that politics is too often influenced by business. When money starts flowing, many stop thinking democratically' (Frederick, EG). It would appear, therefore, that, in all three countries, young people engage in what Beck and Beck-Gernsheim (2002: 158) term 'a highly political disavowal of politicians'.

In this section, it has been suggested that, although varying in degree across the three locations discussed, and notwithstanding an underlying acceptance that there is no better alternative on hand, the level of satisfaction with democracy as it works today is relatively low. The data presented reveal, moreover, that the institutions that are least trusted are the classic institutions of liberal democracy (parliament, political parties, the press), which epitomize the practice of the

214

democratic principles of voicing multiple viewpoints and expressing and resolving difference through debate. What this discomfort with such democratic institutions and practices tells us about young people's engagement with 'the political' more widely is considered in the following section.

## All talk but no real fight: the politics of silencing?

One explanation for young people's lack of trust in parliament, political parties and the media might be their own discomfort with the articulation of political difference, and its rational resolution, because they feel ill-equipped to understand politics.

Qualitative data confirm that young people's engagement in politics is affected by the inaccessibility of the political to them. Some respondents from the eastern German research sites said they found political processes too complex to follow (Guderjan and Grimm, 2013) while for Russian respondents politics can appear impenetrable. Marina explained that she had given up trying to understand the anti-Putin protests (2011–12) because:

> I realised that, in fact, it is virtually impossible. Probably because we just don't know everything that goes on there. They tell us one thing, but what happens is something else. That makes it very difficult to find the truth amidst all this porridge [*kasha*]. So I abandoned any attempt. (Marina, Russia)

Indeed, the language of politics itself can be a mechanism of exclusion:

> The language of politics [...] can be damaging, I think it stops some people from getting involved, if they don't understand the terminology, I think it can make it quite difficult, for some people, to interact with it. (Pam, UK)

In all three countries, respondents expressed a critical attitude to the realm of politics in terms of it being characterized by exclusive rather than inclusive 'talk'. Among UK respondents, the word 'politics' is frequently associated with parliamentary debate and characterized as futile argument:

> [...] that's just the image that comes into my head if you say politics, I just think of [...] a bunch of idiots sat in the House of Commons, just shouting and heckling at each other. They argue about everything, they can never make their minds up. (Nick, UK)

For Russian respondents too 'Politics is chatter about nothing, which has no meaning. They sit there, discussing something. But nothing gets done' (Marina, Russia). This sentiment is echoed by Silke, who articulates how the endless talk of politicians fails to inspire young people:

> I watch those debates and see politicians sitting in various talk shows talking, talking and talking. But when it comes down to it, they rarely succeed in having their finger on the pulse or my personal pulse, so I'd really say: 'Wow, that's what I believe!' (Silke, EG)

*The Sociological Review*, 63:S2, pp. 206–230 (2015), DOI: 10.1111/1467-954X.12269

These associations of politics with 'arguing' for the sake of it evoke the theoretical critiques discussed above that question assumptions that a political process rooted in debate, deliberation and consensus is experienced universally as inclusive. This is most starkly articulated by respondents from the EDL ethnographic case study who deride politics as little more than, 'Debating with other fucking parties man. [ . . . ] What's the point of sitting in a fucking room debating?' (Chris, EDL, UK). However, even interview respondents, who criticized the 'racist' nature of the EDL, admired the movement for demonstrating the passion missing from mainstream politics: '[ . . . ] they ain't scared to go out there and do like a full on fight [ . . . ] We do need a party like to go out there, go on the streets [ . . . ] Protest against real things.' (Craig, UK).

Protest about 'real things' needs to take place on the streets because such issues are perceived to be excluded from mainstream political discourse. Cara illustrates this while explaining why widely held concerns about immigration from other parts of the EU are not given air time:

> [ . . . ] it's seen quite as an issue that working class people care about and not really anybody else. [ . . . ] that's why it's kind of ignored [ . . . ] It just seems to be questions that affect MPs and things and people of the class of politics as it were that seem to get discussed rather than the things that generally affect the working person. (Cara, UK)

In this way, among UK respondents, the class constitution of the political realm acts to exclude politically undesirable debate and real contestation and fabricate an illusion of consensus.

*More voices, more representation: Contest vs consensus in politics*

Young people's own articulation of their scepticism about politics and its institutions suggests that it is not rooted in any profound discomfort with the articulation of political difference but a perceived gap between claims that the democratic sphere is constituted by open contestation between a range of opinions and the actuality of a managed and fabricated 'consensus' politics. This is illustrated by frustrations expressed about (anti)democratic protectionism experienced at first hand in local politics by respondents from one of the UK locations where local councillors had refused to work with representatives of the British National Party[5] (BNP) who had been elected in May 2008.

> [ . . . ] they were elected, we had chose for that person to be elected [ . . . ] and they decided not to work, that really infuriated me. [ . . . ] It's for us, us to put in there, to say like well this is who we believe in, do you know what I mean? Not for them to say well we don't, we don't really like them. (Craig, UK)

This sense of disenfranchisement is reflected in wider support for diversity over false consensus even where respondents disagreed with the views promoted:

> [ . . . ] as much as I disagree with the BNP and some of the other small parties, somebody obviously agrees with them so if you've got them represented then there's more people's views represented as far as I'm concerned. (Cara, UK)

*The Sociological Review*, 63:S2, pp. 206–230 (2015), DOI: 10.1111/1467-954X.12269
© 2015 The Authors. *The Sociological Review* © 2015 The Editorial Board of *The Sociological Review*

These sentiments are also expressed by young eastern Germans, although the very different historical and political context they inhabit – strict legislation prohibiting the display of Nazi symbols as well as the actuality of debates concerning whether far right parties such as the National Democratic Party [NPD][6] should be banned – perhaps shapes a more legalistic approach:

> [...] it is not a normal party [the NPD]. But I think it is difficult to ban it. On the one hand, [...] I think it is important that in a democracy, that other positions, which we perhaps do not like, that they are able to exist. On the other hand it is of course totally dangerous if they get in to local parliament. [...] Banning them is not the right answer because it will not change the political attitudes of people. (Mona, EG)

Among Russian respondents, an emotional response to the denunciation of far right groups is frequently encountered, often evoking historical memories of the sacrifices of the Russian people 'fighting Nazism' during the Second World War. Such expressions, as above, often refer to such groups as 'absolutely abnormal' and their supporters as 'simply not human beings' (Dana, Russia). However, other respondents describe themselves as 'indifferent' (Vlad, Russia) on the question of whether 'radical' parties should be banned or thought all parties should be permitted with the proviso that 'they should not use any violence' (Ignat, Russia). Commenting specifically on (far right) skinheads, Evgenii confirms this position:

> These people have the right to their opinion, to think as they like [...] But they should not be aggressive and should not express their point of view where it is not appropriate. They can say it, but not express it a way that might provoke conflict. (Evgenii, Russia)

### The politics of silencing: unacceptable and taboo topics

This openness to addressing difficult issues is perceived not to be embraced always by those with authority to define the boundaries of the politically 'acceptable'. However, what we call here a 'politics of silencing' is deeply embedded in national cultural contexts and normative politics of localized 'rights' and 'wrongs'; what is and is not permissible depends on historical legacy and the founding principles of different national democratic systems.

In the UK, qualitative data suggest respondents perceive that issues important to 'people like me' are silenced and this confirms their sense that ethnic minority communities' rights are unjustly privileged in the current democratic system. Recounting what she considered to be the unfair exclusion of a friend from school for having 'BNP' written on his hand, Chloe indicates that the impact of immigration on job opportunities is one of those taboo topics:

> It's a party [BNP] at the end of the day. You know, it's open to views [...] You see, I think we should have parties like that because things like Polish people and that coming into the country, I can't get a job sort of thing [...] things like that are affecting me and the people who are around me and the place that I live. So of course I'd join a party like that [BNP]. (Chloe, UK)

Experiences of the political system as one of 'silencing' are most frequently expressed by young EDL activists, although the sites of such encounters are often similar to those recounted above. One respondent reported having been excluded from college for wearing an EDL hoodie (Chas, EDL, UK) while another recounts how the school had prohibited him from even talking about the EDL:

> [...] in one of my lessons in science I was talking about the EDL to another lad [...] and then one of my teachers just got me removed from the lesson [...]There was no-one in that room that was Muslim and there was no way it could have hurt anybody, me talking about the EDL. It's my view, it's freedom of speech. I should be allowed to say it. So I got pulled out in front of four teachers being questioned about my views. (Brett, EDL, UK)

One of the main instruments for silencing, according to EDL case study respondents, is the application of the label of 'racism'. As Peter puts it, 'People are so scared of that word, and being called a racist, aren't they, like when half the things people say and do isn't racist' (Peter, EDL, UK)

Narratives of silencing are evident, albeit less pronounced, in eastern German respondents' accounts. Where silencing is experienced, it is generally in political debate in relation to far right agendas around immigration and 'foreigners'.

> [...] immigration policy [...] is clearly an issue where straight away Second World War, Nazi talk, if you mention anything like, I don't know, asylum rights or something like more control or whatever. In other countries that is not a problem. Here though, it is always said that you cannot do this. (Daniel, EG)

The fact that the historical legacy of National Socialism plays an important role in understanding the perception of respondents that there is a culturally specific taboo on talking about German nationhood and interests is confirmed by members of divisions (from Köln and Berlin) of the German Defence League participating in an EDL demonstration in London in September 2013. When asked whether the German Defence League held similar marches in Germany, one young member laughed and declared that this 'would be impossible'. The problem, he continued, is that you are not allowed to be a German patriot in Germany and you could get arrested for simply saying you are 'proud to be German' (Field diary, 7 September 2013).

In Russia, the qualitative data rarely contain direct reference to the closing down of the political space for discussion of issues of significance to respondents. As noted above, this may be a reflection of a high degree of dissociation from the political as part of individualization processes and the emergence of a new personalized politics of choice (Zhelnina *et al.*, 2013). Thus, where debate is shut down it is narrated as a choice apparently initiated by individuals themselves. This choice may be motivated by the fact that there is 'no point' discussing politics since 'nobody will listen' (Nina, Russia) or by wishing to avoid emotional and unpleasant situations where 'People just argue and that's it – there's no other point to it' (Oleg, Russia). For some individuals, however, the shutting down of space to discuss politics even among friends can feel like being silenced:

> It was just a disagreement. And I said what I thought, straight out, and I knew they would just keep silent about this. And I said, 'You just keep silent about this. That's a

*The Sociological Review*, 63:S2, pp. 206–230 (2015), DOI: 10.1111/1467-954X.12269
© 2015 The Authors. *The Sociological Review* © 2015 The Editorial Board of *The Sociological Review*

real negative on your part.' And one of my friends just took me aside and said that it was better not to ask these questions. So, a lot of lads really won't talk to me because of this. (Mark, Russia)

Of course the fact that silencing is narrated as a personal choice does not constitute it objectively as such. From the adoption of first local and then national legislation to prevent the positive presentation of homosexual relationships to children, to legislative amendments in June 2012 toughening punitive sanctions for organizing unauthorized rallies and violation of the law during public events, which allowed police to regularly detain participants of Russian Run jogging events (Zinoviev, 2014), it is clear that young people are subject to the practice of silencing even if they do not articulate it as such. As Aleksei comments, reflecting on why he has not taken part in the anti-election fraud protests, 'In our country, it is pointless at the moment. However loud people shout, they are not heard' (Aleksei, Russian Run, Russia).

Thus, while young people often lack confidence in negotiating the political field, it does not wholly explain their discomfort with the political. When articulating their experience in their own words, young people in all three countries talk of the constitution of the political as an exclusionary realm in which a different language is spoken. There is evidence, moreover, in at least two of the research locations that young people perceive some degree of the closing down of 'legitimate' political discourse as a result of the social distance between 'politicians' and 'people like us' and the legal and cultural circumscriptions on 'acceptable' issues for discussion. This circumscription is often explained as the consequence of specific political heritages – taboos relating to ongoing 'guilt' about the National Socialist past in the case of East German respondents, the strait jacket of 'political correctness' and obligatory multiculturalism, usually associated with the Blair government in the case of UK respondents – but potentially contains a deeper uneasiness with the democratic system. As Furedi (2005) suggests, a growing authoritarian consensus against offensive speech effectively closes down debate, infantilizes the public and marginalizes nonconformist ideas. Mouffe (2005: 73, 119–20) warns, more specifically, against establishing a 'cordon sanitaire' around right-wing populist movements since this does not pacify society but simply denies the existence of social division and silences 'an ensemble of voices' that is essential to the very constitution of politics.

## Passion and politics: responses to silencing

In the final section of this article, we explore the meaning of the emergent criticisms of democracy identified above. We ask, more specifically, whether the criticism of key political institutions in which political debate is pursued signals a preference for more authoritarian modes of government that remove the ambiguities associated with democratic processes? In this way we consider whether there are associations between the disengagement, perceived silencing, lack of trust and general satisfaction with democracy demonstrated above and populist radical right attitudes. Finally, we consider how young activists in radical right and patriotic movements enact their critique of politics and ask whether this constitutes activism of an extremist fringe or presents a radicalized version of mainstream ideas.

## *A new authoritarianism?*

While there is a range of different responses to dissatisfaction with the democratic system, this article is concerned specifically with the question of whether those who feel their interests are not adequately represented, and who have low trust in the efficacy of the democratic system and its institutions, may reject liberal democracy in favour of more authoritarian forms of government and be receptive to populist radical right movements. Thus, while making no claim that this is the dominant response, it is this that constitutes the focus of this final section of the article.

Both authoritarianism and group focused enmity[7] have been used in quantitative studies as proxies for populist far right and extremist attitudes (Adorno *et al.,* 1950; Stöss, 2000; Decker and Brähler, 2006; Heitmeyer, 2011). Decker and Brähler (2006), evaluating far right extremism in Germany, understand the far right as constituting the antithesis to democratic pluralism and demonstrate that authoritarian attitudes extend well beyond a 'pathological fringe' of German society. This is confirmed by the MYPLACE survey where four markers – support for a strong leader, a multiparty system, military rule and freedom of speech for the opposition – revealed surprisingly high levels of support for authoritarian rule in the UK and Russia (see Figure 3).

Support for a strong leader not constrained by parliament (56.1 per cent) and for army rule (27.7 per cent) is particularly pronounced in UK research locations while rejection of political pluralism (an opposition that can freely express its views and democratic multiparty systems) finds more receptivity in Russia. Creating an 'authoritarian rule' scale based on all four items (where 0 is least support and 5 maximum support for authoritarian forms of government) revealed that eastern German respondents demonstrate lower support for authoritarian forms of government (mean = 1.6) than in the UK and Russia (mean = 2.6 in both locations).

The similarities and differences between locations are reflected in the qualitative data. Interviewees in the UK confirm the importance attached to strong leadership. When talking about contemporary politicians, they are often characterized along a spectrum of 'weak' to 'strong' or from 'cowardly' to 'prepared to fight'. Particular criticism of 'cowardice' relates to the junior position within the coalition government of the Deputy Prime Minister (Nick Clegg) which renders him helpless while positive characteristics (associated with both Margaret Thatcher and Tony Blair) relate to the demonstration of strength, commitment to 'doing something', 'trying their best' and 'passion' even when the policies implemented are seen to be 'wrong'.

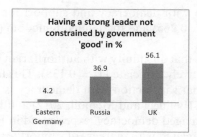

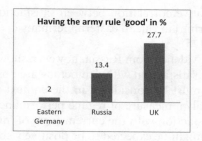

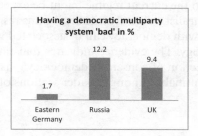

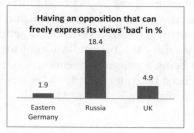

**Figure 3** *Support for authoritarian rule*
*Source:* MYPLACE survey, 2012–13.

Given the place of tropes of strong leadership and 'the iron hand' in Russian political discourse, receptivity to the need for a strong hand to prevent the pulls towards disorder and lawlessness found among MYPLACE respondents is not surprising. A common justification for authoritarian rule articulated in interviews is the territorial size of Russia and its historical exceptionalism:

> Ours is a very big country, you need strong power in order to govern it. For this reason, democracy probably will not come about, and we don't need it – we need some kind of own developmental path and it is irrelevant what it is called. (Serafima, Russia)

There is also confirmation of a heightened scepticism about multiparty systems among Russian respondents. In sharp contrast to the views expressed above by UK respondents, who thought the higher the number of parties, the greater the achieved representation, twelve qualitative interview respondents suggested that less parties, or a single party system, is preferable for Russia.

> [...] when there are many, competing [parties], they start to argue amongst themselves and not put forward any strategies, just engage in all kinds of discussions. And the country moves in different directions [...] But when there is one party, there is at least a set course. (Marina, Russia)

The fact that eastern Germans are more satisfied with democracy than respondents in Russia and the UK appears to confirm the hypothesis that affinity with authoritarian political systems increases with declining satisfaction with democracy. This is partially substantiated statistically. There is a significant, albeit weak, negative correlation between satisfaction with democracy and support for authoritarian rule in eastern Germany ($r = -0.265$) and the United Kingdom ($r = -0.175$).

Evidence from Russia, however, shows that an affinity with authoritarian rule and satisfaction with democracy are positively associated ($r = 0.138$). This finding must be considered in the context that satisfaction with democracy is primarily a measure of regime performance (Bellucci and Memoli, 2012) and thus satisfaction with the current form of 'managed democracy' experienced in Russia might be expected to be positively correlated with markers of support for authoritarian rule while a critical attitude to the current regime might be expected to be consistent with more liberal and pluralist political attitudes. In this respect our survey data suggest that satisfaction with democracy can be associated with a propensity towards radical right ideology. The evidence indicates that rather than being a marginal phenomenon, rejection of consensus democracy – as experienced by young people today – is identifiable among broader sections of respondents from Russia and the UK.

### No longer silent? Youth activism and the populist radical right

Support for populist radical right ideology, as an expression of dissatisfaction with democracy as enacted today is, therefore, far from a pathological 'fringe' view among young respondents in this study. In this final section, however, we draw on data from two ethnographic studies with participants in what are widely considered 'far right' or 'extreme nationalist' organizations – the English Defence League and Russian Run – to explore what the meanings these young people attach to their activism might tell us about the relationship between satisfaction with democracy and populist radical right ideas. Specifically, we ask whether their critique of politics enacted through a practice of standing 'loud and proud'[8] might constitute a call for the extension rather than curtailment of democratic politics. If it does, it may provide some evidence in support of Mouffe's (2005: 3) radical democratic critique of hegemonic notions that a democracy that 'works' for 'the people' is one based not on a universal rational consensus but one in which there is vibrant public sphere of political contestation.

Young activists in the EDL do not see themselves as part of a covert, extremist movement; they want to be seen and heard. Participation, especially street demonstrations, is about 'getting heard' (Sean, Tina, EDL, UK), 'getting your voice out there in the public' (Michelle, EDL, UK), or 'getting your point across' (Chas, Jason, Jordan, Richard, Connor, Chris, EDL, UK). The importance attached to 'speaking out', 'standing up' and 'being heard' reflects a conscious strategy, moreover, for cutting through the perceived silencing imposed in political, and wider public, realms encapsulated in one of the main EDL slogans 'Not racist, not violent, just no longer silent' (see Plate 1).

What is rejected here is a politics constituted by silent, subordinate citizens who drink cups of tea and read the Sunday Times (Ray, EDL, UK). In order to

**Plate 1** *T-shirt with EDL slogan worn by demonstrator, Tower Hamlets, London, 7 September 2013*

*Photo:* Hilary Pilkington.

get their point across, in contrast, EDL activists 'give a chant and make it loud and proud of who we am' (Connor, EDL, UK).

In the activism of young Russians in the Russian Run movement, the emphasis is on being seen as much as being heard. Its main activities are weekly mass jogging events when participants run through central city streets carrying flags and banners (see Plate 2), periodically striking up chants that reflect both the 'sobriety' and 'healthy lifestyle' aspect of the movement ('Do not smoke, do not booze, do not use!', 'Sport is power! Alcohol is the grave!'), as well as its 'nationalist' inclination ('Russians, forward!, 'Russian youth is sober youth!').

Young people are attracted to the movement primarily by the desire to participate in these mass events (where they meet like-minded people and have fun) rather than the appeal of right-wing ideology (Zinoviev, 2014).

**Plate 2** *'Russian Run', St Petersburg, 18 March 2012*
*Photo:* Hilary Pilkington.

I, myself, have several reasons [for participating in Russian Run] – sports, plus social movement, friends. Probably everyone comes for these reasons. (Boris, Russian Run, Russia)

There is a strong choreographic element to Russian Run activities, best exemplified by the break made in the middle of the jogging to undertake physical exercises followed by the formation of the 'circle'; participants form a circle, put their arms on each other's shoulders and perform sets of squats (see Plate 3). This also marks a moment of physical occupation of urban space for the performance of the 'healthy lifestyle' the movement promotes.

This kind of visual symbolic display of standing up for what you believe in is evident in the EDL also. Demonstrations, according to Connor, not only exercise respondents' democratic right to be heard but provide a physical expression of a refusal to 'bow down':

To prove a point like we am there and that we ain't gonna hide, we am gonna go out on the streets and we am gonna prove who we am. We am English and you aye gonna stop us really. You aye gonna make us bow down [...] we are gonna do it whether you like it or not. (Connor, EDL, UK)

Thus for the EDL, too, taking over the city's streets has an important symbolic meaning. A good demo is described as one when 'you get a turn-out' (Ray, EDL,

*The Sociological Review*, 63:S2, pp. 206–230 (2015), DOI: 10.1111/1467-954X.12269

**Plate 3**  *Mass exercise during 'Russian Run', St Petersburg, 18 March 2012*
*Photo:* Hilary Pilkington.

UK) and chants of 'Whose streets? Our streets' provide the soundtrack to this visual claiming of territory. Moreover, although respondents from the EDL case study share with the mainstream youth population a scepticism about their own efficacy, demonstrations constitute a physical display to the government that 'there are still people out there that don't agree with them' (Declan, EDL, UK).

Comparing EDL and Russian Run activists' attitudes to democracy and their own democratic participation reveals the importance of historical legacy and contemporary political and cultural context in shaping attitudes and practices.

Like their counterparts from the survey sample, participants in the Russian Run see themselves as non-political. Trust in the political system and its institutions also reflects the same low level demonstrated among mainstream young Russians. Politicians are viewed as universally untrustworthy and the system as corrupt; one respondent commented that his experience of acting as an elections observer meant that 'Now I treat all political stuff as shit' (Vsevolod, Russian Run, Russia).

The implications of this for embracing or rejecting democracy are also indicative of the views noted above, which deny that the political system in Russia today can be described as democratic. The conclusions drawn from this disappointment in democracy, however, range across the political spectrum. For some, democracy only gets in the way of strong leadership:

I don't believe in democracy at all in this regard. [...] People by nature are not equal. It just gets in the way – of both politicians and of the President – governing. (Anatolii, Russian Run, Russia)

While others call for the popular reclamation of democracy – '[...] democracy here is all talk [...] the people should stand up and say what it wants' (Boris, Russian Run, Russia) – or for greater democratic accountability:

[...] if a bureaucrat cannot manage then he should either be removed or be asked to deliver what he promised. At the moment nobody is doing anything, nobody stands by what they say. It's not right. (Aleksei, Russian Run, Russia)

EDL members, like their mainstream counterparts in the UK, are also critical of the contemporary working of democracy. However, most criticism is directed at governments (past and present) rather than at the democratic system as a whole and the most common suggestion for constitutional change is a call for a mechanism for withdrawing a government's mandate mid-term (Chas, Jordan, EDL, UK). Perhaps more surprisingly, given the striking level of support for markers of authoritarian rule among UK survey respondents, EDL respondents rarely ventured support for authoritarian modes of government. Comparing the relative value of politicians and armed services personnel in the context of widespread government cuts, one respondent stated, 'I'd rather drop the 400 politics [politicians] and have that one soldier. Because that one soldier can make a difference' (Connor, EDL, UK), but there was no reference to military rule as preferable to democracy. In line with survey and interview respondents in the UK, the only alternative suggested to parliamentary democracy was the restoration of the powers of the monarchy.

## Conclusion

This article is an exploratory analysis of the relationship between critical views towards democracy and politics among young people and their receptivity to, or participation in, ultra-patriotic or populist radical right movements through the triangulation of quantitative and qualitative data. Drawing on survey data from three countries with very different political heritages and current constitutions of democracy, we suggest, allows us to see where there are statistically robust correlations that hold across all countries and where attitudes and behaviour differ significantly. Drawing on qualitative interviews with a sub-sample of this survey sample, moreover, allows deeper insight into how young people articulate these associations themselves while ethnographic case studies with activists in ultra-patriotic or populist radical right movements provide the opportunity to explore the continuity or rupture between 'mainstream' and 'fringe' attitudes.

The article demonstrates, first, that the level of satisfaction with democracy as it is today is relatively low in all three countries (albeit that this must be read in the context of an underlying acceptance amongst the vast majority of young people that there is currently no better alternative to democracy). Of particular inter-

*The Sociological Review*, 63:S2, pp. 206–230 (2015), DOI: 10.1111/1467-954X.12269

est was the finding in the survey data that the institutions that are least trusted are the classic institutions of liberal democracy (parliament, political parties, the press), which epitomize the practice of the democratic principles of the voicing of multiple viewpoints and expression and resolution of difference through debate. Drawing on qualitative data, we argue that the particular frustration with parliament, politicians and political parties is not a product of uneasiness with the expression of multiple voices – even those considered 'extreme' by respondents – but of the failure of these institutions to express and represent diverse views across the population when that is what they purport to do. We demonstrate, moreover, that, in at least two of the research locations, young people perceive some degree of the closing down of 'legitimate' political discourse as a result of the social distance between 'politicians' and 'people like us' and the legal and cultural circumscriptions on 'acceptable' issues for discussion. While this experience of 'silencing' in the UK and eastern Germany is articulated in historically and culturally specific ways – and can be found in Russia only at the personal level – it is, we argue, at least suggestive of the radical democratic critique that politics (at least one worth engaging with) is constituted in contestation rather than consensus.

Finally, considering, in this context, the 'seductive' potential of populist radical right movements, we show that survey data – based on four markers of support for authoritarian rule – do reveal surprisingly high levels of support for authoritarian rule in the UK and Russia. The significantly lower level of support in eastern Germany appears to confirm the hypothesis that affinity with authoritarian political systems increases with declining satisfaction with democracy. The fact that in Russia propensity towards authoritarian forms of government *increases* with satisfaction with democracy, moreover, illustrates the significance of context; this association is consistent with the fact that what is being measured here is satisfaction with the 'managed democracy' of the Putin era. In the light of these findings, the views of participants in ultra-patriotic or populist radical right groups in Russia and the UK explored in the final section of the article may be uncomfortable but are not qualitatively distinct from those of their 'mainstream' peers in each country context. Indeed, far from engaging in covert, anti-democratic politics, the meanings attached to their activism by respondents in both movements centre on 'being heard' and 'being seen'. By adopting forms of activism that physically fill urban space — street demonstrations, choreographed 'jogs' and mass exercise, chanting 'loud and proud' – members of the movements studied seek to demonstrate that 'there are still people out there that don't agree'.

## Notes

1  Respondents are referred to using pseudonyms, country of location and, where appropriate, the ethnographic case study in which they participated.
2  The English Defence League (EDL) is widely portrayed in the media and perceived by the public to be a 'far right', 'racist' organization (Extremis, 2012).

3 See Table A1 in the appendix to the contribution to this volume by Pilkington and Pollock for data supporting this.

4 Since ethnographic case studies were clustered in a 'bottom up' process, examples of 'Radical right and patriotic movements' are not present in all countries and a comparable case study is not available for Germany.

5 The success of the British National Party (BNP) (founded 1982) peaked in 2009 (when it held 58 council seats and gained two seats in the European Parliament). The elections of May 2014 saw it lose its representation in the European Parliament and its council representation cut to just two seats.

6 Calls to ban the party increased following claims it had links to the National Socialist Underground whose responsibility for nine murders (2000–2006) motivated by racial hatred came to light in 2011. However, in May 2014, the NPD polled 1 per cent of the national vote and secured the German far right's first ever seat in European Parliament elections.

7 Given that (in)tolerance and group-focused enmity are the focus of other articles in this volume (see, for example, Mieriņa and Koroleva and Pollock *et al.*), here we confine discussion to affinity to authoritarianism as a proxy for receptivity to radical right agendas.

8 The expression 'loud and proud' is found only among EDL activists and is used most widely by respondents connected to football firms. Here it is used as a metaphor for a range of associated meanings of activism discussed in this section.

# References

Adorno, T. W., Frenkel-Brunswik, E., Levinson, D. J. and Sanford, R. N., (1950), *The Authoritarian Personality*, New York: Norton.

Beck, U. and Beck-Gernsheim, E., (2002), *Individualization: Institutionalized Individualism and its Social and Political Consequences*, London: Sage.

Bellucci, P. and Memoli, V., (2012), 'The determinants of democracy satisfaction in Europe', in D. Sanders, P. Magalhaes and G. Toka (eds), *Citizens and the European Polity: Mass Attitudes towards the European and National Polities*, 9–39, Oxford: Oxford University Press.

Blais, A., Gindegil, E. and Nevitte, N., (2004), 'Where does turnout decline come from?', *European Journal of Political Research*, 43 (2): 221–236.

Brooks, R. and Hodkinson, P., (2008), 'Introduction' (Special Issue: Young People, New Technologies and Political Engagement), *Journal of Youth Studies*, 11 (5): 473–479.

Castells, M., (2012), *Networks of Outrage and Hope: Social Movements in the Internet Age*, Cambridge: Polity Press.

Copsey, N., (2010), *The English Defence League: A Challenge to our Country and our Values of Social Inclusion, Fairness and Equality*, London: Faith Matters.

Dalton, R. and Wattenberg, M. P. (eds), (2000), *Parties without Partisans: Political Change in Advanced Industrial Democracies*, Oxford: Oxford University Press.

Decker, O. and Brähler, E., (2006), *Vom Rand zur Mitte. Rechtsextreme Einstellung und ihre Einflussfaktoren in Deutschland*, Berlin: Friedrich Ebert Stifftung, available at: http://www.fes.de/rechtsextremismus/pdf/Vom_Rand_zur_Mitte.pdf (accessed 27 June 2014).

Della Porta, D., (2013), *Can Democracy Be Saved?* Cambridge: Polity Press.

ESS Round 6: European Social Survey Round 6 Data (2012). Data file edition 2.0. Norwegian Social Science Data Services, Norway – Data Archive and distributor of ESS data.

Extremis (2012), 'Under the microscope:pPublic attitudes toward the English Defence League (EDL)', available at: http://extremisproject.org/2012/10/the-english-defence-league-edl-what-do-people-think/ (accessed 5 May 2014).

Furedi, F., (2005), *Politics of Fear: Beyond Left or Right*, London and New York: Continuum.

Guderjan, M. and Grimm, R., (2013), 'WP5: Interpreting Participation (Interviews). Deliverable 5.3: Country-based reports on interview findings. (Rostock/Jena)', *MYPLACE Deliverable Report*, available at: http://www.fp7-myplace.eu/documents/D5.3%20Jena.pdf (accessed 27 June 2014).

Hay, C., (2007), *Why We Hate Politics*, Cambridge: Polity Press.

*The Sociological Review*, 63:S2, pp. 206–230 (2015), DOI: 10.1111/1467-954X.12269

Heitmeyer, W., (2011), 'Gruppenbezogene Menschenfeindlichkeit. Interaktionsprozesse im gesellschaftlichen Raum', in C. Y. Robertson-von Trotha (ed.), *Rechtsextremismus in Deutschland und Europa. Rechts außen – Rechts 'Mitte'?*, 21–38, Baden-Baden: Nomos.

Jackson, P., (2011), *The EDL: Britain's 'New Far Right' Social Movement*, Northampton: RNM Publications, University of Northampton.

Kimberlee, R. H., (2002), 'Why don't British young people vote at general elections?', *Journal of Youth Studies*, 5 (1): 86–98.

Marien, S., Hooghe, M. and Quintellier, E., (2010), 'Inequalities in non-institutionalized forms of political participation: a multi-level analysis of 25 countries', *Political Studies*, 58: 187–121.

Mouffe, C., (2005), *On the Political*, London and New York: Routledge.

Mudde, C., (2007), *Populist Radical Right Parties in Europe*, Cambridge: Cambridge University Press.

Norris, P., (2011), *Democratic Deficit: Critical Citizens Revisited*, Cambridge: Cambridge University Press.

Pilkington, H., (2014), '"Loud and proud": youth activism in the English Defence League', WP7: Interpreting Activism (Ethnographies). Deliverable 7.1: Ethnographic Case Studies of Youth Activism', *MYPLACE Deliverable Report*, available at: http://www.fp7-myplace.eu/deliverables.php (accessed 16 December 2014).

Rancière, J., (1999), *Dis-agreement: Politics and Philosophy* (trans. Julie Rose), Minneapolis and London: University of Minnesota Press.

Rancière, J., (2011), 'The thinking of dissensus: politics and aesthetics', in P. Bowman and R. Stamp (eds), *Reading Ranciere: Critical Dissensus*, 1–17, London: Bloomsbury Publishing.

Sloam, J., (2013), 'The "outraged young": how young Europeans are reshaping the political landscape', *Political Insight*, April: 4–7.

Stolle, D., Hooghe, M. and Micheletti, M., (2005), 'Politics in the supermarket: political consumerism as a form of political participation', *International Political Science Review*, 26 (3): 245–269.

Stöss, R., (2000), *Rechtsextremsimus im Wandel*, Berlin: Friedrich Ebert Stifftung, available at: http://library.fes.de/pdf-files/do/05227.pdf (accessed 27 June 2014).

Wattenberg, M. P., (2006), *Is Voting for Young People?*, New York: Pearson Longman.

Zhelnina, A., Sabirova, G., Krupets, Y. and Omelchenko, E., (2013), 'WP5: Interpreting Participation (Interviews). Deliverable 5.3: Country-based reports on interview findings. Russia', *MYPLACE Deliverable Report*, available at: http://www.fp7-myplace.eu/documents/D5.3%20Russia.pdf (accessed 27 June 2014).

Zinoviev, A., (2014), 'Russian Run', WP7: Interpreting Activism (Ethnographies). Deliverable 7.1: Ethnographic Case Studies of Youth Activism', *MYPLACE Deliverable Report*, available at: http://www.fp7-myplace.eu/deliverables.php (accessed 16 December 2014).

**Appendix**
**Table A1:** *Semi-structured interview respondents' socio-demographic profiles*

| Country | Gender (no. of interviewees) | | | | Age (no. of interviewees) | | | | Employment status (no. of interviewees) | | | |
|---|---|---|---|---|---|---|---|---|---|---|---|---|
| | Male | Female | Trans-gender | Total | 16–18 years | 19–21 years | 22–25 years | Total | In education (including part-time) | In employment (including part-time) | Unemployed (including at home carers) | Total |
| UK | 25 | 35 | 1 | 61 | 19 | 21 | 21 | 61 | 34 | 14 | 13 | 61 |
| Russia | 29 | 31 | 0 | 60 | 16 | 14 | 30 | 60 | 34 | 20 | 6 | 60 |
| E. Germany | 29 | 31 | 0 | 60 | 14 | 13 | 33 | 60 | 49 | 8 | 3 | 60 |

*Source:* MYPLACE semi-structured interviews, 2012–13.

*The Sociological Review*, 63:S2, pp. 206–230 (2015), DOI: 10.1111/1467-954X.12269

# Golden Dawn, austerity and young people: the rise of fascist extremism among young people in contemporary Greek society

*Alexandra Koronaiou, Evangelos Lagos, Alexandros Sakellariou, Stelios Kymionis and Irini Chiotaki-Poulou*

**Abstract:** The contemporary rise of popular support for fascism is investigated in this article through an examination of Golden Dawn's remarkable appeal to a section of Greek youth. This leads to the problematization of mainstream explanatory and inter-pretive discourses that attribute Golden Dawn's electoral and political attractiveness almost exclusively to anger and a will to punish the political system which is regarded as being responsible for the country's collapse and the harsh consequences of austerity and recession. Drawing upon the findings of ethnographic research on Golden Dawn and its young voters' and supporters' ideology and political activism conducted as part of the MYPLACE project, we argue that Golden Dawn's young voters and sup-porters are much more than angry youth. Their choice to support a fascist political agenda and practice cannot be reduced solely to an emotional reaction to the crisis but rests on wider ideological and political affinities and links that have been building over the previous two or three decades. In this sense, the contemporary rise of fascism in Greece appears as not merely a straightforward and simple outcome of the crisis but the complex result of previous socio-political transformations, sharpened, magnified and accelerated by the current systemic crash.

**Keywords:** fascism, crisis, ideology, Greece, Golden Dawn, youth

## Introduction

The economic and social collapse Greece has been experiencing since 2010 has been strongly felt in all aspects of social and political life. The consequences of successive waves of austerity measures (dismantling of social welfare ser-vices and dramatic rise in unemployment, poverty, homelessness and suicides) have had a widely felt impact on living conditions. Young people were among the first and most severely affected (ELSTAT, 2013c; Bank of Greece, 2012;

*The Sociological Review*, 63:S2, pp. 231–249 (2015), DOI: 10.1111/1467-954X.12270
© 2015 The Authors. Editorial organisation © 2015 The Editorial Board of the Sociological Review. Published by John Wiley & Sons Ltd, 9600 Garsington Road, Oxford OX4 2DQ, UK and 350 Main Street, Malden, MA 02148, USA

Petmesidou, 2011, 2013; Malkoutzis, 2011). According to official figures, un-employment for the 15–24 age group reached 50 per cent, while for those aged 25–29 it was 34 per cent in the fourth quarter of 2011 (ELSTAT, 2013a); since then it has skyrocketed to 57 per cent and 44 per cent respectively (ELSTAT, 2013b).

The social turmoil triggered by this long period of austerity and recession has led to profound realignments in Greek politics. These crystallized in the outcomes of two successive national elections in May and June of 2012 when the domi-nant two-party system was severely challenged by the electoral success of the left coalition. Public attention was drawn also to the significant breakthrough made by the hitherto pariah neo-Nazi political organization Golden Dawn. Golden Dawn (GD) succeeded in capturing 6.9 per cent of the vote (from a starting point of just 0.3 per cent in the 2009 national elections and 5 per cent in the 2010 local government elections for the city of Athens) and in gaining 18 seats in the Greek Parliament.

The GD debate became charged when voter analyses revealed the party's success in attracting a high proportion of the youth vote; the second high-est among all parties. In the May/June exit polls, the GD youth vote ranged from 10 to 14 per cent for the 18–24 age group and from 13 to 16 per cent for those aged 25–34. This sparked questions and anxiety about the extent and depth of young people's receptivity to fascism. Such concerns were further in-tensified by evidence from subsequent opinion polls that the proportion of the 18–34 vote gained by GD was systematically higher than the party's average rate in the national elections.[1] Concerns about the interest shown by a section of young people in GD rhetoric and practice escalated when the party's influ-ence became evident within the educational system, particularly in secondary schools. School students appeared to openly express their support for GD, dis-playing the party's symbols (including swastikas and the Nazi salutation), in-timidating and attacking political opponents, teachers and classmates of non-Greek origin, and recruiting fellow students. The situation quickly took the form of fierce antagonism and conflict between groups supporting GD and anti-fascist groups that were formed in reaction to the party's aggressive presence in schools.

This article investigates the characteristics and the sources of young people's receptivity and support for GD's ideological discourse and political practice. To this end we trace and analyse the discursive threads that connect GD with its young voters and locate the areas of ideological convergence or divergence that characterize their political connection.

The material drawn on here comes from an ethnographic case study conducted as part of the MYPLACE research project and combines an analysis of GD's ide-ology and activism, as publicized on the Internet, with the study of the views of young people who support, and had voted for, the party in the 2012 elections. The data used consist of the content (texts and audiovisual material) of the official GD website (www.xagr.net) and its youth division webpage[2] and 10 semi-structured interviews with GD's young voters and supporters. Clearly, the interviews do not

*The Sociological Review*, 63:S2, pp. 231–249 (2015), DOI: 10.1111/1467-954X.12270

provide a representative sample of the party's young supporters, but nor was this our intention. The aim was to investigate how the party's young supporters and voters relate to GD's ideology and political practice to which end a combination of Internet ethnography and semi-structured interviews with young GD supporters was employed.

The party's conflictual relationship with the traditional media, as well as the high proportion of young people among its members and supporters, has led GD to place great emphasis on building and maintaining a strong internet presence. GD's preference for the Internet and social media, exemplified in the call to 'turn off your TV, you can find us on the Internet', has contributed to increasing the visibility of, and interest in, the party among youth as well as to confirming and strengthening GD's anti-system profile. Most of our interviewees, particularly those who feel closer to the party and participate in its activism, prefer to follow political developments and events related to the party via the Internet and social media. In fact they discredit and reject, as 'the system's propaganda', almost everything that the traditional media, especially the TV, broadcast or publicize about the party. Their hostility is directed both towards the owners of media and the journalists; the latter are described by one respondent as 'the soldiers of the hustlers in the parliament' (Minas). They are perceived to lie, distort and devalue everything that does not suit their interests. In contrast, respondents evaluate positively, and tend to trust, information from the Internet as well as from their friends and links with the party.

The party's discourse and activity is disseminated widely across the Internet, providing a range of different media and texts for in-depth study of GD's ideology and politics. The web-content studied and analysed for this ethnographic research included: the periodical *Counter-Attack*; the official ideological and political texts of the party; announcements and reports on events including the activities of local branches; audiovisual material from party activities; reports and audiovisual material on various political developments; activist materials (photos, leaflets, etc.); texts and audio on nationalist music; texts on history; ideological contributions by party members and officials; the party leader's announcements and speeches; texts on ancient Greek and nationalist art; and various texts on the party's policies and political programme. Interviews were conducted with young voters and supporters of the party with whom contact was established in the course of the fieldwork. All interviews have been anonymized in order to protect the identity of respondents. None of the respondents had joined the party formally, although three self-identified as active supporters. The interviews focus on the respondents' views, understanding and experiences of GD's ideological and political activity and explore their links to party ideology and politics. Eight respondents are male and two are female. They range in age from 21 to 28 years old. Seven were unemployed at the time of interview, one was a businessman and two others were in full-time employment.

# The crisis, young people and fascism

*The question of fascism[3]*

Soon after GD's electoral success in 2012, the issue of its ideological and political orientation was raised along with the question of its voters' relationship to fascism and neo-Nazism. GD has rejected repeatedly its identification as fascist, neo-Nazi or even far right. Nevertheless, its neo-Nazi history (Psaras, 2012; Hassapopoulos, 2013; Katsimardos and Roubanis, 2013a, 2013b) as well as the willingness of its leadership and its members to make public use of classic Nazi symbols, slogans and salutations have made the question of fascism central to the 'GD debate'.

GD defines its ideology as 'People's Nationalism', where nationalism represents 'the third great ideology in history' and a counter force to both 'communism-internationalism' and 'liberalism-ecumenism'.[4] The nation 'constitutes the ruling Idea and Faith' of the party's ideology and comprises the cultural aspect of the People's Community which is characterized by its common biological origin and is politicized in the 'People's State'.[5] Thus, race and nation, biology and culture are the main substance of the People's Community, which is understood as a homogenous and exclusionist, primordial collective, indelibly marked by 'the vast range of ethnocentrisms which arise from the intrinsic ambiguities of the concept 'nation', and from the many permutations in which racism can express itself as a nationalized form of xenophobia' that Roger Griffin understands as 'ultra-nationalism' (2003: 118). GD consistently rejects all egalitarian principles and values, stressing its faith in 'the spiritual, national and racial inequality of humans'[6] and describing the mixing of races as 'the last step in the racial destruction of Greeks' leading to the loss of a distinctive Greek identity.[7] The 'superiority of the Greek Civilization', as well as of the 'white race' (Karaiskos, 2013a) is persistently promulgated, while multiculturalism and immigration are denounced as constitutive elements of a global capitalist/communist/Jewish conspiracy aimed at destroying the nation (Karaiskos, 2013b). Indeed, GD draws attention to problems related to the repeated waves of mass immigration into Greece over the last three decades and refers to undocumented migrants as 'invaders' and 'a disorderly army that disintegrates social structure and alienates our national identity'; they are 'a foreign body in Greek society' and the source of unemployment and crime as well as a threat to national unity and identity.[8] In response to accusations of xenophobia and racism levelled at it, the party argues that 'the only existing racism is that against the Greeks',[9] who suffer the consequences of the treason of the politicians and the criminality of the immigrants.

For GD, the nation constitutes the ultimate guiding principle of political action.[10] By equating race, nation and people the party is able to develop a homogenizing rhetoric that denies any totalizing principle other than that of the national/racial/people's unity (politicized, through the state). It follows that GD firmly opposes all other political and ideological persuasions and divisions as well as the institutions and the processes that regulate their democratic antagonism and representation. It expresses extreme hostility towards the entire political system through its central political slogan, 'Against all' (Mihaloliakos, 2013). Thus, politicians, parties, unions, the parliament, but also all kinds of democratic processes and institutions, are denounced as responsible for the nation's decline. At the same time, the two dictatorial regimes that have marked Greek history since the mid-1930s are enthusiastically praised and endorsed.[11] Thus GD presents itself as an anti-system political force, comprised of common people and true patriots, struggling for, and representing, the people's true interests (Alexandrakis, 2012).

The notion that the nation is under threat of destruction and in decline is central and recurring. GD describes our times as '[...] an era of complete social, political, economic and above all moral and cultural decline and fall of the modern world'. It is a world of grief, pain and despair, '[...] a world of ruins, in which the ones responsible for our misfortune, the long standing enemies of Hellenism, have managed to execute an elaborate plan to lead world affairs into a real abyss'.[12] Thus, GD consistently calls upon the Greek people to rebel against those responsible for their fate and to side with the party in the imminent 'Nationalist Revolution' that will redeem the nation, avenge its enemies and save the people. GD's nationalist revolution is 'the only absolute and real revolution, because it aims at the birth of new moral, spiritual, social and mental values'; in order for such a radical transformation to be effected, the party's nationalism 'does not seek to salvage any of the established economic and social interests that drive Nations, Peoples and the Civilisation to decline'. Instead, the party's ultimate mission is to tear down the present decadent state and construct a new and radically innovative reality. This entails 're-Hellenizing' the Greek people and nation and creating a 'New Man', a 'New Nation', a 'New People', a 'New State' and a 'New Civilization' through the ultimate defeat of the nation's enemies and the 'final eradication of those Semitic elements which have been cultivated for many decades in our People. Individualism, selfishness, political opportunism, the rampant pursuit of profit, indifference to the future of the Race and of the Homeland cannot exist in this New People'.[13]

The analysis of GD's ideological texts reveals a political discourse structured around the central themes identified in academic literature as constitutive and peculiar to the ideology of historical fascism. The revitalization of academic research on fascism in the last two-three decades owes much to a sizeable body of work that treats fascism as a distinct 'genus' of political ideology (Griffin, 2008a) and defines it as a 'generic' term through the construction of a Weberian ideal type of fascist ideology. This debate on the ideological 'fascist minimum' (Eatwell, 1996, 2009; Copsey, 2004; Griffin, 2008b) has located and analysed a set of ideas peculiar to fascism that constitutes its 'ideological core' (Griffin, 2008b: 185). Fascism is, according to one of the main proponents of this argument, 'a genus of political ideology whose mythic core in its various permutations is a palingenetic form of populist ultra-nationalism' (Griffin, 1991: 26). Griffin's formula refers to fascism as a political ideology characterized by the vision of a homogenous nation that is under imminent danger, in a state of decadence and in need of salvation through a people's revolution that will result in its rebirth. Here, fascism appears as the 'revolution of the right' (Payne, 1995; Griffin, 2000), the core mobilizing myth of which is 'the vision of the nation's imminent rebirth from decadence' (Griffin, 2003: 107). Griffin's version of the 'fascist minimum' has had a significant impact on the study of fascism and has been used by, or has influenced the work of, scholars holding a range of theoretical orientations.[14]

The ideology of GD conforms remarkably closely to such conceptualizations of fascist ideology. It is founded on a mythologized conception of the Greek nation as an organic (biologically unmixed and culturally homogenous) community that exists in a state of degeneration and decline confronting internal and external enemies who threaten its unity and survival. The enemies of the 'People's Community' – capitalists, international usurers, politicians, communists and internationalists, liberals and conservatives, immigrants, minorities of all types, neighbouring nations, and, of course, the Jews – are repeatedly denounced as being responsible for the present crisis and the dangers that it represents for the nation and the people (Karakostas, 2012). Thus, revolutionary national rebirth (palingenesis), which redeems the nation from its present septic state of decline by mobilizing 'people's power' against internal and external enemies that are perceived to threaten the unity and the survival of a mythic organic community, emerges as the discursive core of GD's ideology and places the party at the centre of historical fascism's legacy.

Distancing itself from Italian Fascism and German Nazism, the party's officially endorsed political ideology is that of Revolutionary People's Nationalism. When asked to characterize the party's ideology, the young GD voters and supporters interviewed all accepted the party's self-identification as primarily 'nationalist' and many of them expressed their own pride in being nationalists. Some of them dismissed outright the view that GD is a fascist or neo-Nazi party and emphasized its nationalist identity, but most of them recognized the existence of links connecting GD with fascism and Nazism. Thus, of members of the party, it was said that 'some of them are neo-Nazis, a part of them are nationalists, others are National Socialists, while others are just supporters of the far right. I would say it is a nationalist party, even though I don't think that this label is the best description' (Harilaos[15]) while another respondent said she would not like to see the party in the country's government because 'no matter what they say, that we are not Nazis and stuff, they are heading toward that direction' (Domna).

Regardless of their suspicions about Nazism, however, the majority of respondents believe that this is something that is emphasized primarily by opponents of the party and the mainstream media which feel threatened by GD's nationalist fervour and the people's support for it. Thus, even those who recognize fascism within the party appear prepared to accept it as long as the party remains a patriotic force that fights actively against the treasonous politicians and the murderous immigrants.

*Explaining young people's support for fascism: crisis, austerity and ideology*

The ideologically and politically charged debate about GD's influence on a segment of Greek youth usually centres exclusively on the role of the crisis, austerity and especially of youth unemployment. It interprets GD's youth vote solely as a consequence of young people's feelings of anger and despair due to the economic and social collapse of the country. According to such arguments, the impulsive nature of youth has led to this anger and despair being transformed into electoral support for an extremist organization as young people seek to punish the political system for the destruction of their future. Ignorance about historical fascism and lack of personal experience and memories of the tragedies of World War II are added as further 'extenuating' factors for young people, thus reproducing the mainstream perception and understanding of the phenomenon as constituting a conjunctural, superficial, emotional and misguided reaction to extreme circumstances.

It is worth noting here that both supporters and opponents of the austerity policies have adopted and propagated this conceptual scheme adjusting it to their own particular views and needs. What both sides share in their understanding of GD's attractiveness to a part of Greek youth (and, indeed, for an increasing section of the general constituency) is a direct connection between the rise of fascism and the crisis; this reflects the traditional explanatory scheme for the rise of historical fascism. According to this approach, the economic crisis and its consequences on society and the political system (unemployment, poverty, prolonged recession, social unrest, acute political conflict and the inability of the ruling elites and the state to preserve social cohesion) constitute the necessary structural and political preconditions for the emergence and development of fascism and for large parts of the population to break with the established institutional arrangements and the mainstream political forces and seek radical, even extremist, alternatives (Eley, 1983; Drucker, 1995; Renton, 1999; Morgan, 2003).

The adequacy of this approach has been challenged by other students of fascism who point to the lack of a convincing analysis and explanation of the specific political choice that the victims of the capitalist crisis made when they supported fascist movements, parties and political programmes (Payne, 1995; Paxton, 2004; Griffin, 2008c; Laqueur, 1996). Such criticisms underline the immanent sociological-conceptual tension between the subjective and the objective determinants of political choices and behaviours which characterizes the traditional understanding of the capitalist crisis-fascism link. In other words, they pinpoint the insufficiency of the postulated direct and unidirectional connection of the capitalist crisis with the rise of fascism in interwar Europe and they stress the need for the development of alternative theorizations that are able to account for the specific ways that the macro-analysis of the capitalist crisis and its effects on society can be connected to, and informed by, the micro-analysis of individual political choices and preferences.

Such questions emerge also in the case of the contemporary return of fascism in crisis-ridden Greek politics and society. Again, the contemporary mainstream explanations that connect directly the present rise of fascism with the long-lasting crisis are not sufficient as they fail to account not only for the specificity of developments in Greece but also for the lack of a similar situation in other countries also hit by the crisis and austerity policies, particularly in the European South. In this respect neither Spain nor Portugal, with which Greece is usually compared, demonstrate an analogous situation, or indeed any rise of far right electoral rates whatsoever (Goodwin, 2014).

Furthermore, the traditional capitalist-crisis-rise-of-fascism approach focuses exclusively on the present situation and misrecognizes important wider trends and processes among Greek youth that had been developing for a long period prior to the crisis. Such trends and processes have been identified repeatedly in social surveys on Greek youth since the late 1990s and include, in particular, the strengthening of nationalism, authoritarianism and xenophobia along with an acute delegitimization and rejection of the political system and an intense dissatisfaction with the functioning of representative democracy. In these studies, Greek youth ranked the army and 'love of homeland' very highly, while, at the same time, they distrusted public administration, the government, trade unions, political parties and politicians. They did not rate social action as important and exhibited very low rates of civic participation and engagement (GSY and VPRC, 2000; IEA, 2001; Demertzis and Armenakis, 2001; GSY, 2005; Stratoudaki, 2005; Koulaidis and Dimopoulos, 2006; Kerr *et al.*, 2010).

More specifically, surveys conducted in 1997 and 1999 by the General Secretariat for Youth located and described a sizeable part of youth as exhibiting intolerant and authoritarian attitudes toward immigrants, sexual preferences and delinquency whilst supporting the view that the educational system should teach submission to authority and unconditional obedience to laws, even where such laws were wrong or unjust. The 'authoritarians', as they were labelled by the researchers, accounted for almost a third of the sample and they shared with the rest a highly critical attitude toward Greek society as a whole, a high level of dissatisfaction with the political system and the functioning of democracy, an acute alienation from political institutions as well as the demand for deep, even revolutionary, changes in society and the political system (GSY and VPRC, 2000). These trends had been strengthening far right politics in Greek society long before GD's electoral breakthrough, as is evident from the electoral successes, from 2004 onwards, of the nationalist and xenophobic political party Popular Orthodox Rally (LAOS) (Georgiadou, 2008; Kolovos, 2005). Indeed, LAOS's collapse in the 2012 elections, following its support for the imposed austerity policies, contributed both electorally and ideologically to GD's success (Mavris, 2013).

The necessity for thinking differently on the relationship of Greek youth to GD became evident after the impressive and alarming further rise of GD's level of support in the 2014 local-regional government and the European elections in which GD managed to increase considerably its electoral gains: 11 per cent for the region of Athens, 16 per cent for the Athens Municipality and 9 per cent and 3 seats in the European Parliament elections. It now has seats also in many regional and local governments around the country. Such electoral gains appear

*The Sociological Review*, 63:S2, pp. 231–249 (2015), DOI: 10.1111/1467-954X.12270
© 2015 The Authors. Editorial organisation © 2015 The Editorial Board of the Sociological Review

even more notable as they were achieved despite the adverse conditions that the prosecution of a large part of the party's leadership, on charges of constituting and directing a criminal organization, has caused. The party's leadership had been put under judicial investigation several months before the election period, following the murder of a young antifascist rapper, Pavlos Fyssas, by members of GD. Since the beginning of the judicial investigation, half of the party's MPs, including its leader, have been in pre-trial detention facing charges relating to 32 more criminal acts against immigrants and political opponents. The prosecution of the party's leadership contributed greatly to shedding light on GD's organization, action and ideology and helped establish its neo-Nazi character in the public domain. It also revealed a paramilitary wing involved in a wide range of crimes, systematically propagating National Socialism, racism and hostility towards all democratic institutions (Deputy Public Prosecutor, 2013). Again the proportion of young people's support for GD was higher than the party's average level of support and GD remained the second most popular party among young people.[16] GD's official discourse hails such developments, boasting that 'we have won the youth from you once and for all' (Antiochos, 2012), and proclaiming that in future elections an 'intergenerational battle' will take place with the majority of Greek youth taking the side of Golden Dawn.[17]

In light of these developments, GD's electoral success could no longer be attributed to ignorance, misunderstanding of its character or a misguided desire to punish the mainstream political parties for the country's collapse. It became apparent that GD's voters were not making merely an angry, symbolic gesture, but a conscious political choice that cannot be reduced to sentiments, though it encompasses them. Undoubtedly, the feelings of rage and despair at the dire consequences of the crisis and the imposed austerity policies play an important role in triggering the extensive and profound challenging of the mainstream bipartisan political system that characterized the Third Greek Democracy established after the fall of the military dictatorship in 1974. The profound nature of this challenge – visible in the inability of the one-party government model to maintain its grip on the Greek political system in the context of the crisis as well as in the remarkable delegitimization of the main players (PASOK and New Democracy) of the political mainstream (Teperoglou and Tsatsanis, 2014) – is certainly linked to the effects of the crisis upon Greek society and the feelings of rage and despair that accompany them.

However, these sentiments cannot, on their own, account for the conscious ideological and political choice that GD young voters make by supporting the party. In other words, they cannot explain why these young people choose to support and to vote for a fascist organization and not for any of the other parties also opposed to those the young people blame for the country's plight. This question makes the assumed direct connection of capitalist crisis with popular support for fascism appear to be less self-evident, while the need to further investigate what makes such a connection possible and realizable emerges. In this context, the investigation and understanding of the meanings, the values and the attitudes that the voters associate with their choices and preferences can be of great value in analysing and explaining the conscious ideological and political choice that GD young voters make by supporting the party. In this sense, instead of taking for granted that support for fascism is a normal consequence of the capitalist crisis, we need to examine what makes GD's ideology and political agenda 'make sense' and appeal to young Greeks in the context of the present crisis.

## A fascist political movement of young people

Historical fascism had a special relation to young people; not only is it suggested that '[a]bove all, the early fascists were young [...] heated by insurrectionary fevers [...] (Paxton, 2004: 49, 83) but it has been repeatedly stressed by academic research that fascist movements and regimes placed great emphasis both on controlling mass youth organizations and institutions and on integrating young people to their militant groups (Griffin, 2008c; Paxton, 2004; Payne, 1995; Laqueur, 1999). Youth is for fascism an absolute value and it becomes a symbol of the 'new', of national rejuvenation and of the nation's rebirth that the future nationalist revolution will bring. It is the symbol of a creative force and of the omnipotence of the forces of life; it is worshipped through images, hymns and music (Richard, 1999: 244) and the fascist state seeks to control and manipulate it (Paxton, 2004).

GD seems to be no exception to this socio-historical connection as it 'loudly declares' that it is a 'political Movement of the Greek Youth and of the Greek Workers' (Karakostas, 2014), the members of which 'are mainly young people, workers, students, scientists, farmers, artists, employees but also unemployed'.[18] Golden Dawn has put great emphasis on its relationship to young people, carefully planning and organizing the diffusion of its political ideology and identity in social milieus where young people are found in high numbers; football fan clubs, gyms, secondary schools, music-based youth cultures as well as the Internet and social media have been key sites for the party to forge its ideological and political bonds with sections of Greek youth (Psaras, 2012). It is no accident, then, that of the party's 18 MPs, four have been (or still are) leading members of Greek white power and black metal bands or that a further three had been leading figures in three major football fan clubs.[19]

### A generation of young nationalists

GD relies heavily on its young members and supporters both ideologically and for political activism. On the ideological level, it is only 'the clean hands of Greek Youth and of Greek Workers' that can build the 'authentic Nationalist State'. Young Greeks are seen as the party's driving force and the vanguard of the Nationalist Revolution.[20] Their inexhaustible energy, courage, fighting spirit, reaction and resistance, their idealism, honesty and love for the homeland make them the natural leaders of the Nationalist Revolution that will regenerate the nation. Thus, youth is, for GD, a vital force with respect to radical change and to establishing a 'New Nation' and a new political regime. GD calls systematically upon

*The Sociological Review*, 63:S2, pp. 231–249 (2015), DOI: 10.1111/1467-954X.12270

a nationalistically awakened new generation to oppose and fight party democracy, in both its liberal and socialist variants, to crush Greece's enemies and save the people and to rebuild the nation from the ruins of the present decadence (Karakostas, 2014; Mihalarou, 2014).

All young respondents interviewed for this study agree that GD is a true patriotic-nationalist party that cares for and 'prioritise[s] the Greeks above all' (Minas). Moreover, all of them expressed pride in being nationalists, firmly believing that the Greek people are superior to all others. Only one rejected the idea of Greek superiority, while two others expressed doubts about the current situation and the political choices made by Greek citizens in recent times. Nevertheless, they believe that contemporary Greek people are above others because of their glorious past history and civilization. The view that 'we had a civilization when others were still in the trees' (Voula) is a recurrent trope in GD texts and is repeated frequently by respondents.[21] It is also widespread across Greek society as a whole, regardless of political persuasion. This is the chief locus of mainstream Greek nationalism; a mythologized glorious past envisaged as being continued through to contemporary Greece, which remains bathed in the power and glory of the ancient civilization (Fragoudaki and Dragona, 1997; Tsoukalas, 1995). This can be seen also in the inability of respondents to envisage the possibility that second or even third generation immigrants could be justifiably considered Greek citizens and their readiness to invoke the importance of a biological link to glorious Greek ancestors in order to reject any such thought.

Despite delighting in past grandeur, all respondents in this study feel that our times bear little resemblance either to glorious antiquity or to the potential for power and prosperity that the Greek nation has due to its history and its natural resources. The current period is characterized by decadence and sepsis in which the Greeks have been subjected to the interests of foreign powers which, in other circumstances, would be seen as in permanent cultural debt to the Greek nation and civilization. The idea that contemporary Greeks are direct descendants of the ancient Greek civilization and the heirs to the cultural debt owed by the rest of Europe to their renowned ancestors is widespread across Greek society and has been strengthened during the country's collapse and the imposition of austerity measures. It is also central to GD's promise to restore past glories to a reborn Greece. Prioritizing the Greeks, demanding what is rightfully theirs, fighting for the nation's rebirth from decadence and achieving the nation's supremacy is what nationalism means for both GD and our young respondents who consistently point to the political system's responsibility for not having established and secured Greece's superiority and prosperity. The distance between this fantasy and current reality evokes feelings of injustice and resentment that are complemented by those of humiliation, guilt, shame and anger:

> I believe that history shows we gave everything to the whole world but are left with nothing. Civilization, culture, everything. The Germans were still hunting pigs with slings when we had the Olympic Games. (Nikodimos)

Domna regretted 'the votes I gave to PASOK all these years. I regretted them because I felt like I had contributed somehow to the country's destruction', while Stamatis too is disdainful of the Modern Greeks:

> The Modern Greek people is the most stupid currently on the planet, in my view [...] Modern Greeks are the dumbest and have low IQ because they are lost and they have degraded their culture and cannot be compared with the ancient Greeks [...]. Modern Greeks are worthless, because there is no education [...] and the only thing that they are occupied with is Facebook and dope, nothing else. (Stamatis)

Resentment, self-pity and self-condemnation are complemented by anger at the corruption of the political system and the treason of the politicians that is perceived to have brought about the country's destruction. All respondents in this study expressed anger and hostility toward the political system holding it responsible for the crisis and challenging its democratic character. This dissatisfaction of young people with liberal democracy is a recurrent theme in the MYPLACE findings (Pilkington and Pollock, this volume) as very often 'the institutions that are least trusted are the classic institutions of liberal democracy' (Grimm and Pilkington, this volume). The majority of respondents justified their vote and support for GD as a reaction against it and 'in order to show that those who are in power now are traitors' (Nikitas). For them, GD was the only possible electoral choice, since they had rejected the two mainstream governing parties and had also dismissed the left either because of its positive attitude towards immigrants or because they viewed them too as hypocrites. However, four respondents attributed their vote and support to a deeper commitment to the values of nationalism and racism. Voula, for example, voted for GD because 'I am racist, clearly, no bullshit, no nothing'. Three others had supported Golden Dawn for several years due to their strong nationalist beliefs and values. While not being official members of the party, they maintain a close connection to the party and participate in its activism.

For all respondents – even for those who disagree with the party's focus on violence – GD is an honest people's party that has remained firm in its views and policies openly opposing the 'treasonous' and 'hypocritical' politicians whose greed for wealth and power is responsible for the country's present state since their only interest is '[...] how they are going to gain votes and money' (Domna). Contrary to all other parties, GD is truly anti-system as it always 'stresses many of the social problems that the others conceal' (Nikitas) and 'they haven't stolen people's money, as the other parties have' (Harilaos). In contrast, GD is a patriotic, nationalist party comprised not of politicians but of 'common people' who themselves suffer the harsh reality:

> [...] they are not a party, in the sense that has been debased in our times. The difference is that it is not comprised of politicians [...] They are people from Kypseli, from Agios Pateleimonas who are fed up. People who, before entering parliament, were unemployed probably for one or two years, they could be starving. This is the difference; it's like if I or you had entered parliament. (Marios)

*The Sociological Review*, 63:S2, pp. 231–249 (2015), DOI: 10.1111/1467-954X.12270

*An army of young militant activists who defend and prioritize the Greeks*

Despite the party's denial that it systematically recruits young people in schools, Golden Dawn's political activities attract young people of all age-groups and the party has been organizing 'history courses' for the nationalist education of children, even at primary school level.[22] GD's public activities reveal that young people are involved in much of its social activism, particularly in food and blood donations 'for Greeks only' and in public events and commemorations. Moreover, the rise in racist violent attacks against immigrants by young people during the last four years has raised concerns that actually GD encourages such attacks as a kind of 'initiation rite' to the party's political practice. Although this accusation is officially rejected by the party, such charges can be read in the recent public prosecutor's request that led to the arrest and pre-trial detention of its leadership. Moreover, the surge of violent attacks against immigrants has been repeatedly attributed to the rise of GD's political influence as well as to the existence and action of informal but organized militia groups, comprised mainly of young people, which are responsible for much of the anti-immigrant aggression (RVRN, 2013, 2014; The Greek Ombudsman, 2013).

On the level of political activism, the party organizes and mobilizes its young members and supporters through its strict hierarchical structure that has repeatedly been characterized as 'military-like' or 'paramilitary' (Psaras, 2012; Hassapopoulos, 2013; Deputy Public Prosecutor, 2013). GD's army of young people was created in the late 1990s under the title 'Youth Front' and since then has fought in the streets of Athens and other Greek cities against the nation's internal and external enemies, mainly the left and immigrants. Until the detention of the GD leadership, such militia had succeeded in establishing a peculiar regime of control in areas with high levels of immigrant residents and/or unemployment rates. The average age of the members of such storm-troops is estimated at 27 years (RVRN, 2013). The intensity of GD's violent presence in the streets was dramatically reduced from the moment of its leadership's prosecution. This also led to a dramatic reduction in the number of racist attacks; only 18 attacks were recorded during the fourth quarter of 2013 compared to 148 cases in the previous 9 months (RVRN, 2014).

The majority of respondents agree with the violent treatment of immigrants meted out by GD. All believe that immigrants are a huge social problem and should leave the country and only a minority expressed dissatisfaction with the party's violent methods towards them. Despite such reservations, all agree that Greeks and not immigrants are the victims of racism, and they are outraged that the latter have more rights and benefits than the former. Immigrants in Greece represent, for respondents, a source of fear and are an easy target for their feelings of resentful racism which they justify on the grounds of the rise in crime and unemployment:

> I have been forced over the last years to become a racist. They have forced me to become a racist, because it can't be real that I am afraid to move around in the country where I was born and in the neighbourhoods where I grew up [ . . . ] why don't they put them on a boat and sink it somewhere in the Aegean Sea? (Voula)

For Nikitas 'the attacks against immigrants are definitely fewer than the attacks of immigrants against Greeks' and for Nikodimos immigrants are to be blamed for the rise of violence. For the majority of informants, violence against immigrants is always preventive/self-defensive and is accepted because 'extreme circumstances require extreme measures' (Marios). Violence (physical and symbolic) is a central characteristic of GD's activism and general public presence. It is also one of the most accepted and admired qualities of the party. If immigrants constitute the first major target of violent activism, then, the second is the left and the anarchists. Again, the vast majority (all but one) of respondents wholeheartedly endorsed the most widely broadcasted such attack, when a young spokesperson of the party physically attacked two women MPs of the left in a TV studio nationally broadcasting live one of the mainstream morning TV shows. Where respondents did not endorse the attack wholeheartedly, they justified it with feelings of hurt masculinity and strong temper. Sexism, even misogyny, as well as hatred of the left was common in their talk; some even expressed their wish that the attack had been harsher.

Militancy, fighting for the nation's rebirth and waging an everyday war against the nation's enemies are a fundamental aspect of GD's young members' and supporters' engagement with the party. A second key site of participation for young people is in the party's cultural and solidarity activities. The party's leadership often encourages the confrontational and violent spirit of its audience in party rallies and events where young members participate in militaristic rituals under the command of the party's young spokesman who is also one of the younger members of the Greek Parliament.[23] This sentiment is articulated by the party leader as he threatens the political system at one of the most famous such party events:

> [...] we are waiting for the time when we will be strong enough to claim the rights of the Greeks. But I am telling you that we are not having a good time at all in the parliament. We feel uncomfortable; it disgusts to be there. If they want, we can leave at any moment and go out onto the streets and then we will see who is going to win. They will see, then, what storm-troops means, what fight means, what it means for bayonets to be sharpened on the pavements.[24]

For the young supporters of GD, the party's violence is embedded in an authoritarian vision of the new Greece that be built in the future. Thus, praising past authoritarian regimes in Greece, advocating the violent suppression of opponents and imagining a regime of absolute power are very common in the discourse of respondents. This is exemplified by Nikandros's advocation of a junta:

> I don't agree with the political system. I am in favour of extreme systems. A very good example is a junta; only one person to make decisions and that's it. We don't like him? He is overthrown. We like him? We keep him. (Nikandros)

Minas hopes for absolutism in order for Greece to thrive again: 'There will not be much of a democracy I think [...] It will be for Greece's benefit. Greece will advance both economically and socially [...] It will be absolute dominance [...]'.

Apart from 'sharpening the bayonets' for the time of the Nationalist Revolution, GD organizes cultural activities and events such as youth festivals, Greek history classes, summer camps, open mass gatherings, speeches and rallies, most of which have an apparent militaristic ritual character with parades, uniforms, military formations and night-time torch processions. All these activities focus on the ideological, political and physical training of the participants as well as on strengthening loyalty and commitment to the party; they play a crucial role in identity formation and personal engagement in a militarized community of 'brothers-in-arms' that simultaneously prepares for and is at war with all party adversaries.

Finally, GD has been active in solidarity activities organized 'only for Greeks'. In these activities of nationalist solidarity – mainly donations of clothes, food and blood – young people participate in numbers allowing the party to declare that 'the Nationalist Youth is the pioneer of the solidarity activities of our Movement'.[25] Food donations are by far the most appreciated and praised GD activity by interviewees; only one commented negatively on the fact that food is given only to Greek citizens while the rest showed no dissatisfaction at all. Nevertheless, half of the respondents are reluctant about or even negative towards participating in GD activism and only two would consider joining the party. The majority does not wish to be actively involved and engaged with the party, invoking anti-partisan feelings and views, although they agree with its core political agenda and behaviour.

## Conclusion

Our research on the party's ideology and political practice as well as on its young voters' views about the meaning of their support for GD, has revealed the existence of important ideological characteristics and political attitudes shared by the party and its voters. The question of GD's political success in Greece, and particularly the investigation of young people's support, needs to take into account both the party's young voters' rejection of the mainstream political forces as a result of the crisis and austerity and wider ideological and political developments and trends that transgress the boundaries of the current crisis.

It is precisely the interplay between the processes of delegitimization of the mainstream political forces, as a consequence of the crisis outbreak and the austerity policies, and wider ideological trends and political developments that has shaped the demand for fascist discourse and political agenda in the context of the crisis. Thus, GD's young voters cannot be seen simply as 'angry youth', though anger is clearly triggering their rejection of the mainstream parties; their political choice should also be understood in terms of a deeper ideological and political affinity to the party's discourse and practice.

Golden Dawn's young voters have been faced with making political choices in the harsh and extremely pressurized conditions created by the crisis and austerity. Their choices have been shaped, it is argued here, by both their desire to punish those they see as responsible for the country's ills and by specific ideological and political predispositions that define the 'horizon' of choices available to them.

## Notes

1 See 'The popularity of Golden Dawn before and after the elections-social characteristics', *Public Issue*, 12 October 2012 (in Greek), available at: http://www.publicissue.gr/2054/gd_popularity/. See also Vernardakis (2012).
2 Initially this was: http://resistance-hellas.blogspot.gr. From March 2013 onwards, it was: www.antepithesi.gr
3 Here Roger Griffin's distinction between 'fascism' and 'Fascism' to refer to the generic concept and to the specific Italian political movement of the interwar period respectively is employed.
4 'Ideology' (in Greek), available at: http://www.xryshaygh.com/index.php/kinima/ideologia (accessed 27 February 2014).
5 'Identity' (in Greek), available at: http://www.xryshaygh.com/index.php/kinima (accessed 27 February 2014).
6 'Identity' (in Greek), available at: http://www.xryshaygh.com/index.php/kinima (accessed 27 February 2014).
7 'The problem of immigration in Greece' (in Greek), available at: http://antepithesi.gr/index.php?option=com_k2&view=item&id=553:to-provlima-tis-metanastefsis-stin-ellada&Itemid=303 (accessed 29 March 2013).
8 'Political Positions' (in Greek), available at: http://www.xryshaygh.com/index.php/kinima/thesis (accessed 15 May 2014). 'Ideology' (in Greek), available at: http://www.xryshaygh.com/index.php/kinima/ideologia (accessed 27 February 2014).
9 'The only existing racism is the one against the Greeks' (in Greek), 31 January 2013, available at: http://www.xryshaygh.com/index.php/enimerosi/view/o-monos-uparktos-ratsismos-einai-autos-enantion-twn-ellhnwn (accessed 15 May 2014).
10 'Movement, ideology' (in Greek), available at: http://www.xryshaygh.com/index.php/kinima/ideologia (accessed 15 May 2014).
11 Namely the 1936–1941 para-fascist dictatorial regime of Metaxas and the 1967–1974 military dictatorship of Colonel Papadopoulos. See also 'Ideology' (in Greek), available at: http://www.xryshaygh.com/index.php/kinima/ideologia (accessed 27 February 2014).
12 'The new generation of Greeks and a supposed dilemma', 24 March 2013, available at: http://antepithesi.gr/index.php?option=com_k2&view=item&id=536:i-nea-genia-ellinon-kai-ena-ypotithemeno-dillima&Itemid=303 (accessed 27 March 2014).
13 'Identity' (in Greek), available at: http://www.xryshaygh.com/index.php/kinima (accessed 27 February 2014). See also Karakostas (2012).
14 See, for example, the inclusion of Griffin's core conception of fascist ideology in Paxton's (2004) influential definition of fascism.
15 All interviewees are referred to using pseudonyms to protect anonymity.
16 'Who are Golden Dawn's voters: young, farmers or unemployed', *iefimerida*, 24 May 2014 (in Greek), available at: http://www.nooz.gr/greece/to-profil-ton-psifoforon-tis-xrusis-augis (accessed 25 May 2014).
17 'Golden Dawn sweeps among youth', 27 November 2012 (in Greek), available at: http://www.xryshaygh.com/index.php/enimerosi/view/sarwnei-h-chrush-augh-sth-neolaia#.UhRkMGew69s (accessed 1 August 2013).
18 'Youth Front' (in Greek), available at: http://www.xryshaygh.com/index.php/kinima/neolaia (accessed 1 May 2014).
19 These bands are: Iron Youth, Hellenic Stompers, Pogrom and Naer Mataron. See also Georgakis (2013) and Hassapopoulos (2013).
20 'Political Soldier 8 – 'Victory is ours' (in Greek), available at: http://www.antepithesi.gr/index.php?option=com_k2&view=item&id=712:politikos-stratiotis-8&Itemid=408 (accessed 7 May 2013).

*The Sociological Review*, 63:S2, pp. 231–249 (2015), DOI: 10.1111/1467-954X.12270

21 'Ideology' (in Greek), available at: http://www.xryshaygh.com/index.php/kinima/ideologia (accessed 27 February 2014).
22 'The courses on Greek History by Golden Dawn start today', 15 March 2013 (in Greek), available at: http://www.xryshaygh.com/index.php/enimerosi/view/jekinoun-ta-mathhmata-ellhnikhs-istorias-apo-thn-chrush-augh (accessed 15 May 2014).
23 'Golden Dawn at Thermopylae', 8 September 2013 (in Greek), available at: https://www.youtube.com/watch?v=U43BbApS8uQ (accessed 21 May 2014).
24 'The distortion of the truth that 'evidenced' the flimsy indictment', 23 January 2014 (in Greek), available at: http://www.xryshaygh.com/index.php/enimerosi/view/h-diastreblwsh-ths-alhtheias-me-thn-opoia-stoicheiotheteitai-to-sathro-kath#ixzz32rV9PBi2 (accessed 21 May 2014).
25 'Political Soldier 8 – 'Victory is ours', 7 May 2013 (in Greek), available at: http://www.ante pithesi.gr/index.php?option=com_k2&view=item&id=712:politikos-stratiotis-8&Itemid=408 (accessed 15 May 2014).

# References

Alexandrakis, K., (2012), 'What is the Golden Dawn supporter', 26 July (in Greek), available at: http://www.xryshaygh.com/index.php/enimerosi/view/ti-einai-o-chrusaugiths (accessed 27 February 2014).
Antiochos, (2012), 'Observatory for the containment of Golden Dawn set up by the Ministry of Education', 25 November (in Greek), available at: http://www.xryshaygh.com/index.php/enimerosi/view/parathrhthrio-gia-thn-anaschesh-ths-chrush-aughs-sta-scholeia-ftiachnei-to#.UhRljGew69s (accessed 1 August 2013).
Bank of Greece, (2012), *Social Policy and Social Cohesion in Greece in Conditions of Financial Crisis* (in Greek), Athens: Bank of Greece.
Copsey, N., (2004), *Contemporary British Fascism: The British National Party and the Quest for Legitimacy*, Basingstoke: Palgrave Macmillan.
Demertzis, N. and Armenakis, A., (2001), *Student Youth: Crisis of Politics and Political Communication* (in Greek), Athens: Sakkoulas Editions.
Deputy Public Prosecutor, (2013), 'Conclusion of the Deputy Public Prosecutor of the Supreme Court, Athens', 28 September (in Greek), available at: http://www.tovima.gr/files/1/2013/09/29/porisma.pdf (accessed 15 May 2014).
Drucker, P. F., (1995), *The End of Economic Man: The Origins of Totalitarianism*, New Brunswick and London: Transaction Publishers.
Eatwell, R., (1996), 'On defining the "fascist minimum": the centrality of ideology', *Journal of Political Ideologies*, 1 (3): 303–319.
Eatwell, R., (2009), 'The nature of "generic fascism": the "fascist minimum" and the "fascist matrix"', in C. Iordachi (ed.), *Comparative Fascist Studies: New Perspectives*, 134–161, Abingdon: Routledge.
Eley, G., (1983), 'What produces fascism? Preindustrial traditions or a crisis of capitalism', *Politics and Society*, 12 (1): 53–82.
ELSTAT (Hellenic Statistical Authority), (2013a), *Labour Force Survey – 4th Quarter 2012* (press release), Piraeus, available at: http://www.statistics.gr/portal/page/portal/ESYE/BUCKET/A0101/PressReleases/A0101_SJO01_DT_QQ_04_2012_01_F_EN.pdf (accessed 3 January 2014).
ELSTAT (Hellenic Statistical Authority), (2013b), *Labour Force Survey – 3rd Quarter 2013* (press release), Piraeus, available at: http://www.statistics.gr/portal/page/portal/ESYE/BUCKET/A0101/PressReleases/A0101_SJO01_DT_QQ_03_2013_01_F_EN.pdf (accessed 3 January 2014).
ELSTAT (Hellenic Statistical Authority), (2013c), *Statistics on Income and Living Conditions 2012* (Income reference period 2011), Risk of poverty (press release), Piraeus, available at: http://www.statistics.gr/portal/page/portal/ESYE/BUCKET/A0802/PressReleases/A0802_SFA10_DT_AN_00_2012_01_F_EN.pdf (accessed 3 January 2014).
Fragoudaki, A. and Dragona, Th. (eds.), (1997), *What Is our Country? Ethnocentricism in Education* (in Greek), Athens: Alexandreia.

Georgakis, G., (2013), 'When Nazism kills also football', 9 May (in Greek), available at: http://www.tovima.gr/sports/article/?aid=511718 (accessed 10 May 2014).

Georgiadou, V., (2008), 'Voting for the far right: the electoral choice of LA.O.S' (in Greek), *Science and Society*, 19: 243–256.

Goodwin, M., (2014), 'How Europe's far-right will – and won't – flourish in 2014', *New Statesman*, January, available at: http://www.newstatesman.com/politics/2014/01/how-europes-far-right-will-and-wont-flourish-2014 (accessed 15 March 2014).

Greek Ombudsman (The), (2013), *Special Report: The Phenomenon of Racist Violence in Greece and its Treatment*, Athens, September.

Griffin, R., (1991), *The Nature of Fascism*, London: Pinter.

Griffin, R., (2000), 'Revolution from the right: fascism', in D. Parker (ed.), *Revolutions and the Revolutionary Tradition in the West 1560–1991*, 185–201, London: Routledge.

Griffin, R., (2003), 'The palingenetic core of generic fascist ideology', in A. Campi (ed.), *Che cos'è il fascismo? Interpretazioni e prospettive di ricerche*, 97–122, Roma: Ideazione editrice, available at: http://www.libraryofsocialscience.com/ideologies/docs/the-palingenetic-core-of-generic-fascist-ideology/index.html (accessed 3 January 2014).

Griffin, R., (2008a), 'Hooked crosses and forking paths: the fascist dynamics of the Third Reich', in M. Feldman (ed.), *A Fascist Century. Essays by Roger Griffin*, 83–113, Basingstoke: Palgrave Macmillan.

Griffin, R., (2008b), 'Fascism's new faces (and new facelessness) in the "post-fascist" epoch', in M. Feldman (ed.), *A Fascist Century: Essays by Roger Griffin*, 181–202, Basingstoke: Palgrave Macmillan.

Griffin, R., (2008c), 'Fatal attraction: why Nazism appealed to voters', in M. Feldman (ed.), *A Fascist Century: Essays by Roger Griffin*, 71–82, Basingstoke: Palgrave Macmillan.

GSY (General Secretariat for Youth) and Institute VPRC, (2000), *Young People of our Time: Values, Attitudes and Opinions of Greek Youth, 1997–1999* (in Greek), Athens: Papazisis.

GSY (General Secretariat for Youth), (2005), *Youth in Greece Nowadays: Final Report of the Project 'YOUTH'* (in Greek), Athens: General Secretariat for Youth.

Hassapopoulos, N., (2013), *Golden Dawn: The History, the People and the Truth* (in Greek), Athens: A. A. Livanis.

IEA (International Association for the Evaluation of Educational Achievement), (2001), *Citizenship and Education in Twenty-eight Countries. Civic Knowledge and Engagement at Age Fourteen*, http://www.iea.nl/cived.html (accessed 3 January 2014).

Karaiskos, A., (2013a), 'Collaboration: the wretched polymorphous racism of the "anti-racists"', 25 February (in Greek), available at: http://www.xryshaygh.com/index.php/enimerosi/view/sunergasia-o-athlios-polumorfos-ratsismos-twn-antiratsistwn (accessed 29 March 2013).

Karaiskos, A., (2013b), 'The unholy war against the Nation', 29 August (in Greek), available at: http://www.xryshaygh.com/index.php/enimerosi/view/o-anieros-polemos-enantion-tou-ethnous (accessed 15 May 2014).

Karakostas, E., (2012), 'Nationalist revolution', 20 October (in Greek), available at: http://www.xryshaygh.com/index.php/enimerosi/view/ethnikistikh-epanastash#.UhixNNK-18E (accessed 3 January 2014).

Karakostas, E., (2014), 'The people drawn up under the nationalist banners, seeking freedom and work!', 1 May (in Greek), available at: http://www.xryshaygh.com/index.php/enimerosi/view/zhtw-h-ellhnikh-ergatikh-prwtomagia (accessed 1 May 2014).

Katsimardos, T. and Roubanis, Th. (eds), (2013a), *The Black Book of Neo-Nazism: The Real Golden Dawn Brought to Light ('I'm not gonna be afraid')*, Athens: 'Ethnos'-Pigassos Ekdotiki (distributed free of charge with the newspaper *Ethnos on Sunday*, 29 September 2013).

Katsimardos, T. and Roubanis, Th. (eds), (2013b), *The History of Neo-Nazism in Greece: The Evidence on Nazi Violence*, Athens: 'Ethnos'-Pigassos Ekdotiki (distributed free of charge with the newspaper *Ethnos on Sunday*, 6 October 2013).

Kerr, D., Sturman, L., Schulz, W. and Burge, B., (2010), ICCS 2009. *European Report: Civic Knowledge, Attitudes, and Engagement among Lower-secondary Students in 24 European Countries*,

*The Sociological Review*, 63:S2, pp. 231–249 (2015), DOI: 10.1111/1467-954X.12270

IEA, available at: http://www.iea.nl/fileadmin/user_upload/Publications/Electronic_versions/ICCS_2009_European_Report.pdf (accessed 3 January 2014).

Kolovos, Y., (2005), *Far Right and Radical Right in Greece and Western Europe 1974–2004* (in Greek), Athens: Pelasgos.

Koulaidis, V. and Dimopoulos, K., (2006), *Greek Youth: Aspects of Fragmentation* (in Greek), Athens: Metaichmio.

Laqueur, W., (1996), *Fascism: Past, Present, Future*, London and New York: Oxford University Press.

Malkoutzis, N., (2011), 'Young Greeks and the crisis: the danger of losing a generation', Friedrich Ebert Stiftung, available at: http://library.fes.de/pdf-files/id/ipa/08465.pdf (accessed 3 January 2014).

Mavris, Y., (2013), 'Snapshot of Golden Dawn: emergence and stabilization of the right-wing phenomenon', *Public Issue-Efimerida ton Syntakton*, 1 July, available at: http://www.mavris.gr/en/298/snapshot-of-golden-dawn/ (accessed 3 January 2014).

Mihaloliakos, N. G., (2013), 'Golden Dawn –June 2013- Against all', 25 June (in Greek), available at: http://www.xryshaygh.com/index.php/gengramateas/view/chrush-augiounios-2013-enantion-olwn-arthro-tou-n.g.-michaloliakou (accessed 15 May 2014).

Mihalarou, A., (2014), 'Soul of the Nationalist Movement, the iron Greek Youth', 21 May (in Greek), available at: http://www.xryshaygh.com/index.php/enimerosi/view/psuchh-tou-ethnikistikou-kinhmatos-h-sidhra-ellhnikh-neolaia (accessed 21 May 2014).

Morgan, P., (2003), *Fascism in Europe, 1919–1945*, New York: Taylor & Francis.

Paxton, R. O., (2004), *The Anatomy of Fascism*, New York: Knopf.

Payne, S., (1995), *A History of Fascism 1914–1945*, London: UCL Press.

Petmesidou, M., (2011), 'Is the EU-IMF "Rescue Plan" dealing a blow to the Greek welfare state?' *CROP Poverty Brief*, CROP, January, available at: http://www.crop.org/viewfile.aspx?id=228 (accessed 3 January 2014).

Petmesidou, M., (2013), 'Austerity and the spectre of "immiseration" on the periphery of Europe', *CROP Poverty Brief*, CROP, August 2013, available at: http://www.crop.org/viewfile.aspx?id=479 (accessed 3 January 2014).

Psaras, D., (2012), *The Black Book of Golden Dawn* (in Greek), Athens: Polis.

Renton, D., (1999), *Fascism: Theory and Practice*, London and Sterling, VA: Pluto Press.

Richard, L., (1999), *Nazism and Culture* (in Greek), Athens: Astarti.

RVRN (Racist Violence Recording Network), (2013), *2012 Annual Report of the Racist Violence Recording Network*, UNHCR, available at: http://www.unhcr.gr/1againstracism/en/2012-annual-report-of-the-racist-violence-recording-network/ (accessed 15 May 2014).

RVRN (Racist Violence Recording Network), (2014), *Racist Violence Recording Network 2013 Annual Report*, UNHCR, available at: http://www.unhcr.gr/1againstracism/en/racist-violence-recording-network-2013-annual-report/ (accessed 15 May 2014).

Stratoudaki, H., (2005), 'Nation and Democracy: aspects of teenagers' national identity' (in Greek), *Journal of Social Research*, 116 (A): 23–50.

Teperoglou, E. and Tsatsanis, E., (2014), 'Dealignment, de-legitimation and the implosion of the two-party system in Greece: the earthquake election of 6 May 2012', *Journal of Elections, Public Opinion and Parties*, 24 (2): 222–242.

Tsoukalas, K., (1995), 'History, myths and oracles: the narration of the Greek continuity' (in Greek), in *Nation, State, Nationalism* (conference proceedings), 287–303, Athens: Association for the Study of Neo-Hellenic Culture and General.

Vernardakis, Ch., (2012), 'The June 17th elections and new cleavages in the party system', *Avgi*, 24 June (in Greek), available at: http://www.vernardakis.gr/uplmed/File/AYGI%2024-6-2012.pdf.

# Notes on contributors

**Tom Brock** is a lecturer in the Department of Sociology at Manchester Metropolitan University. He holds a doctorate in sociology from the University of Durham. Tom's research interests include social and political theory, social movements and popular protest and digital and virtual cultures. He has written on a variety of contemporary social and political issues, including student politics, Internet activism and the relationship of academia to social change. Tom is currently working on projects that examine how technology and social media influence young people's political engagement.

**Britta Busse** (PhD) worked as a research assistant and lecturer (2008–2012) at the Department for Social Science Research Methods at the University of Kassel and the Darmstadt University of Technology (project funded by the German Research Foundation: 'Experimental Mobile Phone Panel'). Since March 2012 she has been Research Assistant at the Institute for Labour and Economy, University of Bremen, working on the EU-funded projects MYPLACE, MYWEB and SAHWA. Her research interests include survey research methods, lifestyle and well-being. Recent publications include: (with M. Fuchs) 'Telephone surveys using mobile phones', in U. Engel, B. Jann, P. Lynn, A. Scherpenzeel and P. Sturgis (eds), *Improving Survey Methods* (Routledge, 2014); and (with M. Fuchs) 'Recruiting respondents for a mobile phone panel: the impact of recruitment question wording on cooperation, panel attrition, and nonresponse bias', *Methodology: European Journal of Research Methods for the Behavioral and Social Sciences* (2014) 10 (1): 21–30.

**Irini Chiotaki-Poulou** is a sociologist. She holds a PhD in gender studies from the Department of Sociology, Panteion University of Social and Political Sciences of Athens (2007). Her doctoral thesis explored the way gender representations were reproduced by the Greek political discourse at the beginning of the 1980s. She lectured for six years on quantitative methodology and applied sociological research at the Department of Sociology, Panteion University of Athens. She currently holds a research position on the MYPLACE (Memory, Youth, Political Legacy and Civic Engagement) research project as well as on the MYWEB

*The Sociological Review*, 63:S2, pp. 250–256 (2015), DOI: 10.1111/1467-954X.12259

(Measuring Youth Well-Being) research project. Her main research interests are sociology of gender issues, sociology of youth, right-wing extremism and applied social research.

**Dušan Deák** studied history and philosophy at Comenius University and holds a doctorate from the University of Pune. Currently he is associate professor at the Department of Comparative Religion, Comenius University in Bratislava. While his research primarily focuses on the Indian subcontinent, conceptually it considers the way in which discourses of past and present are entwined and how interpretations of the past are central to the constitution of (different) present(s). His recent publications include 'Spirituality in the post-communist religious marketplace', in G. McKay *et al.* (eds), *Subcultures and New Religious Movements in Russia and East-Central Europe* (Peter Lang, 2009).

**Mark Ellison** is a research associate at the Policy Evaluation and Research Unit (PERU) at Manchester Metropolitan University. He is PERU's Business Manager who manages many of PERU's projects. He is a specialist in managing, analysing and visualizing large data sets. Mark is currently working on the European FP7 MYPLACE project, managing the UK survey and is currently analysing the consortium dataset of 17,000 records. Mark previously worked in the public sector for 11 years in a range of organizations and policy areas, and has led Information, Analysis and Research teams at Cumbria Constabulary, Blackpool Council Children and Young People's Department, and Government Office for the North West. Mark's main research interests are in geographical information science (GIS) and crime and criminal justice.

**Mariona Ferrer-Fons** is a full-time researcher at the Political and Social Sciences Department of Universitat Pompeu Fabra (UPF). She holds a PhD in political sociology from the European University Institute (EUI) and a postgraduate diploma in data analysis and collection from the University of Essex. She is the lead partner for Spain of two current FP7 projects: MYPLACE (Memory, Youth, Political Legacy and Civic Engagement) and MYWEB (Measuring Youth Well-being). Her research focuses on political participation and consumption, participatory mechanisms and youth studies.

**Robert Grimm** currently works as a senior lecturer in the Department of Sociology at Manchester Metropolitan University where he is also a member of the Policy Evaluation and Research Unit. Robert studied history, sociology and human geography in Germany, France, Belgium, Finland and the UK and received a PhD in sociology in 2008 for which he investigated the informal income generating strategies among Algerian migrants in Marseille. More recently, Robert has been exploring political participation among young people in eastern Germany as part of the MYPLACE research project. Robert is also interested in far right movements and the recent rise of the conservative Alternative für Deutschland which is a new Eurosceptic party in Germany.

**Alexandra Hashem-Wangler** (PhD) has been a research assistant at the Institute for Labour and Economy, University of Bremen since June 2011. She works on the EU-funded projects MYPLACE, MYWEB and SAHWA. Her former doctoral research at the Bremen International Graduate School of Social Sciences (BIGSSS) focused on youth culture and transitions, life course research methods, social change, transformation processes in Eastern Europe, and identity construction. Recent publications include *Rethinking History, Reframing Identity: Memory, Generations and the Dynamics of National Identity in Poland* (VS Verlag für Sozialwissenschaften, 2012).

**Ilze Koroļeva** (Dr.sc.soc) is deputy director and lead researcher at the Institute of Philosophy and Sociology, University of Latvia. She is currently working on the ESF project 'The emigrant communities of Latvia: National identity, transnational relations, and diaspora politics'. Her scientific work is largely focused on youth, social exclusion and identities research. She has been a leading researcher in the Latvian Science Council grants (2004–2012), contributed to, and led more than forty research projects, including several international comparative studies. She is author of many scientific publications, the most notable of which are five chapters in a collective monograph *A Portrait of Latvian Youth Today: Integration in Society and Marginalization Risks* (LU Apgads, 2009); and (with R. Rungule and I. Mieriņa) *Occupational Prestige and Youth Occupation Choice: Comparison of Two Generations* (LU Apgads, 2014).

**Alexandra Koronaiou** teaches undergraduate and postgraduate courses at the Department of Psychology, Panteion University of Social and Political Sciences, the University of Athens and the Greek Open University. Since June 2011, she has been responsible for the Panteion University MYPLACE research team, coordinating and conducting research on youth political activity and civic engagement. She has directed and conducted research on sociology of work and free time, education, youth socio-political participation and engagement and the media impact on youth and gender issues. She is a member of the Scientific Committee of the 'Observatory on Gender Equality in Education' and of KETHI (Research Centre for Women's Equality). She is the author of more than 50 articles and book chapters and several books including: *Youth and Media of Mass Communication* (1995); *Sociology of Leisure Time* (1996); *Educating outside School* (2002); *The Role of Fathers in Balancing Professional and Family-Private Life* (2007); and *When Work Becomes Illness* (2010).

**Stelios Kymionis** is a media historian and researcher and a member of the Panteion University MYPLACE research team. He received his Bachelor's degree from the Faculty of Philosophical and Social Studies and his MA in history and theory of cinema from the School of Philosophy, University of Crete. He worked as Head of the Cinematographic Archive at the Hellenic Ministry of Foreign Affairs (2000–2007) and as Manager of the Archiving, Cataloguing and Documentation Department at the Hellenic National Audiovisual Archive (2008–2011).

*The Sociological Review*, 63:S2, pp. 250–256 (2015), DOI: 10.1111/1467-954X.12259

Currently he is Documentation Manager at the Telecommunications Museum. He has participated in several audiovisual projects and academic programmes. He has several contributions in edited volumes and academic journals on Greek cinema and the audiovisual archives. He has organized a number of conferences on Greek cinema and he is co-editor of the academic journal *Filmicon: Journal of Greek Film Studies* (http://filmiconjournal.com/journal).

**Evangelos Lagos** is a researcher in sociology and a member of the Panteion University of Social and Political Sciences research team for the FP7-MYPLACE research programme. He is currently doing research on youth political activity and civic engagement focusing on youth political activism, young people's receptivity towards far right and fascist ideologies and the political agenda, and young people's participation in the 2011 Greek Indignant movement. He has done research on immigration, unemployment and job training, youth subcultures, youth radicalism, cultural politics and policy, social policy and free time and modernization processes in Greek society. He has published and presented papers on youth radicalism, contemporary neo-fascist ideology and cultural politics, youth's receptivity toward far right and fascism, social policy and culture, modernization processes and social policy.

**Klaus Levinsen** (PhD in political science) is associate professor of political sociology at the Department of Political Science, SDU, Denmark. He has published on a variety of issues in political sociology, especially on political attitudes, political participation, voluntary associations, youth political engagement, and youth and media. Most recently he has published in *Journal of Youth Studies*, and *Scandinavian Political Studies*. He is among the editors of the Danish journal of sociology *Dansk Sociology*. Currently he is involved in the European FP7 project MYPLACE and two Danish research projects focusing on the voting age and young people's electoral participation.

**Inta Mieriņa** is based at the Institute of Philosophy and Sociology at the University of Latvia, where she is a principal investigator of the European Social Fund research grant 'The emigrant communities of Latvia: National identity, transnational relations, and diaspora politics'. Her research interests include: youth, migration, national identity, social capital, political participation, right-wing radicalism, Central and Eastern Europe, cohort analysis and quantitative research methodology. She has been involved in a number of large-scale international comparative studies concerning youth, participation, well-being and addictions. She has been a visiting researcher at the Aarhus University, the University of Illinois at Chicago, and GESIS EUROLAB. Her work has been published in journals including: *European Societies, Europe-Asia Studies*, *Polish Sociological Review and Social Science Research*.

**Phil Mizen** teaches sociology and policy at Aston University. He has a long-standing research interest in children and young people, and has published extensively in these fields. As well as his involvement in the MYPLACE project, he is currently involved in a large ESRC-funded project examining unpaid and involuntary part-time and temporary working in young people's transitions from education to the labour market.

**Hilary Pilkington** has a long-standing research interest in youth and youth cultural practices, post-socialist societies and qualitative, especially, ethnographic research methods. She has been coordinator of a number of large collaborative research projects including the FP7 MYPLACE project. She was previously director of the Centre of Russian and East European Studies, University of Birmingham and is currently professor of sociology at the University of Manchester. Most recently she is co-author of: *Punk in Russia: Cultural Mutation from the 'Useless' to the 'Moronic'* (Routledge, 2014); and *Russia's Skinheads: Exploring and Rethinking Subcultural Lives* (Routledge, 2010).

**Gary Pollock** is professor and head of sociology at Manchester Metropolitan University. He has been involved in youth research for over twenty years, and is interested in using survey data to examine young people in society in terms of their social and political outlook as well as their employment and family trajectories. He is currently the coordinator of the FP7 project MYWEB which examines the feasibility of developing a Europe-wide longitudinal survey of children and young people's well-being.

**Anton Popov** is a lecturer in the School of Languages and Social Sciences, Aston University. He graduated in history from Kuban State University (Russia), studied ethnology at the Institute for Ethnology and Anthropology in Moscow and defended his PhD on the cultural production of identity among Greeks in southern Russia and the North Caucasus at the University of Birmingham (UK). His research interests are in: history and memory studies; social anthropology (especially postsocialist societies); identity and transnationalism; ethnicity and (non-Western forms of) civil society; youth culture; and qualitative research methods. He has conducted ethnographic research on nativist and ethno-cultural revivalist movements, migrant and ethnic minority communities and youth's mnemonic socialization in southern Russia, the Caucasus, Turkey and Britain. Recent publications include: 'Re-making a frontier community or defending ethnic boundaries? The Caucasus in Cossack identity', *Europe-Asia Studies* (2012) 64 (9): 1739–1757; and 'making sense of home and homeland: former-Soviet Greeks' motivations and strategies for a transnational migrant circuit', *Journal of Ethnic and Migration Studies* (2010) 36 (1): 67–85.

**Alexandros Sakellariou** holds a PhD (2008) in sociology from Panteion University of Social and Political Sciences of Athens. He studied at the School of Philosophy of the National and Kapodistrian University of Athens (1996–2000) and in 2003 he obtained his MA in sociology from Panteion University of Athens. He is currently working as a researcher at Panteion University of Athens in two

European Commission Research Projects (MYPLACE, *Memory, Youth, Political Legacy and Civic Engagement* and MYWEB, *Measuring Youth Well-Being*) and he is a postdoctoral researcher at the same university studying the forms of atheism in contemporary Greek society. His scientific interests include youth activism and civic participation, right-wing extremism, politics and religion, Church–State relations, religious communities in Greek society, religious freedom, religion and globalization and atheism.

**Domonkos Sik** is a sociologist and philosopher, currently working as an assistant professor at the University Eötvös Loránd, Budapest. His research focuses on critical theories of modernization in post-transition countries, with special attention to the political formation of youth. His most relevant recent publications include: *A modernizáció ingája* (*The Pendulum of Modernization*) (Eötvös Kiadó, 2012); *Demokratikus kultúra és modernizáció* (*Democratic Culture and Modernization*), (L'Harmattan, 2014); 'Civic socialization in post-transition condition', *Politics, Culture and Socialization* (2011) 2 (3): 257–271; and 'The transformation of action coordination? A critical interpretation of the Hungarian transition', *Review of Sociology of the Hungarian Academy of Science* (2010/2).

**Roger Soler-i-Martí** works as a researcher at the Catalan Youth Observatory of the Catalan Youth Agency (Generalitat de Catalunya) and is a part-time researcher at the Universitat Pompeu Fabra (UPF). He graduated in Political Science from UPF and is a PhD candidate at the Universitat Autònoma de Barcelona (UAB), where he is finishing a thesis on the transformations of youth political activism in European democracies. He also has postgraduate qualifications in Qualitative and Participatory Research (UAB) and in Immigration and Diversity Management (UAB). He has participated in several national and international research projects on youth and political behaviour. He has recently published the book *Democràcia, participació i joventut* on political involvement and mobilization of Catalan youth. His main research fields are political participation, sociology of youth, public policies and social movements.

**Jochen Tholen** (PhD) is research director at the Institute for Labour and Economy, at the University of Bremen, Germany. He holds Masters degrees in economy and sociology and his research areas include: labour relations; management; labour market structure; EU economic development and its impact on society; and young people's participation. His regional focus is on Europe and transition countries. Recent publications include: (*et al.*) 'Transition to Adulthood in Rural Villages during the transition from Communism in the South Caucasus', in C. Leccardi *et al.* (eds) *1989 – Young People and Social Change after the Fall of the Berlin Wall* (Council of Europe Publishing, 2011); and (*et al.*) 'Young people's education to work transition and inter-generational social mobility in post-Soviet Central Asia', *Young Nordic Journal of Youth Research* (2009) 17 (1): 59–80.

*The Sociological Review*, 63:S2, pp. 250–256 (2015), DOI: 10.1111/1467-954X.12259
© 2015 The Authors. Editorial organisation © 2015 The Editorial Board of the Sociological Review

**Carsten Yndigegn** holds a PhD in cultural studies. He is an associate professor at the University of Southern Denmark, Faculty of Social Sciences, Department of Border Region Studies. He has completed research projects on interdisciplinary cooperation in social work on youth at risk, and the organization of youth work in Danish municipalities. He has investigated young people's expectations and attitudes to life conditions and life possibilities with a special focus on youth in the Danish–German border region, and he has studied young people's migration and its influence on their collective identities. Recently, he has been the Danish project leader of MYPLACE.

# Index

*The Sociological Review*, 63:S2, pp. 257–260 (2015), DOI: 10.1111/1467-954X.12315

*The Sociological Review*, 63:S2, pp. 257–260 (2015), DOI: 10.1111/1467-954X.12315